Rise Up!

INDIGENOUS MUSIC
IN NORTH AMERICA

Craig Harris

Foreword by Stephen Butler

UNIVERSITY OF NEBRASKA PRESS   LINCOLN

The University of Nebraska Press is part of a land-
grant institution with campuses and programs on the
past, present, and future homelands of the Pawnee,
Ponca, Otoe-Missouria, Omaha, Dakota, Lakota, Kaw,
Cheyenne, and Arapaho Peoples, as well as those of the
relocated Ho-Chunk, Sac and Fox, and Iowa Peoples.

Library of Congress Cataloging-in-Publication Data
Names: Harris, Craig, 1953 December
20– | Butler, Stephen (Sound recording
producer), writer of foreword.
Title: Rise up! : Indigenous music in North America
/ Craig Harris ; foreword by Stephen Butler.
Description: Lincoln : University of Nebraska Press,
2023. | Includes bibliographical references and index.
Identifiers: LCCN 2023021462
ISBN 9781496236159 (paperback)
ISBN 9781496237927 (epub)
ISBN 9781496237934 (pdf)
Subjects: LCSH: Indians of North America—Music—
History and criticism. | Indian musicians—North
America—Interviews. | BISAC: SOCIAL SCIENCE
/ Ethnic Studies / American / Native American
Studies | MUSIC / Ethnic | LCGFT: Interviews.
Classification: LCC ML3557 .H3805 2023 | DDC
780.842/36107065—dc24/eng/20230605
LC record available at https://lccn.loc.gov/2023021462

Set and designed in Questa by N. Putens.

The music of the Indian . . . springs from our own continent, and is thus, of all music, distinctively American.

—NATALIE CURTIS, *The Indians' Book*

CONTENTS

PHOTOGRAPHS

FOREWORD
Stephen Butler

The songs and music of North America's original inhabitants have been part of the lifeblood of hundreds of tribes, thousands of clans, tens of thousands of communities, and millions of families for millennia. Indigenous musicians have long infused individual artistry with their heritage, but even the most contemporary Indigenous musician uses traditional narratives, beliefs, and language to express how they relate to the world around them. This is the context that informs the music of traditional cultures the world over and demonstrates why it is such a crucial part of global heritage and life.

Rise Up! beckons a world that has, for the most part, systematically worked to silence, marginalize, and ignore Indigenous voices to listen now more than ever. The Standing Rock protests and grassroots movements like Idle No More, Missing and Murdered Indigenous Women (MMIW) and Missing and Murdered Indigenous People (MMIP), and those focused on addressing and healing from the devastating legacy of residential schools have resulted in Indigenous peoples no longer being hidden from the headlines of the day. At every step, the message and activism have been supported and driven by music.

We are being asked to recognize, respect, and revel in Indigenous peoples' musical and cultural beauty, called upon to finally start listening and learning in earnest. By doing so, we have a chance to reconstitute our world and our own humanity. And in that process, some of us will surely tap our feet to a beat or hum a melody that we had never known could move us so deeply.

We're not going to be quiet anymore.

—**Bear Witness** (Cayuga), the Halluci Nation

Preface

Members of more than three hundred Indigenous nations gathered at the Standing Rock Reservation, North Dakota, from April 2016 to February 2017. Concerned that the "Black Snake" (Energy Transfer Partners' Dakota Access Pipeline), stretching from North Dakota's oil fields to Illinois, would contaminate waterways and come close to sacred burial grounds, they joined with thousands of non-Indigenous protesters or "water protectors." According to LaDonna Brave Bull Allard (Lakota/Dakota), whose reservation land served as ground zero, the protest drew "spiritual leaders from every facet of Indigenous people—Mongolians, the people out of Africa, India, China, Australia, and New Zealand,"[1] as well as South America and Canada.

A similar awakening had begun in Canada four years before. Enraged when an omnibus bill (C-45), formerly known as the Jobs and Growth Act, threatened to weaken environmental laws, cancel waterway protection, and endanger First Nation sovereignty, Saskatchewanians Jessica Gordon (Pasqua), Sylvia McAdam (Cree), Nina Wilson (Kahkewistahaw), and Sheelah McLean formed Idle No More in November 2012. Voicing their opposition through Facebook, Twitter, Instagram, and other social media, they drew large crowds to protests, teach-ins, and spontaneous round dances. With the resulting media coverage, the grassroots organization grew into a powerful movement. "We were everywhere," said rapper, producer, and tattoo artist Sten Joddi (Muscogee), "and it was because of cell phones and the internet. We could say, 'We're going to be at this mall. Natives, show up. We'll be singing and dancing.'"

In both Canada and the United States, the attention was long overdue. According to the 2020 U.S. census, more than 9.5 million people identified themselves as full or part Indigenous North American, Native Hawaiian, or Native Alaskan—close to doubling in a decade. Indigenous peoples account for nearly 3 percent of the country's population. There are 574 federally recognized nations, tribes, bands, pueblos, communities, and villages and hundreds without official designation. Over a million Indigenous peoples live on 326 reservations.

In Canada over 1.5 million people comprise Inuit and Metís communities and six hundred First Nations (4.9 percent of the population). But on both sides of the border, forced assimilation, involuntary sterilization, subsidized migration to the cities, and restrictive boarding schools long muffled Indigenous voices.

When *Heartbeat, Warble, and the Electric Powwow* was published in 2016, my prognosis for the future of Indigenous music was bleak.[2] Five years before, the National Academy of Recording Arts and Sciences (NARAS) purged its Native American Grammy category, along with thirty other categories, and established a regional roots category pitting Indigenous musicians against Hawaiian, polka, zydeco, and Cajun artists. The excitement of *Bury My Heart at Wounded Knee: An Indian History of the American West* and the American Indian Movement (AIM) in the 1970s; R. Carlos Nakai's million-selling flute recordings in the 1980s; and Kevin Costner's *Dances with Wolves* in the 1990s was waning. Floyd Westerman and John Trudell were gone, and Joseph FireCrow and A. Paul Ortega would follow. New artists had limited opportunities for exposure. Indigenous record labels were folding or turning exclusively to their archives.

Yet Indigenous music continued to lure me, whether it was the flute melodies of R. Carlos Nakai, Mary Youngblood, or Robert Mirabel; the ballads of Buffy Sainte-Marie, Joanne Shenandoah, or Keith Secola; the powwow and round dance songs of Randy Wood and his brother Steve's drum group, Northern Cree; or the thought-provoking lyrics of saxophonist and three-time poet laureate Joy Harjo or sharp-tongued rapper Litefoot. Despite mainstream resistance, new recordings continue to be released as good as or better than anything on the hit parade.

A suggestion to revisit Indigenous music inspired this book. Compiling a list of recent winners of NAMA (Native American Music Awards) and Grammy Awards in the United States and JUNO Awards and Polaris Music Prizes in Canada, I began making phone calls. After three years of interviewing artists, conducting hours upon hours of research, and listening and relistening to some amazing music, I present the following with a much more optimistic view.

Indigenous identity continues to evolve. I honor current tribal designation while respecting how individuals refer to themselves. The tribes formerly known as the Sioux (a distortion of the Ojibwe word for "enemy") are the Dakota, Lakota, and Nakota. The Iroquois ("Snake") are the Haudeno-saunee ("People Who Built the House"). The Cherokee ("Those Who Live in Caves") are the Tsalagi ("People of Different Speech"). The Navajo ("Farm Fields in the Valley") are the Diné ("The People"). Known as the Ojibwe ("Puckered Moccasin People") in Canada, the Chippewa call themselves Anishinaabe ("Original Person") in the United States. The Papago ("Bean Eaters") became the Tohono O'odham ("Desert People") in 1986. The Muscogee or Mvskoke (possibly derived from Shawnee words referring to residents of an ancient town along Alabama's Coosa River) recently dropped the Creek designation from its name.

Generalization, however, remains problematic. "'American Indian' and 'Native American' have colonial roots," explains Peter d'Errico of the University of Massachusetts Amherst's legal studies department. "Neither is more 'correct' than the other.... There is no unproblematic word to refer generally to the people we are discussing. Every term— including 'Tribal,' 'Indigenous,' and 'Native'—has a history of use and abuse as a function of colonialism, invasion, genocide, marginalization, exploitation, and so on."[3]

"Works on American Indian history and culture," Northern Arizona University professor of applied Indigenous studies and history Devon A. Mihesuah (Choctaw) reminds us, "should not give only one perspective. The analysis must include Indians' version of history."[4]

In that spirit, I was determined to let these pacesetting artists speak with minimal intrusion. Some editing was done, but the following is a rare glance into what it means to be Indigenous in a complex world.

1

Fingerprints

Indigenous fingerprints are all over North America's music. The birthplace of jazz, New Orleans's Congo Square (now Louis Armstrong Park), was an ancient Indian portage way and the site of an annual Houmas Indian corn festival. It's easy to imagine the polyrhythms of African Americans and people from the Caribbean melding with the chop of Indigenous drums. "The music is . . . an integral part of spiritual, social, moral, and cultural events," said Juliette Appold of the Library of Congress.[1]

Country music legend Kitty Wells (1919–2012); Frankie Laine's pianist, Carl Fischer (1912–54); and rock and roller Ronnie Spector (1943–2022) shared Tsalagi roots. Willie Nelson's mother, Myrle Marie Greenhaw Nelson, was three-quarters Tsalagi. Hank Williams (1923–53) had Tsalagi and Muscogee ancestry. Tina Turner's mother, Zelma Currie, was Tsalagi and Diné.

Indigenous blood flows through jazz and the blues. The Mississippi-born Father of Delta Blues, Charlie Patton (1891–1934), had a Tsalagi grandmother. Delta bluesman David "Honeyboy" Edwards (1915–2011) was Choctaw. West Coast blues pioneer Lowell Fulson (1921–99) was Muscogee. Chicago bluesman Eddy "the Chief" Clearwater (born Harrington) (1935–2018), whose grandmother was full-blooded or half-Tsalagi, sometimes wore a Plains Indian war bonnet onstage.

During a fifty-year span that began in the early 1930s, Arizona-born Russell "Big Chief" Moore (1912–83) (Akimel O'odham) played trombone for Lionel Hampton, Louis Armstrong, Sidney Bechet, and others. "Almost all Indians," Moore said, "have a natural musical talent."[2]

Some Indigenous musicians have been reluctant to acknowledge their roots. Born on the Muscogee Nation Reservation, in Okmulgee, Oklahoma, jazz bassist and cellist Oscar Pettiford (1922–60) had a Choctaw mother and a Tsalagi–African American father. "Like many African Americans with Native American ancestry," claimed the website All about Jazz, "[Pettiford's] Native heritage was not generally known except to a few close friends (which included David Amram)."[3]

Mildred Bailey (née Rinker) (1907–51)
(Coeur d'Alene, Swiss, and Irish)
Al Rinker (1901–82) (Coeur d'Alene, Swiss, and Irish)

Jazz vocalist Mildred Bailey was another whose Indigenous heritage was little known. The *New Grove Dictionary of Jazz* called her "the first white singer to absorb and master the jazz-flavored phrasing . . . of her Black contemporaries."[4]

It had it wrong. Born in Tekoa, Washington, and the sister of Bing Crosby collaborator Al Rinker, the multioctave songstress was half–Coeur d'Alene (her devout Roman Catholic mother, Josephine, was full-blood). Though she moved to Spokane, the state's second-largest city, when she was thirteen, Bailey often credited the songs she sang as a youngster on the tribe's Idaho reservation. "It removes the boom from the contralto voice," she said, "this Indian singing does, because you have to sing a lot of notes to get by, and you've got to cover an awful range."[5]

Bailey's light soprano vocals, clear articulation, and precise timing influenced Tony Bennett, Billie Holiday, and Frank Sinatra. "[Bailey] struggled with obesity," said John McDonough of *DownBeat*, "but she was gifted with a musician's ear for rhythmic amendment and could produce a sunny, optimistic timbre that shivered with gentle, shimmering vibrato on high notes."[6]

She was "a much better singer than Billie,"[7] said pianist Teddy Wilson, who played with both.

Bailey and her brothers, Al and Miles, grew up with music. Their father, Charles, played fiddle and called square dances. Their mother played piano.

The Rinker brothers were still in high school when they formed the Musicaladers with nineteen-year-old crooner Harry Lillis "Bing" Crosby in 1923. During the summer of 1925, the group (reduced to a duo) began a five-month engagement at the Clemmer Theater (now the Bing Crosby

Theater) in Spokane. Accompanied by Al's piano, Crosby entertained audiences between films.

Following a stint on KMTR in Bakersfield, California, in the early twenties, Bailey continued to Los Angeles. Visited by her brother and Crosby in October 1925, she introduced them to her contacts, resulting in them being signed to appear in a revue (*The Syncopation Idea*) for thirteen weeks. The duo's show-stealing performance led to an invitation to join Paul Whiteman's Orchestra. Initially struggling to fit in with the orchestra, they hit their stride after pianist and composer Harry Barris joined them. As the Rhythm Boys, they featured in Whiteman's 1929 biopic, *The King of Jazz*, singing "Mississippi Mud," "So the Bluebirds and the Blackbirds Got Together," "A Bench in the Park," and "Happy Feet."

Joining her brother in Whiteman's Orchestra in 1929, Bailey became the first woman to sing with a jazz big band. She was still new to the group when the Rhythm Boys were fired following Crosby's automobile accident and DWI arrest. The Rhythm Boys went on to appear nightly at the Ambassador Hotel, in Los Angeles, with the Gus Arnheim Orchestra. Embarking on a history-making solo career, in January 1931, Crosby recorded his first hit, "I Surrender Dear," with Arnheim's band. The Rhythm Boys split shortly afterward. Their only reunion came on the *Paul Whiteman Presents* radio show on July 4, 1943.

Bailey continued to sing with the Whiteman Orchestra until 1933, the year she married Kenneth "Red Norvo" Norville from Beardstown, Illinois. Initially a stride pianist and vaudeville tap dancer, Norvo had found his niche as a jazz vibraphonist and bandleader.

Affectionately known as the Queen of Swing, the Rockin' Chair Lady, and Mrs. Swing, Bailey sang with Norvo's band from 1935 to 1939. Starring on the CBS Radio series *Mr. and Mrs. Swing*, they topped the charts in 1938, with "Please Be Kind" and Norvo's "Says My Heart."

Bailey recorded the stereotype-laden "Wigwammin'," by Henry Nemo and Irving Mills, on May 2, 1938. "Of course, as a Native American woman, it was a little jarring [to hear] at first," said her niece, Julia Rinker-Miller, more than seven decades later, "but I think it was just one of those things you had to do. You break down the walls you can, but you also had to play the game."[8]

The same year, Bailey covered "Rock It for Me." Written by Alabama twins Kay and Sue Warner, it had been a top-twenty hit for Chick Webb and His Orchestra, featuring seventeen-year-old Ella Fitzgerald, a year before. A portent of things to come, the song included such prophetic lines as "Won't you satisfy my soul with the rock and roll?"

Billboard wouldn't use the term for another four years. Disc jockey Alan Freed would popularize it in the 1950s.

When the Norvo group disbanded in 1939, Bailey hooked up with Benny Goodman's Orchestra for a few months. Recording eight tracks, they topped the charts in March 1940 with "Dam That Dream."

Although she joined Norvo's re-formed band in late 1940, Bailey participated in only one recording session before she and the vibraphonist separated. They would divorce but remain friends.

Hosting a CBS radio show, *Music 'til Midnight,* from 1942 to 1943, Bailey continued to record. Suffering from diabetes, she was hospitalized in 1949. She attempted a comeback a year later but experienced a fatal heart attack in December 1951. She was forty-four.

Bailey was inducted into the Big Band and Jazz Hall of Fame in 1989. Five years later the U.S. Post Office issued a twenty-nine-cent stamp in her memory.

Jean Baptiste "Illinois" Jacquet (1922–2004)
(Dakota and French Creole)

Nineteen-year-old Illinois Jacquet touched lightning on May 26, 1942, when his tenor saxophone playing propelled Lionel Hampton Orchestra's "Flyin' Home," composed by the vibraphone-playing bandleader and clarinetist Benny Goodman. Hampton played on the original, by Goodman's Sextet featuring guitarist Charlie Christian, in early 1939, and he reprised it during their set at John Hammond's *Spirituals to Swing* concert in Carnegie Hall that December. Hampton recorded it again with his band in 1940, but with the tune lifted by the passionate playing of the reedman from Broussard, Louisiana, history was made. Bridging big band jazz and R&B, "Flyin' Home" has been called the first rock and roll tune. It received a Grammy Hall of Fame Award in 1996.

Jacquet's hard-driving approach became known as the "Texas tenor" style of saxophone playing. "It was so musical," said saxophonist Frank

Foster. "It swung. It was soulful; it seemed as if every note was planned . . . that solo was so great."[9]

"Something was with me at that moment," Jacquet told an interviewer. "It all came together for some reason."[10]

Raised in Houston, Jacquet was the son of a Dakota mother and a French Creole father. Taking his stage name from the Dakota tribal name Illiniwek ("Those Who Speak in an Ordinary Way"), he started as a tap dancer in his father and older brothers' band. He played drums before switching to saxophone and bassoon.

Recording for more than sixty years, Jacquet left a discography of 240 tracks as a bandleader (often with his brother Russell on trumpet); sideman for Hampton, Nat King Cole, Count Basie, Cab Calloway, Kenny Burrell, and Buddy Rich; and soloist for Norman Granz's Jazz at the Philharmonic. "God gives you talent," he said. "It's a struggle, but if it's there, it'll come out."[11]

James Gilbert "Jim" Pepper II (1941–92) (Kaw and Muscogee)

Jim Pepper played with guitarist Larry Coryell and Pat Metheny's future drummer Bob Moses in the late-sixties jazz-fusion group the Free Spirits. Encouraged by free jazz pioneers Don Cherry and Ornette Coleman, the Oregon-born reedman and composer continued to blend Indigenous roots and jazz on solo albums, including *Pepper's Pow Wow* (1971) and *Dakota Song* (1987). "I wish I could have met him," said two-time NAMA-winning saxophonist-turned-flute-player Vince Redhouse (Diné and Filipino). "If he had lived longer, he might have blazed more of a trail."

Pepper's signature tune, "Witchi Tai To," was based on a Native American Church (NAC) song that he learned from his grandfather Ralph Pepper, a ceremonial leader of the Kaw Tribe in Oklahoma and one of the last speakers of its language. "Pepper's grandfather never did tell him what [the words] meant in English, [but] he sings them anyway and adds English lyrics which emphasize the roots in the peyote ritual, especially speaking of the Water Spirit, who carries the visions brought by the peyote."[12]

Recorded by the Free Spirits featuring Chris Hill in 1967, "Witchi Tai To" was transformed into a folk-pop classic two years later by Brewer and

Shipley (Michael Brewer and Tom Shipley). The midwestern duo, however, "got all the Native American lyrics right but misheard the adapted English lyrics."[13]

The nine-minute-plus definitive version of "Witchi Tai To" was the pinnacle of *Pepper's Pow Wow*. The Supremes, Harper's Ferry, Paul Winter, Oregon, Jack DeJohnette, the BMX Bandits, Shadowyze, and Joy Harjo are among those who have covered it. Norwegian saxophonist Jan Garbarek and pianist Ben Stenson used it as the title track of the Garbarek-Stinson Band's 1974 album on the Munich-based ECM Records label. "Those who think that contemporary music from Europe lacks soul-fire," said *DownBeat*, "are hereby advised to listen to *Witchi Tai To*."[14]

It had certainly traveled far.

2

Anthropologists

Scientific American reported an apology from the American Anthropological Association (AAA) in November 2021, for "the field's legacy of harm."[1]

It was a long time coming. More than a century before, William John "W. J." McGee, president of the AAA (1902–12) and the National Geographic Society (1904–5), declared, "The savage stands strikingly close to sub-human species in every aspect."[2]

Anthropologists were relentless in their quest to acquire artifacts for New York's Museum of Natural History and elsewhere. "Indians have been cursed above all other people in history," said Vine Deloria Jr., whose aunt Ella Cara Deloria collaborated with the AAA's third president, Franz Boas. "Indians have anthropologists."[3]

"We participated in racist ideologies," admitted Ramona Pérez, president since 2021, "and called it science."[4]

"The apology is the start," Pérez continued, "but now it's up to us to really start moving forward in collaboration with our tribal leaders and our tribal communities to ask them how we work together in empowering them today."[5]

Alice Cunningham Fletcher (1838–1923)

Inspiring scores of researchers who followed, Alice Cunningham Fletcher was extremely complex. A fundraiser for the Carlisle School since 1881, she contributed to a Senate report on Indian education and civilization in 1885. Two years later, she helped Massachusetts Republican senator, and the chair of the Senate's Indian Affairs Commission, Henry Dawes craft the controversial General Allotment Act (Dawes Severalty Act). Not only did it divide tribal land into individual allotments—160 acres for the head of the household, 80 acres for unmarried adults—but it opened the remaining "surplus" land to non-Indigenous settlement. "The General Allotment Act is a mighty pulverizing engine to break up the tribal mass," President Theodore Roosevelt would tell Congress on December 3, 1901. "It acts directly upon the family and the individual."[6]

As a special Bureau of Indian Affairs (BIA) agent from 1882 to 1884, Fletcher was responsible for dividing the Omaha's land into individual plots. "[She] genuinely believed allotment would empower reservation Natives," said University of Nebraska at Omaha history professor Denny Smith, "but she was gravely mistaken. . . . [It was] a legal land fraud perpetrated by the federal government to steal tribal lands from within existing reservations."[7]

Fletcher was born in Havana, Cuba, where her ailing father, a prominent attorney, was hoping to recover. When he died after her first birthday, she and her mother, a former Boston debutante, returned to New York. Raised in exclusive Brooklyn Heights, she attended the elite Brooklyn Female Academy. A fervent feminist, she became a member of the Soro-sis Women's Club, co-founder and secretary of the Association for the Advancement of Women, vice president of the American Association for the Advancement of Science, and president of the Anthropological Society of Washington and the American Folklore Society.

Fletcher's documenting of Indigenous music countered her more controversial views. Her interests sparked after meeting Omaha chief Joseph "Iron Eyes" La Flesche's twenty-five-year-old daughter, Susette (Inshata Theumba, or "Bright Eyes"), and her three-year-younger half brother, Francis, in 1879. A graduate of the Elizabeth Institute for Young Ladies, a private school in Elizabeth, New Jersey, Susette had returned to the Omaha Reservation, in Macy, Nebraska, to teach, before being hired to translate for Ponca chief Luther Standing Bear (Óta Kté, or Mathó Nážiŋ) during his maltreatment suit against the U.S. government. Ruling in the chief's favor, and affirming his demand for equal treatment, Judge Elmer Dundy declared, "An Indian is a person within the meaning of the law, and there is no law giving the Army authority to forcibly remove Indians from their lands."[8]

Shortly afterward, Standing Bear's brother, Big Snake, "tried to move from the Ponca Reservation in Oklahoma to one occupied by the Cheyenne.

Indian agent William Whiteman ordered a detail to arrest him. When Big Snake resisted, he was shot and killed. Following a U.S. Senate investigation of Big Snake's death, Standing Bear and the Ponca were allowed to return to Nebraska. Standing Bear traveled the country telling his story through the Omaha interpreter Susette La Flesche."[9]

Francis had been an interpreter and research assistant of ethnologist, linguist, and Episcopalian missionary James Owen Dorsey.

Reconnecting with the half siblings in early 1881, Fletcher was encouraged to experience tribal life firsthand. She gladly accepted their invitation to visit them on the Omaha Reservation. While there, she met their sister (Susan La Flesche Picotte), whom she would help obtain a loan from the Connecticut Indian Association to attend the Woman's Medical College of Pennsylvania and become the first female Indigenous physician in the United States.

The *History of American Women* blog describes what Fletcher would have found at the time of her visit: "The Omaha economy ran on corn (maize) agriculture along with hunting and gathering. In spring and autumn, they lived in permanent villages with earthen lodges; during the hunting season they lived in tepees that could be easily moved."[10]

After attending a reservation dance, Fletcher recalled being initially "startled by a sudden mighty beating of the drum, with such deafening yells and shouts that I feared my ears would burst."[11]

Her opinion changed quickly. "[After] the last vestige of the distraction of noise and the confusion of theory was dispelled," she said, "and the sweetness, the beauty, and the meaning of these songs were revealed to me, . . . I ceased to trouble about scales, tones, rhythm, and melody."[12]

Accompanied by Francis, Susette, and *Omaha Herald* reporter Thomas Henry Tibbles (Susette's future husband), Fletcher spent six weeks on the Rosebud Reservation, becoming the first non-Indigenous female ethnologist to live on a reservation.

Francis went on to work as a translator for the Senate Committee on Indian Affairs. Fletcher provided him with a room in her Washington DC home and encouraged him to study at George Washington Law School. After graduating in 1893, he worked for the Smithsonian Institute's Bureau of American Ethnology, from 1910 until 1929, writing about the Omaha and Osage, lecturing, and producing wax recordings. He cowrote *A Study* of *Omaha Music* (1893) and *The Omaha Tribe* (1911) with Fletcher and authored *The Middle Five: Indian Boys at School* (1900), *Who Was the Medicine Man?* (1904), and *A Dictionary of the Osage Language* (1932) on his own. "Almost everything Fletcher knew about the Omaha," asserted Margery Coffey, assistant director of the Omaha Tribal Historical Research Project, "came from La Flesche."[13]

Mentored by Frederick Ward Putnam, director of Harvard University's Peabody Museum of Archeology and Ethnology, Fletcher became the first woman appointed to a research position at the Cambridge, Massachusetts, school in 1882—eighty-five years before female undergraduates were admitted. She continued to focus on Omaha music but also documented songs of the Pawnee, Sioux, Arapaho, Cheyenne, Chippewa, Oto, Osage, Nez Perce, Ponce, and Winnebago.

The earliest documentation of Indigenous music was limited to written transcription, but things changed after Jesse Walter Fewkes, a Harvard University zoology student turned anthropologist, recorded Newell Joseph (Passamaquoddy) in Calais, Maine, in March 1890, on an Edison cylinder recording machine. Stomping feet accompanied Joseph's song. There are roughly twenty thousand wax recordings still in existence.

Frances Densmore (1867–1957)

Documenting Indigenous music from the 1890s to the 1950s, Frances Densmore amassed an archive of more than one thousand recordings and transcriptions. "I heard Indians sing," said Densmore, "saw them dance and heard them yell, and was scared almost to death."[14]

An ethnologist born in Red Wing, Minnesota, Densmore said her fascination stemmed from reading "what Miss Alice Cunningham Fletcher was writing at the time about Omaha music." She described, "[I became] acquainted with John Comfort Fillmore who transcribed [Fletcher's] phonograph records. For the next ten years I soaked my receptive mind in what army officers wrote about Indians, and what historians wrote about Indians, with some of the publications of the Bureau of American Ethnology, with which I was later to be connected. All this was preparation for my life work."[15]

More than a half century after her passing, Densmore remains controversial. "In the decades since her death," said poet Dorian Brooks, "some critics—with the growth of Native sovereignty and increasing recognition of Native rights, and with the passage of the Native American Graves Protection and Repatriation Act (NAGPRA) in 1990—have questioned Densmore's practice of 'salvage anthropology,' the imperative for non-Natives to capture elements of Indian culture before they would presumably disappear; and to preserve them in non-Native facilities. Some have alleged that she pressured Indians to share sacred songs and teachings that tribal members thought should be kept secret."[16]

On the other hand, Brooks continued, "others, including Indian educators and scholars, have valued Densmore's work highly, consulting her recordings and books to learn about forgotten aspects of their cultures that were hidden for generations because of fear of government retribution."[17]

Natalie Curtis Burlin (1875–1921)

Natalie Curtis viewed Indigenous music as a musician. "No civilized music," she wrote in *The Indians' Book* (1907), "has such complex, elaborate, and changing rhythms."[18]

A classically trained pianist and singer, she had previously published transcriptions of Yuma, Navajo, Zuni, Winnebago, Apache, Kiowa, Pawnee, Cheyenne, Arapaho, Dakota, Mojave, Kwakintl, Pima, San Juan Pueblo, Wabanaki, and Penobscot tunes in *Songs of Ancient America* (1905).

Born in New York, Curtis was introduced to Indigenous music in 1903, a year after joining her librarian brother, George, in Arizona. "She and George were at the Rose Festival in Pasadena, California," said Jane Kirkpatrick, author of the biographical novel *The Healing of Natalie Curtis*, "and they saw Navajo singers brought in by [outdoorsman and author] Charles Loomis. He had spent some time with Indigenous peoples in South Dakota and done some recordings."

Curtis later met the singers at Loomis's estate. "She hadn't performed or sung much in five years," Kirkpatrick said, "but she asked if they'd like to hear her sing and they said they would. She chose Wagner's 'Ride of the Valkyries.' It was this spirited, heavy kind of song. When she finished, they sang. Their music was so different, she was almost embarrassed that she had plunged forward into her performance the way she did. It was so dissimilar from Indigenous music."

Natalie and her brother stayed with Loomis for a few weeks, spending hours listening to his recordings. Then they continued to Yuma, Arizona. "I speculate that George was working on a book," Kirkpatrick said. "There was a great library at the Yuma prison."

From the Quechan Reservation, Curtis "heard someone singing a lullaby" on the other side of the Colorado River, Fitzpatrick said, "and made her way over; she was so taken by what she heard. Remarkably, the woman singing spoke English and Spanish, as well as her Native language. She had been to Washington DC and had some awareness of the outside world. They struck up a relationship. That was the beginning of [Curtis's] interest."

Acquiring an Edison recorder, Curtis visited reservations to collect songs, "even though she knew that was, at that point, a violation of law," Kirkpatrick said. "She used her unique relationship with Teddy Roosevelt to try to get him to give her permission, which ultimately she was able to do."

Curtis's passion for Indigenous music was a personal awakening. She had been on the threshold of a promising music career in 1897, when she experienced a breakdown. "It was a combination of factors," Kirkpatrick explained. "She realized that if she married, all she'd be able to do is teach piano. There's also been some discussion about her relationship with one of the conductors. She was emotionally involved with him, but he may have never reciprocated. She was in this malaise for five years. She composed a few things, but she didn't perform."

Curtis married expressionist painter Paul Burlin in 1914. Three years later, she and her husband relocated to Virginia. At Hampton Institute (now Hampton University), she extended her research to African American music. A four-book series, *Negro Folk Songs*, in 1919, was followed by *Songs and Tales from the Dark Continent* a year later. In her introduction to the former, she explained, "A group of earnest colored men . . . asked me to do for the music of their race what I had tried to do for that of the Indian: to present it with entire genuineness and in a form of publication that could readily be grasped by all people."[19]

On October 16, 1921, Curtis debated Edward Burlingham Hill, the future author of *Modern French Music*, at the International Congress of Art History Convention in Paris. She countered the Harvard professor's argument that there was no true American music by singing tribal songs. "The Europeans had no idea," she said, "we had such interesting folk music in America."[20]

Curtis's excursion abroad ended tragically. Stepping off a streetcar, a week after the debate, she was struck by a taxi and seriously injured. She died shortly afterward. "I just couldn't put it into my novel," Kirkpatrick said, "because I wanted people to experience her life and what she attempted to do, without having to think about her life being cut so short. She never regained consciousness."

The Hampton Institute dedicated a monument to Curtis's memory in 1926. "It was her almost divine quality of understanding," said New York attorney Elbridge L. Adams, "and entering into the inner spirit of another race or individual which gave her tremendous influence."[21]

3

Assimilation

Being Indigenous doesn't mean surrendering cultural identity, but it isn't easy.

"Sometimes it seems you and I are living in two very different worlds," said Ron Gurley (Tsalagi) of the Amber Alert in Indian country initiative, "the tribal community, which is based on thousands of years of language, drum, stories, traditions, etc., and the dominant society which is fast-paced, technology-driven and constantly changing."[1]

"Holding onto my culture in the modern world," explained Diné hoop dancer Patrick Willie, "is about identity and remembering where I come from."[2]

"I can be a Sisseton-Wahpeton Dakota," added Murray Lee of *Partnership with Native Americans*, "descended from and existing because of my ancestors and what they did for me so many generations in the past. I can also be an American citizen that offers his culture to those around him and accepts theirs with understanding and a willingness to face the future . . . a future that is forged one day at a time and can be exactly what I strive to make of it."[3]

The mere existence of Indigenous music defies over five hundred years of attempts to assimilate Indigenous peoples. Initially, it was through treaties. During the Revolutionary War, the Second Continental Congress authorized Benjamin Franklin and Patrick Henry to negotiate agreements. Congress established the Committee on Indian Affairs in 1775, to oversee trade and treaty relations. The War Department took it over in 1789.

Believing them "vital to the national security" and partly responsible for "the very survival of the fragile republic,"[4] the first president, George Washington, dined with Mohawks, Senecas, Oneidas, Cherokees, Chickasaws, and Creeks. He attempted to purchase Indigenous land, but "when Indians refused to sell, [he] was ready to wage war against them."[5]

Washington's successor, John Adams, continued his policies, but the third president, Thomas Jefferson, took things further. The chief architect of the Constitution "was fascinated by Indians," said Gaye Wilson of the Robert H. Smith International Center for Jefferson Studies at Monticello. "He had a curiosity, an admiration. He had a romantic streak, and the Indians caught his imagination, so he was interested in studying them, being with them, collecting languages, and determining their origins."[6]

The Sage of Monticello was anything but benevolent. A decade and a half before taking the presidential oath, he recommended the removal of Indigenous peoples from the East. "I would never cease pursuing them," he wrote in 1776, "while one of them remained on this side of the Mississippi."[7]

As president, Jefferson reminded Congress that, since Washington, the federal government's goal of replacing "the Indian's culture with our own" had been "the cheapest and safest way of subduing the Indians, of providing a safe habitat for the country's white inhabitants, of helping the whites acquire desirable land, and of changing the Indian's economy so that he would be content with less land."[8]

After acquiring 828,000 square miles, from the French First Republic, via the 1803 Louisiana Purchase, Jefferson added nearly 200,000 square miles more through treaties with a dozen tribes in nine states. He obtained additional land by driving the Indigenous into insolvency. "To promote this disposition to exchange lands," he wrote to future president William Henry Harrison, then provincial governor of Indiana, "which they have to spare, and we want . . . we shall push our trading uses and be glad to see the good and influential individuals among them run in debt. We observe that when these debts get beyond what the individuals can pay, they become willing to lop them off by a cession of lands."[9]

Inviting tribal leaders to the White House in January 1809, Jefferson warned, "The tribe which shall begin an unprovoked war against us, we will extirpate from the earth or drive to such a distance as they shall never again be able to strike us."[10]

Addressing assimilation, he continued, "You will become one people with us; your blood will mix with ours . . . spread with ours over this great land."[11]

The Indian Civilization Act of 1819 provided funding to "civilize" the Indigenous by "getting rid of their traditions and customs and teaching them reading and writing in the missionary schools to replace . . . Lakota Iyapi with Wasicuya (Caucasian) and Christian practices."[12]

In June 1876 Canada passed the Gradual Civilization Act, or Act for the Gradual Civilization of the Indian Tribes. Along with similarly repressive edicts, it consolidated into the Indian Act. Sacred ceremonies, including the potlatch and sun dance, were banned. First Nation members who were designated as "civilized" could vote and were given farmland. "Civility," however, was determined by a board of commissioners who "reported in writing to the Governor any such Indian of the male sex, and not under twenty-one years of age . . . able to speak, to read and write or instructed in the usual branches of school education; and if they shall find him able to speak readily either the English or the French language, of sober and industrious habits, free from debt, and sufficiently intelligent to be capable of managing his own affairs."[13]

The assimilation of Indigenous peoples was sanctioned by fifteenth-century papal bulls, edicts, and decrees collectively known as the *Doctrine of Discovery*, or the *Doctrine of Christian Domination*. "The European nations claimed for themselves the entire Western Hemisphere," said Oren Lyons (Onondaga), "a demonstration of the incredible arrogance of the time."[14]

Pope Nicholas V's *Dum Diversas* (While different) set the doctrine's principles on June 14, 1452, four decades before Columbus's maiden voyage, by granting Portugal's king Afonso V authority to "capture, vanquish, and subdue all Saracens [Muslims] and pagans whatsoever, and other enemies of Christ wheresoever placed, and the kingdoms, dukedoms, principalities, dominions, possessions, and all movable and immovable goods whatsoever held and possessed by them and to reduce their persons to perpetual slavery."[15]

The 1455 *Romanus Pontifex* further bestowed "suitable favors and special graces on those Catholic kings and princes . . . athletes and intrepid champions of the Christian faith."

Applied in Africa, Asia, Australia, New Zealand, and three Americas, the doctrine encouraged colonizers to take over any non-Christian land considered "terra nullius," or unoccupied by Christians. The doctrine, however, authorized more than land acquisition. Issued in May 1493, two months after Columbus's return to Europe, Pope Alexander VI's *Inter Caetera* emphasized that "if Native inhabitants refused to convert, they could be displaced, enslaved, or even killed."[16]

Inter Caetera set the missionary movement into full gear; calling for the appointment of "God-fearing, learned, skilled, and experienced men . . . to instruct the aforesaid inhabitants and residents in the Catholic faith and train them in good morals."[17]

"If [the Indigenous] converted . . . they would be saved," said the founder of *Lakota Times* and Indian Country Today, Tim Giago (Oglala Lakota), sarcastically, "and much more, they would be civilized."[18]

The doctrine didn't go unchallenged. Pope Paul III's *Sublimis Deus: On the Enslavement and Evangelization of Indians* (1537) declared that "the said Indians and all other people who may later be discovered by Christians, are by no means to be deprived of their liberty or the possession of their property, even though they be outside the faith of Jesus Christ; and that they may and should, freely and legitimately, enjoy their liberty and the possession of their property; nor should they be in any way enslaved; should the contrary happen, it shall be null and have no effect."[19]

When Pope Paul III withdrew ecclesiastic penalties for violating the document, missionaries weren't the only ones emboldened. Before becoming the seventh president, nearly three centuries later, Andrew Jackson (1767–1845) would use it to justify leading military forces against tribes throughout the southeastern United States.

Practicing law in Salisbury, North Carolina, since his teens, Jackson was admitted to the bar in 1787. After representing the new state of Tennessee in the U.S. House of Representatives (1796–98), he was elected to the Tennessee Supreme Court in 1798, where he served until 1804. Military strategy was Jackson's passion. Thirteen years old when he joined the community militia to fight the British during the American Revolution, he was appointed as a colonel of the Tennessee Militia in 1801 and promoted to commander a year later. As major general during the 1813–14 Creek War, he was victorious at the Battle of Horseshoe Bend in the Mississippi Territory (now Alabama). He rose to national prominence by defeating the British at the 1815 Battle of New Orleans. Commemorated by a much-played fiddle tune, it inspired a chart-topping hit (with lyrics) for Jimmy Driftwood in 1959. Lonnie Donegan, Pete Seeger, the Royal Guardsmen, Johnny Cash, Leon Russell, Dolly Parton, Nitty Gritty Dirt Band, and Deep Purple are some who have covered it.

Jackson next turned his attention to the First Seminole War (1817–18), which would result in the annexation of Florida from Spain. Without authorization, he retaliated against the Seminole Indians for aligning with the Spanish. After attacking the Spanish fort at St. Marks, Jackson "marched east to the Suwanne River and attacked the village of [Seminole principal chief] Boleck. Many Indians escaped into the swamps."[20]

As federal military commissioner of Florida from March to December 1821, Jackson negotiated treaties with what were considered the Five Civilized Tribes—Choctaws, Chickasaws, Creeks, Seminoles, and Cherokees. He acquired fifty million acres of tribal land using military threats and bribery.

The Supreme Court affirmed the doctrine in its decision of *Johnson and Graham's Lessee v. M'Intosh*. "The principle of discovery," asserted Chief Justice John Marshall, "gave European nations an absolute right to New World lands."[21]

In that same year, 1823, James Monroe stirred the belief that the country's expansion was divinely ordained. Speaking to Congress, the fifth president presented what would come to be known as the Monroe Doctrine, written primarily by the secretary of state and future president John Quincy Adams. "The American continents, by the free and independent condition which they have assumed and maintain," Monroe claimed, "are henceforth not to be considered as subjects for colonization by any European powers."[22]

In 1825 Monroe proposed relocating Indians east of the Mississippi River to the new Indian Territory, in present-day Oklahoma, obtained in the Louisiana Purchase. "Experience has . . . demonstrated," Monroe argued, "that, in their present state, it is impossible to incorporate them in such masses, in any form whatever, into our system. Their degradation and extermination will be inevitable."[23]

Despite scoring the most popular and electoral votes, Jackson was defeated in his first presidential bid, by John Quincy Adams, in 1824—an election decided, after backroom deals, by the House of Representatives. Successfully running again four years later, as the first candidate of the new Democratic Party, Jackson became chief executive on March 4, 1829. A year later Congress passed the Indian Removal Act. Jackson addressed legislators that December. "It gives me pleasure to announce," he proclaimed, "that the benevolent policy of the Government, steadily pursued for nearly thirty years, in relation to the removal of the Indians beyond the white settlements, is approaching to a happy consummation."[24]

The elimination of Cherokees, Choctaws, Chickasaws, Creeks, and Seminoles made room for southern mansions and slave plantations. The owner of hundreds of slaves, Jackson "expressed his loathing for the abolitionists vehemently, both in public and in private."[25]

"Jacksonian Democracy . . . was about the extension of white supremacy across the North American continent," said historian Daniel Walker Howe.[26]

Under military invasion, the Choctaw became the first nation expelled from their land in the winter of 1831. In that same year, the Cherokee Nation pleaded with the Supreme Court to reverse their forced removal from Georgia. Defining the tribe as a "domestic dependent nation," the court refused to hear the case.[27] Later that year, Vermont-born missionary Samuel Worcester and other non-Indigenous settlers were indicted in Georgia for "residing within the limits of the Cherokee nation without a license."[28]

Sentenced to four years of hard labor, Worcester appealed the verdict. In September 1831 the Supreme Court ruled that "the Cherokee nation . . . is a distinct community occupying its own territory in which the laws of Georgia can have no force."[29]

Ignoring the decision, Jackson continued to apply the Indian Removal Act. Pushing through the Treaty of New Echota, in December 1835, he purchased the Cherokee's 4,366,554 acres, as well as "many rich gold mines and many delightful situations and though in some parts mountainous, some of the richest land belonging to the state" for $5 million, relocation assistance, and compensation for lost property.[30] Despite being rejected by the Cherokee National Council and opposed by a majority of the tribe, led by Chief John Ross, the sale remained valid.

Numerous tribes adopted what settlers considered civilized ways. But according to the Constitutional Rights Foundation, "the Cherokees embraced [them] enthusiastically. The Cherokees believed that, if they became more like their white neighbors, the Americans would leave them alone on their remaining land. By the 1820s, most Cherokees were living in family log cabins, cultivating fields on tribal land. Some owned stores and other businesses. A few borrowed from southern whites the idea of establishing large cotton plantations complete with a mansion and Black slaves. The Cherokees also welcomed white Christian missionaries to set up schools to teach English and agricultural skills."[31]

A silversmith and farmer, Sequoyah spent a dozen years developing an eighty-six-character alphabet based on spoken syllables of the Cherokee language. In 1828 the *Cherokee Phoenix*, the first Indigenous newspaper, began publishing in Cherokee and English. The same year, the tribe adopted a constitution. It didn't matter.

Many Chickasaw, Choctaw, Seminole, Creek, Quapaw, Sauk, and Kanza left voluntarily, but the Cherokee resisted. In 1838 Martin Van Buren, who succeeded Jackson a year before, oversaw the mandatory removal that would be memorialized as the Trail of Tears. General Winfield Scott "forced the Cherokee into stockades at bayonet point while his [7,000 soldiers] looted their homes and belongings. Then, they marched the Indians more than 1,200 miles to Indian Territory."[32]

The routes of the trail spread more than five thousand miles through Alabama, Arkansas, Georgia, Illinois, Kentucky, Missouri, North Carolina, and Tennessee before ending in Oklahoma Territory. More than 25 percent of the approximately sixteen thousand Cherokee making the four-month trek failed to reach their destination. "Whooping cough, typhus, dysentery, cholera and starvation were epidemic along the way."[33]

Contrasting views about national growth fueled the 1844 presidential election. The new Whig Party's candidate, Virginia-born Henry Clay, opposed the call for westward expansion from the Democrats' North Carolina–born James Knox Polk.

In May 1845, two months after Polk took office, journalist John Louis O'Sullivan addressed the annexation of Texas (which would lead to a war with Mexico) and the acquisition of Oregon Territory. Declaring that it was the nation's "Manifest Destiny . . . to possess the whole continent," O'Sullivan's editorial in the *United States Magazine and Democratic Review* reaffirmed Monroe's belief that a higher power intended the United States to span from the Atlantic to the Pacific.

Meanwhile, in Canada, the country's first prime minister, Sir John A. Macdonald, spoke of stretching the railroad "from sea to sea," the Latin translation of which (*a Mari usque ad mare*) remains the country's official motto.

Assimilation was the goal of 408 federally funded Indigenous boarding schools in the United States and 139 church-supported residential schools in Canada. Secretary of War John C. Calhoun established the Office of Indian Affairs, without Congressional authorization, in 1824, to administer funds for the schools. Transferring to the Department of the Interior, it was known by various names before becoming the Bureau of Indian Affairs (BIA) in 1947.

Opened in 1860, a school on the Yakima Reservation, in Washington, was the first to be federally funded. By the end of the 1880s, a government-supported school was on every reservation.

The off-the-reservation Carlisle Indian Industrial School took over the grounds of a former military college between Philadelphia and Pittsburgh in 1878. Before it closed, thirty years later, it was attended by 10,500 youngsters from 142 Indigenous nations. More than 180 lost their lives to a combination of malnourishment, abuse, and disease.

In Canada an amendment to the Indian Act made it mandatory for Indigenous children to attend a residential school and illegal for them to attend any other. Between 1894 and 1947, more than 150,000 First Nation youngsters attended a boarding school.

Arriving by train, students on both sides of the border prepared for "civilized life." After their hair was cut (a symbol of mourning for the Lakota), boys changed into military-like uniforms and girls into Victorian-style dresses. Assigned Christian names, they were forbidden from speaking their language, singing tribal songs, or observing rituals. Rule breakers faced severe punishment. Carlisle's Indiana-born founder and superintendent, Colonel Richard Henry Pratt, believed strict discipline would "kill the Indian and save the man."[34]

Pratt crafted his disciplinary approach while overseeing seventy-two Cheyenne, Kiowa, Comanche (Niminu or Nemene), Arapaho, and Caddo Indian prisoners at Fort Marion in St. Augustine, Florida, in 1875. Accused of killing white settlers, they had been sentenced without a trial. "I believe in immersing the Indians in our civilization," Pratt explained, "and when we get them under holding them there until they are thoroughly soaked."[35] (Pratt would supervise Carlisle until retiring in February 1903. A year later he would become a brigadier general on the retired list.)

Canada's Truth and Reconciliation Commission documented 3,200 deaths and 38,000 sexual and physical abuse claims from residential school survivors. Media attention increased after more than one thousand unmarked graves were uncovered at three former schools in July 2021. Prime Minister Justin Trudeau claimed to be "horrified and ashamed of how our country behaved."[36]

In a May 2022 report, the U.S. Interior Department acknowledged the deaths of five hundred Indigenous Americans, Alaskan Aleuts and Inuits, and Native Hawaiian students at boarding schools. "Each of those children is a missing family member," said Interior Secretary Deb Haaland (Laguna Pueblo), the second Indigenous American to serve on the cabinet, "a person who was not able to live out their purpose on this Earth because they lost their lives as part of this terrible system."[37]

Indigenous peoples became tenants at will in the United States, in 1886, after the Supreme Court declared, "The soil and the people within these limits are under the political control of the government of the United States, or . . . the States of the Union. There exist within the broad domain of sovereignty but these two."[38]

Indigenous women married to U.S. citizens became citizens in 1888, but it would take another quarter of a century before World War I veterans were eligible for citizenship. The 1924 Indian Citizenship Act extended to all Native Americans, but the right to vote was determined by state laws until 1957.

Authorized by President Harry S. Truman in 1948 and directed by his predecessor, Herbert Hoover, the Hoover Commission's Indian Affairs Committee reported, "Assimilation must be the dominant goal of public policy. On this point there can be no doubt. . . . The basis for historic Indian culture has been swept away. . . . Assimilation cannot be prevented."[39]

Truman's "solution to the Indian problem," contended Philleo Nash, a former commissioner of Indian Affairs, was "to wipe out the reservations and scatter the Indians and then there [wouldn't] be Indian tribes, Indian cultures, or Indian individuals."[40]

Between 1952 and 1972 the BIA provided "one-way transportation and a couple hundred dollars to Native Americans willing to move to a city,"[41] especially to the San Francisco Bay Area, Los Angeles, Phoenix, Dallas, Minneapolis, Denver, or Cleveland. The program was anything but a success. A BIA commissioner called it "an underfunded, ill-conceived program . . . essentially a one-way ticket from rural to urban poverty."[42]

In August 1953 the U.S. Congress enacted House Concurrent Resolution 108, also known as the Termination Act. Over the following decade, more than one hundred tribes in eight states lost their official recognition, thus depriving them of tax-exempt status and grant opportunities. The act would be repudiated by the Federally Recognized Indian Tribe Act in 1994, but there are still many tribes without official designation.

Appearing on the radio series *Indian Country* in 1957, one misguided white BIA official claimed, "I've always felt that the only real solution for the Navajo was to cease to be a Navajo—to get off the reservation and become a citizen just like everybody else, and make his living the same way as other people."[43]

Christianity's dominance of Indigenous North America reached its peak at the end of the twentieth century. According to the *Tribal College*, in 1994 "more than 80 percent of native Americans claim membership in a Christian church."[44]

"I was told I needed to become a Christian too," said Dr. Richard Twiss (Sicangu Lakota Oyate), author of *One Church Many Tribes: Serving Jesus the Way God Made You*, "specifically a Euro-American Christian. I learned that only English speakers had the 'authorized' version of the Bible. I discovered the Christian culture complete with Christian music, Christian T-shirts, and even Christian haircuts. It was almost as if the Bible read, 'When a person becomes a Christian they become a new creation. Old things pass away, and all things become white.'"[45]

Since the enactment of the 1978 American Indian Freedom of Religion Act, Indigenous peoples have increasingly returned to tribal roots. Some Christian denominations have adjusted. "It isn't uncommon to hear traditional drumming at the Catholic church that serves the Lummi Nation in Washington State," explains Carolyn Casey.[46]

In 2004 the United Methodist Church resolved, "There are many Native traditions, languages, customs, and expressions of faith; that in the best of Native traditions, the church, and the spirit of ecumenism, we allow for the work of the Spirit of God among our communities and tribes without prejudice."[47]

Membership in the NAC has increased exponentially. Blending the spiritual beliefs of northern Mexico's Indigenous cultures (specifically the Huichol and Tonkawa) and Christianity, the monotheistic church developed among the White Mountain Apache in Oklahoma Territory in the 1870s and spread to other southern Plains tribes by the end of the century. The last (federally appointed) Comanche chief and a veteran of the Plains Indian Wars, Quanah Parker joined religious leaders, including Jim Aton, Jonathan Koshiway, and John Wilson, to expand the church's popularity. Today the NAC is the most widespread Indigenous religion in the United States, Canada, and Mexico, with more than 250,000 adherents. Michael Waasegiizhig Price (Anishinaabe) wrote in *Tribal College*, "Somewhere back in time, our ancestors learned that certain rituals or medicines can heal a person from physical pain or emotional trauma."[48]

The church's sacramental use of the hallucinatory mescal (peyote) flower or "button" (*Lophophora williamsii*) gets the most non-Indigenous attention, but its music traditions are deep. "In the mystery of the spirit world of Native American people," said multi-instrumentalist and composer David Amram, "there is the same quality of timelessness that there is in all true music."[49]

In *The Encyclopedia of Native Music*, Brian Wright-McLeod discusses the instruments used during the all-night prayer, meditation, and song ceremony, including "the cast-iron kettle water drum, the eagle bone whistle, which is used twice during the meeting by the road when calling for midnight and morning water; the gourd rattle; and the human voice."[50]

"The mescal songs are all esoteric," observed Natalie Curtis in 1907. "They contain no words, the meaning usually being known only to the members of the same lodge or fraternity, or sometimes only to the singer or to the man who made the song. . . . The mescal songs are invocations that the truths of the universe may be revealed."[51]

"Peyote chants are generally uniform from one tribe to another," explained Canyon Records' liner notes for *Healing Chants of the Native American Church* (1972), "which make them unique in American Indian music. They are also unlike any of the traditional songs of the Plains

Indians where the Native American Church developed. The high degree of tension, breaks, quavers, and accents typical of Plains music are absent. They are sung in quiet unstressed style similar to the tribes of the Sonoran Desert and parts of Mexico."[52]

"To us, [peyote] is a portion of the body of Christ," said Carlisle survivor Albert Hensley (Winnebago), "even as the communion bread is believed to be a portion of Christ's body by other Christian denominations. Christ spoke of a Comforter who was to come. It never came to Indians until it was sent by God in the form of this Holy Medicine."[53]

Despite growing opposition, the *Doctrine of Discovery* remains the law of the land. Though known for her progressive views, Supreme Court Justice Ruth Bader Ginsburg cited it in opposing Haudenosaunee land reclamation efforts in New York State (*City of Sherrill v. Oneida Indian Nation of New York*) in 2005. "Ginsberg's legacy presents profound realities on reconciliation," said a poster on University of Alberta's law blog, "that even those with the sharpest eye towards 'equality under the law' can fail to move past the historic legal frameworks that dehumanize Indigenous communities and invalidate their autonomy."[54]

During the Standing Rock protest, an interfaith congregation of 524 clergy people burned copies of *Inter Caetera*. "There are moments in a life of faith," explained Rev. Noah H. Evans, rector of Grace Episcopal Church, Medford, Massachusetts, "where we have to stand with a larger community in solidarity with people who are being marginalized and this is one of those moments."[55]

4

Stereotypical

Searching for the legendary golden cities of Cibola in Zuni Territory (present-day Cibola County, New Mexico), in July 1540, Francisco Vasquez de Coronado y Lujan ordered his 500 Spanish soldiers and 1,500 Native and African American allies to ransack Pueblo Hawikuh. Inhabited since the 1200s, the pueblo became the first permanent Indigenous settlement invaded by a Spanish conquistador. Its attacker would be "disappointed to find the rumored golden city to be nothing more than a dusty, crowded Zuni village."[1]

Eighty-nine years later, Mission La Purísima Concepción opened in Hawikuh in 1620. It was the fourth new mission in Zuni Territory that year. In addition to Bible study, Natives were instructed in musical counterpoint, bassoon and organ playing, and Gregorian chant. The Spaniards' efforts proved futile, in 1672, when an Apache raid resulted in a priest's death and the mission being burned.

Conflicts between the Rio Grande's original inhabitants and the Spaniards continued to intensify. In 1675 forty-seven spiritual leaders from the pueblos were arrested for "witchcraft." Three were executed, and one committed suicide. The rest were severely beaten and threatened with being sold into slavery. Angered by the injustice, seventy warriors stormed the governor's office demanding the prisoners' release. Already dealing with Apache and Diné war parties, the governor agreed.

One of the men freed was Popé or Po'pay (ca. 1630–ca. 1692) (Tewa) from Ohkay Owingeh (renamed San Juan de los Caballeros from 1589 to 2005) in Rio Arriba County, New Mexico. Calling for a return to the old way of life and the expulsion of the Spaniards, Popé secretly visited each pueblo. Despite their separation by languages and beliefs, he managed to convince all but two to join what would be the colonies' first rebellion, set for August 13, 1680. Although the days remaining were counted down by a deerskin rope with knotted cords, the revolt ignited three days before schedule. Continuing for eleven days, it was extremely successful. Popé's battalion of 2,500 warriors easily defeated the 1,000 Spaniards, killing 400, including 21 of 33 priests. The remaining Spaniards retreated to El Paso, Texas, or to Mexico. Zuni warriors destroyed Mission La Purísima Concepción a final time. Spain wouldn't return to the area for a dozen years. Popé proclaimed the God of Christianity dead. A statue of the religious leader and activist would be added to the U.S. Capitol's Statuary Hall in September 2005. Sculptured from Tennessee marble by Cliff Fragua (Jemez Pueblo), it stands seven feet tall.

For Christianity, Popé's rebellion had little impact. London-born Roger Williams (ca. 1603–83) continued to convert Narragansett Indians in Rhode Island. His dictionary, *A Key to the Language of America; or, An Help to the Language of the Natives in That Part of America, Called New England* (1643), was the first in-depth study of a Native language printed in the colonies.

Williams's views set him apart. "He believed that Indians had the same property rights as Englishmen," explained *Smithsonian Magazine*, "and therefore just because the crown gave an Englishman land didn't mean it had any legal authority."[2]

An editor of the first book published in the colonies, *The Bay Psalm Book* (1640), Thomas Mayhew the Elder (1593–1682), born in Wiltshire, England, colonized Martha's Vineyard, Nantasket, and adjacent islands south of Cape Cod in 1641. Befriending the three thousand Wampanoags who lived in permanent settlements on Martha's Vineyard, Mayhew's son Thomas Mayhew the Younger (ca. 1621–57) established an Indian school in 1652. After his death by drowning, while sailing to England, his father assumed his missionary work. Taught the Wampanoag language by Hiacoomes, possibly the colonies' first Christian convert, the self-proclaimed "Governour and Chiefe Magistrate" of Martha's Island preached to the Indigenous in their language. On some days, he would "walk twenty miles through uncut forests to preach the Gospel . . . in wigwam or open field."[3]

Mayhew's assistant, Peter Foulger, became Benjamin Franklin's grandfather.

Between 1646 and 1690, Puritan minister Rev. John Eliot (1604–90) sang hymns with Wampanoags and other Natives in Nonantum (Newton), Massachusetts. Devising a written Algonquin lexicon, the "Indians' apostle" from Widford, England, translated and published editions of the Old and New Testaments. Eliot is credited with converting more than 1,100 Natives and setting up fourteen singing communities.

"Neither Cordeliers nor nuns ever sang as do our Iroquois men and women," observed a Franciscan missionary in 1763. "Their voices are both mellow and sonorous, and their ear is so correct that they do not miss a halftone in all their church hymns, which they know by heart."[4]

Born in Charlestown, Rhode Island, and a veteran of singing communities in Oneida, New York, and Calumet County, Wisconsin, Thomas Commuck (1804–55) (Narragansett) included 120 original hymns in *Indian Melodies* (1845), the first book published by an Indigenous American. Non-Indigenous singing teacher Thomas Hastings harmonized Commuck's tunes in shape note notation. Commuck titled his hymns "as a tribute of respect," he explained, "to the memory of some tribes that are now nearly if not quite extinct."[5]

The musical exchange flowed two ways. One of the first missionaries to New France's Huron Country (Great Lakes region), Gabriel Sagard (baptized Theódat) (fl. 1614–36) published four-part transcriptions of Mi'kmaq and Tupinamba songs in 1636.

More than 250 years later, New York–born Theodore Baker (1851–1931) collected songs from the Senecas in New York and students at Carlisle (one of the rare times they got to express their culture). Graduating with a doctorate from University of Music and Theater in Leipzig, Germany, in 1881, Baker published his dissertation, "Über die Musik de Nordeamerikanischen Wilden" ("On the Music of Native American Indians"), in 1888. Themes from Baker's book would be interpolated into Edward MacDowell's *Indian Suite for Orchestra* (1892). A year later Antonín Leopold Dvořák (1841–1904), Czechia-born director of the National Conservatory of Music in New York, composed Symphony no. 9 in E Minor (*New World Symphony*), op. 95, B. 178, by writing "original themes embodying the peculiarities of the Indian music . . . [and developing] them with all the resources of modern rhythms, counterpoints, and orchestral color."[6]

Composed between 1898 and 1900, Samuel Coleridge-Taylor's cantata trilogy, *The Song of Hiawatha* op. 30, transformed Henry David Longfellow's poem about the Iroquois Confederacy into music. Sheet music of its most successful section, "Hiawatha's Wedding Feast," fared well, but, before publication, its London-born, Anglo-African composer (1875–1912) sold his rights for fifteen guineas (less than a dollar) and did not benefit any further.

In 1905 cornet player and vocalist Thurlow Weed Lieurance (1878–1963) began touring reservations with a Chautauqua tent show. Born in Oskaloosa, Iowa, and raised in Kansas, the future University of Wichita dean of fine arts immersed himself in Indigenous culture, teaching himself to make and play Native American flutes.

Polio may have hampered Lieurance's walking, but it didn't stop him. Two years after acquiring a portable cylinder recorder from Edison Records, he recorded Sitting Eagle (Mortimer Dreamer) on the Crow reservation, in Montana, in October 1911. Adapting one of Sitting Eagle's songs, he composed "By the Waters of Minnetonka." Theodore Presser subtitled it "An Indian Love Song" when he published it (with lyrics by J. M. Cavaness) in 1913. Glenn Miller recorded a big band version in 1938. Lucille Ball and Desi Arnaz lampooned it on an episode of *I Love Lucy*. "The work itself is a perfect vehicle for interpretation," Lieurance said. "It just seems to roll on when played."[7]

Along with *Indian Suite for Orchestra* and *New World Symphony*, "By the Waters of Minnetonka" sparked a fad for Indianist music. Non-Indigenous composers, including Charles Sanford Skilton, Arthur Nevin, and Charles Wakefield Cadman, began incorporating Native themes into their music. Edward MacDowell used two of Commuck's hymns in his compositions. The movement flourished into the 1920s. Even John Philip Sousa's brass band played Indianist tunes ("Red Man" and "Hiawatha"). "Sousa enjoyed being made an honorary chief in three different tribes," said Paul Mayberry of the Chatfield Brass Band, "and given the Indian names: 'Great Music Chief,' 'Chasing Hawk,' and 'Chief Singer.'"[8]

Arthur Farwell published transcriptions of Indianist compositions in a subscription magazine, the *Wa-Wan Press*, from 1901 to 1912. Its name was derived from the Omaha word for peace and friendship. "When one race conquers, absorbs, or annihilates another," the Minnesota-born publisher and composer based in Newton, Massachusetts, contended in 1903, "the spirit, the *animus* of the destroyed race invariably persists, in the end, in all its aspects,—its arts, customs, traditions, temper,—in the life of the conquering race."[9]

Broadway added to the appropriation. Sung by Ethel Merman in *Annie Get Your Gun*, Irving Berlin's "I'm an Indian Too" prompted protests when the fictionalized portrayal of Wild West sharpshooter Annie Oakley premiered at New York's Imperial Theater on May 16, 1946. The musical would run for 1,147 performances.

Chosen to play Oakley in the Academy Award–winning 1950 film, Judy Garland was fired after clashing with director George Sidney and choreographer Busby Berkeley and being repeatedly late. Betty Hutton took her place. Garland's deleted scenes are available on YouTube.

Accompanied by an orchestra and chorus directed by Franz Allers, Doris Day included Berlin's tune on an album of songs from the soundtrack recorded with Robert Goulet in 1963. Don Armando's Second Avenue Rhumba Band released a disco version in 1979.

On the silver screen, Disney's animated *Peter Pan* (1953) included "What Makes an Indian Red?" by Sammy Kahn, Frank Churchill, Sammy Fain, and Ted Sears. Sung by Thurl "Tony the Tiger" Ravenscroft and the Mellomen, its lyrics included the terms "squaw," "paleface," and "Injun." In 2015 Frank Waln (Sicangu Lakota) did a stereotype-busting update. "I owe it to my ancestors," the Rosebud-born rapper and producer told me, "to not waste my gift of music."

Non-Indigenous musicians poked fun at love-struck Indians ("Little Bear") and cowardly warriors ("Mr. Custer"). Bill Haley and the Comets, the Beach Boys, and Harry Nilsson revived Septimus Winner's deceptively racist minstrel show and preschool ditty, "Ten Little Indians" ("Ten Little Injuns"), from 1868.

Movie and TV commitments prevented Shelby Frederick "Sheb" Wooley from recording Lorene Mann's "Don't Go Near the Indians" before Rex Allen scored a hit with it in 1962, but the singer and actor from Erik, Oklahoma, was undeterred. Famous for his million-selling novelty 1958 hit "Purple People Eater" and regular appearances on TV's *Rawhide*, Wooley parodied Mann's tune with the similarly derogatory "Don't Go

Near the Eskimos." Credited to Wooley's inebriated nom de plume, Ben Colder, the single reached number sixteen on the country charts. It would plague him. "For the rest of his career, Wooley—in a manner anticipating the lot of David Johansen/Buster Poindexter—had to split his time between appearances as 'straight' country/cowboy singer Sheb Wooley and drunken comic Ben Colder."[10]

Dressing in fringed buckskin and beaded headband, Marvin Karlton Rainwater (1925–2013) capitalized on his part-Indigenous ancestry. "It wasn't quite true," confessed the Rockabilly King from Wichita, Kansas. "I've got a little bit of Cherokee blood . . . [but] I got into all kinds of problems when promoted as a full-blooded Indian chief, which was ridiculous. Just look at me. I've got blue eyes and all American Indians have brown eyes. Everyone was getting mad at me, and it wasn't a problem of my doing."[11]

Rainwater's twangy country hits included "Half-Breed" and the chart-topping "Whole Lotta Love." A year before Johnny Preston's chart-topping 1958 hit, Rainwater recorded "Running Bear" by Jules Perry "the Big Bopper" Richardson. Introducing it during shows, he would joke, "Since the Indians tore my clothes off, they call me . . . Yes, you've got it!"[12]

In 1960 Rainwater became the first to record John D. Loudermilk's "Indian Reservation (Lament of the Cherokee Reservation Indian)." When we spoke in September 2012, a year before his passing, he still regretted renaming it "The Pale-Faced Indian." "I just went out of my mind," he said. "What did that have to do with the song?"

Eight years after Rainwater's barely noticed recording, a West Coast rock band sporting Revolutionary War–era garb, Paul Revere and the Raiders featuring Mark Lindsay, restored the song's title and topped the charts.

5

Defiance

Breaking stereotypes was tough. Despite riding high on one of his biggest hits, "Ring of Fire" (number one for seven weeks), and a chart-topping *Best Of* compilation, Johnny Cash had to plead with radio stations, in a full-page open letter in *Billboard*, to play his 1964 Columbia Records follow-up, *Bitter Tears: Johnny Cash Sings Ballads of the American Indian*. After Cash's appeal, the album rose to the runner-up chart position.

"The Ballad of Ira Hayes" was the album's masterpiece. Reaching number three on *Billboard*'s country singles chart, it recounted the tragic saga of a U.S. Marine from the Gila River Pima Reservation in Arizona. A participant in the American flag raising that climaxed a fierce World War II battle on the Japanese archipelago of Iwo Jima (Iō Tō) in March 1945, Hayes (1923–55) was included in a memorial statue (based on a Pulitzer Prize–winning photograph by Joe Rosenthal of the Associated Press) that stands outside of Arlington National Cemetery in Virginia. He played himself in a 1949 film, *The Sands of Iwo Jima*, starring John Wayne. It would be the high point of his life.

Possibly suffering from what would be diagnosed as post-traumatic stress disorder, Hayes drank excessively. After a night of heavy imbibing and poker playing in Bapchule, Arizona, he stumbled into a drainage ditch on January 24, 1955. He would never get out. Two weeks after his thirty-fourth birthday, he succumbed to alcohol poisoning and exposure to the cold. He would be buried with full military honors.

Oliver Albee "Peter" LaFarge (1931–65)

"The Ballad of Ira Hayes" was one of five songs on Cash's album by Peter LaFarge, who had been born in New York but mostly raised in New Mexico and Colorado. The former rodeo cowboy, wrestler, and repertory theater actor's time in the spotlight, however, would be brief. A little over a year after *Bitter Tears*' release, the songwriter was dead. The cause of death was officially listed as a stroke, but Liam Clancy (of the Clancy Brothers) claimed, "He committed suicide in my bathtub. . . . Dylan lived next door."[1]

Gored by a bull at a rodeo, LaFarge was nursing his injuries in Colorado when his songs caught the attention of touring folk singers Josh White and Big Bill Broonzy. Persuaded to return to the Big Apple in the late 1950s, he settled in pre-Dylan Greenwich Village. Mentored by folk singer Cisco Houston, he was immersed in a Woody Guthrie–influenced music scene that included Pete Seeger, Ramblin' Jack Elliott, Dave Van Ronk, and myriad others.

In addition to cowboy and miner songs, LaFarge sang about the sharp realities of Native life, including discrimination, alcoholism, broken treaties, and poverty. Signed by Moses "Moe" Asch's Folkways, he released *On the Warpath* (1961), with "Johnny Half Breed," "If I Could Not Be an Indian," "White Girl," and "I'm an Indian."

"The Crimson Parson" lambasted Colonel John M. Chivington, leader of the Third Colorado Calvary during Colorado Territory's 1864–65 Indian War. A former Methodist preacher, Chivington directed the massacre of more than two hundred peaceful Cheyenne and Arapaho Indians (all but sixty women, children, and elderly, including twelve chiefs) on November 29, 1864. "I have come to kill Indians," he explained, "and I believe it is right and honorable to use any means under God's heaven to kill Indians."[2]

As Long as the Grass Shall Grow (1962) extended the theme with "Damn Redskins," "Tecumseh," "Custer," and "The Trail of Tears." The album's title came from "Seneca (As Long as the Grass Shall Grow)," which lamented the broken promises of the 1794 Treaty of Canandaigua, signed by President George Washington and the Seneca Nation on the New York–Pennsylvania border.

A fifth-generation descendant of Commodore Oliver Hazard Perry, LaFarge was inspired by his father, Oliver Hazard Perry LaFarge, author of Indigenous-themed books including a Pulitzer Prize–winning novel,

Laughing Boy (1929), and president of the Association of American Indian Affairs. His passion for Indigenous peoples, however, went even deeper. His grandfather, Christopher "C" Grant LaFarge, a beaux arts architect who designed New York churches, subway stations, and several Bronx Zoo buildings, wrote anthropological treatises and books about Native tribes.

LaFarge organized an activist group, FAIR (Federation for American Indian Rights), in early 1965, but "the FBI raided his apartment at midnight," said Gordon Friesen in *Broadside*. "They scattered and tore his papers. They put handcuffs on him and dragged him to Bellevue [Psychiatric Hospital] in his pajamas. They put pressure on Bellevue to declare him insane, but Bellevue could find nothing wrong and turned him loose."[3]

"I think it was the police," LaFarge biographer Sandra Schulman told me, "not the FBI. He was planning rallies at a time when there were radicals and Black Panther groups. The police were getting very uneasy about it."

Regardless of who's to blame, a few months after the raid, LaFarge was gone. He was thirty-three.

Beverly "Buffy" Sainte-Marie (1941–) (Piapot Cree)

Born on the Piapot 75 Reserve in Saskatchewan's Qu'Appelle Valley, on February 20, 1941, Buffy Sainte-Marie has provided a more enduring voice. Adopted as a baby and raised north of Boston by parents of part Mi'kmaq ancestry, the multioctave songstress continues to set ripples in the world of Indigenous music.

Sainte-Marie started singing in the coffeehouse at the University of Massachusetts, Amherst. She would earn an undergraduate degree in oriental philosophy and religion in 1963 and a PhD twenty years later. "I knew I was a musician before I knew I was an American Indian," she wrote me in July 2011.

Attracting attention in Greenwich Village, Sainte-Marie signed with Maynard Solomon's Vanguard Records. Opening her debut album, *It's My Way* (1964), with "Now That the Buffalo's Gone," a heartbreaking chronicle of the near extinction of the American bison, she was named *Billboard*'s Best New Artist.

Elvis Presley, Morrissey, Janis Joplin, Gram Parsons, the Charlatans, Jimmy Gilmore, and Courtney Love have covered Sainte-Marie's songs. Scottish folk-pop singer Donovan scored an antiwar hit in 1965 with "Universal Soldier." Two years later, San Francisco's Quicksilver Messenger Service covered "Cod'ine," based on the songwriter's struggle against addiction during treatment for bronchial pneumonia.

As cowriter of "Up Where We Belong," sung by Joe Cocker and Jennifer Warnes in *An Officer and a Gentleman* (1982), Sainte-Marie shared an Oscar, Golden Globe, and British Film Academy Award with Jack Nitzsche and Will Jennings. More than two hundred artists, including Elvis Presley, Barbara Streisand, and the Boston Pops, have recorded it. "The words are about honesty," Sainte-Marie told me, "and freedom inside the heart."

Sainte-Marie's Indigenous-themed tunes include "My Country, Tis of Thy People, You're Dying," "Bury My Heart in Wounded Knee," and the uplifting "He's an Indian Cowboy in the Rodeo." "Most singers are like Volkswagens," she said. "I'm more like a 747. I go longer, farther, stronger, and higher—combining rock and roll with the power of Plains Cree singing. I invented powwow rock forty years ago."

Sainte-Marie's impact has gone beyond music. "She's a total influence on me," said Jeremy Dutcher (Wolastoqiyik), "not only for her songwriting but also because of her activism and the way she moves through the world."

During a 1970s radio interview, Sainte-Marie learned that she had been blacklisted in the United States. "The interviewer apologized," she told me, "for going along with letters from then–President Johnson's administration thanking him for suppressing my music."

The blacklist barely slowed the songstress down. Continuing to record intriguing albums, she reevaluated her "life and career and decided to keep on with [her] original goals—to be a complete artist in two worlds: Native America and the great stages and concert halls around the world." Accompanied by her son, Dakota "Cody" Starblanket, Sainte-Marie appeared semiregularly on *Sesame Street* from 1977 until 1981. "I wanted to show that Indians existed," she said, "that we're not all dead and stuffed in museums like dinosaurs."

Still active in her eighties, Sainte-Marie collaborated with A Tribe Called Red (who later became the Halluci Nation) on a remix of her song "Working for the Government" in 2015. She sang with Nunavut-based throat singer Tanya Tagaq (Inuk) on the title track of her 2017 album, *You Got to Run*. "It's a great life," she wrote me, "and it keeps getting better and better."

Floyd "Kanghi Duta" ("Red Wolf") Westerman
(1936–2007) (Dakota)

Titled after Vine Deloria Jr.'s bestseller, Floyd Westerman's debut album, *Custer Died for Your Sins* (1969), provided a soundtrack for Indigenous resistance. "Some people call us radicals or leftists," said Westerman, "but we are not left or right. We just want the Indians to survive, to help the old Indian way survive because it is the true and tried way."[4]

Born on the Lake Traverse Indian Reservation, home of the Sisseton Wahpeton Oyate branch of the Great Sioux Nation in Northeast South Dakota, Westerman was taken from his mother at the age of ten and placed in the Wahpeton Indian School. "At first, he thought he was on the bus because his mother didn't want him anymore," said Charla Bear of NPR, "but then he noticed she was crying."[5]

Befriending classmate and future AIM co-founder Dennis Banks (Ojibwe), from the Leech Lake Indian Reservation in Northern Minnesota, Westerman would perform at many benefit concerts. "He was really, really politically conscious," said his son Richard Tall Bear Westerman. "He said the Iraq war is just another land grab, like they did with Oklahoma and the Midwest in America. Back then it was about land and gold, and now it was about oil."[6]

Graduating with a secondary education degree from Northern State University, in Aberdeen, South Dakota, Westerman spent two years in the U.S. Marines before settling in Denver and becoming a Johnny Cash–influenced country singer (his fourth and final album would be *A Tribute to Johnny Cash* in 2006). His original songs continued to address Indigenous issues.

Westerman's acting eclipsed his fame as a musician. Portraying nineteenth-century Oglala Lakota leader Red Cloud in *The Renegades* (1989), he appeared as Chief Ten Chiefs in *Dances with Wolves* (1990) and a shaman in Oliver Stone's *The Doors* (1991). He was a guest on TV's

Northern Exposure and *The X Files* and had recurring roles on *Walker, Texas Ranger* and *Dharma and Greg*.

During more than sixty foreign tours, Westerman not only promoted Indigenous rights but also joined Harry Belafonte, Jackson Browne, and Bonnie Raitt to speak out against nuclear power. He raised awareness about endangered rainforests with Sting.

"We are all from the earth," he said. "And when earth, water, and the atmosphere is corrupted, then it will create its own reaction. Mother is reacting."[7]

In September 2000 Westerman launched Red Crow Creations, the first Hollywood studio to focus on Indigenous films, TV shows, multimedia programs, and educational curricula. Its first release was *Exterminate Them! The California Story*. "The Indian point of view in America is so important today," Westerman explained. "We have agonized for several centuries now over why the Indian point of view is not mentioned."[8]

Willie Dunn (1941–2013) (Mi'kmaq, English, and Cornish)

Willie Dunn directed Canada's first music video, *The Ballad of Crowfoot*, in 1968. Based on a song from the Montreal-born singer-songwriter's debut album, the ten-minute film presented an Indigenous view of colonialism. Making an immediate impact, it scored seven international awards, including a Gold Hugo for Best Short Film at the 1969 Chicago International Film Festival.

Dunn went on to direct such films as *These Are My People* (1969) and *The Other Side of the Ledger: An Indian View of the Hudson Bay Company* (1972), but he also continued to write and record meaningful songs. "Charlie" relayed the tragic tale of a twelve-year-old boy who froze to death after running away from a boarding school.

Condemning "buyers of bigoted news" and "fascist town criers," "I Pity the Country" resurfaced in 2021 on the Grammy-nominated *Native North America*, volume 1, *Aboriginal Folk, Rock, and Country 1966–1985*, compiled by Kevin Howes, a deejay and music historian. (Other artists on the album were Duke Redbird, Shingoose, Sikumuit, and the Saddle Lake Drifting Cowboys.)

Eight years after Dunn's 2013 passing, his son, Lawrence, collaborated with Howes on a twenty-two-track retrospective, *Creation Never Sleeps, Creation Never Dies: The Willie Dunn Anthology.* "He was always grinding the ax," Lawrence remembered of his father, "and trying to push his music out to a wider audience, but he ended up hitting a lot of walls. . . . I think part of that has to do with the content of the kind of music he was singing and the message he was putting out."[9]

John Trudell (1946–2015) (Santee Sioux and Mexican)
Jesse Ed Davis (1944–88)
(Kiowa, Comanche, Seminole, and Muscogee)

John Trudell, born in Omaha, Nebraska, arrived on San Francisco Bay's Alcatraz Island in November 1969. Along with Indigenous activists and community members calling themselves Indians of All Tribes (IAT), the twenty-one-year-old San Bernardino Valley College radio announcer, attending school under the GI Bill, remained at the former federal prison until the occupation's conclusion, nineteen months later, on June 11, 1971. His Radio Free Alcatraz reports on Pacifica stations in California, Texas, and New York drew more than one hundred thousand listeners and linked protestors with the outside world. "Alcatraz is more than just a rock to us," he explained. "It's a stepping-stone to a better future. We have a chance to unite the American Indian people as they never had the opportunity to do."[10]

Trudell's broadcasts provided a springboard for direct action. After participating in the Longest Walk, or Trail of Broken Treaties, from California to Washington DC, and a six-day occupation of the BIA building, in late 1972, he served as AIM chairperson from 1973 to 1979.

In February 1976 the Royal Canadian Mounted Police (RCMP) arrested Leonard Peltier (Lakota, Dakota, and French) in Hinton, Alberta, Canada. Extradited to the United States, the AIM member from the Turtle Mountain Indian Reservation, St. John, North Dakota, was one of four accused of murdering FBI special agents Jack R. Coler and Ronald A. Williams on June 26, 1975, the peak of the occupation of the Oglala Lakota's Pine Ridge Indian Reservation in South Dakota. Led by AIM members, including Russell Means, two hundred Oglala Lakota activists demanded "that the U.S. government make good on treaties from the 19th and early 20th centuries." Emily Chertoff explained in the *Atlantic*, "In particular, they sought the removal of tribal chairman Dick Wilson, whom many Oglala living on the reservation thought corrupt."[11]

Coler and Williams were attempting to serve arrest warrants stemming from what they claimed to be robbery and assault with a dangerous weapon on the reservation when they were shot.

Tried in Iowa, codefendants Robert "Bob" Robideau and Darrelle Dean "Dino" Butler were found not guilty after pleading self-defense. Charges against James Theodore Eagle were dropped. Peltier was not as fortunate. Despite witness perjury and a ballistic test proving that his gun hadn't done the killing, he was found guilty following a five-week jury trial. More than four decades and many appeals later, he remains imprisoned in Coleman, Florida. "He was convicted of aiding and abetting murder," said former federal judge Kevin Sharp, "but who did he aid and abet? His co-defendants were acquitted based on self-defense."[12]

On March 23, 2022, seventy-seven-year-old Peltier made his first statement in five years. "Peltier's family says he is struggling with diabetes, hypertension, partial blindness from a stroke and an abdominal aortic aneurysm," reported NBC News, "and that he tested positive for COVID in late January."[13] Peltier remains steadfast. "They're going to try and make me die here," he claimed. "I have a last few years, and I got to fight."[14]

Attempting to attend Peltier's trial in Fargo, North Dakota, in January 1977, Trudell was turned away. Refusing to leave, he was arrested. The FBI had already begun compiling what would be a file of more than one thousand pages. Sentenced to six months, he shifted between five jails in three states. A federal prison inmate warned him of danger if he continued his political activities.

Disregarding the warning, Trudell resumed his fight for Indigenous rights after being released. On February 12, 1979, he defiantly burned an American flag on the steps of the J. Edgar Hoover Building, the FBI's headquarters, in Washington DC. "I burned the American flag," he said, "as an act of protest against the injustice being extended against all of the people."[15]

That night, as Trudell's pregnant wife (Tina Manning-Trudell), children (Ricarda Star, Sunshine Karma, and Eli Changing Sun), and Tina's parents (Leah and Arthur Manning) slept, his in-laws' house on the Duck Valley Reservation, in Nevada, was suspiciously burned. The local BIA claimed that it was an accident. Seriously burned, Trudell's father-in-law, tribal chairman of the Shoshone-Paiute Tribes, was the only survivor. Kris Kristofferson wrote about it in "Johnny Lobo." Trudell followed with "Tina Smiles." "They say she was compassionate, and intelligent—a remarkable combination," remembered Tina's niece, Sarah Sunshine Manning, on Indian Country Today. "She was an activist of water rights, and Native American civil rights, but she was also a tender mother, a skilled craftsman of traditional arts, and a devoted relative to old ones, and friends, and sisters, and cousins, nieces, and nephews."[16]

The loss left Trudell unsure of where to go or what to do. Getting into his car, he drove aimlessly for the next six months. Somewhere in the middle of Canada, he pulled to the side of the road, took out a pad and pen, and started to write. It would be his first poem. A seventy-one-page booklet, *Living in Real: Songs Called Poems*, came out in 1982.

Before producing his 1983 cassette debut, *Tribal Voice*, German American singer-songwriter Jackson Browne encouraged Trudell to add musical accompaniment. The poet and activist began reciting to the drumming and singing of Milton "Quiltman" Sahme from the Warm Springs Reservation, home of the Confederated Warm Springs, Wasco, and Paiute Tribes in Oregon.

The addition of Jesse Ed Davis, who had been born in Norman, Oklahoma, made the sound complete. An accompanist of folk-bluesman Taj Mahal in the late sixties, Davis had become one of the era's busiest session guitarists. He recorded with Bryan Ferry, Albert Collins, Charles Lloyd, John Lee Hooker, Albert King, Gene Clark, Leon Russell, the Steve Miller Band, B. B. King, Harry Nilsson, the Pointer Sisters, the Fifth Dimension, Keith Moon, Cher, Jimmy Cliff, the David Bromberg Band, Rod Stewart, Neil Diamond, Leonard Cohen, Ry Cooder, Arlo Guthrie, Van Dyke Parks, Rick Danko, Emmylou Harris, and three Beatles—John Lennon, George Harrison, and Ringo Starr. His solo on Browne's 1972 hit, "Doctor My Eyes," helped to propel it to the eighth slot on the *Billboard Hot 100*. "If [Eric] Clapton was known as God," said Stevie Salas, "then [Davis] was right up there with the disciples somewhere."[17]

"He had a different way of playing," remembered drummer John Ware, who played with Davis as early as 1959, "a light touch with his left and right hands."

Trudell's collaboration with Davis and Quiltman was magical. Bob Dylan and the Grateful Dead added AKA Grafitti Man (1986) to their pre-show playlists. "[Dylan] told me," Trudell said proudly, "that what I was doing with music was revolutionary."[18]

The opportunity for a follow-up was lost when Davis overdosed in June 1988. "I was so mad at him," Mahal remembered three decades later, "but I flew to Oklahoma to pay my respect. I remember they smudged the room with sage."

A limited-release collection of AKA Grafitti Man demos (Heart Jump Bouquet) came out in 2015. The Native American Music Hall of Fame inducted Davis three years later.

Renewed by a late-1988 tour with Midnight Oil, from Sydney, Australia, Trudell contributed two tracks to Oyaté (1990), British keyboardist Tony Hymas's tribute to poet, songwriter, and AIM member Barney Bush. Jeff Beck played guitar on Trudell's "Crazy Horse." The song would be recut for Bone Days.

After participating in Peter Gabriel's 1993 WOMAD tour, Trudell went back to recording. St. Louis–born Mark Shark played guitar and mandolin on the Browne-produced Johnny Damas and Me (1994). Neil Ullestad praised the album for mixing "traditional sounds, values, and sensibilities with thought-provoking lyrics, this time with urgent rock and roll."[19]

"[Trudell] has good reasons to be mad," added Entertainment Weekly, "and they boil up through these tracks like oil-well fires."[20]

Like Westerman, Trudell had a second career in acting. He appeared with actor and blues musician Gary Farmer (Haudenosaunee) in Smoke Signals, a 1998 comedy filmed on the Coeur d'Alene reservation, and he made several TV appearances.

The National Association of Native American Music presented Trudell with a lifetime achievement NAMA, or "NAMMY," in its inaugural year (1998). Founded by music-industry professionals, record labels, and publicist Ellen Bello, the New York–based organization continues to "celebrate the rich music heritage of the nation's first people."[21] The association "helped generate an international market through international awareness," said Bello.[22]

Trudell was far from done. On the strength of *Blue Indians* (2000), he scored Producer of the Year and Artist of the Year NAMAs. The title track was the Song of the Year. *Bone Day* (2001) kept the momentum going. Executive produced by Academy Award–winning actor Angelina Jolie, *Bone Days* set Trudell's recitations to the hard-driving accompaniment of Bad Dog—Quiltman and his son (Teewhanee "T" Sahme) (vocals), Ricky Eckstein (bass), Mark Shark and Billy Watts (guitars), Debra Dobkin (drums), and Chicago-born and San Diego–based singer-songwriter Joel Rafael. "[Rafael's] voice is unmistakably his own," said Browne, "a conductor for the human emotions that connect us all."[23]

Trudell recorded several spoken-word albums, but his involvement with music never ceased. *Madness and the Moremes* (2007) included new tunes and previously unreleased tracks with Jesse Ed Davis. Seventeen new and reworked songs appeared on *Crazier than Hell* (2011).

A guest on recordings by the Mighty 602 Band, the Cody Blackbird Band, and A Tribe Called Red, Trudell collaborated on his final album, *Through the Dust* (2014), with Kwest (Jonas Leuenberger), drummer of the Swiss hip-hop group, Die Mundartisten. Additional tracks were released posthumously on *Like Broken Butterflies* (2016).

A year after Trudell's December 2015 passing from cancer, Minneapolis-based alt-folk trio the Pines released "Time Dreams." It was the poet's final recording.

Bad Dog continued, with Rafael taking over as a leader. In 2019 Rafael teamed with Virginia-born Jason Mraz to record "Strong," which Rafael says was written in support of "the Water Protectors at Standing Rock, people who risked all they risked to make an issue visible to people who weren't aware of it."[24]

The circle continues.

6

Beating of the Heart

The land that became the United States and Canada was already buzzing with song and dance when Europeans arrived on Turtle Island. According to an ancient Abenaki legend, the Creator heard a loud BOOM shortly after the earth's creation and went to investigate. Arriving at the source of the thunderous sound, he asked, "Who are you?"

The reply was swift. "I am the spirit of the drum . . . I would like to accompany the singing of the people."

Drums provide the heartbeat of a powwow, or *wacipi* (Dakota for "they dance"). "Our whole culture centers around the drum," said Paul Gowder, founder of Powwows.com. "[It] brings the heartbeat of our Earth Mother to the powwow for all to feel and hear. Drumming brings everyone back into balance."[1]

After a flag ceremony, acknowledgment of military veterans and special guests, and a prayer or invocation, most powwows begin with a Grand Entry. "When the Indian tribes were forced onto reservations," Gowder explained, "the government forced the Native Americans to have dances for the public to come and see. Before each dance, they were led through the town in a ceremony or parade, which is the beginning of the Grand Entry."

Dancers enter the circular dance arbor (arena) in pairs, introduced by a quick-tongued emcee. Before long, the floor is packed with Plains-style dancers, grass dancers, Eastern Woodland dancers, and fancy dancers in their respective regalia. Jingle dancers add to the spectacle. "It's so powerful to see that arena full of the dancers you've invited," says Denni Woodward, associate director of Stanford University's Native American Cultural Center, "and in every seat . . . [there's] someone sitting. It's amazing."[2]

The dancers move to the rhythm of ten to fifteen drummers who encircle and beat a large buffalo- or moose-hide drum and sing in Native languages, occasional English, and nonlexical vocables. "Vocables were sung long before the First Encounter," explained Jamie K. Oxendine of the Black Swamp Intertribal Foundation to me. "Think of the Christmas carol 'Deck the Halls.' Fa-la-la-la-la are vocables."

"We sing vocables," added Wayne Silas Jr., "because that's the language we speak when we're born. It brings us closer to the Creator."

The Grand Entry was a staple of Buffalo Bill's Wild West, the most successful of more than one hundred similar shows at the turn of the twentieth century. Directed by ex–buffalo hunter, Pony Express rider, and army scout William Frederick "Buffalo Bill" Cody, it toured North America and Europe from 1884 to 1913. Over its twenty-nine-year span, more than one thousand Indigenous men, women, and children—including Hunkpapa Lakota spiritual leader and Little Big Horn participant Sitting Bull (Tatanka Ioyate), Apache medicine man Geronimo (Goyahkla), and Chief Luther Standing Bear—participated in the show. Like dime novels and penny thrillers and later Hollywood westerns, it presented a Euro-American view of "savage" Indians and the Wild West. "While [most of the] Indians belonged to the [Lakota] tribe," Standing Bear said, "we were supposed to represent four different tribes, each 'tribe' to ride animals of one color."[3]

"They generally were treated and paid the same as other performers," said Paul Fees, former curator of the Buffalo Bill Museum. "They were able to travel with their families, and they earned a living not possible to them on their reservations."[4]

Encouraged to "retain their language and rituals," Wild West performers "gained access to political and economic leaders," Fees said, "and their causes were sometimes argued in the published show programs. Yet they were stereotyped as mounted, war-bonneted warriors, the last impediment to civilization."[5]

Four decades before Buffalo Bill's first show, Phineas Taylor "P. T." Barnum showcased Sac and Fox dancers at his American Museum in Manhattan. For six weeks in April and May 1843, the legendary impresario presented fifteen members of the tribe, including Chief Nan-Nouce-Push-Ee-Toe and his eighteen-year-old daughter, Do-Hum-Me, as they demonstrated war dances and re-created ceremonies. The group had traveled east from their Iowa reservation to participate in treaty negotiations in Princeton, New Jersey. During the negotiations, Do-Hum-Me fell in love and married warrior and delegate Cow-Hick-Kee.

In New York the chief and his daughter were feted as visiting dignitaries. After attending a ball in their honor, they were heading back to their hotel when their carriage broke down, forcing them to walk the rest of the way in rain and snow. On that trip, Do-Hum-Me contracted influenza and died shortly afterward. Married for only five weeks, she was interred in the Green-Wood Cemetery in Greenwood Heights, Brooklyn. A graveside monument consists of "a white marble base [with the] die and capital supported on a granite plinth. . . . Set in the face of the die is a bas relief plaque depicting a Native American male in mourning."[6]

There are no records of the first powwow. Most researchers attribute it to a ceremony of the battle-honored veterans who comprised the Heth'uska Society of the Omaha or Ponca. "The grass dance societies," Oxendine said, "[provided] an opportunity for the warriors to re-enact deeds for all the members of the tribe to witness."[7]

Received through a vision, the ceremony spread to other tribes, transforming into a nonreligious celebration. At a time when sacred ceremonies were outlawed, powwows gave Indigenous peoples a chance to gather. "'Inter-Tribalism' began to emerge," Oxendine said, "with the sharing of songs, dances, clothing, food, and art."[8]

The definition of the word *powwow* has gone through changes. According to the Online Etymology Dictionary, it was used in the 1620s to signify "a priest, conjurer, [or] sorcerer."[9]

"Powwow comes from the Narragansett Eastern Algonquian language," says the Nanticoke Indian Tribe's website, "[and] is defined as any gathering of Native people. However, in Indian Country, we define it as a cultural event that features group singing and dancing by men, women and children."[10]

Powwows combine "love for song, music, dance, rhythm, grace of motion, prayer, chant, ritualism, body decoration, and symbolic design."[11]

"The powwow is one vehicle that is keeping our children 'Indian,'" said Presidential Medal of Honor recipient, author, and the "last living Plains Indian war chief," Joe Medicine Crow (1913–2016). "Of course, they go to school, but during the Crow Fair, you'll see even little kids all dressed up, dancing, parading on horses, going back to the old Indian ways, and enjoying themselves."[12]

A massive powwow was held on the Salish and Pend d'Oreille's Flathead Indian Reservation, in Arlee, Montana, on July 4, 1888. Sponsored by the Confederated Salish and Kootenai Tribal Nation, the Arlee Powwow Esyapqeyni (Celebration) continues to be held annually. The choice of date has little to do with Independence Day. "The BIA found it difficult," the Esyapqeyni's website points out, "to argue that it should be illegal to celebrate the Fourth of July."[13]

On the same weekend, a Kiowa gourd dance (Tdiepeigah) takes place at the American Indian Exposition in Anadarko, Oklahoma. Tracing back to the 1700s, it was originally part of the sun dance. Resurrected after a two-decade hiatus on Armistice Day (November 11), 1946, in Carnegie, Oklahoma, it has been held at its current site since 1955. "Whether you attribute *Tdiepeigah* to the Kiowa warrior who was taught the songs by a red wolf who instructed him to teach them to his people," said Indian Country Today, "or to the honoring of battles fought by Kiowa warriors during their migration from the northern plains to what is now Oklahoma, both oral history and flesh make it clear this is a warrior dance."[14]

"If you listen to the Kiowa gourd dance songs very closely, you can hear the wolf yelp," said Andy Cozad, of the Cozad Singers. "That yelping sound *Gui-Goodle-Tay* (Red Wolf) had made out there when he was singing, and at the same time a holler or shouting sound at the end of the song that the warriors made on their journey."[15]

Several tribes in the Southeast hold a Green Corn Ceremony in midsummer when the second crop of corn (maize) ripens. The four-to-eight-day celebration combines "Thanksgiving, New Year's festivities, Yom Kippur, Lent, and Mardi Gras."[16] Centered in the town plaza, the ceremony starts with a feast that does not include corn. Sacred plant-based drinks, or "medicine," are consumed, and sacred songs are sung. Afterward, men deprive themselves of food until "the second sunrise."[17]

Women, children, and the elderly eat a restrictive diet.

The Green Corn Ceremony is a time of renewal. Public buildings are restored, and homes are freshened. Repairs are made on tools, clothing, and utensils. Nonmurder criminal charges are dropped. "When the town celebrates," observed naturalist William Bartram in 1773, "they collect all their worn-out cloths and other despicable things, sweep their houses, squares, and the whole town of their filth."[18]

On the final day, all fires in the town are extinguished. A priest relights the plaza flame, and the world is restored. Another large feast is consumed, followed by a celebratory dance. "I've gone to the Green Corn Dance," said Joy Harjo, "and seen stomp dances."

Some powwows are limited to tribal members and invitees, but most welcome non-Indigenous attendees. North America's largest powwow, the Gathering of Nations, draws more than ninety thousand people to the Expo New Mexico event in Albuquerque every April. Over three thousand dancers, singers, and musicians, representing more than five hundred tribes from Canada and the United States, participate. In addition to the dancing, the "Superbowl of Powwows" includes a traders' market, horse and rider parade, contemporary music showcase (referred to as Stage 49), street fair, food court, world's tallest tipi, and the crowning of Miss Indian World. During the pandemic, the Gathering of Nations switched to virtual programming. "We needed to keep the bright light on," said founder Derek Matthews.[19]

Powwows attract a diverse but recognizable range of participants. "The conservatives are the Indians who lived and retained the old culture," said non-Indigenous dancers and authors Reginald and Gladys Laupin. "The traditionalists are the products of modern schooling who have not actually lived the old Indian way but are now aware of their heritage and are endeavoring to preserve it. A large group of non-Indian students of Indian lore also call themselves traditionalists."[20]

Growing up in the San Francisco Bay area, Vince Redhouse didn't experience his first powwow until he was twelve. "I remember going into the gym where it was being held and hearing a drum," he said. "It was so powerful, I cried before I even walked through the door. Something struck me at a deep level; it was who I was."

Some powwow attendees come to gamble on the stick game (also called the hand game). Predating written history, the game traditionally uses a pair of bones, one plain and one striped. The guessing team bets on which of their opponent's hands is holding the plain bone. "The meaning behind stick games, as I was told," said Fawn Wood (Cree), a two-time

NAMA-winning round dance singer and a member of her fiancé Dallas Waskahat's drum group, Cree Confederation, "is that we were given them as a way to battle other tribes without going to war or counting coup on people."

Stick game songs are fast-paced and energetic. "You could tell which tribe someone is from by their songs," said Wood. "There are stick games among the Dene in the north, the Northwest Territories and Alaska, along the coast of British Columbia, all the way down to California, across the prairies to the East Coast."

Wood's father, Earl Wood, founded Northern Cree with his two brothers in Maskwacis, Alberta, Canada, in 1982. Comprised of drummers and singers from the region defined by Treaty 6, Northern Cree is the recipient of five NAMA awards and nine Grammy nominations and continues to lift powwow and round dance songs to a new level of musicality. "I remember watching rock and roll bands," said Steve Wood, the only one of the founding three brothers still with the group, "and thinking that powwow music should be as good."

Young Spirit
Jacob Faithful (1980–) (Cree)

Influenced by Northern Cree, Frog Lake First Nation's Young Spirit plays "high spirited Pow Wow Dances that make it very difficult to stand idle."[21]

Keeping it "old-school" is about remembering songs and practices and sharing as much as we can with the younger generation, but there was nothing fancy about pre-European-contact music. It had a constant rhythm and a certain way of chanting. Contemporary powwow music, like what we play, incorporates English words and has a spin and twist to the melody. We strategically put hooks in our music so that when people listen, they'll say, "That sounds cool."

I had been part of Blackstone, a group known for winning drum contests at powwows, since 2000, and competed with them everywhere on the circuit.

Young Spirit came together in June 2001. I was twenty-one. My younger brothers were fifteen and sixteen. I had recently entered into a relationship

with the woman who would become my children's mother, and we were just getting to know each other. I wanted a break from all the contests, so I said to myself, "I'm going to give myself a weekend off. I'm going to go to a powwow [in Hubbema, Alberta] and spend time getting to know my girlfriend."

My younger brothers had their own drum group [High Spirit] consisting of teenyboppers who wanted to sing traditional music. I thought it was awesome that people that young were interested in performing, but at the powwow, they asked me, "Would you be our lead singer?"

I wasn't planning on singing that weekend—I just wanted to sit back and relax—but I ended up talking to some friends who were, like me, at the powwow but not singing with anybody. The next thing I knew, I was singing with them and my brothers. After teaching them our first song, I decided that we might as well kick it old-school and have fun. We wound up putting a good crew together.

I asked, "What name are we using?"

One of my brother's friends [Carla Red Star] said, "Young Spirit."

In my mind, it was a good name.

On Friday, there was a laid-back contest so people could warm up and get a feel for the weekend. Then, on Saturday, when the powwow started, one of my brothers entered us in the singing contest. I wasn't planning on that, but I found myself in a situation where I had to compete. We ended up taking first place. It was fun being part of a group of a younger generation. That weekend turned into another, and we kept going for the rest of the summer.

We have a tradition called "feeding the drum." We hold a feast, after the summer, and feed the drum spirit. At this feast, I told an elder, "We used a drum group name this summer, but we don't have an actual name given to us. There was no prayer put into the naming, no offerings—nothing. We put it together at the last minute to have fun, but my brothers, our friends, and I want to do this full-time. Our primary focus is empowering young people and being part of a bigger picture."

The elder thought about it that whole ceremony. Afterward, he said, "I want to call you Oskíyak Kīsak."

Oskíyak is a group of young people, and Kīsak is the spirit or inner soul of a human being. That was already our name. For the cover of our Grammy-nominated eighth CD, *Mewasensational: Cree Round Dance Songs* [2017], we had a University of Alberta professor do the proper spelling in Cree.

Frog Lake First Nation is in the northeastern part of Alberta, Canada. It has three thousand members. Before European contact, we spoke the Athabaskan language. The six nations in Mohawk Territory [Mohawk, Oneida, Onondaga, Cayuga, Seneca, and Tuscarora] are all descendants of the Athabaskan people.

In the Plains, we call ourselves "Nehiyawak." In Cree it means a four-direction person. We exist north of us, south of us, east of us, and west of us. There's a ton of us everywhere.

"Cree" was the European name for a Christian Indigenous person. Of the people in my territory, we were the first to adopt Christianity. It's still very dominant in Frog Lake, but the majority have gone back to their original roots and are living old-school. No one goes to the churches in my community anymore. There are more sweat lodges and prayer ceremonies than anything. I'm proud to be part of the group that said there's more to who we are and what we stand for.

My parents played the stick game. A lot of singing went with it. My grandfather traveled the powwow circuit with the Frog Lake Handgame Singers. I idolized him. I didn't know about Creedence Clearwater Revival or contemporary music until I was well into my teens, but I went through whatever a teenager goes through—traveling, talking to girls, trying to figure out who I was. I became a fan of old-school rock. That turned into liking grunge, but I didn't forget about traditional music; I still practiced.

Preserving our traditional beliefs and practices is easy for me. I learned from the elders at a young age. A lot of their messages are lost, but I speak the language fluently. I remember those conversations.

Language has the power to heal. It was given to us by the Creator. It's ours, and nobody can take it away. We incorporate Cree words into songs with a modern powwow feel. Audiences sing along without knowing they're singing words that aren't spoken today.

I was once driving through the Arizona desert, on my way to do a recording in Apache Territory, and looking at the plateaus. It's a beautiful landscape, and I made a song about what I was seeing. The lyrics said, "I feel a tremendous amount of joy being asked to sing in this beautiful territory, the beautiful earth, the beauty of this land."

Another time, I had to make a song for a young boy who lost his mother. He wanted to quit traditional dancing and stop being part of the circle. His family approached me and said, "Hey, Jacob, we have a young man who's quitting life. Could you put together a song to encourage him to continue doing what his mother loved watching him do?"

That was a heavy request, but I took the tobacco they gave me, went to the fire, and said a prayer to all the spirits in our vicinity. When I talk about spirits, I don't mean humans who have passed away. I'm talking about eagle spirit, buffalo spirit, wind spirit, fire spirit, thunderbird spirit, and the spirits that live in the heavens and do the Creator's work. I prayed, "If you have something to encourage this young man in this tough time, let me be the medium."

Driving home from that powwow, a melody came into my head. I smudged myself, purified myself with sweetgrass, and started humming. In a matter of three to four minutes, that song was complete from start to finish. It said, "Don't quit dancing, do it for your mother. Keep trying, our baby boy."

The last word in the song, "akameyimoh," told the young man to believe in himself, the spirit in his soul, and his ability to succeed and accomplish. I repeated it three times—for the mind, body, and spirit—and prayed for him. The song didn't come from putting together patterns of words and melodies; it came from somewhere else.

We named our 2016 CD *Akameyimoh Baby Boy (Keep Trying Baby Boy)*. Fast-forward and that guy's still dancing. He has a wife and a child. He's a strong, vibrant young man.

Athabaskan people are known for our tea. We use traditional herbs from our Mother Earth. There's a tea my family makes that helps people with diabetes and mental illnesses. It has so much power. It was a remedy given to us prior to European contact. The main component of Tylenol, aspirin, heart medication, and diabetes medication comes from that drink. We used to have a ceremony, the tea dance, where we danced in a circle and sang while exchanging tea remedies. We brought the pipe into the tea dance as we do with every ceremony. We put our own variations into the songs, adding Cree words and our way of singing, and made it our own. Our variation of the tea dance is what people now call the round dance.

Some of my earliest memories of round dances were dancing to a big drum. A man from my community, the late Andrew Abraham, changed that. He was a craftsman and good with wood. He was known for building houses. He had a dream of this hand drum. In his dream, an elderly person told him, "You need to make as many of these drums as you can. They're travel friendly; everybody could have one in their home."

A hand drum's tone is higher than a powwow drum. At the same time, it has a different power. The round dance beat represents the heartbeat of Mother Earth. Then, there's a scratch that you do on the inside of the drum with your finger. It makes a vibrating sound that represents the roots of the trees and how they connect. If you look at it as a human form, it's our heartbeat and blood flow.

The form of a round dance song is consistent. It starts with a high-pitched lead solo, and then everybody comes in at that same pitch in unison. Then, we get into the body of the song using vocables. These aren't words but sounds that are quite familiar. Sometimes, we come in with English lyrics. They can be about anything from heartbreak to going for a walk on a Sunday afternoon, whatever the song makers are feeling.

Choreographing the crew is as simple as sending a sound file via email. I'll sing into my phone and send it to everybody. I'll say, "Learn this song for next weekend."

With live recordings, we're not able to overdub. Everything has to be done right, but the finicky little things that happen add to the live feeling. When you listen to those albums, it feels like you're sitting at the drum. In the studio, we get to experience the magic of recording. We overdub riffs here and there. We'll lose track of time, and it'll be three or four in the morning before we know it. We're proud that the creative juices are flowing, but after eighteen hours, we need sleep.

Canyon Records has had the respect of Indigenous communities since 1951. It was our goal to be recorded by them. Stephen Butler, who produced our albums on Canyon, now runs Buffalo Jump Records. He has an ear for what we're trying to attain. I don't even have to listen to a mix before it goes out; I know he's got it figured out. He's got so many ideas.

Our music was initially very traditional, but fast-forward to *Angel Eagle—Cree Round Dances* [2021]. One of our singers [Lucas Ernest] treated a song, "The Only Girl I'll Ever Love," with a guitar. We added piano to other songs. It's contemporary with a traditional feel.

There's a huge cry for our young people to take the music, the knowledge, and the traditional practices and harness them, so they're not lost. That's what we're doing, pushing forward without forgetting the foundation that's been set.

Spirit of Thunderheart

Donna Coane (1961–) (Chippewa Cree, Mohawk,
Mohegan, Schaghticoke, and German)

Based in New York's mid–Hudson River Valley, Donna Coane's Spirit
of Thunderheart was the first NAMA-winning women's powwow drum
group to play a big drum and they did it twice (2014 and 2019).

Most of our songs are sung in our Native languages. We do a few in English
when we want people to understand what we're singing, but you don't
have tradition without language. It lets us tell a more accurate story.

We had a prophecy that when the maple trees die, the women would
take back the drum. There were always women drummers. They drummed
so other women could dance. Men weren't always around.

We have an easier time in the Northeast than if we were in the Midwest or down South. I know a women's drum group in Georgia. They
have a really hard time being accepted. Being Native women, we're often
forgotten about, even though we're professional musicians, actors, and
writers. We have doctors, lawyers, nurses, social workers, and teachers.

When I was growing up, it wasn't cool to be Native. We practiced our
ceremonies behind a stockade fence, trying to not be seen or heard. The

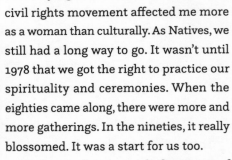

civil rights movement affected me more
as a woman than culturally. As Natives, we
still had a long way to go. It wasn't until
1978 that we got the right to practice our
spirituality and ceremonies. When the
eighties came along, there were more and
more gatherings. In the nineties, it really
blossomed. It was a start for us too.

I led two other groups before Spirit of
Thunderheart. The first was for a local
community. I was the one who got the
women to be around the drum as backup
singers. The men didn't want them, but
there was no reason why we shouldn't
sing along, with rattles, around the drum.
That's what got it started. After that, I got

the women to dance. The men didn't think dancing should be done around a drum. Why not? It's an honor for a drum to have people dancing around it.

Then the women decided they wanted their own drum group. We put it together with community members and women I knew. We set up next to the men's drum group; it was a huge breakthrough.

Eventually, our group dispersed, and everyone went their own way. I bought the drum. I had to pay my mother back; she let me use her credit card to buy it. I got a tribal discount. My daughter sold her car to pay my mother back.

The drum is twenty-eight inches around, with a depth of thirteen and a quarter inches. The wood is maple. The skin is moose. Moose hide never changes because of the humidity or the cold. You don't have to warm it up. It has the most beautiful sound.

An elder told me, "That drum will take you places."

I said, "Thank you," and started taking the drum to the lodge. A couple of women said, "Maybe, we should start something," and that's where we are today. We started with seven women; two left. Then we had five women, and one left. We have four women now. I have a few backup singers who fill in. I try to always fill the four directions, no matter what.

Our first CD was *Rising* [2014], our second was *Unity* [2015], and our third was *Tradition* [2019]. Our logo is "Rising with Unity and Tradition." I'm thinking of using that for our fourth CD.

In the beginning, I was the lead singer, drummer, and producer. Brenda Martin-Buffa came first. Then, Debbie Fichtner and Wyona Decker. Wyona's a former member now, but she was with us when we won the NAMA and when we were nominated the second time. Mary Griffin and Wyona joined together; they're sisters. Brenda, Debbie, and I came from other drum groups.

We come from the four directions. Brenda is from the east, the Taconic area. Mary is from Hudson, further north. Debbie is from the west, in Plainville, and I'm originally from the mid–Hudson Valley. I grew up in LaGrange, New York, five minutes from Hyde Park, in the south. That's where the four sections of our medicine wheel logo come from, the four directions.

Debbie is Mohawk. Brenda is Metís. My grandmother on my father's side was Chippewa, Cree, and Mohawk. My grandfather was Mohegan and

Schaghticoke. My great-grandfather and my great-uncle were Mohegans who married Schaghticokes. I grew up Mohawk, so I know more about my Mohawk heritage than I do the Mohegan, Chippewa, or Cree.

My other grandmother was from Germany, the Black Forest area. As for my grandfather, I've learned as much as I can, but it's funny when your DNA thinks you're more than you are. We've never been able to figure it out.

On my mother's side, my grandmother loved the cello. When I got into elementary school, I took it up and played up to the middle of my high school years. I entered competitions to play with philharmonic orchestras. I learned to play guitar in high school and switched. My father played electric guitar, my uncle played xylophone and guitar, and my aunt played the ukulele. My father also played xylophone. My aunt was a great storyteller. My father's other brother wasn't into music.

My father was also a country music drummer. That's where the drum came into play. It was taboo to us, as women, but I would take my knife and fork and drum away at the table. My mother used to say, "Stop! Stop!" but anything I could use for a drum, I'd play. I made myself a hand drum in junior high.

I remember one song I played. I found it in an old book. I went to an elder and asked if she'd translate it for me. She said, "It means 'Beautiful Mountain Towers.'"

I told her, "I like that, but I don't know the melody."

She said, "Study those words, think about it, and it will come to you."

The next thing I knew, "Oh my God, I got it!"

We recorded it on our *Tradition* CD.

For a while, videographer Pamela Timmins [Pamorama Productions] documented our travels. She started booking us too. We'd go to New York, and she'd say, "I've got you an interview here, a gig there."

This went on weekend after weekend. We were exhausted. By the time she finished the documentary, we needed a vacation.

To get to the NAMAs in 2012, we had to get up at four in the morning and be on the road by five. During the intermission, we met some amazing people, some I already knew. People thought we were really something because of our matching Nehru jackets. They were black with buffalo bone and silver, with lots of fringes.

After the awards show, we were so hyped up we didn't want to go back to the hotel. We stood outside the Three Sisters Café and sang. This woman turned around and said, "That was beautiful. I loved it."

It turned out that she worked for Donald Blackfox [Spirit Wind Records], who was sitting by himself at a table. I told the girls, "I'll be right back," and sat down with Donald. "Hi, I'd like to introduce myself. This is who I am; this is who we are."

He said, "Stop right there," and put out his hand. "I like what I see, and I like what I hear. I want to sign you."

In my head, I was going, "Don't act like an idiot—ask questions." So I said, "Tell me about your company; tell me about royalties. What do you charge, and how long a contract?"

I waved the girls over and told them, "Donald would like to sign us."

They looked at me like deer in headlights. I repeated it. Then I began to sense more excitement. I gave them some money and told them to get me a bottle of water, just to get rid of them. I could see they were getting antsy. Then Donald and I continued talking. He said, "I'd like to invite you to our after-party at the Hard Rock Cafe as my VIP guest."

Later on, the girls and I tried hashing out what happened. We had already been recording. I had come into a little money and invested in a good sound system. It had an equalizer and lots of plug-ins. I had mics for different purposes and a computer that I built myself. We recorded in the basement of the VFW Hall [American Legion Post 398] in Harlem. There weren't any windows, but the sound was awesome.

I emailed Donald that we had agreed to work with him and sent him a couple of tracks. He put them on Spirit Wind's website and asked for pictures and a bio. Two weeks later we were in a studio in Nyack. We recorded eight songs in one sitting. A year later *Rising* won the NAMA for Best Traditional Recording.

I bought a case for the drum—we needed to protect it—and my husband made two sit-down stands. One can be broken down for traveling. We also have a stand-up stand that we love. As a singer, it's easier to stand than it is to sit. It's a blessing to have a stand like that. Then he made a breakdown stand-up stand. We use it when it's just us and not the whole entourage.

I write on my mother's piano. She passed on in 2012. I also have a piano app on my phone that I use when I'm out. I like the way it sounds.

I come up with tunes when I'm showering, driving, running, or biking. Then I just need words.

In June 2019 I helped to produce a musical, *Hymn to the Earth*, at the Diamond Sokolow Dance Theater in Woodstock. Spirit of Thunderheart played our music. The play was about Native Americans pre–first contact, what happened, and what could have happened. Modern dancers played Europeans. It was beautiful. I had had cancer and gone through radiation, but here I was—singing and drumming—glad that I didn't need to go through that again.

Last year I got a part in my third movie, *High Hopes*. Unfortunately, we couldn't finish filming because of the virus. We're waiting to start again. I play a Native woman. She's the leader of her tribe, but she owns a brothel. She kidnaps some white guys and takes advantage of them. We tied those poor guys up at least five times.

We've started thinking about our next CD. We're going to be bringing in other musicians, including a non-Native violinist. We want to record more English-language songs, so we can get out more messages. I've already written most of the songs. They're on the political end, and they tell the truth.

Fawn Wood (1986–) (Cree and Salish)

Buffalo Jump Records describes Fawn Wood as seeking "to encourage hope for the betterment of all indigenous people, especially by encouraging indigenous women to connect to their identity through song."[22]

Saddle Lake, Alberta, is in the heart of Treaty 6 Territory in Alberta, Canada. We're only a couple of hours from big gatherings. We used to be one of the higher-populated communities. We struggle with the aftereffects of what we've been through as Indigenous peoples—genocide, residential schools—but there's another side to our community. We're rich in culture, and we have many talented people.

I'm fortunate to have musical families on both sides. Seeing where my uncle Steve has taken Northern Cree has been inspirational. Uncle Randy has been nominated for a Grammy a couple of times too. He's won NAMAs for Best Traditional Recording [2004, 2011] and Best Male Artist

[2018]. Music is something they were exposed to as kids, and here they are doing big things.

My dad was one of the founders of Northern Cree. He and his brothers started it after losing a stick game. They needed money. A powwow was coming to town, and they got the gig. They played songs they learned as kids. Northern Cree was stenciled on the drum they borrowed.

Dad met Mom [singer Cindy Jim-Wood] at a powwow that Northern Cree was hosting. He shifted away from the group and started a family. Mom's side was musical too. It was everyday life for me—hearing music and seeing beautiful things happen to my family with music. I never knew how embedded it was until I got older and started creating my own songs.

For the longest time, I would only sing at home for my family. When I started traveling, carrying music with me, and getting recordings out, people I went to school with were surprised that I sang. I'd say, "It's always been a part of my life."

We used to practice singing in our house. I remember my dad telling my sisters and me to come and practice. He's a powwow emcee, so he'd announce us. He gave me support to be a female singer. It's not common in this style, but my dad, being a Plains Cree man, pushed me. I don't think I would have been able to pursue what I do if it weren't for that kind of support.

Round dance music originated with our Plains Cree people, but you see it common now across the U.S. and Canada. People are picking up the custom of having round dances at gatherings. The songs depend on what type of gathering it's going to be. There are protocol songs that we have for memorials, but sometimes they're celebratory songs for birthdays or graduations or for communities wanting people to dance and sing with them.

Another style on my albums is the West Coast type of song. They're much different from Plains Cree songs; you don't hear as many words. They come from my mom's family—the Salish people from the mountains. They're all singers, but they started the same way I did, at a big drum with their mom and dad.

I don't know how many times I've told this story, but at the end of 2007, I came home from college for Christmas break and met Dallas Waskahat through my cousin. They had just started the drum group we

3. Fawn Wood

sing with [Cree Confederation] and were starting to pull people together and get their crew set. My cousin kept telling me, "You should sing for us. We need a backup singer."

I didn't know how to backup sing, but he said, "We want a backup singer that hasn't sung with anybody yet. We'll help you."

I tried it, and that's how I met Dallas and started traveling with Cree Confederation. I had to learn to sing higher, but I found my own style. I had good mentors and teachers who encouraged me to learn the tradition but put my own flare to it.

In our teachings, the reason a woman sings higher and stands in the background is that she signifies an angel. When you're singing all weekend and the guys' voices start to go, the backup singers keep that energy going. Most people focus on the drummers, but if you take those backup female singers away, they notice. When women's voices ring out, you can feel how passionate they are about the music. You feel it in your heart when you hear beautiful backup singing.

At first Dallas and I were just friends. He'd show me songs over the phone or when we hung out. I didn't know he liked me, but he pursued me once I figured it out. It's amazing to find someone who shares the same passions. He's about creating music, and he's passionate about our language. We share a passion for working with youth and empowering them through culture. Twelve years later we're still happily engaged and have two kids. It's been a journey for sure. We've recorded with Cree Confederation and done two albums on our own—'Til the End [2010] and Blessings [2013].

Dallas grew up when Northern Cree was already doing big things. He looked up to them the same way I did. When I asked him why he wanted to start Cree Confederation, he told me that he had a dream about a drum.

When he started telling people about it, they laughed, but he ended up being given a big powwow drum during a sweat ceremony in Maskwacis, Alberta, where my uncle Steve lives. There are singers all over that area. They ended up having a practice that night.

Dallas wanted the group to represent the whole confederation, so he named it Cree Confederation. People again laughed, but he was set on the name. He also wanted his own sound and style. When people heard the group, he wanted them to know who it was.

I've been lucky to see everything he's gone through since the beginning. It takes a special person. My hat goes off to people like Dallas, Jacob Faithful, and my uncle Steve. It takes a lot of work to keep a group going.

What makes Cree Confederation different is our beat. Dallas takes a lot of pride in it. He said it's like a horse trotting, like when our warriors were riding horses.

There's a traditional aspect to my music, but it's constantly evolving. I want to project a female perspective. Growing up hearing songs, they were all by male composers. Whether it was a funny song or a love song, it would always come from a male perspective.

In the early days, my dad helped me to create songs, but he also encouraged me to compose my own. That's what pushed me. He even encouraged me to start learning my language. I currently hold a bachelor of arts degree in the Cree language, and I'm going after my master's degree.

When I create a song, before I show it to anybody, I let it sit for a while. I want to make sure that the melody is something people want to listen to. Melody sets a song's energy and mood. A big influence on that was my uncle Randy. His recordings are sweet and flowing. I practiced every day with those recordings. They were easy to listen to. To me, he sounded like Elvis in a round dance form.

I do a couple of funny songs, but most of my songs are about love or heartbreak. If it's a love song, I want it to sound smooth, like it was made out of love.

A lot of the songs on my first solo album, *Iskwewak—Songs of Indigenous Womanhood* [2012], were composed early on. Of my albums, that's the one that's been shared the most, the one people gravitate to. There are songs on that album that I'm always being requested to sing, like "Mommy's Little Guy," about motherhood and the love I felt for my firstborn son.

When it came to *Kikāwiynaw* [Our mother] [2016], I was more seasoned and knew what kind of sound I wanted. I was blown away by the people who contributed to that album—Anthony Wakeman, Kevin Yazzie, and especially R. Carlos Nakai. I grew up listening to him. My mom's a flute player. I was so floored that he wanted to work on it. Having people like that contribute to the songs brought my music to a level that I couldn't even imagine.

The song I recorded with R. Carlos and Uncle Randy, "Remember Me," started being used by the Missing and Murdered Indigenous Women [MMIW] movement. To bring awareness, they made a video showing a red handprint over their mouths. It went viral, and many people found their way to my music.

Working on new recordings for Buffalo Jump Records, I've found the sound I want to share. I'm better at portraying the stories, my feelings, and the intent of the songs.

The NAMAs named me Female Artist of the Year twice [2013, 2016]. The first time, I went to the awards by myself. I didn't think I had a chance—I was up against Radmilla Cody, who was up for a Grammy the same year—but I thought I'd make connections. When it came to my category, my heart was pounding. It blew me away when they announced me as the winner. I was speechless. I had nothing prepared; I didn't think I had a chance. When I started my acceptance speech, I remembered words my dad taught me and ended up speaking in my language. It was surreal.

The second time I won, I didn't go. I was pregnant with my second son, but I listened on internet radio. I remember being nervous. My second album was different from my first; I wasn't sure how people would take to it. When they announced me as the winner, I jumped off the bed.

Knowing that people like the way I'm putting things together drives me. I want to create music that makes people feel good, regardless of whether they're Indigenous or not. I want to leave a legacy not just for myself but for my kids, my family, and my people. That's why I put so much thought into the way I let my music come across. When I'm gone, I want people to hear my songs and know what my intentions were.

The Halluci Nation (formerly, A Tribe Called Red)
Thomas Ehren "Bear Witness" Ramon (1977–) (Cayuga)

Powwow and round dance music has been revolutionized by the Halluci Nation. Known as A Tribe Called Red (ATCR) since 2007, the Ottawa-based DJ collective changed its name in 2020. Regardless of what they call themselves, by incorporating archival drum tracks and new recordings into electronic dance music, they've plugged Indigenous sounds into the world of nightclubs, concerts, and festivals. "I saw ATCR in Vancouver in 2015," said Fawn Wood. "My uncle was hosting the show, so I got to hang out backstage. I remember looking at the crowd and seeing all these different nationalities vibing with Indigenous music. It not only changed the game to where everybody wanted to create powwow music, but it changed how our Indigenous youth saw themselves; it made them proud of who they were."

Canada holds [the Halluci Nation] as an example of its success. As unapologetically Indigenous as we are, we're able to be as subversive as we want. We've never been asked to dumb it down.

Before we started, our cultural history wasn't being heard. Nobody was interested in what our community was doing. That's why we started the Electric Powwow at the Babylon Nightclub [317 Bank Street, Ottawa]. It was magical. After the first night, we were told we couldn't stop. We kept it up, the first Saturday of each month, for almost ten years [2008–17]. There was no other place for young Indigenous people to go where they could feel comfortable and safe.

In the beginning, we just did regular club deejaying. After a year or so, we started doing mash-ups with powwow tracks to give something back to our community. The time was right. Not only was the Indigenous community waiting for something like us, but the rest of the world had finally come to a point where it was willing to listen. We struggled, at first, to get people to understand what we were doing, but once they got on board, it really changed. Our idea was to create something everybody could enjoy, something that would be instantly recognizable as Indigenous, something that Indigenous youth could hold up and say, "That's mine."

I grew up listening to Redbone, XIT, and a group out of Ottawa that mixed rock, reggae, and poetry, Seventh Fire. There was all this hip-hop by people like Julian B [Muscogee], but the one thing that no Indigenous artist had done before us was electronica, and that had been my love since the midnineties.

When we started, I was already in my thirties, the oldest member of the group. I was born in Buffalo, New York, but we moved to Toronto in 1983, when I was six, and I grew up in the Indigenous arts community. My mom's an actor and playwright. She was the artistic director of the Native Arts Centre in Toronto. My dad [Jeff Thomas] is a well-known photographer.

I started as a video artist, not a musician. I can't write a melody. I'm learning by working closely with Tim "2oolman" Hill [Mohawk] from the Six Nations of the Grand River in southwestern Ontario. He was producing hip-hop tracks for fifteen years before joining ATCR.

I've always connected music and video. When I was teaching myself to deejay, I'd put movies on mute and deejay to the movie. Incorporating video into our live performances makes sense. It was the same as what my father did. He'd look at historical photos of Indigenous peoples and give them a different narrative, and I look at racist, one-dimensional depictions in the media and give them Indigenist context. We've always been represented through the lens of others.

Growing up, I made up my own heroes. I found ways to take the negativity and stereotypes out of these characters and used my imagination to recontextualize them. That was a way of taking the pain out of it and turning it into something positive. That's the message of the videos we put out for our community. The images are fun, but we're exposing non-Indigenous people smack in the face with racist images. I don't wiggle my finger at anyone. That doesn't work—you end up in standoffs—but there's nothing more powerful than allowing somebody to use their own experience to reach a realization. If I show a racist image, people laugh, but on some level, they realize this is messed up. They come up to me afterward and say, "I thought that image was hilarious all my life, but the more I looked at it, the more I realized it was racist."

Our first single was "The Electric Powwow Drum." "Northern Girl," with Northern Cree, came next. We worked with their original recording. It was rocking the community. At one of our electric powwows, they were in town and came. We didn't know if we should play it or not, but they requested it. An hour later they requested it again. That was a good feeling.

We released *A Tribe Called Red* [2012] as a free internet download. So much of what we've been doing has not only been to give as much as we can to the community but also to get the visibility that Indigenous people haven't had.

When *Nation II Nation* [2013] was in production, we signed with Tribal Spirit Music. We were able to build good relationships with drum groups on the label, and they started sending us recordings. It changed the way we sampled powwow vocals. The idea was to work collaboratively with drum groups,

not just with recordings of their songs. The CD was nominated for a Polaris Music Prize and a JUNO as Electronic Album of the Year.

We've been trying to get drum groups to sing contemporary pop songs in a powwow style. It hasn't been released, but we worked with the Black Bear Singers from the Atikamekw Nation in Manawan [Quebec] on a powwow version of Redbone's "Come and Get Your Love." We didn't have a chance to finish it before *Guardians of the Galaxy* [2014] came out and Redbone made the charts again.

Our first session with Black Bear was done in their community. They speak Atikamekw [Ah-tik-ah-mek] and French. English is their third language, but they're young, and we connected. They understood what we were trying to accomplish and were willing to push their comfort level to record with us. We took them to a studio—the first time we got to record powwow music the way we wanted. We've been able to do a few experiments with them since. We've also been working with an Anishnaabeg family group, the Chippewa Travelers. We've gotten them to try different things too.

I met Buffy Sainte-Marie when I was working with a stage crew in Ottawa. She had heard ATCR and said, "It's awesome, what you're doing. Maybe we can do something in the future."

A year or so later we were contacted to do a remix of "Working for the Government" from her NAMA-winning *Medicine Songs* [2017]. It was an incredibly difficult process, very daunting. What were we going to do with a song that was already as close to perfect as you could get?

Fortunately, Buffy and ATCR were in Winnipeg at the same time. She came to the studio to hang out with us. She wanted to know how we were doing, how the industry was treating us, how we were taking care of ourselves, and whether we were learning the business side of things. It was a schooling session, but at the same time, it was her giving us permission to do whatever we wanted with her music.

A huge storm hit the studio in Hawaii where Buffy was working and destroyed the original tapes, except for one that was damaged but still playable. If you listened closely, you could hear a distorted bass line. We took the track apart, found that bass line, brought it up in the mix, and used it at the beginning of our track. It was like finding gold. It was such an interesting sound.

We released "The Road" before *Nation II Nation*. People were already playing our music at protests, but they needed songs for the movement. We dedicated it to Idle No More and Attawapiskat chief Theresa Spence [whose hunger strike protesting C-45 was announced on International Human Rights Day, December 10, 2012]. It was speaking to the relationship Canada needs to have with Indigenous people—the kind of conversation that Idle No More is about, at least in my eyes. We need a place at the table, we need our voices to be heard, and we need to be counted.

John Trudell was another on our dream list. Before we met, we heard through the grapevine that he was impressed with what we were doing and wanted to meet us. It didn't fall into place until we were playing at the Art Institute in Santa Fe. He was in town for the Indian market. He introduced us at the show. I was the only one at the venue when he arrived. When he came into the greenroom, I jumped up to shake his hand and introduce myself. I started telling him how much his work meant to me, and he stopped me. He knew about me, and he started telling me what he had accomplished—spokesperson during the Alcatraz takeover, chairman of AIM, setting his poetry to music. One thing that stuck with me was that he said it took him half his life to realize what ATCR had done intuitively, which was to use music to reach people. Before I could even bring up the idea of collaborating, he pulled out a notebook and started reading things. "Could you do something with this . . . would you be interested in that?"

It was close to a year before we started production of what became *We Are the Halluci Nation* [2016]. I hit John up and asked if he was still interested in contributing. We wanted the album to be a collaborative work, but we also knew that we wanted it to be more than just a collection of tracks. We wanted it to tell a story and be more than just club music. I'd been working on different story lines, but they all revolved around the theme of reaching out to people and telling them to become heroes, outlaws, and bandits and work together.

We set up a recording session in San Francisco, something easy for John to get to. He had recorded poems on a portable tape recorder. One of them was "The Halluci Nation." It wasn't the main one; that was supposed to be "A Tribe Called Red." When we got in the studio, he said, "I put another little poem at the end of the tape."

That turned out to be "The Halluci Nation." We very much identified with what it was saying. We were thinking of superheroes, and he was seeing this nation in what we were trying to create. We went to Ernesto Yerena Montejano, who designed the cover of *Nation II Nation*, and explained that we were going to have this new nation and wanted a national seal. He said, "I've already made four or five of those."

He knocked it out of the ballpark, and then I had the idea to turn that image into a patch. Very quickly, our manager got a test patch made. It looked like a national logo. Then I realized we had moved so quickly, we hadn't told John. I quickly wrote him an email explaining what we had done and sent a picture of the patch. He said, "Thank you so much, the Halluci Nation is real."

We did "Land Back" with A Northern Voice [Atikamekw] and DJ-producer Boogey the Beat [Les Boulanger] [Anishinaabe]. It came out as a free download in February 2020 [and, later, on *One More Saturday Night*] in between a protest in solidarity with Wet'suwet'en chiefs who were blocking the Coastal GasLink Pipeline from illegally going through their territory and an invasion by the RCMP [Royal Canadian Mounted Police].

Actions across the country shut down traffic. It was a big moment. Ottawa became the epicenter of the largest Indigenous protest ever in Canada. People came from all over the country. You saw a rise in the number of Indigenous people on the streets, on the buses, and in the restaurants. It was more than a feeling.

We wanted more tunes for our live set, so we reached out to Keith Secola [Anishinaabe and Italian] from the Leech Lake Indian Reservation in northern Minnesota. Every few years, someone records his "NDN Kars." He was super into the idea of an official remix. He's cut the song differently on every one of his albums. We went with his original recording [and included it on *One More Saturday Night*].

Interesting things took place on *One More Saturday Night*. One of my favorites was getting to use a modular synthesizer, TONTO [The Original New Timbral Orchestra]. British American bassist, producer, programmer Malcolm Cecil created it in the 1970s. He and his partner [Bob Margouleff] worked with Stevie Wonder for three and a half years. It provided the signature sound of "Superstition," "You Are the Sunshine of My Life," "Boogie on Reggae Woman," and many others.

The National Music Center, in Calgary, is a hands-on synthesizer museum. We've gone there on residencies to work with their synthesizers. They purchased a TONTO and restored it over four or five years. Not only were we the first group to work with it, but we also got to work with its producer and creator. It looks like something out of *Dr. Who*, but it was like having a studio musician with this warm, amazing sound.

"Tanokumbia" was a collaboration with Black Bear and Corpus Christi, Texas–based DJ [and] producer El Dusty Oliveira, the originator of cumbia electronica, or nu cumbia. It was another reminder that Indigenous people have no borders. It was one of the first times we got to use TONTO as well as work with somebody doing cumbia music.

I have hopes and dreams that the Halluci Nation will continue, but we're not young. There'll come a time when we get off the road, but we want this thing to continue and grow bigger. This next generation of artists is so far beyond where we started. When I talk about creating heroes out of racist imagery, I see a generation that doesn't have to do that anymore.

Dan "DJ Shub" General (Mohawk)

Competitive turntablist and former producer of ATCR, DJ Shub continues to connect on "emotional, physical and spiritual levels through music."[23]

I've been called the Godfather of PowWowStep, but I first heard it played by ATCR [at the time, Bear Witness, Ian "DJ NDN" Campeau, and Jon "Dee Jay Flame" Limoges] at one of their early electric powwows. It was like any DJ showcase, but I witnessed something I had never seen before—a club full of Indigenous people going crazy over music played by DJs. The music was mash-ups, nothing produced. They were playing tracks and throwing traditional songs on top. There was a lot of dubstep [a subset of electronic dance music (EDM) emphasizing syncopated drum or percussion patterns and sub-bass frequencies], but the BPM [beats per minute] lined up with traditional powwow music. Hearing that music and seeing people going crazy gave me chills. I told them, "I've been producing hip-hop for a couple of years. I'd love to take this idea and run with it."

They said, "Go for it."

I went home, started messing with the sounds, and came up with "Electric Pow Wow Drum." That's the one that put ATCR on the map.

We were worried that we'd get slack for what we were doing, and we did. It was brand-new to a lot of people, especially to the elders. The biggest problem was that it was played in clubs where alcohol was served. That was the biggest no-no, something we had to overcome.

We made music and put on parties. Students from the reserves came to Ottawa for our party. It snowballed from there, and we started getting gigs, especially after we were nominated for a JUNO.

Drum groups realized this wasn't just something we were trying to make money from. We were taking what they were doing and showing it to a different audience. They started sending us a capella studio recordings, which had never been done before. When they record, they don't sing a capella. It's live, or if it's in the studio, they record it all at once. We changed the way they record.

I grew up in the city [Fort Erie, Ontario], fourteen minutes from Buffalo. I had cousins and other family on the reservation an hour away and went there for powwows, but it wasn't until I started mixing traditional and

5. DJ Shub

contemporary music that I got into my culture. It's why people like this music so much. It's bringing culture back into their lives.

I got the nickname "DJ Shub" in high school, and it stuck. It started as "Shubba," but we shortened it. It came from [Jamaican dancehall musician] Shabby Ranks's "Mr. Loverman." It's too late now—I've got to keep it— but I should tell people a better story.

I have a six-year-older brother who deejayed in college bars in Buffalo. He used to take me with him. He noticed how much I loved it and bought me my first setup [two turntables and a mixer].

DJ battling is still one of my favorite things to do. I used to lock myself in my room and practice. My goal was to become a world champion. I won back-to-back Canadian titles [in 2007 and 2008] and represented Canada at the DMC [Disco Mix Club] DJ Championship, the DJ Olympics, and the best of the best. That's what caught the attention of A Tribe Called Red. I was the only Indigenous DJ to ever get that far. I placed fifth out of thirty-two, of which I was proud. The guys who won were fantastic, way above my skill set. I was happy just to make it to the world championship. If I can inspire a kid on a reserve that has nothing but two turntables and a dream, I've done my job, and I'm happy.

ATCR's first album, *Electric Pow Wow*, was masterminded by our manager at the time. He wanted something to send to award shows. We had songs scattered all over the internet, but he compiled everything. It was a mash-up; there wasn't a real direction.

Nation II Nation was about striving to make an official powwow step album. We were at our best, and it shows. It won a JUNO and other awards. We were proud of that album.

Our live shows were amazing. We told a story without audiences knowing it. The visuals were projecting, the music was playing, and audiences were getting bombarded by culture. We set up in spaces where Natives wouldn't normally feel comfortable. I remember a gig at an art gallery in Toronto. How often do Indigenous people get to play there?

I wouldn't have a career if not for ATCR, but after a while, I wanted to explore different genres and work with other people. I wanted the freedom to do what I wanted without having to get votes from the rest of the group, so I left in 2014.

I did tracks on my EP *PowWowStep* [2016] with Northern Cree [smoke dance singer] Frazer Sundown and a northern-style drum group, the Black Lodge Singers. It received an Indigenous Music Award for best instrumental album in May 2017. The Canadian Organization of Campus Activities [COCA] named me DJ of the Year a month later.

"Indomitable," with Northern Cree, was my first video after leaving ATCR. It was important to get it right. We hired a video team from Montreal, and they took my concept and ran with it. They did an excellent job. I wanted to convey a story about an Indigenous person who's tired of city life and wants to get back to his culture. He's renewed by returning to the Six Nations Reserve and going to a powwow. My mom's a good friend of the chief, so we were allowed to fly drones over the reserve. We got shots that a normal person wouldn't get. It won the Best Video NAMA and a Canadian Screen Award.

I've continued working with Northern Cree. If you made up a team of the best players, they'd have a lot of spots on the team. There's power behind their songs and voices, and they think outside the box, which is fantastic. We've continued to have a great relationship. They record tracks and send me tapes. We meet a few times a year. They'll tell me, "I've got this great hook."

As DJs, you've got to be into what's current. Otherwise, you're going to get lost in the mix. ATCR used music that was happening and mixed it with traditional tracks. It worked every time.

I don't know if we started it or if it's something someone else started and got pushed forward after we got mainstream recognition, but traditional powwow music is being mixed with all kinds of music. I sample classic rock and disco records that my mom and dad used to play. My heart is based on jams by Michael Jackson, the Doobie Brothers, and Donna Summers.

My music's a continuation of what I was doing with ATCR. I knew they were going to keep going after I left and didn't want to be in their shadow, but I received a ton of messages saying, "You started powwow step—you need to continue. People are listening to you for it."

That made me realize that this was something I had to do. Don't get me wrong. It's not that I don't want to do it. It got me to where I am, and I'm so thankful for it.

I just finished a new video, "Calling All Dancers." We did it at Six Nations as well. I like incorporating where I come from in my music. Six Nations has one radio station that plays nonstop country music and bluegrass. When I was a kid going back to the reserve, that's all I would hear. There wasn't any Indigenous rap or dance music on the radio. It's the same today.

I do workshops for young people and tell them that the EP that won a JUNO in 2018 [*PowWowStep*] was made in my basement, with little studio gear. It's all about attitude.

Keeping your culture is the most important thing. I didn't realize that until I started making music, but that's why I push on. Buffy Sainte-Marie and Robbie Robertson opened the door for us. Hopefully, we're opening the door for the next generation. It's a continuance; young people are the future.

7

Sound of the Wind

In 1995 a Neanderthal flute was found in a cave in what is now Slovenia's Divje Babe Archeological Park. Estimated to be at least fifty thousand years old, the bear-bone woodwind has four finger holes and produces four distinct pitches. "These pitches," said musicologist Bob Fink, "match four notes of the traditional scale we use in music today, the diatonic scale."[1]

In North America's Southwest, the Anasazi decorated rocks with images of a humpbacked flutist, Kokopelli (Hopi for "wooden backed"), as early as AD 1000. The fertility god can also be seen on pottery attributed to the Hohokam, predecessors of the Pima and Tohono O'odham. "The flute that Kokopelli carries symbolizes joy and music," explained Dani Rhys. "It carries the idea of merriment and laughter during feasts . . . a muse to inspire creative individuals to produce songs, poems and literature."[2]

Kokopelli has a darker side: "Sometimes crops fail. Sometimes couples fail to have children no matter how hard they try. Sometimes plans fall apart and success slips away. When these things happen, it's easy to blame Kokopelli as the trickster, who failed to deliver."[3]

Most researchers connect Kokopelli to Pochtecas, an Aztec representation of a trader, but Kevin Brewer of Ouachita Baptist University, in Arkadelphia, Arkansas, disagrees. "The humpbacked flute player," he claims, "[appeared] hundreds of years before the great influx of these traders."[4]

Alternate theories range from Kokopelli being "an actual person inflicted with Pott's disease, a spinal chord [sic] deformity which results in priapism, a humped back and a club foot" to the most widely held belief that "the humpback flute player is a depiction of the Hopi fertility katchina, *Kookopolo*." (The Pueblo referred to spirits of the invisible forces of life as *katchinas*.)[5]

In 1823 Italian explorer, art collector, and former soldier in Napoleon's army, Giacomo Costantino Beltrami was seeking the source of the Mississippi River in present-day Minnesota when he found what is considered to be the oldest, extant cedar flute. Displayed at the Museo Civico di Scienze Natural in Beltrami's birthplace, Bergamo, Italy, the E-flat flute and accompanying zufolo (small flute) are still playable.

Woodwinds continued to be unearthed. An archeologist from the Carnegie Institute, Earl Halstead Morris found four Anasazi flutes (AD 599–AD 769), in 1931, in what is now known as the Broken Flute Cave in the Prayer Rock district of Navajo Nation. Made of box elder maple, the flutes with six finger holes are displayed at the Arizona State Museum.

The following year another prototype of the modern Indigenous woodwind, the Breckenridge flute (AD 1020–AD 1160), was found along the shores of Beaver Lake in Arkansas's Ozarks, by Samuel Dellinger, the director of the University of Arkansas Museum. A two-chambered river cane flute, its sound chamber is decorated with elaborate designs.

For the continent's original inhabitants, flutes and whistles served a variety of purposes. Shamans played them during ceremonies, and they were used as a warning signal or hunting call. In some tribes, young men hoped to lure a sweetheart with their melody. Eagle-bone whistles are still used in the sun dance.

One of four shipwrecked survivors, from what started as a three-hundred-man voyage, Álvar Núñez Cabeza de Vaca listened to "flutes of reeds" along the west coast of Florida in April 1528. "We heard, all night long, especially after midnight," he wrote in his journal, "a great uproar, the sound of many voices, the tinkling of little bells, also flutes and tambourines and other instruments, the most of which noise lasted until morning, when the storm ceased."[6]

Chronicler of de Coronado's 1540–42 excursion to present-day New Mexico, Pedro de Castañeda reported that "people came out of the village with signs of joy . . . with drums and pipes, something like flutes, of which they have a great many."[7]

Castañeda also recalled seeing Pueblo women grinding corn and singing to the accompaniment of a flute player.

Oklahoma-born Belo Cozad (1864–1950) (Kiowa) and Joyce "Doc" Tate Nevaquaya (1932–96) (Comanche) were among the first flute players to record. After being recorded by ethnologist Willard Rhodes for the Library of Congress in 1941, Cozad told an audience, "I got this music from way back in, in, eh, Montana. One of the poor boys, he, he ain't got no home, and he went up on the mountain and stayed out four nights there, and he learned, learned this music and got it—he got it from some kind of spirit . . . show him to make it this way and make it good music. And keep it, keep it long as you live and you make you good living."[8]

Traveling across the United States, Nevaquaya presented flute concerts and visual-art workshops at places like Brigham Young University in Provo, Utah (1972), and Georgetown University in Washington DC (1974). The Fort Sill boarding school survivor released two albums—*Indian Flute Songs from Comanche Land* (1976) and *Comanche Flute Music* (1979)—and made more than twenty-five television appearances. He received a National Heritage Fellowship from the National Endowment of the Arts in 1986. "He played in the old style," Jerod Impichchaachaaha Tate told me. "It was shriller than recent flutists."

Despite the efforts of Cozad, Nevaquaya, and a few others, including James Poweshiek (Meskwaki), Richard Fool Bull (Lakota), and Dave Marks (Dakota), interest in the Indigenous flute continued to fade. By the last quarter of the twentieth century, the instrument appeared to be headed toward extinction.

Raymond Carlos Nakai (1946–) (Ute and Diné)

Enter R. Carlos Nakai. Raised on the Navajo Reservation, Nakai's childhood dream of playing the flute was dampened by his high school music teacher. Instead, he trained as a cornet player before switching to trumpet. A featured soloist with the Navajo Tribal Band, he auditioned for the Royal Hawaiian Band while in the U.S. Navy, but he was turned down. "I passed the audition," he recalled in 2013, "but they said, 'We'd love to have you, but there's one problem—you're not Hawaiian.'"

Returning to the reservation after being honorably discharged, Nakai felt out of place. "All my classmates were in the ground," he said, "victims of the Vietnam War. People resented me for coming back."

Turning to drugs and alcohol, Nakai headed toward self-destruction. A serious auto accident in 1972 altered his path. "I damaged my embouchure," he told me, "and thought my world had ended."

It was, instead, an awakening. Abstaining from substance abuse, Nakai began to pull his life together. Unable to play trumpet, he began tinkling on a girlfriend's "meant to hang on a wall" flute (he would acquire his first well-built woodwind in 1974). He knew some traditional Kiowa songs, but he was free to explore the instrument's possibilities. "I had years of music theory and practice behind me," he explained, "and thought I could transfer that knowledge to the flute."

Debuting with *Changes: Native American Flute Music* in 1982, Nakai exceeded everyone's expectations with million sellers *Earth Spirit* (1987) and *Canyon Trilogy* (1989). Their success lifted Ray and Mary Boley's Phoenix-based Canyon Records to the international level and opened doors, not only for Indigenous flute players but also for peyote singers (e.g., Louie Gonnie, Cheevers Topper, and Verdell Primeaux), round dance singers (e.g., Randy Wood and Jay Begaye), classical guitarists (e.g., Gabriel Yacoub), and powwow drum groups (e.g., Black Lodge, Northern Cree, and Tha Tribe). Stephen Butler signed on as a producer in the mid-1980s.

Often linked with new age music, Nakai's discography reflects much more. In addition to recording more than a dozen solo flute albums, he's led trios, quartets, and quintets (often with guitarist and luthier William Eaton and percussionist Will Clipman) and appeared as a guest of symphony orchestras. His collaborators have included German-born, Los Angeles–based pianist Peter Kater; ambient saxophonist Paul Horn; avant-garde composer Phillip Glass; Hawaiian slack-key guitarist Keola Beamer; Israeli cellist Uri-Bar David; Tibetan flutist and vocalist Nawang Khechong; Japan's Wind Traveling Band; and choreographer Martha Graham. He shared an experimental fusion group, Jackalope, with synthesizer player Larry Yañez and guitarist Steve Cheseborough, which played what they dubbed "SynthacousticpunkarachiNavajazz."

Nakai's Grammy-nominated ninth album with Kater, *Ritual* (2015), featured oboist Paul McCandless (Paul Winter Consort, Oregon); Brazilian cellist Jacques Morelenbaum; and vocalist from York County, Pennsylvania, Trisha Bowden. "My music," Nakai said, "has to do with my perspective of being in the world at the moment. Seeing the beauty and even ugliness of life, you've got to keep your perspective about being a participant in the world as it grows and changes all the time."

The Indian Arts and Crafts Act

Nakai's success inspired flute players of every ethnicity. A distinction needed to be made between instruments built or played by an Indigenous person and those that were not. Seeking a solution to the misrepresentation was a factor in the 1990 Indian Arts and Crafts Act, which made it illegal to market or sell any artwork or musical instrument as Native American unless it was made or played by a "member of any federally or officially State recognized tribe of the United States, or an individual certified as an Indian artisan by an Indian tribe."[9]

"It's not so much the fact that they're playing the flute that bothers me," said Darren Thompson of the Lac du Flambeau band of Lake Superior Chippewa in northern Wisconsin. "It's the fact that a lot of them are non-Native and try to play the part of a Native, wearing what they think is Indian attire."[10]

Acknowledging and respecting an instrument's origins are important, but personal expression transcends geographical borders. "It's a matter of respect," said Seattle-based flutist Gary Stroutsos, who plays Chinese, Afro-Cuban, and Indigenous woodwinds. Despite his Greek and Italian American ancestry, Stroutsos was a founding artist of the otherwise all-Indigenous Makoché label in 1996. His forty albums include Zuni, Salish, and Diné melodies. He's currently working with the director of the Hopi Cultural Preservation Office, Stewart Koyiyumptewa, to extend the tribe's flute tradition. "Some of the elders recognize what I've done," he said proudly.

The plaintive tones of the Native flute captured the fascination of Austria-born flute player Bearheart Kokopelli (Bernhard Mikuskovics). Intrigued by the world beyond his homeland, the 2017 recipient of a Native Heart NAMA (for an outstanding contribution by a non-Indigenous artist) traveled as soon as possible. "I met many musicians," he told me via Skype. "It didn't matter if they were from Austria, Turkey, America, or anywhere else—we were connected by our native hearts."

Calvin Ishoni Standing Bear (1949–) (Oglala and Sicangu Lakota)

Descended from nineteenth-century Oglala Lakota war leader Crazy Horse (Tashunca-uitco) and Ponca chief Luther Standing Bear, Calvin Standing Bear expresses his deepest soul through music. His mix of "traditional Lakota music and . . . contemporary Lakota Flute songs" are "grounded in the concept of spirituality."[11]

I'm full-blooded Lakota. There aren't many of us left, fewer than two hundred. I was born on the Rosebud Indian Reservation in South Dakota, but reservation life was tough, without opportunities, so Mom moved us near my grandmother in Denver.

My mother's father, Silas Standing Bear, was a chief. He died the year before I was born. I'd talk to my mother and not only ask about my grandpa but also about why we were living in Denver. Why weren't we on the reservation? She'd explain that the federal government relocated Native Americans to the cities for a better opportunity. My grandpa had been one of those relocated. My grandma was taking a journey to California when

they met. A couple of years later, a relative talked them into heading to Denver. That's how my family ended up there today.

Chief George Standing Bear, my great-grandpa, had two wives. Of course, if you've got two wives, they'd better get along. A chief with more than one wife built the tribe that way. George had three sons who became chiefs—Silas, Henry, and Luther—and a couple of daughters.

Seven tribal bands make up the Lakota council fire—the Sihasapa [Blackfoot], Brulé [Upper and Lower], Hunkpapa, Mincinjou, Oglala, Sans-Arcs, and Oohenonpa [Two-Kettle]. You can't marry within your tribe. It's against the rules. If you're an Oglala, you can marry a Blackfoot but not an Oglala. My father was Oglala, and my mother was Sicangu. So they could marry. They had many in-laws.

We don't think of families the way white people do. There are no great-uncles or great-aunts. Your mother's or father's father and his brothers are your grandpas. Their sisters are your grandmothers.

My grandfather Silas was a catechism reader in the Catholic Church. He stayed on the reservation and became an interpreter. People on the reservation couldn't speak English and didn't understand when the government was talking to them. My grandpa would listen to it in English and tell it to the people in the Lakota language.

Luther was an author, educator, and interpreter, as well as a horseback rider and dancer with Buffalo Bill's Wild West. He and his brother Henry went to boarding schools.

When Gutzon Borglum started carving out the sacred Black Hills for the Mt. Rushmore National Memorial, Henry wrote to [Polish American sculptor and former Borglum assistant] Korczak Zlokowski and told him that what he needed to do was carve a memorial to our great Crazy Horse, George Standing Bear's father. Nobody knows what Crazy Horse looked like; there are no photographs of him. His appearance was kept secret. When [Zlokowski] started carving the Crazy Horse Memorial in 1948, he used the face of my grandpa Henry.

I started dancing northern style when I was around seven; my grandma made my outfit. Around the same time, Mom put me in a cathedral choir. I not only learned to sing, but I got to listen to great piano playing.

I was the only Native American in the choir. Watching TV, I'd seen cowboys killing Indians because Indians were no good. There was bad name-calling directed at Native people, but it wasn't just on TV. I was bullied because I was Native, so I kept to myself. I was quiet and wouldn't talk to anyone. When I'd walk down the cathedral aisle, I wouldn't turn my head or look at anybody. I wondered why my mother put me in the choir with the white kids. She'd tell me, "I want you to grow up to be a good boy."

After school on Monday, Wednesday, and Thursday, I'd go to choir practice for two hours. On Sundays, we'd go into the choir practice room and get ready for the 11:00 a.m. service in St. John's Cathedral. I always wore a white shirt, tie, and suit pants. We sang out of the Episcopalian hymnbook, along with a big pipe organ. I did it for four or five years. When

I was thirteen, the choirmaster told me, "Your voice is changing. You're no longer a soprano; you're an alto. You're welcome to sing with the altos."

I told my mother. She said, "Son, you're growing up."

My grandfather was Catholic, but Grandma didn't like Catholicism and became Episcopalian. I told her that I hoped to become a minister. I had good grades and loved going to school. I learned spirituality and the Christian way. I learned catechism. I was confirmed and baptized. I still have my grandpa's Masonic Bible—it's five inches thick—but growing up, I didn't believe the Christian way of life. I felt sorry that my people couldn't practice their spirituality until the American Indian Religious Freedom Act in 1978.

We lived in the ghetto, the poor side of town. There were lots of cockroaches—sometimes mice—but Mom went back to school and studied to be a linguistics teacher. After graduating, she got a job teaching the Lakota language. Things got better, so she bought a house further north, thirty miles from Denver. We ended up living among white people in the farm area. There were five or six homes, but they were still building houses.

In 1961 Mom sent me to an Episcopal school on the reservation in Mission, South Dakota. I had to walk a mile and a half from the dormitory to the school, even if the snow was two feet high. On Saturdays, we'd go for catechism with the minister. After that, we could do anything we wanted. We could go to town or the movies. I hardly did much, because money was hard for my five brothers and four sisters. We didn't have a father, and my mother had a hard time raising us. She'd get a welfare check for $300-and-something a month and try to feed eleven people.

During a school break, some students and I went to Minneapolis. We dressed in suits and ties and carried duffel bags with the rest of our clothes. We wanted to experience something different, and people in Minneapolis wanted to experience Native boys. We ended up staying in different homes. We went to church and had dinners together. We didn't talk much to white people, but we went along with them. They learned about us, and we learned about them. We had that opportunity for a week, but during that week, I heard the Beach Boys. If you've been in a choir and experienced harmonies, you could hear that that was what they were about. Then I heard the Beatles. They could harmonize and play rock and roll. I started buying their albums and singing along. I got into the

Supremes, the Four Tops, and the Temptations. I had so many albums. I listened to James Brown, Marvin Gaye, and Stevie Wonder. I liked the way Black people sang. They were gospel singers; that's why they sang so good. I loved them all.

One day my uncle showed up at the boarding school. He was going to be a counselor. He came to my dormitory and brought his guitar and amp. He said, "C'mon, I want to show you something," and started walking to a second dormitory. I followed him into the basement. He started hooking up his equipment and playing "Pipeline." I watched him, thinking, "Wow, that's cool!"

I hoped that I could someday play the guitar; I wanted to play Beatle tunes. I started when I was fifteen. I played by ear; I couldn't afford a guitar teacher. Fortunately, a Spanish man taught me. I played rhythm guitar for him. He played lead and sang, but his singing wasn't too good. He tried to sing like Elvis. He had the right voice, but he was in the wrong tuning on the guitar. It didn't sound like the right chords.

My younger brother introduced me to a guy who had a drum set. Another guy had a guitar. I talked to both, and we formed a band. We had to find a singer. I wouldn't sing, even though I had experience, because I was shy. I played the lead guitar. We played Beatles and Rolling Stones songs and other things happening in 1966 and '67.

As soon as I finished school, I was drafted and sent to Vietnam. After nine months, I was medically discharged. I don't talk about it much; it was sad. I saw many soldiers fall. I was on the flight lines for the carriers that came in and went out.

After I got home, I wound up having an alcohol problem for a good six or seven years. I didn't like it and cried every day. I went to meetings in churches, trying to change my life, but it wasn't working. I got married but lost my family. I should have never gotten married in the first place.

I tried going to Metropolitan State College to study law, but that didn't work out. I tried doing music, but I couldn't concentrate. I was just having problems. I did everything I could to stop drinking, but I couldn't do it.

I finally thought about studying construction and carpentry, which is what I did. I went to the community college in Littleton, got my degree, and went to work doing construction. I was still drinking, but I had responsibilities. I said to myself, "I'm going to take care of my family and do my best."

After the Freedom of American Indian Religion passed, Indigenous people started going back to their roots. I figured that was what I needed to do—go back to my culture and spirituality. That chance came in 1989 when my little brother got into a head-on collision and was almost killed. His daughter called me, waking me on a Saturday at about 4:00 a.m. I had been drinking the night before with my wife Irene's uncle, but I didn't have a hangover. I hadn't drunk much, three or four cans of beer, and that was it. My niece said, "Your brother's in the hospital; he's dying. The doctor wants you to sign papers."

I don't know why she got hold of me. She could have gotten in touch with my other brothers and sisters, but I said, "Okay, I'll get dressed. I'll throw some water on my face and get the hay out of here."

I woke my wife's uncle and asked, "Do you want to come with me to the hospital?"

When we got there, I spoke with the doctor. He said, "Someone's got to sign these papers, but let's wait. Come back in thirty minutes."

It was around eight o'clock. My mom and other brothers and sisters soon showed up.

My wife came down with multiple sclerosis in 1985, and I had to take care of her and our kids. By 1987 I had to push her around in a wheelchair. I could have burned out, but I was hanging in. We were in the visitors' room praying for my little brother when something just came to me. I looked at my mom and said, "I want to sun dance."

Sun dance is when they pierce you in the chest with pencil-sized pegs. They pinch the skin on your chest, cut it on both sides in a diameter, stick the pegs through your flesh, put a rope on them, and tie them to the arbor [tree]. You've got to break that flesh off your body. Mom looked at me and said, "Do you know what you're saying?"

I told her, "Yes," and she asked me why. I said, "Because of my wife and my brother."

One of my other brothers turned to me and said, "What did you say?"

"I want to sun dance."

"That means we both have to sun dance."

The doctor came over and told my mom, "Your son's sleeping, everything's going to be fine. In a day or two, there'll be visiting hours, and you can come back."

I told my mother to get in touch with the traditional healer. She said, "Okay," and we all left and went home. When the weekend was over, I took Monday off. My mother called and said, "Son, what are you doing?"

"I'm pacing the floor, thinking about what I said about sun dancing."

"Are you drinking?"

"No. I told you what I want to do."

"Well ... a healer from South Dakota and his wife are coming to bring you a peace pipe; you need to prepare yourself. Sun dancing is a serious thing. Once you start, you can never drink for the rest of your life. Once you go to a ceremony, it's over. Do you understand?"

"Yes, Mom."

She called again on Friday and told me that the healer and his wife were there. My brother and I went to the sweat lodge on Saturday to get cleansed. When we came out, they had a ceremony for us. We were invited to South Dakota for a sun dance.

That sun dance changed my life. My kids were still little—three, four, five, six, and seven. My wife couldn't walk, so I carried her to the car and put her in the passenger side. I took her wheelchair and put it on top of the car. We had a trunk full of camping gear. We were heading back to Rosebud.

Everybody helped me get ready. My mom made a skirt for me. I made sage bracelets for my ankles and a sage wreath to put around my head, with two eagle feathers in it. I was given an eagle-bone whistle, a medallion, and an eagle fan.

I danced for four days without food or water, dancing for forty-five minutes, taking a fifteen-minute break, and doing it again, from six in the morning until five in the afternoon, in a sun that was almost one hundred degrees. I didn't feel tired but energized.

I was scared the first time. Before the sun dance, I walked around the camp and talked to my grandpas and grandmas, aunts, and uncles. I was trying to get out of piercing, but they said, "Uh-uh, you've got to pierce."

The first day was hard. When the sun dance began, I was asked where my wife was. I told them that she was over by our camp, a couple of hundred feet from the dancing circle. They went to get her. They put her in her wheelchair and brought her back to the circle. They carried her inside and brought her to the tree.

It was time to get my rope, and I did. They laid me down and cut my chest. They put the pegs in. I didn't think anything of it, but they hooked those ropes on and started singing. I was pulling on my flesh with the ropes, but I couldn't break free. People told the other dancers not to touch me. I had to do it by myself. I went to the tree and started praying, "Help me, God."

I tried again but still couldn't break free. I said, "I'm coming back next year."

When I came back, I broke that flesh.

They told me, when I started sun dancing, that it would be a lifetime commitment. You come back and pierce every year, four years for each direction—east, west, north, and south.

When the sun dance was over, we rolled up camp and headed home. We stopped at a motel for the night and got to our four-bedroom apartment the next day. We pulled in around 10:30 in the morning. We hadn't been home for eight days. I needed to open the windows and air the apartment out, so I told Irene, "I'll come back and take the wheelchair off the top of the car, put you in, and roll you home afterward."

She said, "Okay," and I went to the apartment. I started opening windows until I got to the third bedroom window, overlooking the parking lot. I heard my kids teasing their mother. She was going, "No, no, no, quit that."

I went into the master bedroom, opened the window, and walked out. I started up the sidewalk to the parking lot, focused on getting to the car. Suddenly a shadow went by. I stopped, turned around, and my wife was chasing the kids. I said, "Irene! Irene!"

She stopped and said, "What?"

"Look at you, you're standing, you're running!"

I went three feet from her, held my hands out, and said, "Come here."

She started walking toward me. I looked at her and said, "Are you okay?"

"I'm fine; let's walk a little."

She walked with me to our apartment, and then she said, "I want to use the bathroom."

It looked like everything was going okay. When she came out of the bathroom, she walked into the living room, looked at me, and said, "I'm going to make some fry bread."

"What!? You haven't cooked in years."

"I know what I'm doing."

Since that day, I haven't touched alcohol. Everything was cool. I was working; my wife was fine. She'd walk the kids to school and back home afterward. I was so happy, so grateful, I knew I had to pierce again.

I continued learning about my roots and going to sweat lodges. I learned the spiritual songs I do today in my language.

I went to a ceremony in 1993. It was springtime. The healer said, "Calvin, the spirits say they have a gift for you."

"What is it?"

"They're not telling you; you have to find out yourself."

When I left that ceremony, I went home to get my carpenter tools. Irene got my lunch ready. I said, "I'll see you later," and left. I was walking up the sidewalk when I heard somebody playing flute. "Who goes there?"

The flute stopped. I went back to the apartment and told Irene. "Am I hearing things?"

She said, "Everything will be all right," so I went to work. I drove to the job site and started working on a three-story apartment building. I took my lunch break in a breezeway, sitting on the steps. I was eating lunch when I heard somebody playing the flute again. "Who's that?"

It stopped.

All that week, I heard flute playing. When Saturday came, Irene and I got a babysitter and went to a Native American exhibition. When we walked in the door, she saw all these flutes. She took my hand and pulled me to the flute area. We walked up to a table with flutes. "See what they sound like."

I picked one up. It had six holes. I put my fingers on them and started blowing. I started moving my fingers. Then I looked at the flute and said, "Yep, this is what I've been hearing."

I put it down, and a lady who was selling flutes said, "That's beautiful music you're playing."

"I've never played before; I don't know how to play."

She looked at me and said, "Nah, you ain't pulling my leg."

She went to another table, picked up a flute, and said, "Play this one." I started blowing into it and moving my fingers. "This one sounds good."

She picked up another flute and gave it to me. I blew through it and moved my fingers. It sounded good. She said, "Come here," and I walked with her into the back where there were glass counters with flutes in them. She pulled one out and said, "Play this."

It sounded good, too, but I said, "Lady, I've been here a long time. My wife and I are anxious to see other vendors."

"Wait a minute! Turn around. See that table by the entrance door? Pick any flute off that table and bring it to me."

I went over to the table and picked up a flute. It was the first flute I had played. I came back and said, "This is the flute I like."

She looked at it, wrote its number down, and said, "It's yours."

My eyes got big. "What!? You're giving me this?"

"I used up all your time. Take your flute and have a nice day."

Whoa! I couldn't believe it. I held the flute as we walked all over, seeing all these vendors—turquoise makers, jewelry makers, all kinds of Native American artists—but I couldn't wait to go home. When we finally got there, I went into the back bedroom and looked inside the flute's barrel like I was looking into a shotgun. I started taking deep breaths and blowing into it, moving my fingers. A tune ["Morning Song"] came to me, and I played it.

It kept growing from there. On Sundays, I'd take my wife and kids to church at the Four Winds community center in Denver. There were giveaways. This guy gave me a drum thirty inches in diameter. I was really surprised.

When we started going to the church, around 1988, I was the only one to sun dance. The next thing you knew, all those people—the ministers, my brothers, and the board of directors—wanted to sun dance. They all pierced—my mother, everybody. Everything changed. At first there were twenty-five long pews on each side of an aisle. They removed them and left a big space. The minister told me, "We're going to put chairs in a circle. Put your drum over there, and people can sing with you."

Indians on the streets of Denver would hear that drum, come up the stairs of that church, and look in. The minister would say, "C'mon in."

Some Indians started coming every Sunday, doing their best to not be drinking. It doesn't feel like a church anymore; it's a whole different thing.

One day I brought my flute. I played one song, and that was it. After church was over, this guy came over to me and said, "I'm John Torres [Chiricahua Apache and Mexican American]. We're putting on an event.

We'd like you to come with your drum and sing some songs. Bring your flute. I wrote this song, 'Buffalo's Heart.' I wonder if you could play the flute to it."

"I can't play your song unless it's in F minor."

"That's what I wrote the song in. How about you and I get together?"

We went to my mother's house, and he started playing the piano. I started playing my flute. Suddenly he stopped. I turned around and looked at him. He looked at me. His eyes got big, and he said, "We have something in common."

After months of practice, I said to my mom, "We've got to have a name for our duo."

Mom said, "How about Red Tail?"

"That sounds good."

My first cousin is Michael Chasing Hawk. I wanted to honor him. "How about Red Tail Chasing Hawk?"

After working out seven songs, John and I went to see Tim Tickerner, who had a studio in Parker, Colorado. He said, "I like what you're doing; let me record you."

We played all the songs we had been practicing. Tim gave us a cassette and said, "It's yours; you don't have to pay me. Do what you want with it."

I put that cassette in my pocket and went home. Howard Bad Hand [Sicangu Lakota] was having a ceremony in my mother's house. He's a traditional healer whose spirit name is Anunkasan Wakinyan [Thunder Eagle]. After singing together, everybody started praying. Then it was my turn. I started talking to the Great Spirit, telling him that my partner and I had completed all these songs. "I want to know if you'd bless these songs and give me permission to share them with the world."

I had never asked for permission to expose my music to the world before, but it was a good thing to do. I submitted the cassette to Canyon Records. They listened to it and sent a letter to John and me saying that we could sign with them. *Eagle Dances with the Wind* [1995] came out, and we started playing all over. We went to Japan. It was quite an experience. We recorded a second album, *Brother Hawk*, and again took the tapes to a ceremony. I asked the Great Spirit to bless the songs. Do you know what the elders told me? They said, "You can bless these songs yourself. What you do is already a blessing."

I met Tony Palmer at the Hollow Bear Sundance in Saint Francis, South Dakota, in 1999. He came up to me and said, "I have a record company. I sell CDs for artists and help them out."

He wanted me to sign a contract for a year, but it sounded like he wanted to be in control of me. I didn't know if that would work, so I tried finding another manager. Tony Palmer sent me a letter saying that I breached his contract. I hadn't signed anything with him, but he took off with my CD *Wakan Olewan—Lakota Pipe Ceremonial and Sacred Songs* and kept selling it for five or six years. He must have made hundreds of thousands of dollars. Finally, I told someone about it, and he said, "Well, I'm going to call Tony Palmer and tell him to give your music back, or he's in some heavy trouble." And that's what he did. Tony Palmer turned the account over to me. I hadn't given him the original tapes. Now that I'm married for a third time, my wife holds the copyrights for the songs. She's a graphic designer. We put a different photo on the CD, added two songs, and reissued it as *Sacred Songs: Channupa and Ceremonial*. It's a powerful album. You'd be surprised what those songs sound like with piano.

Approximately four hundred years ago, the Great Spirit brought a messiah, the White Buffalo Calf Woman, to the Cheyenne River Reservation in South Dakota. The story goes that two warriors were buffalo hunting when they saw this woman two hundred feet from them dressed in white buckskin. She was by herself out on the plains. One of the warriors wanted to make love to her. He told his brother, who said, "No, this woman is sacred."

The negative brother said, "Okay," but he approached the woman anyway. He was going to touch her when a cloud came over them. The positive warrior stood back. When that cloud disappeared, the negative warrior was a pile of bones. The woman looked at the positive warrior and said, "Do not be afraid. I have a gift for you and the Lakota Nation. Go back to your village and tell your people what you've seen. Tell them to make a big circle with their tipis."

He hurried back to his village and told the chief. Everybody dressed in their finest clothing and did what they were told. When the woman came, she was carrying a buffalo robe. When she came into the circle, the warriors' assistants took it off her arm. They laid it down and unrolled it. There was what we call a *channupa* in the Lakota language. It means peace pipe. It had been first offered to the Egyptians. They didn't want it, so it was given to the Lakota Nation.

White Buffalo Calf Woman stayed with the people and taught them how to pray with the pipe, how to load it, how to offer it to the four directions, Father Sky, and Mother Earth, and how to have a ceremony with it. She taught the people sacred songs. She stayed for twenty-eight days, and then it was time for her to go. Before leaving, she said, "Spread the channupa throughout the world so there will be peace and love."

Virtues come with that channupa—love, compassion, generosity, humility, respect, and prayer. They were given to us with the channupa.

The Great Spirit, Wakan Tanka, gave me a special life. When I started to play music, I was blessed, because that was the gift given to me. "Recognize it; it's yours. You know what to do with it. Keep yourself disciplined; everything's going to go right for you. Forget about the past and move on with your life."

"Fly Eagle Fly" came from a dream. When I woke, I got a pencil and paper and started writing it out. In the dream, I was traveling across the plains on my horse and saw an eagle. I sang "Fly eagle fly, fly so high in the sky."

In our language, that line means so much.

We prayed when *Fly Eagle Fly* was nominated for the Best Debut NAMA in 2019. I knew it was going to win, and it did. We won the Global Music Award too.

I was grateful when the Colorado Symphony Orchestra wanted me to do a youth concert with a seventy-seven-piece orchestra. The music would be heard like thunder in the sky and touch the hearts of the people.

They bused in children from different counties of Colorado. Some traveled as far as thirty miles. I had to play two concerts a day. That's a lot of work, but I've done that before. You must have spirituality, be with the Great Spirit, and discipline your life to do it. You can't be involved with alcohol or drugs. That's the only way the Great Spirit is going to work. If you're going to create music, you've got to pray about it.

When the Colorado Symphony Orchestra started the concert, kids were talking to each other. I could hear them from my dressing room, through a speaker. The teacher would say, "Be quiet; listen to the music." But they kept talking . . . blah, blah, blah. When the orchestra stopped, nobody clapped until the conductor said, "Come on, everybody, give them a hand."

The orchestra continued to play, but the kids kept talking and carrying on. The conductor announced, "We have a guest who's Native American. His name is Calvin Standing Bear, and he plays Native American flute. Please welcome him."

I walked on stage, and the kids all went, "Yay!"

I waited for them to calm down. The lights lowered, and the spotlight came on me with a light-blue color. The orchestra started playing. Those kids got so quiet you could hear a pin drop. Nobody said a word. I could hear all seventy-seven instruments. I saw little kids looking over seats, trying to see me.

I played each song for about a minute and thirty seconds. Before we moved on to the next song, the kids clapped but calmed down afterward. When I ended my last song and the lights turned on, those kids jumped up and down. I put my left hand out, waved it to all the orchestra players, and thanked them for backing me up. I bowed and walked off the stage. All those orchestra players started crying. I've appeared with the orchestra sixteen times since.

After eight years of sun dancing, my body was light. Alcohol left my body; it took a while. I'm an elder now, but I learned so much from my elders. I was taught how the Creator created this world. He made a ball and blessed it. It was a ball of red—a ball of blood—and he made it Mother Earth. She was a spiritual world from day one of creation, but she was in orbit all by herself. It was dark in the universe. She pleaded with the Great Spirit for light. The Great Spirit put a moon out so there'd be light in the dark. Mother Earth met with the Great Spirit again and said, "Wakan Tanka, it's cold. I need warmth." So he put the sun out. Now, we have the earth, moon, and sun.

In the Lakota way, we call the earth "Unci Maka" [Grandmother Earth]. We call the moon "Hanhepi Wi." Wi means woman. The sun is "Wi," so it's female too. That's why we call the sun dance "Wiwanke Wachipi." We're talking to the sun so she's part of our life.

The sun, moon, and earth are all sacred; they talk to each other. Mother Earth said, "People are out of control. They're being disrespectful. There's pollution, drilling for oil, all kinds of abuse of the things I love."

She communicates this to the sun so the sun will throw flares toward the world.

The Creator put Native people in this world first. They know about taking care of Mother Earth, and they know all the medicines.

Amazon Indians have their own lives and don't want to be bothered by anybody, but last year, the Brazilian government set their forests on fire to wipe them out. Even though all these things are happening, we pray for our people: the Black-Red-Yellow-White Nation. We pray for the four-legged, two-legged, and two-winged creatures—the *mato* [bear] and the *tatanka* [buffalo].

We're in the fourth world today. When the world was in the third world, the Creator destroyed the world by water. Why? Number one, there were giants upon this world; archeologists know that. They found giants all over the world. Even our tribe, our own people, were giants. The Creator didn't like it. He said, "That's not what I created upon this world."

Who were those giants? They were aliens, the Anunnaki, who came to this world and had intercourse with our Native women. They took DNA and made giant animals—rabbits, deer, and buffalo. The Creator saw this and said, "No, I didn't create that either. I did it my way, but you took it the other way. I'm going to destroy the world."

He did it by a flood. I don't know about forty days and forty nights, but it rained every day. And the water started getting high. The giants saw the water coming, but they were kicking back and thought everything was cool. They got on their spaceship, took their DNA, and got the hell out of there. While the rain was flooding the world, the Hopi people cried out, "Great Spirit, if you spare our lives, we will teach the people to discipline themselves."

The Great Spirit said, "Okay, I'm going to present four ears of corn, and you're going to pick one of them."

The Hopi picked the little ear of corn, and the Great Spirit said, "You have done well. You were wise to pick the small ear of corn. Therefore, I'm going to spare your lives, and you're going to teach the world. I am going to give you a tablet with prophecies on it. And the prophecies on that tablet? Before I tell you, I'm going to communicate with the Spider Woman."

The Spider Woman told the Great Spirit, "I have two women, an older one and a younger one."

"Bring them forward."

When they came, he gave them two tablets—one for here and one to take over the waters. Those tablets had prophecies about what's going on in this world today, prophecies about trains, planes in the air, and pollution. If the tablets come back, everything is going to be good, but if not, the world is going to be destroyed. We're at end-times. I'll be praying for you, praying for all of us. We're waiting for the Great Spirit to take us home; it's time.

Jack "Crazy Flute" Holland (1972–) (Tsalagi, Lakota, and Scot)

A seven-time NAMA nominee and the recipient of the Best Instrumental Recording Award for *We Belong to the Music*, in 2019, Crazy Flute blends "world tribal rhythm and North American Native flutes."[12]

My dad and my grandfather were flute players. I wanted to play, but they wouldn't teach me. They said that if they taught me, I'd play like them. If I genuinely wanted to play the instrument, I'd find my own song; that's how they worded it to me. I was angry about it throughout my teenage years. I didn't want to have anything to do with my grandpa

or my father or any traditional ways. I got on a high horse like young people do when they don't get what they want, and I threw a fit.

After I was married, I met a friend of my wife's father. He was a flute maker. I loved the way his flutes sounded. He had me come with him to the Memorial Day Powwow in Tahlequah, Oklahoma. I was living in Fort Smith, Arkansas, about an hour and a half away. I helped him with his booth. At the end of the day, he told me that he was having a problem figuring out which flute sounded the best of the ones he had left. He played them for me and asked, "Which one do you like?"

I picked one, and he said, "Take it."

I told him I couldn't afford it, and he went, "You're not going to buy it from me. You're going to trade me. In one year, you're going to come back to this same powwow and play me a song."

That's all I owed him, but it took a while to learn to play. I got exiled to the front porch. I knew almost nothing about music other than being part of a medieval reenactment group, the Society for Creative Anachronism, that had Middle Ages–type drum circles with people playing *doumbek* and *djembe*. I had a sense of rhythm, but that was all. I sat on that porch with my flute and played and played and played, trying to figure out what to do, until it sounded right to me. I went back to the powwow the next year and played the flute maker a song. I planned to give up the flute afterward.

A few years later I was at a powwow in Oklahoma. There was a row of flute makers hawking their flutes. I was walking by the booths, talking to a friend. He was going, "These flutes are cool," but I said, "No, they're a limited instrument."

One of the flute makers [Tom Minton] heard what I said and came out from behind his booth, stopped me in my tracks, and said, "What do you mean it's limited?"

He picked up a flute and started playing. He completely blew my mind with the stuff he did. It totally invigorated me.

I would sometimes toot around on a flute, trying to look cool in front of my friends, but I had gone a couple of years without really playing. I could make a mournful sound, but Tom Minton reeducated me. I spent a lot of time around him. I'd see him at powwows selling flutes, and he would rearrange my goofy attitude. I jokingly call him my "Flute Yoda."

The more that I played flute, the more I got into drums. They go perfectly together. My flute sounds as good as it does because I have drum tracks that I record of myself or another drummer. It adds spice. I've used everything from hand pans to tongue drums. We use congas, bongos, and timbales, trying to layer the sound and make it have more of an impact.

I'm known as a speedy flute player. I've gotten comments like "the fastest fingers in the business" and "the heavy metal rocker of the Native flute," but I have my style. I like a happy vibe. It's a traditional sound, but the drums add a driving, aggressive beat.

No one in my family was musically inclined, but Mom was the classic in-the-car singer. My little brother picked up a guitar. It's funny. I play esoteric New Age music on the flute, but we're fans of roaring heavy metal.

On my mother's side, we come from Scottish and Norse roots. She was born in Shipley, Virginia. The family came there in the late 1600s and married Cherokee people. At a young age, she was taken north to Boston. My biological father is Lakota from South Dakota—the Pine Ridge, Wounded Knee, American Indian Movement people. My family is deep into that.

Mom and my biological father split up when I was five. They had gotten together while he was serving in Vietnam. They were both in the Outlaws Motorcycle Club. He was born in D'Iberville, Mississippi, and was a dyed-in-the-wool southerner who didn't like being north of the Mason-Dixon Line. My stepfather [Marvin] served in Vietnam too. After he got out, he joined a smaller motorcycle group, the King Cobras. He and my biological father got to be friends. In the midst of that, my mother decided that she liked my stepfather better. You know how those things go. She and my biological father wound up getting divorced. We headed to Mississippi, where my stepfather was from, for a while.

We went to Massachusetts next. I went to elementary school in a little town west of Boston [Chicopee]. I never felt comfortable there; Mississippi was where I was accustomed to being. I got picked on because of how I talked. I was quite different from everyone else. We moved there because Mom wanted to be closer to her family, but it wasn't long before she and my stepdad decided to move back to Mississippi. On our way, we broke down in Trenton, Georgia, where I live now. It's in the northwest corner of the state, twenty miles south of Chattanooga, Tennessee, and an hour and a half north of Atlanta. If I go to the end of my driveway, make a left, go half a mile, and make a right, I'm at the Alabama state line.

Mom and my stepdad bought a house. He worked in the oil fields for the Global Marine Drilling Company as a welder. He worked a lot overseas. He'd go to Egypt and places like that.

I experienced a lot of the traditional way growing up. I'd go to the reservation during the summer and spend time with family. I learned to speak the language. I consider myself to be following a traditional path. If you go far enough back, every race was Indigenous, living a tribal existence and believing in spirits and ceremonies.

Mom took her own life in 2004. She was eaten up by cancer and wanted to go on her terms. It was rough, but I could respect it.

Flute player and dancer Ryan Little Eagle and I went to Peru for the first time in 2013. He had won the debut artist NAMA a year before. The promoters in Peru picked him out of the blue. They wanted him to work with a project [Perusa] that mixed Peruvian, South American, and North American Indigenous music. He hadn't been out of the country before.

Ryan knew me from when I was doing security at powwows. I'm a chapter leader for the Guardian Angels. I'd volunteer our chapter to work security at powwows. Ryan's dad wanted me to go along to watch out for his son. The organizers were hesitant when they were asked if I could come. It's a lot of money to fly somebody to Peru and back home. They got in touch with me and asked, "Do you play any music?"

I sent them a couple of pieces so they could hear me play. Suddenly it was, "You're not coming as a bodyguard; you're coming to be part of the group."

We went to Peru two years in a row. The first year, we filmed music videos and did some recordings. When we went back, we did TV spots and Peruvian news programs. We played at a five-thousand-seat arena [Estadio Huancayo] in Huancayo, Peru, on top of the Andes Mountains. That put the bug in me. It was awesome to be able to share my culture and music.

I'm a martial artist, an ex-cop. I did bail enforcement and bodyguard work for three years, but I saw how badly people treated each other. I saw too much garbage on the police end with which I didn't agree. I didn't belong there and left. I taught martial arts for a while. But the insurance will kill you, and it's hard to get students and charge them enough to pay the bills.

My wife kept asking me why I wasn't doing more with flute music. I had all these reasons—I'm not good enough, I don't have the time. She said, "I love you, but you're an idiot."

She kicked me in the rear when I needed it. I started street performing with a tip bucket. I made enough the first year, along with a little help from my wife and her family, to build a home studio.

My friend Keith "Professor" Talley came over one day to check out what I was doing. We had gone to high school together. I was trying to figure out how to record drums and flute at the same time. I remember thinking aloud, "I need a drummer," when he goes, "I can play drums."

I didn't know it, but he had been in the high school band. He played trumpet, but he had a set of drums. He brought them over, and it blossomed from there. He's got a mellow attitude, while I'm more frenetic about things. I'm high-energy, just zoom, zoom, zoom all the time.

We started busking every weekend, doing whatever we could to get notoriety, and it took off from there. We've won five major music awards and had more than thirty nominations.

Neither of us can read or write music. I write it down in a way that I can understand it and remember what I'm doing. I mark down the key; the flutes are all in minor pentatonic. I describe the vibe and how I want the drum to sound. Professor will peck around for a minute and come up with exactly what I'm looking for. A lot of our improvising turns into written pieces.

Echoes from the Mountain [2016] was Crazy Flute's first album. We didn't know what we were doing. I was lost in the world of digital recording, trying to learn how to use the software. I spent a year studying recording and getting more and more electronic gear. We finished the album, but we didn't know if we were going to do anything with it. It had a traditional vibe, with drums and flute, but not much of anything else. We started adding other instruments and sounds. I have a friend, Brandon Whetbruk, who's a death metal guitarist, but he plays beautiful acoustic guitar. He played on "Summer Breeze" and alerted me to other players.

Right out of the gate, Crazy Flute was nominated for a NAMA as the Best Debut Group of 2017. That really sparked us, so we got creative on our next album, *Tribal Groove*. Rather than a repetitive drumbeat, there was more personality in the drumming, and the flute got more hyper. By then, I understood how to use recording software and was starting to understand mixing and mastering. The album came out sounding better than the first one. "Coyote Tears" won the Indian Summer Award as the year's Best Modern Contemporary Recording.

We Belong to the Music came out in 2017 and did well. "Unity" won an Indian Summer Award as Best-Spoken Word Recording, and "Wistful Soul" won as Best Modern Contemporary Recording. We added keyboards and ambient backgrounds. I added an instrument called a strum stick.

It's a three-string, banjo-like instrument that's tuned G-C-D. It has a low string, a midstring, and a high string. You strum it. It doesn't have the fretboard action of a guitar, but it's designed so that, no matter what you're doing, you're getting notes out of it. I heard it in a shop in South Pittsburg, Tennessee, and fell in love with its weird sound. I thought it would make our music stand out.

I'm not knocking other flute players, but I don't want an emotionally sad sound. When I'm playing, I want to demonstrate that the Native flute is a modern instrument. It's not just for the sad, lonely Indian on a hill or for when the Indians exit stage right on an old western show. It can be traditional and emotive of Indigenous identity and still have a modern flare to it. I try to evoke emotional content with my songs.

Now and then, I'll throw in a spoken-word piece, but I don't do a lot of singing. My wife, who's biased, will tell you that I'm a good singer, but I'm not comfortable doing it. I stick with things I'm passionate about. I want to play music that strikes a chord in me. No pun intended.

Instrumental music isn't dictated by lyrics. Twenty people can listen to a tune and come away with twenty different ideas of what it's about. They wouldn't be wrong. When I'm creating something, I have a basic idea, but it changes sometimes. I may start out wanting a plaintive feel, a tense vibe, but it'll come out being a song about journeying. I have one called "The Road Ahead." It's a chanting song. The vibe I started going for was this warrior who's on a mission. It's paramount that he gets to where he's going. As I put it together, it became more about this guy who's not going anywhere. He's already got everything done.

Star Brite is Crazy Flute's latest CD. We released it in December 2019. The title was inspired by my cat. I had her for ten years. She was an outside cat. She got hit by a car in front of my house and passed away. I played a happy tune on the flute, because whenever we'd pull up to the house, my cat would trot up the roadway to meet the car. She was a Maine coon cat, a big cat. Her fur had a bounce to it, and she had a little sway to her backside when she ran. That was the whole point to the song.

The album had a lot more guitar. We tried to knuckle down and focus more on the technique of what we were doing musically. We're constantly trying to improve, thinking of how we could make an album that's not like the last one.

I've got fifty flutes or so. My wife jokes that whenever I go to a show, I buy another flute. There are always flute makers at powwows. Sometimes they give me flutes and want me to promote them; I do a lot of shout-outs.

Steven Rushingwind-Ruiz (1960–) (Cahuilla and Opata)

Steve Wildsmith wrote of Steven Rushingwind, in the *Blount County Daily Times*, "No doubt it's the Native American blood that runs in his veins that sees and hears the call of wild places that were once sacred to his fellow natives."[13]

People go through anguish, anxiety, and fear of the unknown. That's why music's so important. Keeping to a theme of healing helps people know they're not alone. I purposely don't play a concert every week. It could become redundant if you do it too much. You can't force healing on anyone. You've got to let it naturally occur. By spreading it out, it gives people a chance to feel good. Then they can listen again.

When I was a kid, we were told not to tell anyone we were Native or Mexican. We had to assimilate into the white world, but, in 1970 or '71 my dad went full turn and said, "Be proud of who you are."

We got more and more into the Native world. My dad was very dark-skinned. He was tired of trying to assimilate. By that time, my older brothers and sister had moved out. I was the one who took to heart what my dad was saying. I stood up for what we were.

My father was born in 1915, a year after Arizona became a state. My grandfather, great-grandfather, and great-great-grandfather were born in Phoenix. They were Opata. The tribe wasn't recognized on the

U.S. side of the border, but we go back hundreds of years. Suddenly, a line was draw: "You're Mexican, and you're Native American."

I've been working on a blues album with guitarist Tom Matranga. It's dedicated to my mother. She was from Mexico, of Spanish descent. She looked whiter than white and spoke Spanish. As I got older, I embraced my Spanish heritage.

My grandmother was born in 1880 in San Diego. She moved to Phoenix when she was ten. She was Cahuilla, so she was considered Native American. She and my grandfather moved to East LA in 1920 and bought a house. They were there for decades. I spent my summers there.

I have a slight case of bipolar disorder. I'm not a crazy person who throws things around, but I've suffered from depression since I was a kid. I keep myself uplifted. It's important to let people know they're not the only ones fighting depression. It takes its toll, at times, but you wake up the next day, put your best foot forward, and keep going.

My eleven-year-older brother, Gilbert, was like a second dad to me. We called him Berto. He played bass in the sixties, but he didn't continue. He drove a truck for forty years and loved his Harley Davidson motorcycle. He drove all over the United States. He was a great guy, and he loved life. It was tough to lose him to esophageal cancer in 2017. He was sixty-eight when he passed, much too young.

When I was sixteen, my bipolar disorder got bad. A lot of it had to do with the food I was eating; we had no money. My brother made sure I went to a nutritionist. He had a job and paid for everything. He was always there when something was going on in my life. Before he died, the entire family went to Park City, Utah, and had a party. He came in a wheelchair. I got to perform for him for a half hour. I have the setlist pinned up in my studio. Afterward, we did a living eulogy. We all went home, and he died two days later. Before he passed, my wife snuck into his room and took a video of him telling me that everything was going to be okay.

When I went to grade school, I wanted to play trumpet, but we had six kids in my family. We didn't have the money to rent a trumpet. I had to start with a recorder, because it was free. That went on until my junior high school years. When I hit thirteen and fourteen, it wasn't cool to play the recorder, so I picked up a guitar. It was cooler with the girls.

After playing guitar for a few years, I was watching a movie and heard a Native flute. I was intrigued. A week or two later, I was at a festival in Monterey. Odell Borg was selling High Spirits Flutes. I walked up to him and said, "I want to buy one."

I wanted a bass flute, but he told me, "No, I don't want you to buy that one. Buy this one first. Learn it, come back next year when you're ready, and I'll sell you the bass flute."

I bought the flute he suggested, took it home, and played it for a year. I went to the next festival, and Odell Borg was there again. I walked up to him and said, "I'm ready to buy the bass flute." He handed it to me. I played it, and he said, "You're ready." I still have that flute twenty years later.

A Native flute isn't a clarinet. There's no reed, but two chambers. The first one, you blow into, and then the air goes out and back into the flute. It's like picking up a blade of grass, putting it between your thumb and finger, and blowing into it. It makes a whistle.

There are two types of Native flutes. One has a wooden block on top. You can move it. It's called a fetish [an inanimate object worshipped for its magical power]. It lets you change the brightness of the sound. If you want a windy, raspy sound, you move the block away from the square hole. The farther it goes back, the raspier it gets. If you take the block off, nothing comes out. It's just air, no sound. When the block is on the square hole, you get a brighter sound. The other type of flute doesn't have a fetish, or block. You blow directly into it.

Some people are true traditionalists. I applaud them, but being an artist, I like modern life and looking to the future. I was in high school when Redbone came out. Their music was rocking, and I was drawn to it. I liked the way they portrayed themselves. They had a top-five dance hit ["Come and Get Your Love"], but they embraced their heritage. They were proud of who they were, but they didn't fall into any cliché.

I've been painting for twenty years or so. I paint with oil. It's not only therapeutic, but it's in my blood, like music. In my twenties, I was in a band that covered top-forty hits. I got so tired of the arguments, by my midthirties, that I decided to paint instead. I did a lot of art exhibitions, but I kept playing music.

I recorded *Cloud Runner* in 2009. My wife and I live in Joshua Tree, California, two hours east of Los Angeles. We had a neighbor who was a record producer. He heard me play and said, "You should do an album."

I didn't want to get back into the music business. But he encouraged me, and I agreed. I played all the instruments myself. It was more synthesizers and guitars than solo flute.

My neighbor recommended fingerstyle guitarist Michael Mucklow, a third cousin of Roy Acuff, to me. When we got together, it evolved into more structured music, not as free-flowing. Our albums had themes. Our fourth album, *Strong Horse* [2013], was rocking. We played one of the songs at the NAMAs. We won the Best New Age Recording NAMA in 2013 and 2014, but Michael wanted to stop. I formed my band, Native Groove.

We toured Japan in 2015 and performed in Takasaki. It's a spiritual city. My oldest brother had passed away a couple of weeks before. A woman walked up to me and started talking fast in Japanese. I had no idea what she was talking about. My translator told me what she was saying. She had "seen" my father, who died in 1998, and he told her to tell me to break my music into pieces and take it further. I still don't know what she meant, but then she said, "Your brother was there too. He had nothing to say, but he was very emotional. He wanted you to know he's okay."

I was taken aback. How did she know? It wasn't the first time that's happened to me. A couple of days after I did a show in Ohio, someone called and told me, "I saw something when you were performing—your ancestors. They were moving around you really fast, but they were focusing on your chest area. Do you have any problem with your lungs?"

I said, "No," and the conversation ended. A week later I was in the hospital with chronic asthma. I've been on medicine for the past seven or eight years.

When I played in Ohio again, the same guy was there. He came up to me after the show and said, "I saw your ancestors again. You're fine, but I saw a woman walk up to you. She had a big smile on her round, moon face, but she had her hands on her back like she had something wrong with her kidneys."

My hair stood up, because my dad used to call my mother "Moon Face" and she had kidney problems. She always had her hands on her back. How do you explain that?

We live in Paloma, twenty-two miles east of Los Angeles. It's died and come back many times. I was born and mostly raised here. It's a large city, but there's not a whole lot happening. I go to LA quite often, but I spend

95 percent of the rest of my time in Montclair, ten minutes away. I lived there for a while and had a business, but Paloma has always been my home.

I can do anything with a flute. I collaborated with Norwegian song-writer, multi-instrumentalist, and producer Åge Reite on *Nordic Passage* [2016]. It brought out the flavor of everybody's music.

My percussionist, Nelson Rios, played with Gloria Estefan and the Miami Sound Machine for twenty years. He's Puerto Rican and lives in Philadelphia. I went there, and we sequestered for a week, writing songs. Then we flew to San Francisco and recorded *Fuego* [2017]. It had a Latin feel to it.

Rushingwind: Keeper of Secrets: Native Flute [2018] received a Best Instrumental Recording NAMA. Two of my songs were used in Larry Hott's PBS documentary *Warrior Tradition*, highlighting Native Americans in the U.S. military. One was "Wind Traveler," and the other was "Call of the Crow." I was impressed with how they incorporated them into the show; they fit. I got to perform at the world premiere in Washington DC.

I came close to not recording again. When I hit sixty, in 2020, I told my wife, "I'm done. I just want to paint." But my publicist kicked my butt and said, "Sixty doesn't mean you're old. You're not done yet."

"Okay ... I'll give it five or six more years."

Retirement isn't in my vocabulary. I'm going to be kicking off a new album with Nelson Rios. We're going for a more mainstream sound.

Vince Redhouse (1955–) (Diné and Filipino)

Prefacing her Voice of America interview with Vince Redhouse, Kimberly Haas pointed out that "some of the licks he does on the Native American flute are influenced by the saxophone."[14]

Smooth jazz stations play my CD *A Long Way Home* [2013], and it fits right in. That's what my brothers [Tony, Lenny, and Larry], sisters [Mary and Charlotte], and I heard when we were growing up. We formed the Redhouse Family in 1969, when I was fourteen. Mary was seventeen. Charlotte was sixteen. Tony's a year older than me. Lenny's two years younger than me, and Larry, the youngest, is three years younger than me. We were all close. We were a musical family like the Osmonds, Jacksons, and

Nevilles, but we didn't get as much recognition because of demographics. There aren't many Indians, and they mostly listen to country and western, not jazz.

The Redhouse Family Singers played Super Bowl XLI, in Miami Gardens, Florida, in 2007. The Indianapolis Colts beat the Chicago Bears, 29–17. Prince played the televised halftime, but we played at a party for commissioner Roger Goodell and the NFL team owners. It was incredible. We played jazz from our album [*Urban Indian*], but we mixed in traditional stuff. The commissioner and the owners were floored.

My siblings did traditional dances while we played. They've done that most of their lives. It was an amazing show about the Southwest and how Native Americans have a gift and the potential to do something special.

9. Vince Redhouse

We were raised in Seaside, California, fifteen minutes from Monterey, home of the longest-running jazz festival in the world. We heard jazz all the time. I remember hearing Miles Davis's *Bitches Brew* when I was thirteen. We listened to Weather Report, Return to Forever, and the Mahavishnu Orchestra—progressive things.

Each of us chose an instrument so we could have a complete band. Everybody practiced in a different room; it could drive you nuts. Tony memorized drum solos by David Garibaldi [Tower of Power] and Steve Gadd. He had them down. Mary has a five-octave voice. I'd listen and go, "Uh-oh, better up my game."

Some of us went to music school, where German professors taught us to play classical music on the piano. They trained us well. We did ear training for hours, transcribing what we heard. That's where we excelled. We could learn solos and play them, even as kids. Our ears were sharp and tuned in. When we play together, even now, we're on the same page. It set us up for musical careers. Mary played with R. Carlos Nakai's Quartet for ten years. She and I went to the music school after the rest of the family moved to Arizona.

When I was eighteen, the whole family went into a studio to record Donny Hathaway's "Valdez in the Country." We learned it from Cold Blood's version. It was our first time in a studio, and we didn't do as well as I thought we could. There were no retakes, just BOOM ... record. That was difficult. We got better at it; a few of us still record. We're familiar with recording now.

I did studio work playing tenor sax. At twenty-one I was a soloist for the U.S. Air Force Band in Central California, which was unheard of.

For Native people, there are lots of people who tell us, "You can't do this. You can't do that." But you're the only person who can stop you from living your dream.

Dad was a Diné healer. He met my mom [Maria Icasiano] in Manila, during World War II, as a U.S. Army quartermaster. Her grandmother ran a honky-tonk piano bar, the Three Sisters, for the GIs. They married after he got back from the Philippine Islands.

Mom was born in 1925. When she needed a break, she'd put us down for a nap and play piano. When we got up, we'd come to the piano. She taught us four-part Christmas carols. She was amazed that none of us were distracted by the other harmonies. That told her something was happening here. She got the six of us to perform in churches for different functions. At Christmas we still sing. We'll be at a restaurant, Mom will call out a song, and off we go.

I was born off the rez, but it was tough. I couldn't figure out why, but I was different. There weren't many Natives in the San Francisco Bay Area, but there was a lot of prejudice. At school, when they called my name, the whole class would start laughing and do the Indian whoop. I felt like I wasn't good enough.

When I talk about prejudice, young people on reservations don't know what that is. They haven't gone to a city where they're the minority. They have strength in numbers. I tell them, "You may wonder why someone's looking at you like they're mad, but what you're looking at is prejudice. Don't return that spirit—allow the circle to change."

Seaside has the largest population of Black people between Los Angeles and Oakland. Most of my friends, growing up, were Black. I felt like I was going through what they were going through.

Native Americans took over Alcatraz Island on November 20, 1969, and occupied it until June 11, 1971, nineteen months later. We lived so close that my dad said, "Let's go."

I had never even been to Oakland on the other side of the bay. We got in the car and headed out. When we got near the shore, my dad talked to a few people. We waited in the station wagon. The next thing we knew, we were on a ferry going to Alcatraz. It was the day after it had been taken over. It was intense. I had never been around a large group of Native people before. Helicopters were flying all over the place. It was a disorganized scene. There wasn't enough food.

I felt like an outsider looking in. That's the identity issue we have as Native Americans. We're called "the Invisible People" and not seen as significant. I was ashamed of being Native American for a long, long time. I had gone the corporate route, working for a Fortune 200 company, but I couldn't rise to the upper levels. I was thinking of changing my last name, but when I was forty, I looked in the mirror and said, "God, you didn't make a mistake. I'm Navajo. I'm going to accept who I am and be proud of it."

In that moment, everything changed. Shortly afterward, the Native flute came to me. I had never even held one before. I saw one at someone's house and asked if I could play it. The person who owned it gave it to me. Things happen for a reason.

Native flutes have been around a long time; they weren't something that came over in the boats. The first time I picked one up, I wanted to play it like I played saxophone, where I could play everything on the same instrument. People told me I was crazy. That made me want to do it more, so I spent twenty years creating a technique that allows for a chromatic, three-octave range on the flute.

Native Americans talk about walking in two worlds, respecting tradition while paying attention to what's going on in the world. Lenny Pickett played saxophone for Tower of Power. He had complete control, even in the upper register. I spent years doing that and used the technique to develop fingerings for the Native flute.

I wanted to break the stereotypical image of Native Americans playing music and make people think, "I wonder what he's going to play—classical, jazz, or whatever," rather than knowing beforehand. Lately, I've been playing Willie Nelson's "Always on My Mind." I'm going to record it and see what people think about the Native flute then.

Even if it's an instrumental, a song can remind someone of an experience. When people hear it, it brings them back to that moment. I write a song and see how it makes me feel before I give it a name, rather than feeling something and having to write a song about it.

Hozhooji: The Beauty and Blessing within Us [2011] was about the link running through each person, animal, plant, tree, and everything else around us. We're connected to all of it. That's what we believe in our hearts. We may be better at believing it than doing it, but it's what we strive for.

My mom has lived in the Tucson area since the army transferred my dad there in 1973. I lived there for fifteen years. I met my wife, Diane, there in 2009 and fell in love. She's a professional photographer. She's done all my album covers. Her parents live in Washington; there are twenty-nine federally recognized tribes in the state. Diane started bringing me to visit her parents. She'd cry on the way home. She missed the beauty of the area.

I wasn't a fan of the California heat, but I don't have to worry about that in Washington. The air is cleaner; the green is more conducive to creativity. It rains, but it's like having a sprinkler. It's why everything's so green. Cedar trees are all over this place. I'm more connected to the earth than when I was living in the city. We see hawks and eagles all the time. We live by the water; I play for harbor seals. They poke their heads out of the water and listen. There were songs on *A Long Way Home*, "Kokopelli's Day" and "The Wind Song," and a song on *Songs for the Earth* [2016], "Dance of the Tide," about being connected to nature.

NARAS allowed *Appear to Be* [2014] to compete in the Grammy's jazz category, even though the flute was the primary instrument. It was the first time that's happened, but I was playing the flute like I would saxophone.

Sounds of the Earth: Meditations of Love and Nature [2016] was more soothing and not as structured. I held notes longer. I like that kind of playing, where I'm expressing something of myself.

I've taught over a thousand young people on reservations to play the Native flute. I like teaching in high schools, but I've worked with kids as young as third grade. They get flutes at no cost. I teach lessons online and go once a month to encourage the kids to play their songs from their hearts. There's a lot that they can't talk about but can share through music. Reading music disciplines their thinking and helps them in all their classes. One student is becoming a neural surgeon; and another, a cardiac surgeon. Last year, one of my students went to the Utah State music finals. Other competitors were playing violin or metal flute. He played an entire classical piece on the Native flute and got the highest score he could get from the judges. He floored them. The first time he went to the finals, four years earlier, they looked at his instrument and said, "That's impossible."

My next album is going to be *Songs of the Wind*. People could do other things while listening to it. I also want to do soundtracks to my wife's stories. I want to keep teaching too. That's my gift; it was given to me for a reason.

Ancestral Voices

Many of today's Indigenous artists meld centuries-old traditions and modern sensibilities. Scholars Dana Lepofsky, Álvaro Fernández-Llamazares, and Oqwilowgwa Kim Recalma-Clutesi describe this dynamic, saying, "Music carries the word of the ancestors across time, transmitting key knowledge from deep in our sacred memory."[1]

Roman Orona (1975–) (Apache, Pueblo, and Yaqui)

Roman Orona's website describes how he uses music "to teach balance in all aspects of life: world peace, equality of men and women, environmental and cultural preservation, racial equality, and the abandonment of all forms of prejudice."[2]

> Music is an ancestral link. If we forget that link, we change our future. My ancestors sacrificed for me to be where I am. That wouldn't have been the case if they hadn't fought or if they had sold off the minerals from the land. They were thinking of future generations. Now, here we are, living representatives of that ancestral voice.
>
> I sing traditional Apache songs. I use them as prayers for grounding myself. I create music that blends that ancestral link with present-day thoughts. *Circling Spirits: Contemporary Apache Songs* [2016] was about combining the music of the powwow with contemporary singing.
>
> R. Carlos Nakai played flute on "Dancing Spirits" [the CD also includes a Dashmesh Khalsa remix]. It started as a very repetitive song in the powwow style. I didn't know if I wanted to keep it like that or let the music breathe. RC was in the studio at the same time. We sat and talked. I asked

10. Roman Orona

if he'd play, and he agreed. The engineer put the drum beat together. The recording came about organically and transformed into something nice. It's one of my favorite tracks.

"Sacred Cave Song" featured the recorded voice of the late Philip Cassadore, son of Chief Broken Arrow. He was Chiricahua from the San Carlos Apache Reservation, in Arizona, like me, and broke a lot of barriers. He sang with his sister [Patsy] and his wife as the Singing Cassadores. Their first album, *Singing Apache Songs*, was released in 1968. Their second, *A Voice Singing Apache Songs*, came out in 1975. Apache women didn't sing at that time, but they broke the mold. That's who I am—breaking molds and creating for future generations.

I formed Medicine Arrow with R. Carlos Nakai's longtime percussionist, Will Clipman, and Aaron White [Diné and Ute] in 2017. Aaron's an amazing flutist, guitarist, and singer. We're comfortable playing in a groove. Music and spirit come through us at different times. If someone feels something, they go for it. We follow.

Medicine is deep, whether it's ingested, applied, or experienced through meditation. An arrow pierces everything. Medicine Arrow is about piercing the negative in our lives. As it's piercing, it's healing.

For me, there's always been music, whether it was jazz, African, Cuban, Mexican, rock and roll, or Apache music. If we were sad, we played sad music. If we were happy, we played happy music. Sometimes, when we were really sad, we played happy music to get us out of our funk.

My dad was a drummer. Drums and singing were who we were. I played drums in a high school rock and roll band. It helped me adapt from living in a small New Mexico town to my mom's home in Yaqui Village, Tucson, and then to Chicago.

My name, Ish Hish Itsaatu, translates as "One Who Dances with Eagles." Whenever I heard music as a child, I'd start dancing, whether it was traditional Apache dancing or break dancing. I learned the country two-step. I was a powwow fancy dancer when I was young and agile. As I got older, I became a grass dancer, which I absolutely loved. As one continues to age and put on weight, they become a traditional dancer. They say once you slow down, you become a singer. Then you go into emceeing before retiring.

Dancing is a way of prayer, a way of teaching the next generation. Hoop dancers teach about our interconnectedness when they display an eagle, a horse, or the sun.

I make my own regalia. I put what I'm feeling spiritually into it. It might be that the four directions have been on my mind, so I'll put four colors into my regalia. I might put the nine-pointed star of Baha'i into it. It's my way of representing who I am.

I developed a curriculum, *Music, Movement, Magination*, for early elementary classes. Education was important to my family. It wasn't that we necessarily had to go to college, but we had to be educated in whatever we were doing. My paternal grandfather had a fifth-grade education, but he did mining and agriculture. He owned his own business with my grandmother. On my mother's side, it was the same thing. They were hardworking, but they had to go out into the world to create their lives.

I had to be proper so people wouldn't buy into stereotypes about Native Americans. I didn't want to be a starving artist, so I went to the University of Hawai'i and got a bachelor of science degree in biology. Then I went to the University of New Mexico and studied civil engineering. I've done what I needed to do. I helped raise my family while my wife went for her medical degree. I work for the tribe doing environmental engineering.

The Baha'i faith enables me to look at everyone as my siblings or aunt and uncle, depending on their age. It allows me to be a better Native, a better Indigenous person, and a better Indian, not materialistically, but spiritually.

I'm going to be releasing a digital album that blends Apache instruments [the water drum, bells], the way I sing, and Baha'i prayers. My sixteen-year-old son, Cahj, and twenty-one-year-old daughter, Kaya, sing with me.

My hour-long show, *Indigenous Café*, airs on KURE-FM in Ames, Indiana, every Monday. I play Indigenous music from around the world and provide an avenue for listeners to get a deeper appreciation.

Spirit Wing
Barry Lee (1950–) (Munsee)

According to the Philadelphia Folksong Society, Barry Lee and Barbara Andrews-Christy's Spirit Wing plays "strong folk/acoustic music . . . with traditional Native songs that date back hundreds of years."[3]

To the untrained ear, Eastern Woodland songs sound no different than powwow songs. But it's like any music. If you're a blues fan, you could tell the difference between Texas blues and Chicago blues.

We play a water drum; it has a ringing sound. The songs we sing aren't longhouse ceremonial songs. People train for a long time to sing those. A lot of the time, we sing vocables in place of words. Each vocable goes with a particular song.

I was born in Quakertown, Pennsylvania, and adopted by a Munsee family. I have no illusions; I don't deserve an enrollment card. But when I'm with Munsee people, I feel a belonging.

The Munsee are a band of the Lenape [Delaware] people; but before the 1700s, they were their own entity. Their territory stretched from the Lehigh Mountains and the Susquehanna River to the Atlantic Ocean, including what is now Manhattan. The Mohegan and Wappinger bordered

11. Spirit Wing

them in the north and east; the Lenape, in the south and southeast.

During the Seven Years' War [French and Indian War], the Munsee sided with the Huron and the French. And then, during the American Revolution, they sided with the English, except for the Stockbridge Munsee, who fought with the colonists. Horrible conflicts separated families. Christian Munsee went north to the lower Ontario Province in Canada. Others incorporated into the Lenape Nation near the Ohio River [approximately sixty-five thousand Haudenosaunee (Iroquois) live in Wisconsin, Ontario, Quebec, and the Onondaga Nation Reservation in northern New York].

My adopted family is all gone now. They were as traditional as you could be in the modern world. Like most Lenape people, they went to sweat lodges but absorbed Western culture. Our ceremonies were lost forever. We know some of the stories but not all of them. I had to follow Eastern Woodland spirituality, so I embraced what the Onkwehonwe [First People] or Haudenosaunee ["the People of the Longhouse"] had.

Some friends built a longhouse in New Jersey. I've been invited twice. The first time, I gave a talk about the wampum belt. I explained how, in Pennsylvania—where my wife and musical partner, Barbara, and I live—there were treaties between the Lenape and Governor William Penn. The 1683 agreement was made of wampum beads and showed two people holding hands. In my mind, that belt still exists; the idea that people could live side by side in peace.

Our ceremonies go on for days and trace the great Peacemaker's journey. We never say his name out of respect. As the stories go, he was born of a Huron [or Onondaga] woman. I don't know if it was influenced by Christian philosophy, but his mother was a virgin. For some reason, his grandmother tried killing him three times before realizing that he was someone special. When he grew old enough, he got a revelation from the Creator about a great peace. At the time, there was horrible fighting going on in what is now New York and New Brunswick, Canada, especially among the people who are now the Haudenosaunee. There was fighting in every village. The Lenape weren't a group yet. They came across the lake in a stone canoe made of white quartz. It shot across the lake like an arrow.

Peacemaker sought a way to bring the nations together. In what is now New York, he ran into the Good Mind, who told him that he should talk out his differences. He also met a woman [Jigonsaseh] who was providing housing and food to warriors. But he got to her, and she became the mother of our nation.

Peacemaker went from nation to nation—the Cayuga, Onondaga, Mohawk, Oneida, and Seneca—to persuade them to accept the peace. In Kahon:ios [Cohoes Falls, New York], he proved to the Mohawk community that the Good Mind was special. He climbed a tree above the falls and cut it down. He fell into the water and didn't come back up. The people went home. The next morning, they smelled smoke coming from near the falls. When they got there, they found him cooking a deer.

People wanted Onondaga leader Hiawatha [Ayenwahtha or Aiionwatha] to learn from the Good Mind [kanikonhri: yo], but Hiawatha had a wife [Minnehaha] and seven daughters and didn't want to leave them. The chiefs summoned Tadodaho [Tha-do-day-ho], a murderous scoundrel whose arms were bent from punching people, a truly ugly, ugly person with snakes in his hair.

Tadodaho decided that the only way to get Hiawatha to leave was to get rid of his family, so he killed his wife and daughters one by one. Hiawatha cried until he had no more tears, but he continued walking until he came to a lake. Across the water, he saw Peacemaker. Hiawatha thought he could get comfort from him, but there was a lake between them. Just then, a flock of geese flew off and took the water with them. Someone once told me, "Most likely the beaver dam broke."

As Hiawatha walked across this now-dry waterway, he used wampum shells to wipe the pain from his throat and scrape the tears from his eyes, the way only spiritual people can. If you tried it, you'd be scarred for life.

Hiawatha and Peacemaker held their first ceremony. The story ends with them going to this vicious criminal, Tadodaho, and forgiving him. Chiefs from the five nations were there [the Tuscarora wouldn't join the Iroquois Confederacy until 1722]. One by one, they took Tadodaho as a brother. It's said that when the evil left him, Tadodaho screamed in pain.

At the beginning of the Iroquois Confederacy, the chiefs needed somebody who was beyond reproach, somebody who wouldn't be bothered by politics but always follow the Good Mind. They decided that their fire keeper, or spiritual leader, should be Tadodaho.

There have been many peacemakers—Buddha, Muhammed, Jesus, and thousands of others. Dr. Martin Luther King Jr. was a peacemaker; Gandhi, too. They never condoned a violent revolution.

I met Barbara in 1998, a year after my first wife left me. We've been together since. She was getting a divorce from her husband. Her birth name was Andrews; ask the Cherokee about that.

When we met, I was playing bluegrass guitar. Barbara was in a new age band. Soon after we got together, we went to a powwow. The woman running it told us that she'd written a song about Indian boarding schools. I put it to music, and Barbara and I performed it as "The Children." We put it on Sprit Wing's first CD, *Ancient Spirit Voices*, in 2002. We also sang a Marty Robbins tune and a couple of environmental songs. We thought we might have something, but we put it aside and didn't talk about it.

Two weeks later we were at a bluegrass festival. Barbara was reading about the Cheyenne trying to get back from Oklahoma during what we call the Cheyenne Trail of Tears. I was reading about the Indian Removal Act and Andrew Jackson. We were sitting by a fire, talking about the similarities between the two books, when I started seeing images in the fire ... or in my head. That's where "Trail of Tears" came from. We sang it, and people started crying. We went back to our campsite and said, "We've got something we have to develop."

A year later we were ready to perform at powwows. Our regalia is different from what you usually see. War bonnets are western—I don't wear one. Instead, I wear a small cap. Barbara beaded it. It has an eagle feather that I got for my service in Vietnam.

We were nominated for a NAMA for "When the Buffalo Comes Back" from *To Future from Past* [2006]. Dave Crossland wrote it. We played at the Susquehanna Folk Festival with him one year and performed his song. When we came off the stage, he told us, "You've got to add energy to it."

He was kidding. When we play, I dance all over the stage and get my frustrations out.

Barbara and I wanted *Flutes, Drums, and Guitars* [2006] to be all-instrumental. It got us our second NAMA nomination. Two submissions, two nominations. Winning is being in the top five.

We haven't done a CD since *Red Kroz Blues Band* [2014]. Barbara's gotten involved with the Carlisle Indian School Project. They're trying to open a museum at the former boarding school, and I've started emceeing at powwows. But we still do a handful of performances together. Last year we spent a week in Indiana teaching Eastern Woodland social dances. They're counterclockwise stomp dances. Someone asked why we were teaching Iroquois dances in Indiana. I told him, "There's a Muncie for a reason."

Stevie Ray Vavages (1983–) (Tohono O'odham)

"When Spaniards came to America in the sixteenth and seventeenth centuries," bajo sexto player Stevie Ray Vavages told me, "they not only converted Natives to Christianity but also taught them music for the church. Within time, Germans came to build the railroads and brought accordions and polkas. Natives began playing them at their own dances, calling their music *waila* [way-la], based on the Spanish word *bailar* [to dance]. The music was also called 'chicken scratch.' Anglos watched as Natives danced and said, 'They look like chickens scratching their feet.'"

My dad had a waila band, Papago Express, with my uncles in the 1980s. Around that time, our tribe did away with the name Papago. It translated as "Bean Eaters." We changed it to Tohono O'odham, which means "Desert People."

Bands had been calling themselves things like the Papago Raiders, the Papago Sunlighters, and Papago Express. When the tribe changed its name, they changed their names too. My dad came up with Thee Express.

Waila songs are mostly instrumental. There are some songs in Spanish, but we don't speak the language. A few bands have started singing, but there are a lot of shy Natives on the reservation. They rarely speak into a

12. Stevie Ray Vavages

mic. It took me a long time to even talk to people without being nervous.

We accompany our traditional music with gourd rattles. The drum skin is either cow or deer hide. We have songs for rain, crops, our health, and strength. There are songs for landmarks on the reservation.

My sister played reggae records when I was a kid. As a musician, when you hear a rhythm, you picture where your instrument would go. When I hear a reggae song, I think that it'd be cool to turn it into a cumbia. A reggae tune might have a schottische feel.

When I was thirteen, my dad's older brother, my uncle, took me aside and gave me a guitar. He changed its strings, tuned it, and said, "Play this."

I thought it was cool, something fun. We sat there for five hours, and he showed me scales. A month later, he said, "We've got a gig."

"Cool, I'll come and hear you play."

"No, you're going to play with us."

That was my first gig. We played at a small bar, the Coyote Club. My dad and mom had split, so I rarely got to see my uncles or my cousins. Being in the band, I got to hang out with my uncle. It was exciting. I sat on a barstool when I played. My leg was shaking, but with the help of my uncle and our bass player, I made it through the night. I kept improving after that.

I got the hang of it by the time I was fourteen or fifteen. By that point, I had become a big fan of regional Texan and Mexican music: Tejano and conjunto. I got into Michael Salgado and Roberto Ayala and practiced their music. Then I got into Albert Zamora and Jamie y Los Charmacos. They had flare. They were doing riffs and hip progressions, adding rock influences.

I got hooked by conjunto music, the more traditional side of Tejano, but Tejano has more progressive changes and chordal structures. It sounds smoother. It's more Americanized, as far as instrumentation [keyboards, horn sections], and a higher level of musicianship. It's a jazzier kind of feel.

The difference between waila and conjunto music is like people speaking with different accents. We play the same rhythms, but there's not a whole lot to waila. We know the basics, but there's no true foundation. It is what it is. Its tempo can be all over the place. It's not always in synch, but it works.

My uncle taught me bajo sexto [a twelve-string plucked instrument that originated in northern Mexico] on an acoustic six-string guitar, but I used electric guitar for gigs. I'd take the first string off and tune the second string to the third, so they sounded double. My mother bought me a Fender twelve-string, and I turned that into a bajo sexto. I didn't know what I was doing, but I used the third string for my first and second strings and the fourth string for my third. For the fourth, I used another fourth string, and so on. I experimented with it for a long time until I got it right. When I was fifteen, my dad bought me an Ovation Applause twelve-string. This time, I used bajo sexto strings. That's how I got my start. I saved money and bought my first bajo sexto for $135.

I've known Max Baca, bajo sexto virtuoso, leader of the Grammy-winning Los Texmaniacs, and longtime Flaco Jiménz accompanist for at least ten years. I was playing with a Tejano band out of Tucson, Pasión [Passion], when we met. They were from the Yaqui tribe. Yaquis are known for speaking Spanish. We played a lot at Casino Del Sol in Tucson. They gave us tribal preference for gigs. We loved playing there. We opened for big shows and the annual Tejano Shootout.

I wasn't playing the night I met Max. The tribal chairperson saw me in the crowd, called me over, and brought me backstage. Max was about to go on. I introduced myself. He went onstage and did his thing. Afterward, we talked. I asked if he'd mind if I held his bajo sexto. It was a white Macias bajo sexto. I was in awe. I told him I had studied bajo sexto players, including him. He said, "Let's get out of here," and I followed him to the dressing room. There was Flaco Jimenéz , Oscar Garcia, and Joe Farias. I was like a kid in a candy store with all these musicians I looked up to. Max gave me his number and said, "Keep in touch."

I was on cloud nine. About a year or two later Max called and said, "We're going to be in Tucson. Bring your bajo sexto; we'll jam."

I was supposed to be playing with my dad's band that night, but I ditched that gig to play at the casino. I called another bajo sexto player to replace me.

By then, I had become friends with a lot of casino employees who worked at the amphitheater. I walked in with my bajo sexto, and they said, "Are you jamming?"

I told them, "Yeah," but I didn't know if I was going to be playing or not. I did get to go backstage and hang out. When it came time for the grand finale, Max brought me onstage. A lot of musicians were playing. They gave me a solo, which was very cool.

I was working full-time and gigging on the weekends, but I had to get out of Arizona. With its conjunto and Tejano scene, San Antonio had always been my dream. I told Max that I'd be heading his way but had no plans. He said, "You have a place with me."

Lo and behold, we wound up living together.

Before I even moved, I had my first gig with the well-known Tejano musician Bobby Pulido, son of the great Roberto Pulido. It was big-time, beyond anything on my bucket list. I've been with him since. He has one group in Mexico and another in the United States. He debuted at the right time, in the mid-1990s, when Tejano was at its peak. He was young and good-looking. The songs he sang became number one hits. When we play, you see a very wide age range in the audience, but it's mostly women. They're into Bobby and his music, and they sing loud on every song.

There are so many musicians I look up to; I mix them all into an Indian taco. I don't copy anyone, but they're in my blood, my memory, and my heart.

9

Sing It Loud

"Among the Indians, music envelopes like an atmosphere every religious, tribal and social ceremony as well as every personal experience," wrote Alice C. Fletcher, in *A Study of Omaha Indian Music*, in 1893. Fletcher continued,

> There is not a phase of life that does not find expression in song. Religious rituals are embedded in it, the reverent recognition of the creation of the corn, of the food-giving animals, of the powers of the air, of the fructifying sun, is passed from one generation to another in melodious measures; song nerves the warrior to deeds of heroism and robs death of its terrors; it speeds the spirit to the land of the hereafter and solaces those who live to mourn; children compose ditties for their games, and young men by music give zest to their sports; the lover sings his way to the maiden's heart, and the old man tunefully evokes those agencies which can avert death. Music is also the medium through which man holds communion with his soul, and with the unseen powers which control his destiny.[1]

"There are songs for the making of rain," added Willard W. Beatty, BIA director of Indian Education from 1937 to 1951, "Guardian Spirit songs for success in hunting, fishing, and gambling, songs for the protection of the home, the curing of the sick, lullabies, love songs, corn-grinding songs, social dance songs, and songs connected with legends."[2]

Country music provides much of the soundscape of today's reservations. Radio stations keep things hopping with steel guitars, fiddles, and truck driver songs. "What people will actually hear from most top Native American country singers," said Manitoba-based vocalist Tracy Bones

(Keeseekoowenin Ojibway), "are stories highlighting struggle, honesty and integrity—the values traditional country music was founded on and ones that it too often lacks today."[3]

"Generally speaking, the genre draws from a canon by country legends including Merle Haggard and Buck Owens," said the *New York Times*, "more tilted, perhaps, to the Southwest than Nashville—sometimes blending Diné phrases into the songs."[4]

"It's easy to see why country music resonates with Diné people," explained the anthropology magazine *Sapiens*. "Navajo communities were ranching in the U.S. Southwest long before Anglo cowboys came onto the scene. . . . Country music is about love, loss, nostalgia . . . and connections to land, family, and rural places. These themes are central to what it means to be Diné. What could be more Navajo?"[5]

"They're singing about mama, trucks, ranching, nostalgia," added Kristina Jacobsen, author of *The Sound of Navajo Country*, "things the Navajo happen to know a lot about."[6]

Dr. Joanne Lynn Shenandoah (1958–2021) (Oneida)

Joanne Shenandoah gave up a six-figure salary in Washington DC to return to Oneida Iroquois Territory in northern New York and sing and write songs reflecting her heritage. She would receive an unparalleled fourteen NAMAs, along with numerous Indie (independent music) and SAMMY (Syracuse Area Music) Awards.

Shenandoah experienced a fatal heart attack at the Mayo Clinic in Scottsdale, Arizona, on November 22, 2021, seven months after we spoke. She was sixty-three. At the time of her passing, her husband, Doug George-Kanentiio, a former board of trustees member of the National Museum of the American Indian and editor of *Akwesasne Notes*, and her daughter, Leah, were beside her.

> Iroquois songs have always been part of my life. There are songs for when a baby is born and songs for when someone passes into the spirit world. We sing for plants, medicine, animals, and the harvest. There are hundreds and hundreds of songs.
>
> I belong to the Wolf Clan of the Haudenosaunee Six Nations Iroquois

Confederacy Oneida Nation. My Oneida name, Tekali Wha Khwa, translates as "She Sings."

My mother, Mary "Maise" Shenandoah, collected antiques and operated a trading post. She served as the matriarch of the Oneida people for thirty years. My father, Clifford Shenandoah, was chief of the Onondaga Nation and played guitar for Duke Ellington.

I'm seven generations from Chief John Shenandoah [Skenandoa or Schenando], who helped George Washington's army during the Revolutionary War. I live on the property where he lived until he died, at the age of 110, in 1816. Across the street, revolutionary soldiers passed by. Washington gave Chief Shenandoah a peace medal, which we still own.

I served on the board of directors of Syracuse University's Hiawatha Institute for Indigenous Knowledge. The institute is the fulfillment of Chief Shenandoah's dream. His wish was to provide a place of learning where the essence of Native knowledge would be shared with the world in a school of higher learning.

I can't vocalize how wonderful my life has been—opening Woodstock '94; singing for Nelson Mandela and the Dalai Lama; wining and dining with Frank Sinatra; being offered the chance to be the next Patsy Cline— but that's not what's important. It's all about the music. I have critics, but I also have people who have been strong mentors. They're full of gratitude for me bringing a centered peace to the sound of what our culture is about.

I started singing when I was young. I won the grand prize in a contest at school when I was in the third grade. I sang "September in the Rain" from *Melody for Two* [1937]. I remember not wanting to go on stage, but my dad was there with his guitar. He whispered, "Sing it like you've always sung it," and I did. People tell me I was too young to know that song, but my dad taught it to me.

I went to a boarding school in my teens and studied Western classical music. I went to school for half a day and worked half a day. Fortunately, I got to work for the music department, setting up the rehearsal room for the school band. I picked up every instrument, tried to play it, and read every book on how to play. I learned clarinet, flute, cello, and piano.

Each album is a different chapter, a different experience. I'm always looking forward to the next offering of what my soul has to offer. I have fifty songs sitting on the shelf that I need to release. I have so much music in me. If I lived in a studio, who knows what would happen? I sure would love to do that.

Neil Young, Bruce Cockburn, Bill Miller, and Mary Youngblood con- tributed to *Eagle Cries* [2016]. "Feather from Heaven" was used in a video documentary about New York City and 9/11. That song is a favorite of many in Indian country. "When the dust of death has settled on your shoulders."

It's more than a folk song. It's powerful and very profound. It's beyond me. It's my ancestral heritage speaking through me.

I had to follow my path. My mother and father instilled in me pride in my culture and how it would make a change in the world and fulfill the prophecies. Against all odds, the Iroquois have continued to survive, but our community has been broken, divided by economic goals, priorities, and principles.

I lived in Washington DC in the late 1980s and early '90s, earning a six-figure salary managing seventy-five people for a computer science corporation. I was young but driven. I was offered $6 million to start my own minority-owned engineering firm. I didn't read *Cosmopolitan*; I was too focused and busy.

I had everything I thought I wanted, including a fantastic boss, but he was diagnosed with leukemia and asked if I'd take over his job. I said, "Yes," and I did. He was so full of gratitude. I told everyone, "Get the work done, no matter what it takes."

One day I watched a tree being cut down from my office window. It uprooted me. I asked myself, "What am I doing?"

I knew in my heart of hearts that it was my responsibility to put out music that was healing—the Iroquois believe everyone was put on Earth for a specific purpose. But I do a lot more than just sing. When I start talking about it, it almost makes me tired. I just narrated a film for Encyclopedia Britannica, *A Seat at the Table*, with Huston Smith, one of the most amazing historians of all time. I love traveling and seeing what people are doing in different countries. I went to Iceland to be in *The Last Winter*, with Ron Perlman, in 2005. It was fantastic. They have high taxes, but people buy less, and they share. They have less pollution. They take care of their elders. Their crime rate is low.

Canyon Records released my first album in 1988. I didn't think I was going to be making any more records, so I sang everything.

Returning to Oneida Iroquois Territory, I turned my full attention to music. I wanted to represent Native people in a good light. It was a huge responsibility.

The title track of Haudenosaunee-based *Peacemaker's Journey* [2000] was nominated for an Emmy when PBS included it in a documentary, *The Native America*, narrated by Robbie Robertson. I also sang harmony on *Contact from the Underworld of Redboy*.

Sacred Ground: A Tribute to Mother Earth [2005], with additional tracks by Robert Mirabel, Bill Miller, and Primeaux and Mike, won a Best Native American Album Grammy and a Best Compilation NAMA—one of fourteen [unmatched] NAMAs I've received. I was the best female artist in 1998 and 1999, the best producer in 2001, and the best artist in 2002. They gave me a Lifetime Achievement Award in 2007. "We Will Rise Up" was the best indie single of 2019. Awards are great, and I'm grateful to receive them. But they're not what it's about. It's not about the money either. It's about how we affect each other and make a better world. I don't take that lightly.

Floyd Westerman was a dear friend; he was special. The last time I saw him was at Vine Deloria Jr.'s funeral in November 2005. Vine's son asked me to sing. Floyd told me, "I just read an interview where you said that A. Paul Ortega [with whom I recorded *Loving Ways* in 1991] was your biggest influence. That's just not right."

I said, "C'mon, Floyd, you know it's always been you."

After he passed, I had a dream. Floyd came through a door, walked over to me, kissed me on the cheek, and said, "Are you okay?"

"Yeah, Floyd, are you?"

He hugged me. It was precious, a nice dream. Floyd was so funny. I used to tease him. We had a great relationship. We were once in the Black Hills of South Dakota, going to a concert, and he got lost. South Dakota is desolate, but he said, "I suppose it's somewhere around here. See any recognizable landmarks?"

A. Paul Ortega was a traditional medicine person and president of the Mescalero Apache, but he was a lot of fun too. I don't know if I bring out the silliness in people, but I love to laugh. That's my mom in me. She'd always try to make people feel better. I spoke with Paul during his last days. Buddy Red Bow [Oglala Lakota] too. Buddy invited me to sing with him at the Paha Sapa [Black Hills] Festival, in South Dakota, in July 1989. Then Floyd asked me to sing with him.

Pete Seeger was always supportive. I sang at his ninetieth birthday at Madison Square Garden in May 2010. At his last Hudson River Revival [June 2014], I was told, "Ms. Shenandoah, Pete requested you to be the only artist he listens to today."

He sat next to the stage, singing along to my songs.

I became severely ill in 2015 and almost died. A couple of years before, I had done a workshop, at a Victims of Violence conference, on the positive effects of musical vibrations on the body. I didn't realize it, but members of the U.S. Department of Justice came to my workshop. I received a letter a month later, from then attorney general Eric Holder, asking me to cochair the National Task Force of Children Exposed to Violence, with Senator Byron Dorgan of North Dakota. How could I say no? I did it for a year, but I can't begin to tell you how difficult and painful it was. I saw not only Native children but all kinds of children across the country suffering from the same traumatic experiences. I listened to testimony from lawyers, doctors, teachers, police officers, and prostitutes. I ingested it all, trying to figure out a way to make a change. We came up with 286 recommendations. President Obama passed a bill for $1.3 billion to oppose child violence, but it was a big undertaking. My immune system was low; my heart was on the ground. I ended up catching a *C. diff* [*Clostridium difficile*] infection. Its symptoms range from diabetes to life-threatening inflammation of the colon and nonalcoholic fatty liver disease [NAFLD]. It's rampant in nursing homes. People usually die within thirty days. Authorities say it's natural causes, but it's a virus. After thirty days, I felt like I was at the end of my life. It had totally depleted my body. I couldn't keep food or vitamins in me. It was rough.

I went to Korea anyway—I had agreed to be on a national television program—but I came home with double pneumonia and ended up in the Mayo Clinic in Jacksonville, Florida, for seven months. They had me on a liver transplant list.

Thank God for friends, family, and GoFundMe. I was able to sustain life. I started eating organic food, exercising, meditating, doing yoga, and going back to my practice of quantum healing. I'm a fighter; I've taken self-defense training.

I had twenty doctors taking care of me. I asked one if anyone came out of this without a transplant. He said, "It's extremely rare."

I said, "In that case, I'm going home," and that's what I did. Doctors and hospital staff were in shock. They promised me a transplant if I stayed. But I have a rare blood type—that was part of the problem—so I went home. I was missing funerals and birthdays, missing my family. I missed being in my own environment, and I needed to do that.

I tried all the techniques I heard about—prayer and song, vibration of the spirit. I started meditating three hours a day, balancing my body and soul, and feeling grounded with nature. I was happy and pain free. You can't get that from a pill.

I released *Shenandoah Country* [2019] with songs on my shelf. Why not share them? I recorded it in my house. I didn't know if I'd be doing any more albums.

I wanted to do a video of the closing track, "Missing You." I wanted a song that would reach out to people and try to help bring change but not be overly sad or make people feel depressed. My relatives helped;

everybody did it gratis. They said that it completely altered their lives. The video showed vulnerability, the potential of what could happen, what does happen, and what can be done to help.

I appreciate the moments I've shared with people from many nations. I'm not trying to boast; that's not our way. But I know I've made some change in the world and affected people's lives. The East-West Interfaith Seminary's website includes me with Huston Smith, Nelson Mandela, Amma, Elie Wiesel, and the Dalai Lama as people who have contributed to world peace and interfaith understanding.

I've led a good life. I was ready to take that journey across the stars, but my daughter told me, "No, Mom, you've got more work to do. You can't go."

Then she had a baby. I've been helping to raise that baby. He's nineteen months old, but he already sings and plays piano, flute, guitar, and harmonica. He's a little celestial miracle; I'm full of gratitude.

Theresa "Bear" Fox (1966–) (Mohawk)

Whether she's writing songs in English or her native Mohawk language, Bear Fox speaks from her heart. "A melody will come to [Bear Fox's] mind," said Sesi King of *Indian Time*, "and [she] isn't able to do anything else until she writes words to that tune."[7]

Akwesasne Mohawk Nation Territory, in northern New York, isn't far from the Canadian border. We're pretty isolated. I can see other houses from where we live, but they're not too close together. I love that we have the St. Lawrence River and can go fishing or use the kayak.

I grew up with the Mohawk language [Kanienkeha], but there was so much English around me, it overpowered the Mohawk. I remember my mother sitting me in front of the television while she did housework. That was my babysitter. I started being called "Bear" after the animated series *The Berenstain Bears*.

I felt a connection to Mother Earth. When I walked outside, everything was alive. I didn't want to be unfair to anything in nature; I wanted to greet everything.

I had eight brothers—six boys in a row—and five sisters. I'm the youngest. My oldest brothers and sisters speak the language. My brothers worked with my father, but by the time us younger ones were born, we couldn't understand or speak it. My sister told me that one time a bus driver was so angry that they were speaking the language on the bus, he came into my house and yelled at my mother. He said, "What are you doing speaking the language to your kids? Do you want them to grow up to be savages?"

She stopped speaking to the younger ones, but she kept speaking to my father in the language. That was all he spoke. When he spoke to me, I couldn't understand him. We weren't close, because we couldn't speak to one another. I felt ashamed that I didn't know my language. That's why I put it in my songs. I would get an idea for the message I wanted to put in a song and ask my friends, who were language speakers, to translate it into Mohawk. I could always find a melody.

14. Bear Fox

My sister-in-law [Katsitsionni Fox] and I formed a women's singing society in 1990 to sing songs in our language. We were always trying to get more women to join us. We alternated between names. Kontiwennenhawi ["Carrier of the Words"] was our name when we performed off the rez.

Some songs come strongly to me. They push on my shoulders to hurry up and write them because they need to be shared with the people. It's like a spirit coming through me.

It's so important to put positive messages about respect and taking care of families into songs. People connect to the songs because of the stories. There's always something that triggers a memory or pulls at heartstrings. It's from my heart.

We had a house fire in 2001. My husband [iron worker Sky Fox], sons [Niharonhia:a, Karoniote, Shatekaronhioten, and Tewenteneh], daughter

[Iahonwa:awi], and I had to move to another house on the other end of the rez. I was going to the Iohahi:io Adult Education and Training Institute to become a teacher and didn't have a permanent job, but I wanted to find a way to bring in an income. I started thinking that a painter paints, a potter creates pottery. Why shouldn't I record a CD and sell it?

English helped me to reach a wider audience. My first song in English, "Broken," was about residential schools. This lady had come to visit me. She was one of my friend's girlfriends. It was the first time we met. We sat at a table, and she told me that when she lived in Alaska, she had to go away to school. She had to fly there in an airplane and be away from her family for months. I could feel her emotions. Her story planted deeply in me. I thought about how hard it must have been when our people had to go to residential schools, the loneliness they must have felt. When she left, I started writing the song. I thought about my grandfather. He had lived with us for a while. He was a product of the residential schools. Now I knew why he thought the way he did. He didn't like anything Native. If we had moccasins or a choker on, he would look at us in disgust, wave his hand, and leave the room.

"Rich Girl," my second song in English, came strongly. When I was growing up, kids were always coming to our house to play. It was the main gathering place for my brothers, sisters, and me. I was happy all the time, so I figured we must be rich. We had everything we needed. I didn't realize that we didn't have a lot of money until I got invited to a friend's house after school. I walked into her house, and it was the first time I saw anything new—new cupboards, new stove, new fridge, new floor. I never saw that before.

My best friend's daughter, Teio Swathe [Mohawk], used to be in our singing group. She's got a beautiful singing voice. Her mom helped me with translations. I did a song, "Sky World," and Teio learned it. She sang it on a YouTube video in 2018. Supaman saw it and asked her to be part of his video of the song. She asked me if it'd be all right. They wound up winning the NAMMY for Best Video Concept. I'm amazed at how many people love it.

It was my third NAMMY. I got one for Best Songwriter in 2014 and one for Debut Artist in 2011. They've helped get my music out there, but I'm not one who goes someplace and says, "I won this," or, "I won that."

We're taught to not boast about our achievements. What makes me feel good is that my nieces and nephews are so proud of me. My community and my students are learning the song.

I dedicated "Say Her Name" to Indigenous women who have gone missing. Corporations are drilling for oil in Canada and the United States. There are camps of men working on pipelines. They're taking women. It happens on the highway. If women are walking, they'll get abducted. I wanted to raise awareness that was happening. When I finished the song and sang it for my granddaughter, she said, "That's such a sad song."

I said, "I know it's sad, but I want you to know that you have to start close to your family and not go anywhere alone. You've got to be with somebody all the time. There are a lot of bad people. You can't trust anyone."

I've been working with a couple of musicians—one in Switzerland—in a contest called Beyond Music. They connect musicians and songwriters from around the world. We work together on a song and submit it. I was invited to participate. I sang "Our Precious Mothers," and the musicians put music to it.

I recorded *Aterosera* [2020] with flute player Mignon Geli. I'd always wanted to record a CD with flute music, something that would put little babies to sleep. Mignon was born in San Francisco of Filipino and Spanish ancestry, but she lives in the California Sierra foothills. She's a member of the Neena McNair Family Singers, a multitribal women's traditional drum group. She played on a couple of beautiful instrumentals, "Friendship" and "Wedding Song," but we sang songs in the language too. It's who we are, our identity, our culture. We're trying to keep that alive.

The government is trying to erase us on both sides, Canadian and American. That's why it's so important to hang on to our language. I'm proud of my son because he's able to speak the language. My father-in-law is the chief. He's able to speak to my son. My son is so much more advanced than my husband or me. He's trying hard to teach the language to his daughter.

I teach Mohawk to Head Start, pre-K, and kindergarten students. I really like singing with the little ones. They love to sing. They don't have barriers yet. They're not self-conscious, they're ready to learn, and they still have a sense of fun.

Desja Eagle Tail (1991–) (Crow)

Hailing from the Crow Reservation in Wyoming, Desja Eagle Tail is "a regionally acclaimed singer known for her bluesy, soulful voice and a style mixing R&B, rock, and pop."[8]

> I feel resilience in my heart. The Crow have pride in our tribe and our language. We have more native speakers than many tribes. We have the Crow Language Consortium and an immersion school that teaches the Crow language to our little ones. We take our practices seriously and pass them down to the next generation.
>
> I was apprehensive about going to Standing Rock, in November 2016, but once I got there, I knew I had to be there. I met people from all kinds of backgrounds. Different religions came together to pray for the people and the land. It was eye-opening. I participated in a benefit concert with Native artists from all over. None of us were compensated; we wanted to help the Standing Rock people in their fight to protect the land and water. I sang "Indian Reservation [Lament of the Cherokee Reservation Indian]," but I made some changes. It originally said, "Native people will return," but I didn't like that. It was like it was saying we were gone. I changed it to "Native people will arrive, we'll rise."
>
> I grew up out in the country, on the Wind River Reservation in Wyoming, with my parents and grandparents. We had horses. I was sheltered from the harsh realities of the reservation, but I've become more aware of people having food insecurity. A documentary is being made about how the Crow Reservation is a food desert. Its only grocery store burned down in February 2019. The owner had just renovated it. The closest grocery store is fourteen miles away. A lot of people don't have cars or enough gas to get there and back. I'm doing songs for the documentary, telling people that we're warriors, we're resilient, and we're working to make the world a better place. I want to expand it into an opera. It won't be in Italian; it'll be from our perspective. It might take a few years, but I've got the inspiration.
>
> My grandparents retired when my mom had me. She had to go back to work when I was a month old, so they were my babysitters. They're the reason I know so much about my culture. My grandma—I called her "Mom"—would sing Crow lullabies and hymns translated into Crow. She made sure all her grandchildren learned those songs.

My mom [Marjean Eagle Tail] also taught me songs. She sings in church, but she's shy about singing.

I always had the radio on, even if I was with other relatives. I'd go out to the pickup and listen to the radio while they were tending to the cattle. I mostly listened to country music, but my mom liked oldies but goodies, and I knew those songs too.

I love a good groove with solid syncopation. I love a brass section. I did a concert with five horn players when I was at Montana State College in Billings. I absolutely love that sound. If I could afford it every show, I'd be the happiest woman in the world.

I love musicals like *Hairspray* and *Sweet Charity*. As I've gotten older, I've acted in local stage musicals. When I was a young girl, I never thought of it for me.

Native Americans have always known God. They just don't spell it G-o-d. In the Crow culture, it's Akbaatatdia, the Creator. I believe that Akbaatatdia brought my dad into my life because, if it weren't for him, I wouldn't have known that singing was an option. I never met anybody who was a singer. It was just something I loved, but my father had prophetic visions of me singing when I was a little girl.

I tried out for Miss Montana in 2010. It's part of the Miss America Organization. I came back in 2013 and got fourth runner-up. I had done singing competitions as part of a choir. I call my high school choir teacher [Maggie Ratliff] and band teacher [Dohn Ratliff] "my musical parents."

They're married. He told me that I should run for the pageant, so I did. I never wanted to win a beauty contest or be Miss America, but it was a great stepping stone. It built my confidence enough for me to say, "I am a singer."

I was able to develop a relationship with what is now the Rocky Mountain Tribal Council. They sponsored me in the pageant and gave me my first paid performance a year later.

I was excited about going to the NAMAs in 2018 and winning the Best Country Recording Award for *Never Let Me Go*. They not only understood the struggles of being Native American but also the challenges of being an artist.

Becoming the first person to sing "The Star-Spangled Banner" in the Crow language [Apsáalooke] was a great honor. My uncle translated it for me. He had gone to a rodeo and heard a woman singing the national anthem in Navajo. On his journey back, he kept going, "We should do that."

People told him, "It's too hard." But he came to where I was working, one day, and said, "You're going to sing the national anthem in Crow," and I said, "Okay."

I met with him and recorded it so I could take it home and learn it. He talked me through every line. I had to meet with female relatives and get their help too. In our language, there are words for men and words for women. I had to change a few words so they would be appropriate. When I sing it, I bring the Crow culture and America together in one song. I ask the Creator for unity for the country and between each other in our tribe and all Native American tribes.

When I was growing up, I had a CD by Native American evangelist Dr. Juanita Byrum [Chahta and Cree]. I loved the way she sang. It was so Native, even if she was singing praise songs. Her voice had a soulfulness that I've always remembered. Sometimes, when I sing, it reminds me of that. Some people think I should just do Native American songs, but my music is eclectic. I don't want to be tied down to one genre.

Many Crow Nation people have Scottish blood. It gives me my light eyes. My uncle has blue eyes. He just had a great-grandbaby with those same eyes.

I've always liked blues and R&B—Aretha Franklin and Etta James. I jokingly say that it's because I have two Black godmothers, but it's just a part of me.

I've stayed alcohol and drug free to show people that they don't have to live with alcohol and drugs to survive. My dad, Leon Eagle Tail, is a recovering alcoholic. It was generational and in the family, but he wanted to know why. He had to understand alcoholism, so he went to school to be an alcohol and drug counselor. He was able to retrain his thinking and abstain from alcohol. He said, "That's not going to help me or my family, my tribe, or my community."

Tribes used alcohol to numb themselves from the pain of having children taken from them and put in boarding schools. It happened decades ago, but it's still impacting us. We had a relocation program, the Termination Act. We had doctors sterilizing Native women without their consent. Alcohol helped people survive these awful conditions, but I've never wanted to drink. I'd rather be doing music. I appreciate people with a natural sense of humor, but I was made to be an "encourager," bringing joy and happiness.

I always knew I was going to be a mother. When it finally came, in December 2018, I said, "Why did I wait so long?"

I get a lot of support from my parents. We live in the same house, five of us—I have a little brother who's ten—and two dogs. I love them. My baby and I took the downstairs: two rooms and a bathroom. Being a new mother, I've got to take care of myself, not only physically, but also psychologically, emotionally, and spiritually, make sure all my needs are met, and then I'm in the position to create life through songs.

We live in Spokane, Washington. There are a lot of urban Indians here. It's where my dad lived during his first marriage. He has four kids; they're all here. There are a lot of tribes in the surrounding area. There's a Native American community center in town.

There are perks to being in a city. I like going to the gym and swimming. I love Zumba. If I were in the country, it'd take an hour to get there, but I love being in the country too. I don't have to worry about my neighbors. I can enjoy a walk or run by myself. I've seen hawks, deer, and all kinds of wildlife. I remember seeing a porcupine eating his Easter dinner after I had eaten mine. I got close, but I didn't scare him, and he walked away.

Cary Morin (1962–) (Crow)

A guitarist, singer, and songwriter from Billings, Montana, Cary Morin mixes blues, bluegrass, jazz, and reggae into infectious Native Americana grooves.

My connection to music came through album covers. I didn't know anything about the artists other than what was written in the liner notes. There was a mystery. I was unaware of musical genres. I knew there was a difference between rock and roll and country music, but there were lots of things I didn't know about, like Creole and Cajun music.

I used to listen to powwow music, especially when my kids were young. I was trying, with the help of my mother, to get them interested in traditional dance. I took them to powwows, but my relationship with Native

15. Cary Morin

music has never gone much beyond that. I've never tried to sing Native music, but I have a different perspective than most non-Native people. Dealing with racism is one thing. You could never understand it until it's right in your face. I don't speak my language, but being around Crow people, I appreciate their humor and the way they communicate with each other. I sometimes use phrases in my songs that only Native people would recognize.

When I was into powwow dancing, I tried combining powwow songs with reggae music. I recorded with powwow guys from back home, but if Native life has influenced my songwriting, it's from me being Native and a songwriter. It's bound to come out.

I was born in Billings. But my dad bought a house ten miles out of Great Falls, and we moved. There wasn't anyone else out there, just us and wheat fields. We didn't take many family vacations, but sometimes we visited my grandparents on the Crow Reservation, three or four hours away. That was my connection to my tribe.

The reservation was unspoiled, beautiful land with mountains, rivers, and valleys. As a kid, I'd hang out with my cousins, spending most of our time on horseback, riding in the mountains, or on our grandfather's property.

There were a couple of radio stations that played commercial hits, but we didn't have access to media the way that people do now. We could only pick up two TV stations. I saw *Hee Haw* and *Don Kirchner's Rock Concert*.

My older brother had a classical guitar. He took lessons when he was a kid, but he lost interest. When he went to college, he left it behind. I had taken piano lessons for six years, but it was surprising when I picked up my brother's guitar and could play it. For whatever reason, it was easy for me. I got really interested in it. I spent a lot of time by myself. I had time to play guitar, so I did.

My dad, an officer in the air force, was a fan of classic country music. He'd sit around listening to Hank Williams, Merle Haggard, Charlie Pride, and Willie Nelson. He had a couple of Chet Atkins albums. I thought it interesting how he played bass lines with his thumb. I tried learning to do that.

I listened to a lot of recordings—it didn't matter whom—Led Zeppelin or Jose Feliciano. We had all the folk music albums—James Taylor, Cat Stevens, Mason Williams, Carole King, and Jackson Browne. I heard Neil Young's early albums and then *Zuma* [1975], a heavily electric album. *Yessongs* [1973] had Steve Howe's amazing acoustic guitar playing. I learned to play by listening over and over and figuring it out.

Jeff Beck's *Blow by Blow* [1975] was one of my favorite albums, but it didn't occur to me, until I was in my twenties, that it was jazz. It was just cool music. New Grass Revival wasn't classic bluegrass, but they played acoustic instruments. I was fascinated by David Bromberg's recordings. He was a ripping bluegrass player but always included blues tunes. I listened to Segovia and other classical guitar players, as well as to all the pop music that was around. Chubby Checker's "The Twist" and "The Limbo Rock" fascinated me, and I learned to play them on the piano. I had all these influences and loved them all.

Bands would pass through Montana on their way to Seattle. Our town was one of the stopovers. Right before I graduated from high school, I became more aware of what these guys were doing. They were traveling around playing clubs, and it sounded great.

After graduation I went to visit friends in Colorado. I got the idea that I wanted to play solo guitar. In the mind of a seventeen- or eighteen-year-old, that seemed cool, so I moved to Fort Collins and started playing solo shows at Keystone Mountain, two hours away. I also played at the Winter Park Ski Area, which was about the same distance.

Bands were playing ski areas all over the Rocky Mountains and clubs in bigger cities like Portland, Denver, and Boulder. That fueled my passion, so I started playing electric guitar. That grew into my own band, the Atoll, in 1989. We had management out of Minneapolis and played colleges, clubs, and bars, and an occasional frat party. I met musicians from Chicago; St. Paul–Minneapolis; Madison, Wisconsin; and Omaha and picked up things by playing shows with them. It was a great education.

I worked with Jessica Freestone, a ballet dancer from Colorado, on a musical, *Turtle Island*. She approached me about writing the story. She was going to direct it and coordinate the dancers. I wrote about a young Native girl [Agnes] in a fictional town called Turtle Island. Once the pride of the town, Agnes appears to be suffering from narcolepsy. She keeps falling asleep, but when she sleeps, she's teleporting to other places and witnessing dance in India, Africa, Brazil, and Mexico. As the story goes on, the town gets more concerned about Agnes's well-being, but from her point of view, she's having a great time.

We rehearsed for almost a year before putting it on in Fort Collins in 2000 and again a year later. The second time, we had a cast of fifty dancers. It was a huge undertaking, a stressful production. I had to take my band off the road. While they were off, a couple of guys got married, so it wound up killing my band and changing my direction. I switched to fingerstyle acoustic guitar, the Piedmont blues style.

In 2013 I got a phone call asking me to be the guitar player for a production of Nina Raines's *Tribe* in Phoenix. It was going to feature an all-Native cast of musicians, actors, and dancers. I made a lot of what've become lifelong friends, including Saskatchewan-born singer-songwriter Pura Fé [Tuscarora]. She was leading Ulali at the time. They did two songs for the production that were incredibly moving. We stayed in touch for years. She was always moving around, doing something different. She called one time and told me that she had been learning to play acoustic lap steel guitar. Another time, she wanted to put a group of Native songwriters together and present a showcase. She had a deal with a record label in Paris, and she said, "I'm going to talk to them and have them let us do an album."

Artists submitted songs for this album, but I didn't have anything ready to send. I wasn't playing solo yet—I was still in a band. But I recorded some tracks in my basement and sent them to her. She picked two. That was my first appearance on a European record.

Pura Fé was busy touring Europe with guitarist Danny Godinez, but he was worn out. They were playing so much, he wanted to quit. She called me and asked if I'd be interested in taking over for him. I agreed. We ended up touring Europe for five years.

I learned a lot from her. She was doing things I had only dreamed about. We played in front of big audiences all over Europe. I couldn't fathom how she could do it without a rhythm section. It made no sense to me, but I watched her do it for years, sitting next to her and learning how it could be done.

Playing with the Subdudes John Magnie and Steve Amedee as the Young Ancients was another fun project. I was one of the first people they met when they moved to Fort Collins in the eighties. We've been friends since. We live in the same neighborhood, so we started a songwriting project. Every day for a year, I'd go to John's house. I'd write a song the day before, and we'd record it. After nine months or so, we started thinking that we should go out and play these tunes. We shifted gears and turned into a performing act. We recorded an album, *Fish Story* [2015], and started doing shows. But they got busy with the Subdudes, and I got busy doing my stuff. It just faded away.

One of my songs on our CD, "Yellowbird," was fictional, though I used my father in it. He was a Vietnam and Korean vet. After he got home, he didn't talk about his experiences in Asia. The rest of the story, I made up. At the time, there were a lot of nonviolent people in prison for marijuana possession and cultivation. Marijuana was suddenly legal; it didn't make sense for people to be serving time.

I was heavily influenced by prison recordings from Mississippi, the prison chants from the 1920s and '30s. If you dig for those recordings, you can still find them. I based some of the words of "When I Rise," the title track of my 2018 CD, on those prison songs. I came up with the story line for the video. I had imagery in my head about a crooked law enforcement officer. We settled on him being a fur trader. We didn't think we could nail a specific time, so we made one up. It's its own time. With limited funding and a small crew, we pulled it off. We filmed in the mountains outside Fort Collins. We filmed my part, and then I took off for a European tour. They did the rest of it while I was gone. My son played the young man.

I try to make every album different from the ones before. Spyro Gyra's bass player, Kim Stone, produced the Rippingtons. We've been friends for twenty-five years. He always said that if I wanted to do a project together, he'd be interested. This was our chance. We did half of the album in Boulder and half in the studio in Fort Collins, where I'd made my other recordings. He helped me gather the players. We got together for four days and knocked out the selections that I had done preproduction for. I wrote the tunes with a band in mind instead of sitting in front of a microphone by myself.

I was doing shows near New Orleans in 2018. A friend took me to the Dockside Studio in Maurice, Louisiana. B. B. King recorded there years ago; it was his "house." His guitar is still there. Driving onto the property was amazing; it was classic Louisiana.

I named my next album *Dockside Saints* and released it on August 7, 2020. Tony Daigle, who produced it, had seen me for the first time at a club in Lafayette. He's Sonny Landreth's producer and soundman. We had eight days booked. After we were done, Sonny's crew came in and recorded *Blacktop Run*.

It was a treat to play with Lee Allen Zeno, Buckwheat Zydeco's bass player for Buckwheat's entire career. He also recorded with Charlie Rich and Bobby Charles. He's got a connection to gospel music, country music, reggae, and the blues. It flows out of him. He's the ultimate Louisiana bass player and an excellent human being, great to be around. We've stayed in touch. We're already talking about the next album.

Brian Brignac, who plays drums for Sonny Landreth, played on the entire album. The list of people he's played with includes Fats Domino, Graham Brown, Jo-El Sonnier, Bobby Charles, Wayne Toups, C. J. Chenier, Chubby Carrier, Cindy Cashdollar, and a friend of mine, Tommy Malone. Corey Ledet played accordion. We met at the Port Townsend Acoustic Blues Festival. John Fohl played guitar for Dr. John's Professor Bizarre's Funknology for twelve years or so. Like me, he's originally from Montana. We met when I was playing in New Orleans a couple of years back. When the project came up, I gave him a call, "Hey, remember me? Are you interested in doing some songs?"

I emailed him a handful of tunes and asked him to pick the ones he wanted to do. He wrote me back fifteen minutes later and said, "I can't decide. I love all of this stuff."

Beau Thomas played fiddle. He grew up around Lafayette. He's one of Louisiana's greats, a positive energy. We had a keyboard player, Eric Adcock. He's the go-to guy as far as boogie-woogie. His playing is like Professor Longhair, Dr. John, and Jerry Lee Lewis. We also had Keith Blair, a great blues guitar player, play Strat on a couple of tunes.

My wife, Celeste Di Iorio, and I sang all twelve tracks. Some had a gospel feel. Others a funky, New Orleans–style groove. There were two instrumentals. We redid "Prisoner" from *Sing It Louder* [2014]. It was inspired by a combination of things. One was incarcerated Native people, including a cousin of mine. I wrote some songs in Italy, France, and Germany. I wrote "Come the Rain" two days before we moved into the studio.

I like performing solo, but I've been doing shows with Celeste. We met around the time that the Subdudes came to town. They weren't instantly popular, but a few of us would go to their shows, fascinated by what they did. Celeste's ex-husband played bass in a band I was in for a year. She and I have been friends for thirty-five years or so. My marriage split up ten years ago, and her marriage split up around the same time. We got together and started playing music. We had all this history. She was the high school principal for two of my kids. She eventually became my manager. She's responsible for my ability to put albums out and tour. Without her, I don't know what I'd be doing.

Growing up in Montana, I've always been around country bands. Even when I was underage, I could walk into clubs. The bands would see me and say, "Get up here," and they'd make me play. I learned to sing harmony because everybody sang. I've always craved that. Celeste doesn't just sing along with me; we sing songs together. We're putting a band together, Ghost Dog. It'll be a rhythm section, Celeste, and me.

I have a band, Rancho Deluxe, with Will Kimbrough and guys from around New Orleans. We do shows in Georgia, Mississippi, and Louisiana when everybody's schedule allows it. Then I have the musicians I just made the album with. I want to do shows with them too. I don't know if I have enough time to do all of it, but I'm going to do as much as I can.

Lucas Ciliberti (2000–) (Tsalagi and Mi'kmaq)

With his youthful charm and natural exuberance, Lucas Ciliberti has found his greatest outlet through music videos. "He's definitely an old soul," said his mother, Bridget. "He just seems to have a great understanding of life and of people."[9]

Native Americana describes my music. It has a Native feel that everybody could relate to, an Americana kind of storytelling.

It's cool to bring music to a picture; it takes imagination. People normally listen to a song and do it themselves in their heads, but I share how I portray that music. I've worked with filmmaker Lance Goodman in Kansas. He's a brother to me. I've done behind-the-camera work for him.

We filmed *Springfield* in Alabama in 2016. It's about a Native American scout during the American Civil War who goes off to fight for the Confederate cause that he believes in. He dies for that cause and never makes it home to his family. It takes time, effort, and passion to fit everything in three minutes, but it can be done.

I love singing by myself, but I love to cowrite. You get to see another person's imagination, thoughts, and experiences. I've been in the studio, working on a sequel to *Rainmaker* [2017], and Macy Ruggiero's been singing with me. She's got an amazing voice. Morgan Snoddy, Brooke Ashé, and Maggie Perry have also been singing with me. My friends and I share a passion for music. It touches people and affects their lives, runs through us in different ways.

No matter who you are, you deserve love and happiness. That's just the way things should be. If my music touches one person, I'm pleased. If it touches more, it's a major blessing. I use my passion to make people happy, give them joy, and share my experiences with them. It's the way I grew up. I'm Christian, and I believe in God. He put a lot of blessings in my life. I wouldn't be here today without the voice he gave me. I grew up singing in church.

Number two is my mom. She's been there for every situation and supported me and my goals, no matter what.

I was born in Rochester, Minnesota, but we moved to my grandmother's farm in Enid, Oklahoma, when I was two. We've had the farm in my family for four generations.

I made my debut performance when I was eighteen months old at a San Jose Sharks hockey game. I sang "God Bless America." My mom has a video of it.

I love being Native American and the traditions that come with it. I've traveled around the country singing at powwows. They're unique opportunities to see people who look like family. I sang at a powwow in Orlando, Florida, and they invited me to drum. I absolutely loved it. I felt a connection with the drum and the people around the drum singing with me. It's indescribable how it affected me. There's meaning behind the songs, whether you understand what they're saying or not. I felt peace while singing them. At the powwow, someone told me, "As individual fingers, we can be broken, but together, we form a mighty fist."

My older brother, Nathan, has autism. It was hard for him growing up, but the love was always there. His situation taught me responsibility and true love for my family. He's currently in a place in Georgia that's helping him. His diet had been Cheetos and spaghetti. Now he eats everything they put in front of him. He said, "I love you," to my mom for the first time in years.

With every song I record, I try to relate it to my life. I want it to be genuine, as full of feeling as possible.

"Face of a Friend" was the first song I recorded; I was ten. It was the first time I was in a studio.

Another song on the first album, *Time for a Real Change*, was "Maybe Jesus Was a Cowboy," by Christian country music singer-songwriter Hunter Erwin from Walker, Louisiana. We filmed a video of it.

I had the chance to go to Pigeon Forge, Tennessee, to perform at the Country Music Association International Championship in 2010, but we didn't have the money. My grandma sold a cow so I could go. I sang "God Bless America," a cappella, and won the awards for Vocalist of the Year and Clog Dancer of the Year.

My grandma recently passed away. Over the past couple of years, I took time off and came home. I helped her on the farm and spent time with her. Of course, I still did things in the studio, but I didn't do as many live performances as I normally do. I don't regret a day of it.

Relocating to Tennessee in 2014 wasn't too hard. I'm not one to sing in a bar downtown for four hours. It's not my calling, not what I enjoy doing. When I went the first time, guitarist Tommy Neal introduced me to a wonderful couple [Ann and Randy Dorman] and their family. Randy played guitar for Kenny Rogers for forty-something years. I recorded *Rainmaker* for their Scenic Ridge label. It got a lot of attention. At the NAMAs in November 2017, I was named Debut Artist of the Year, the youngest [at seventeen] to win the award.

My goal is to touch as many people with my music as I can. If I make a living with it, cool. If I don't, that's cool too. That's not why I make music. I do music because I love it. I love changing people's lives. That's what's important, to be there for each other. It's much needed. I'm going to keep trucking and going the way I'm going. The possibilities are endless; I can do anything if I set my mind to it.

Lac du Flambeau (Lake of Torches)

The northern Wisconsin home of the Lac du Flambeau band of Lake Superior Chippewa Indians (Anishinaabe) since 1745 can be "like the North Pole in the winter," said singer-songwriter and dentist Paco

Fralick. "We're a couple of hours south of Lake Superior. We have lakes all over the place, lots of fishing and wildlife. We've got fifteen thousand people if you count the surrounding areas. Wausau is an hour south, with sixty thousand. We're three hours from Green Bay and four hours from Milwaukee."

"The French named Lac du Flambeau," added NAMA Lifetime Achievement recipient Robert "Bobby Bullet" Hollis, "after seeing people fishing with torches in front of their canoes to reflect light in the walleyes' eyes. The idea of fishing at night came to an old man through the spirits. He passed it to the rest of the tribe."

Robert "Bobby Bullet" St. Germaine Hollis (1942–) (Anishinaabe)

In 2021 the *Minocqua (WI) Lakeland Times* declared, "Bobby Bullet is to Indian Country, what Hank Williams is to country music—a legend."[10]

It's a gift to be able to grab a thought and put it down, giving new life to the spirit. I listen to people talking and try to catch sentences and words. In my first attempts at writing songs, I didn't understand what I was doing. I gained wisdom by shopping songs and getting doors slammed in my face. When I started, it would take a thousand words to get a point across. Simplicity, I found, is one of the keys to a good song.

My father, Milan Robert St. Germaine, was killed during World War II when I was about five, and I was adopted by a white man, Ernest Hollis. He married my mother, Julie Ann Marie LaBarge, of French descent, and we moved to Brooklyn, Wisconsin, and then to Cottage Grove [southern Wisconsin]. My wife, Pamela Nesbit, and I have lived in Iron River, Michigan, since 2003.

My aunt, who passed on years ago, would say, "Ernest Hollis isn't your real father; you were adopted," especially after she got a few drinks in her. It was a hush-hush thing, being adopted, but I never quite fit in with my adopted family. My uncle told me that I looked like my dad. He was an artist and liked to tease girls.

I couldn't understand why, but when my stepfather and biological mother would go to the reservation and take me with them, I'd run into children my age and fit in. They talked and acted like me; it was quite an eye-opener. I remember witnessing ceremonies, but I never understood them until much later.

An aunt and uncle had an act in a traveling carnival. They had a dog show and did tricks like bullwhipping the cigarette out of a partner's mouth from ten feet away. They played trick fiddle.

I was about ten when I started playing music. My uncle taught me chords on the guitar, and I just took off from there. TV had just started coming out, but I listened to the radio a lot, especially the Grand Ole Opry out of Nashville. They played different kinds of country music. I was drawn to it, along with storytelling programs like *The Inner Sanctum* and *The Gene Autry Show.*

My uncle played old-time music—fiddles, banjos, guitars—but along with that came drinking. I was very shy. I drank when I started playing music, and that helped ... or so I thought.

I went to Germany with the U.S. Army in 1961 and heard jazz and the blues. Friends took me to bars where Black musicians played. It was a different kind of atmosphere. People were drinking, but they were also listening to what was happening on that little stage. That impressed me. It wasn't like a country bar, where people went to raise hell. I learned a lot.

The Beatles had a toehold in Germany at the time, and country musicians were being shoved to the side. I ended up playing guitar in a USO theater production, *The Boyfriend,* with a bass player. It was all brand new to me. I was still struggling with my three chords on the guitar, but I enjoyed being in the theater. I didn't get many chances to express myself.

Chet Atkins was my first inspiration on guitar. Then it morphed into Jerry Reed, B. B. King, and a number of great guitar players. A lot of blues guitar players played lap guitar.

As a writer, of course, it was Hank Williams. He wrote in a way that the common person could understand. A lot of singers try to put pain into their voices. Sometimes it works. Other times, it sounds manufactured. Hank was genuinely tormented like the painter who cut off his ear. When a person fasts for days, they put their life on the line. Hank Williams, and some of the great writers, experienced that urgency. They were gifted enough to put it down on paper and recordings.

Guy Clark could tell a story, and country music's all about storytelling. What got me attracted to him was seeing all the artists that sang his songs.

I was impressed by the way that he used words in a simple way to get his point across.

Nashville songwriters used to follow Roger Miller around to catch some of his ideas and throwaway words.

Carole King's got my respect as a songwriter; I've sung a few of her songs. Paul McCartney and John Lennon, Paul Simon, Jimmy Webb, Neil Young, Johnny Cash, Kris Kristofferson, Bob Dylan, the list goes on and on. Those writers, to one degree or another, are in my songs.

I started writing short stories when I was young. They were childlike, but they needed to come out. Songs were in my spirit too. In grade school, I wrote "pretend" music. One time, my music teacher played what I had written to the class. When she finished, she asked me to hold my hands up and said, "These are the hands of an artist."

I've had an insatiable appetite for reading about songwriting. I studied the people who wrote the standards, not understanding the process but absorbing it. The Nashville scene had a whole different approach to songwriting.

My songwriting changed with "Strawberry Island." It was about a twenty-six-acre island in Lac du Flambeau that was allotted to John Whitefeather at the turn of the twentieth century, when he was five years old. He sold the island to Walter Mills in 1910. In the midnineties, Mills's descendants considered building single-family condominiums and an airport on the island. The community opposed the idea, and the family agreed to sell the island to them on December 23, 2013. An elder [Mike Chosa], who has now passed, told me, "Bobby, you should write a song about that island. Our young people don't know the story."

17. Bobby Bullett

On that island, there had been a battle in 1745, between the Ojibwe people, who I am, and the Dakota people. Warriors were killed on both sides. Elders warn us to stay off the island. You can hear the spirits at night. Sometimes you can even see fires.

I included "Strawberry Island" on *Crooked Tear* [2012]. What made me think I was on the right path was doing a concert in Wisconsin and looking at the audience. When I was singing that song, I saw people crying. It made me realize the power of music and words and how they open a dialogue.

I ended up going to Canada, where elders told me they'd been waiting for me for three years. Two elders had the same dream, about a month apart, about sharing their traditional teachings. In their dreams, they saw a young man from the south that would help with their gatherings. Turned out, that was me. I picked up the sacred pipe and followed those ways. I followed the elders' instructions for years to fulfill those dreams. One elder commented that I had two gifts—the pipe and my music.

My first CD was *Scrapbook: The Ol' Sage* in 2009. My cousin [Rusty Ward] talked to Bruce Sharp of Black Scotty Records, who said, "Bring your songs in, and let's make an album."

That was my first CD, but I made my first record when I was thirteen. Back then, you could walk into a studio, pay five dollars, and walk out with a record. I got bit by the creation bug. It's still hovering around me.

The NAMAs gave me a Lifetime Achievement Award in 2010 [the Indian Summer Music Awards would do the same four years later]. When they called my name, an usher grabbed my arm and led me to the stage. On the way, I started getting tears in my eyes, thinking about all the people I'd played with who deserved it as much as me. It was very emotional. When I got on stage, I didn't know what to say, but I try to always be as honest as I can when I'm saying something. Most Native people have humor in them, so I said, "If there's reincarnation, I might win this award again."

I received a Folk Arts Masters of Tradition in Songwriting apprenticeship from the Wisconsin Arts Board in 2012. A year later a Native Arts and Cultures Foundation Artist Fellowship enabled me to conduct oral history interviews with Native peoples in Minnesota, Wisconsin, and Michigan and turn their stories into songs. The CD's title, *Justice in Time*, was suggested by Kimberly Acosta of Indian Country Today. Some songs had a bite to them. There's a reason. I like people to sometimes feel the sting, so they understand what's being said.

One song "Shades of Mississippi" was about the fishing wars of the 1980s and '90s and reflected the nation's systemic racism. When Native fishers exercised their treaty rights to spearfish, they were met by violence on the boat landings from non-Natives who didn't understand that treaties were binding legal documents.

My wife and I were asked to write songs and perform with the Ancestral Women's Performance Project, a collaborative theater group honoring Wisconsin's Indigenous women, in 2019. One of the songs, "Grandma Song," honors the elders. It's about how things were back in the days when they had no water, electricity, or TV. They lived a hard but simpler life. Another song, "Here Comes the Children of the Seventh Generation," encourages respect for traditional teachings and reminds us to make decisions with children and the ones not yet born in mind.

The Ojibwe have seven grandfather teachings—wisdom, honesty, truth, bravery, respect, humility, and love. I haven't done everything yet, but I've done enough to share what I've learned with young people. Teaching songwriting to Native youth wasn't about sitting with a guitar and writing stuff down. The kids were opening their souls and spirit; tears were shed. It was a form of healing. One boy wrote about his father, who's been missing since before he was born. His song expressed the loneliness of not having a father. My wife and I kept telling the boy, "We love you. No matter what happens, we love you."

We continue to tell that to all the kids whenever we get together. We hold hands, stand in a circle, and tell them that we love them. That means a lot to them and us. Love is a powerful thing.

A music educator from Milwaukee, Amanda Satchell, joined Pamela and me to promote songwriting and recording with young people from Lac du Flambeau. Currently, we're working with a wonderful singer-songwriter, Jasmine Plasky, the recipient of a Rising Star NAMA in 2019. In one of her songs, "Changes," she sings of growing into a young woman and facing an uncertain world while rooted in the love of her family.

There's a spiritual awakening going on. Native youth are looking back and picking up on ceremonies. It's part of the prophecy that says that when the people come back together in a circle, we will live in true brotherhood.

Paco Fralick (1967–) (Ojibwe and German)

A dentist by trade, guitarist and vocalist Paco Fralick is adept at "blending notes of country, folk, pop, and Native Americana with original and authentic lyrics."[11]

I'm Native on my mom's side—Ojibwe, Chippewa being the English term. My dad, Len Fralick, is mixed. *Fralick* means "happy" in German. I grew up in two worlds. We visited the reservation—my grandma was there—but I mostly grew up in Rhinelander, which is a small Northwoods town about forty-five minutes from the reservation.

Music is in my DNA. My dad played five nights a week when I was young. He knew a thousand or more Hank Williams–Johnny Cash–type country songs, and he had a beautiful voice. With his guitar, he could carry a show by himself. Music was simpler back then; you didn't need all the electronics. He hasn't been able to perform as much as he's gotten older, but he and my mom are still my biggest supporters. I chose my parents well.

Dad practiced in the house with old reel-to-reel recorders, even when I was in the womb, and I absorbed all that music. When I was about four years old, he brought an upright piano home. He put it on the porch and taught me C, F, and G. With those three chords, I could play many of the songs he had been playing. I had a knack for being able to play by ear.

I took classical piano lessons from five to thirteen. I remember playing "Rhinestone Cowboy" at one of my first piano recitals. I also had four years of Suzuki violin. Phyllis Rheume was my teacher for both. She was a good classical player and one of the more influential people in my life, but that music wasn't necessarily what my heart wanted to play. I wish I had learned more theory, but when I got to my teenage years, I started getting into other hobbies and quit the lessons.

My parents ran a bar on the reservation, the Candlewick Inn, that my grandma owned. Her husband had passed away, and the bar was too much for just her. So we lived on the reservation for a year. You might think a tavern wouldn't be a good place for a kid, but everybody knew me. I met people I still know today. Every day after school, I'd grab a handful of quarters and shoot pool. I was a little pool shark. Of course, I saw the negative side of the bar, but I was too young to process that.

My dad was always playing music there on the weekends. I'd sneak out of bed and crawl under the pool table, listening to the band. The floor would be bouncing; there were so many people dancing. It was always fun.

When I was sixteen, my dad was playing on New Year's Eve. I got the bug to play after watching him. Somebody hocked a bass guitar for ten dollars and never came back for it. It became mine. I played it for quite a few years with the Country-Aire Band. Mauri Big John (Maurice William) was our guitarist and fiddle player. I modeled my playing after him. Gene Ciscek was a good jazz drummer. He had played with Frank Sinatra. We played together for twenty years. Looking back, I'm grateful that I had so many opportunities to play with them and my dad. Having gigs kept me wanting to practice and grow.

My dad encouraged me to be a dentist. When I was thirteen, he told me, "You can use your hands," which I like to do, "and be self-employed versus being on call working for a hospital."

It was a quick conversation; I already had my mind set on being a dentist. I went to the University of Wisconsin–Eau Claire for my undergraduate degree.

I continued playing music when I went to college, but I started playing more folk music and music popular in the eighties. I enjoyed playing around campus, but I'd go home on the weekends and play with the band. Music was a great vehicle to meet people.

My first year at school, I was lonely in the beginning. I'd sit in my dorm room thinking about my grandpa George, on my dad's side, who had recently passed. He had recovered from alcoholism. I hadn't seen much of that side of his life, but I saw the effect it had on his body. I wrote my first song, "Daddy, When Are You Coming Home?," about him and performed it for a talent show on campus. It happened to be the second to last stage that Buddy Holly, the Big Bopper, and Richie Valens performed on before their plane crashed on February 3, 1959. Two girls approached me backstage. They told me about their dad, who was struggling with alcohol, and asked for a recording of that song. They thought it would help their family. That was moving to me. It's still one of my favorite songs.

I've forgotten about this until now, but because of that show, I received letters from agencies wanting my songs. I don't know why I didn't act on them, but even now I have a hard time giving my songs to someone else. It may sound weird, but it feels like I'm cutting off a finger or losing a part of myself.

I wrote many songs during that time. Some I didn't like, but I held on to them and, over the years, kept revisiting them. I think it's cool that as my life evolved and my songwriting abilities increased, I was able to complete them. "I Still Wonder" and "Under the Moonlight" appeared on my first album, *Letting Go*.

I try to not get too critical when I'm writing. I start with a theme, idea, or fragment, but I don't know where I'm going until I pick up the guitar. Sometimes I've got to put the guitar down and grab a pencil. Other times, I write the music first. I try to get my mind out of the way, so the music flows through me. I've gotten better at it as I've gotten older. Later I can focus on fine-tuning and tweaking.

I move around and write in different places until the energy is flowing. I may start in the house, but if I get stuck, I'll sit on the dock by the water. It helps.

My best stuff comes out first thing in the morning. Before I do anything, I grab my guitar and see what wants to come out. That's my morning ritual. Vacations tend to be when I get a lot of writing done. I'm not thinking about work, I guess.

After three years at Eau Claire, I passed my admissions test for dental school. I went to Marquette Dental School in Milwaukee and got my first taste of living in the city. It was shocking after growing up in a small town. I didn't even own a tie. On my first day of school, I ran to the drugstore on the corner and bought a clip-on. In class, a friend taught me to tie a real tie.

I married Heidi Beyer while I was going to dental school. We had two daughters, Kailey and Alleigh, while we lived in Milwaukee. I liked having a family while I was in school. It kept me grounded and gave me something to look forward to after a long day.

I had been to the Indian Summer Festival on Milwaukee's lakefront as a kid and remembered liking it. During my first month of dental school, I was invited to play at the festival, but I didn't go. My wife was nervous that if I went too heavily into music, I might not focus on my dentistry.

Living in the city long-term was never in the cards. My wife had the U-Haul packed the day I graduated, and we moved back to Rhinelander, where both of our families were. Our last child, Colton, was born in Rhinelander in 1997.

In addition to practicing as an associate dentist, I worked part-time at a nursing home and for my tribe. I learned from all three environments. After a year and a half, I decided to build my own office. I've worked for five tribes in Wisconsin during my career, helping them to develop dental programs, but I'm most proud of the work I did to build the Peter Christensen Dental Clinic. It's one of the largest tribal dental programs in the country. At the same time, I've always kept my private practice.

Music took a back seat to my career and family during this busy time of life, but it was always there. Like a lot of bands, we were going through ups and downs, so I stepped away to be a one-man band. I had bought Kailey a child's drum set, but she didn't take to it. I thought, "Well, let me see what I can do with it."

Let me back up a step. One day our drummer, Gene Ciszek, and I were sitting in a bar after a gig. He was a real character and a lot of fun. He was demonstrating how he could take his left hand and tap half notes. Then with his right hand, he doubled it. His right foot tripled it, and his left foot quadrupled it. With his voice, he went a fifth time. Then, he flip-flopped them. It was amazing.

That stuck in my head, and I wondered what I could do with drums by playing with my feet. I didn't like electronic drums. I started out playing the bass drum with my left foot and a tambourine with a pedal with my right foot. Later I added a snare drum and started playing shows at the casino. I kept adding pedals and ended up with fifteen pedals that I could rock with my heel or toes. I put drumsticks on my elbow, so I could play guitar. It wasn't as good as having a real drummer, but it was very entertaining.

I could drag the whole kit in as one piece. I had it attached to a piece of plywood. I had the mics hardwired and could set up fast, but I got away from it. It was a good novelty, but it wasn't going to advance my career. I could keep doing local shows and bars, but I wanted to take my music to the next level.

When I was thirty-seven, I started having vivid spiritual dreams that I'd wake up remembering. Sometimes I'd see things ahead of time. In one dream, one of my patients came to me with a message. The next day, I went to work and found out that she had passed away.

My dreams shifted to Native American ideology and stories and sent me on a new path. I started dreaming about eagles, bears, and wolves. Ancestors came to me. It's when my Native American side woke up. I dreamed of a lodge. But I didn't know what that was, so I asked my mom. She said, "I don't know, but my friend Goldie lives in one."

So I called Goldie. She said I could visit her on the Bad River Reservation on Lake Superior's southern shore where she lived. It was a snowy Saturday morning in February when I got there. It was like stepping back in time. There were people doing ceremonies. I didn't know what was happening, but I decided to immerse myself and just go with it. I was invited inside the lodge and went through the blessing line. They were honoring the grandmothers and smudging. I didn't even know what smudging was. When I came to the second grandmother, she said, "You don't know what you're going to do yet, do you?"

I said, "No," and she said, "I do."

I had to keep moving, because the line was moving, but I went over to her later and said, "How do you know?"

She tapped on her necklace and said, "I'm Wolf Clan."

The wolf was coming to me heavily at that time. That's one of our teachings, as I came to learn.

I knew I was in the right spot because other things unfolded that the spirit had to have guided. I went back to Bad River in June, and more affirmations happened. I declared that I wanted to become a spiritual Ojibwe person. That changed my priorities and life. I wasn't so much about money anymore—I had been pretty career focused—and it opened me up. I could understand things I was receiving from the spirit. It influenced my music and the reason I do things.

Spiritual things started happening to me. I was traveling back from Midewiwin ceremonies in Michigan and saw a sign that said, "Hardwick Pines Road."

A friend had told me, "Paco, you're supposed to meet this man, Bruce Hardwick," so I called. I said, "Bruce, I'd like to stop by and say hello."

He said, "Well, I'm a couple of hours from you. Call me when you get close."

When I visited, we talked for a few hours. He was a very spiritual man, but I was still trying to determine the connection. As I was leaving, he said, "You know, I always thought my name was Hardwick. I just found out it's Christensen."

Wow! My mother's birth name was Christensen.

It's a long story, but months before, a man came to me in two different dreams and showed me the dental clinic I would build for my tribe. It turned out that that man in my dreams was Bruce's mentor, Nowatin. His message was that I wasn't to worry about time or money.

When I was forty, Mauri Big John passed away. I had modeled my guitar playing after him. I used to tape our gigs with a cassette player and listen back, to learn to play like him. He even impacted my fiddle playing, though I hadn't played my violin for a few years and stored it under my bed collecting dust. Up until that point, I had played classical music by reading notes, but I dreamed that I was playing bluegrass style, double bowing, like Mauri. I got out of bed and dug the violin out of its case. Surprisingly, I was able to play like in my dream. I must have absorbed it by being around him. He won the Indian Summer Festival fiddle contest a few times. After his family gifted me with his fiddle at his funeral, I thought a good way to honor him would be to take it back to Milwaukee. I played "Orange Blossom Special" the way he would have and won the fiddle contest. It was such a fun experience; I felt like he was there with me.

After the fiddle contest, I walked to the main stage. Michael Bucher was playing. He's a Tsalagi singer-songwriter. I had never met him, but I loved his percussive guitar playing, his voice, and the message of his songs. I thought to myself, "Someday, I'd like to meet him."

In 2004 I stepped down as health director for my tribe and transitioned back to my private practice. After being so busy for so long, I started picking music up again. I was happy to discover that I still could write songs.

When I work in my dental office, I wear gloves. My hands sweat, so I take my wedding ring off and set it on my desk. One day, between patients, I was sitting with my guitar. I couldn't get the sound I wanted—I didn't have a pick—but I saw my ring sitting there. I put it on my thumb and started hammering the strings like a dulcimer. I've had guitar players ask me how I get that sound. I show them. Some people do harmonics better than me. You could do it that way, but my way is a little more versatile.

Lots of people encouraged my renewed musical efforts. One of my patients who knew I hadn't played for a while asked me to play in a nursing home. I remember being nervous, but everybody was in a wheelchair. I had a captive audience.

Through the Three Fires Midewiwin Lodge, I came to know Maryellen Baker, an elder from the Lac Courte Orielles Reservation. She was inspired by dreams to create the Women and Water Symposiums [spiritofthewater .org]. They teach an Indigenous, spiritual approach to caring for the environment and offer healing ceremonies. In our Native teachings, men take care of the fire, and women take care of the water. I've been blessed to know grandmothers like Josephine Mandamin and others that have walked around the Great Lakes carrying their copper vessels of water. Through their energy, they transform that water. When you drink that water, it goes to every cell in your body and can be very transformational. They do that work to heal the earth. Maryellen reached out to me and asked me to perform for their symposiums. It helped resurrect my musical aspirations. Seven years after playing in the fiddle contest, I was performing for one of the Women and Water Symposiums and saw that Michael Bucher was on after me. I thought, "Well, here's my chance to meet him."

It turned into one of those friendships where I felt like I'd known him my entire life. We talked for hours. Then he went home and brought his wife back. We sat and talked for a long while again.

I hadn't heard from him for about six months, when Maryellen told me that Michael had lost three fingers on his right hand in a table-saw accident and wasn't playing anymore. He was in a dark place. I called him and said, "Mike, we should write a song together."

I didn't hear from him for another six months, but one day, he messaged me and said that a song was coming fast. He sent it to me to finish. I felt so honored to work with him; I put everything I could into it. We called it "Women and Water" and put it on *Letting Go*. I'm proud to say that it won Song of the Year in 2018 at the NAMAs. Mike's name recognition might have helped us win that award—he had won three NAMAs prior—but I'm proud of it. It's the only song I've recorded Native flute on.

Going to the awards ceremony was my first trip to New York. Our category was the first award of the night. Someone tapped me on the shoulder and said, "We want you to present an award."

He brought me backstage, but he really had me up there because Mike and I were going to win that award. It was moving; it still is.

Recording *Letting Go* was a learning experience. We started in Tomahawk, Wisconsin, at Clear Blue Studios, and finished in Wausau at White House Productions. I learned what fits me. I feel blessed that the album received several Indian Summer Music Awards, as well as a Global Music Award for Best of Show. Recognition should extend to all the musicians and people in the studio who brought it to life. I started by trying to play as many instruments as possible but realized there were better musicians than me and started hiring session players.

I wrote a song about homeless people, "Homeless Man." We were visiting my daughter in Seattle. I hadn't seen many homeless people before, but I had come across a few while living in Milwaukee. I'd give them apples and blankets when they huddled by the heater. As my spirituality opened, I started looking at things differently. As I was watching homeless people in Seattle and taking it all in, I noticed so many people passing them by. I remember seeing a man packing up his duffel bag in the morning because he was going to be sleeping on a different bench that night. While we were there, one man climbed a four-story tree and blocked traffic. The streets were shut off. He was homeless and making a statement. After twenty-four hours he finally came down. It was national news. When he came down, they put a restraining order against the tree . . . crazy.

All that stuff was affecting me more than I realized. We went out to dinner our last night in Seattle. When we came out of the restaurant, a Black man came out of the darkness and said, "Hey man, you got thirty-five cents for a doughnut?"

I reached into my pocket and gave him some money. One of the ladies gave him her doggie bag. I touched his hand, and it was worn out like leather. I had never seen a hand like that.

When a song is coming, I can tell. It feels like it's rising in me. I've learned to wake myself up because, most of the time, it won't be there in the morning. It was 2:00 a.m. when I wrote "Homeless Man." I didn't have a guitar, but I wrote it in my head. By 5:30 I had the song. When I got back to Wisconsin, I got to play it with guitar. That song is very meaningful to me.

I wrote "Under the Moonlight" three different times. When I was younger, I had to finish a song in one sitting, or it didn't happen. I don't have that problem anymore. Now when I sit down to write, I eventually get a productive song out of it. That song took thirty years. It has a modern country feel. Melissa Salaam-Horner sang with me on it. She has an extraordinarily strong voice.

The title track, "Letting Go," came out of a four-day spiritual fast on the Lac Courte Orielles Reservation. When we do fasts, our physical dominance is lessened, our spiritual side becomes stronger, and we become more open to receiving guidance. I was shown many things about letting go during that fast, things that had been weighing me down. I had conversations with elders in a nursing home. With my son leaving for college, I was shown some things he was going to go through. The discovery was that it was his life to live and if you hold good things back, they can wither and no longer be good.

We had a CD-release party in my hometown, at Nicolet College, and sold out the venue. I had fifteen musicians on stage that recorded with me, including Mike. It happened to be three years from the date of his accident and the first time he was performing publicly. He was very self-conscious about his hand and how people would look at him. But he came, and we played together. It was very healing for him and moving to all of us. He could still play guitar. He uses adhesives to hold the pick. I couldn't tell the difference; he still sounds awesome. He just put out a new album, *This*. We talked last week, and he said, "Let's do dinner and play our new songs for each other."

Some of my songs come from the Native side. "Where Were You?" was about a powerful man, Walter Bresette, from the Red Cliff Reservation near Madeline Island. He opened doors for me even after he passed away. I never met him, but he came to me in dreams when my tribe was going through a difficult time and there was a lot of political unrest. I'd never been an activist, but he had led many movements to stop mining, trains carrying acid through the reservation, and pollution of the Great Lakes. I didn't know that he was showing me events ahead of time, until there was a peaceful sit-in at the tribal center to bring awareness to important issues. I wanted to help remember him and carry on some of his messages, so I wrote that song. I remember I had a hard time finding an intro I liked.

"In Seven Generations" was about the difficulties our tribe was going through. There were lands at risk and bad investments. I was awoken to it in a dream. There was a healing lodge in the parking lot of our casino. It was full of elders who had passed away. They reassured me about things that we were all stressed about. That song talked about that and captured that moment in time.

Most of my songs have stories in them. I wrote "Home in My Mind" about my best friend growing up. I remembered being in dental school during my first year in Milwaukee. I was waxing teeth with the window open in our second-story apartment. You could sometimes hear shooting and a lot of troubling sounds outside at night. Music helped me feel centered amid the chaos and stress.

On "Take My Breath Away" we had mandolin and violin. I wrote about my wife, Heidi, and the essence of our relationship. We've been together for thirty years. We've gone through a lot and have made a good life for ourselves. I love her more now than I did in the beginning; it's a much deeper connection. She supports my music and takes on responsibilities that allow me to be creative. Sometimes she gets stressed out about the cost of recording, but I think that's normal for spouses of musicians.

I wrote a classical piano instrumental for my wife, "Heidi's Song," in 1989. I wrote it in my biochemistry class, trying to write a song for our wedding party to march down the aisle to. I didn't have a piano, so I just imagined it in my head. I met pianist Connor Chee at the NAMAs. He's helping me embellish this song. I plan to add a string quartet when we record it.

We were halfway through our second album when COVID hit. The studio closed, so we weren't able to finish it yet. I've got twenty new songs, so I might record a double album when we get back to work. I've learned a lot since my first record. This new album has fewer players, but the songs breathe better. I'm learning to appreciate the power of silence in a song.

Kirk Starkey has been producing and managing the strings for me. He plays cello for Quartetto Gelato. His wife's Native, so he identifies with my music and messages. We rented space in a church in Hamilton, Canada, and we've been recording there. It was expensive, but it sounds so good. The songs are even more diverse.

One of my new songs, "Penokee Hills," is about mining in Wisconsin. I wrote it right before they stopped what would have been the world's largest open-pit iron mine, with the waste flowing into Lake Superior and affecting some of the best wild rice beds in the United States.

"That Old Trout Stream" is about the grandfather I mentioned before. Even though he was sick, he'd take me trout fishing when I was a kid. Those are great memories. I still love to fish. After he passed, my aunt Helen found a poem he had written talking about how good he felt when he was out on the stream. It's a moving song. I cried in the studio when I was recording the vocals. That doesn't happen often.

I wrote "The American Dream" a few months ago. It's not meant to be political or anti-American. But let's face it—things could be better. We're not realizing our potential. The song touches on everything—homelessness, greed, the environment, racism, and spirituality. It includes excerpts by Martin Luther King Jr., John F. Kennedy, and John Trudell. I'm hoping to add a gospel choir.

In 2018 I opened for an Irish band, Switchback, in Madison, Wisconsin. Public TV filmed it. They liked my songwriting and, after the show, offered me a James McCandless Scholarship to attend their annual songwriter's retreat in Dubuque, Iowa. I decided to go. Being the recipient of a scholarship, I felt extra pressure on myself. Before the retreat, I purchased a book on songwriting. The retreat was in a beautiful spot, this old bed-and-breakfast house. Rivers were converging, and there were a lot of bluffs nearby. There were Native burial mounds on the property, so I went over and put tobacco down before the retreat began. Kevin Gordon, a songwriter out of Nashville, was our mentor. There were fourteen other songwriters in the house. We each had one day to come up with a song and perform it for the group. I was nervous, because I had never written a song on a strict timeline. I started with an idea—walking in both worlds—and applied the new techniques I had learned. I spent most of the morning mining for data, when the song seemed to take on a new direction on its own. As the day went on, others were saying they were almost done with their song. I only had a few lines by dinnertime. That evening, we attended a concert. I stayed up afterward and managed to write one verse and part of another before I fell asleep. The next morning, I got up early and grabbed my guitar. Immediately, a bridge popped out and a chorus. I had the song finished in time for breakfast. I was relieved. The song is called "The Great Divide." It's very fitting for the political times we're in. We have our differences, but we're all connected by spirit.

Two years ago I was performing at the Indian Summer Festival. Jan Michael Looking Wolf was on after me. He approached me and said, "Hey bro, can I borrow your guitar to play a song before my flute set?"

I said, "Sure," and went into the audience to listen. I was so surprised when he started by saying, "I'd like to gift this song ['We Too Can Shine'] to Paco."

No one had ever done anything like that for me before. What an honor! We've become good friends. He always makes me feel good about my music. He has a gift that way, lifting and inspiring other musicians. That song has gone through evolutions and grown into a fun project. When we recorded it, we had Native singers on it. In addition to Jan and me, we had Michael Bucher, Keith Secola, Sandra Sutter, Kelly Derrickson, and others. Connor Chee played really beautiful piano.

I've worked hard as a dentist. I've been a workaholic and missed out on things at home. The morning my son drove away for college was particularly tough. He was our last child, so it seemed more final. My wife went for a walk, and by the time she got back, a song had come to me. I had it almost all written. It was a combination of the fast and the emotions of Colton leaving, but it was also about the circle of life. As I get closer to retirement, I hope to keep writing good music and getting better at recording and producing. I want to travel and play my original music. I've put family and career ahead of it for a long time, but I want to pursue what I've put on hold, whatever that is, and use my music to heal. There's a whole world waiting.

Canada

Each First Nation played and sang distinct music long before the arrival of the French or English. Prohibitions against Indigenous cultural expression after the Dominion of Canada was established on July 1, 1867, became increasingly restrictive. The Indian Act of 1884 banned the cherished potlatch ceremony. The sun dance and other sacred ceremonies were forbidden shortly afterward. The bans wouldn't be lifted until the revision of the Indian Act in 1951. "Our objective is to continue," swore Duncan Campbell Scott, deputy superintendent general of Indian Affairs, in 1920, "until there is not an Indian that has not been absorbed into the body politic, and there is no Indian question, and no Indian Department."[12]

Dr. Duke Redbird (1939–) (Ojibwe)

Speaking out against the oppression, Duke Redbird used poetry (often set to music) to deliver some of the First Nations' strongest messages. A veteran of the 1960s and '70s folk music circuit and an elder of the Saugeen First Nation, Ontario, he served as vice president of the Native Council of Canada (1974–76), director of land claims research for the Metís and Non-Status Indian Association (1978–80), and president of the Metís and Non-Status Indian Association (1980–83). Founding editor of *The Thunderbird*, Canada's first national Indigenous newspaper, he became the first Indigenous reporter on a Canadian major television network, covering entertainment for CityTV from 1994 to 2006.

Canada's federal government denied our community and people their culture. It was against the law to teach or learn our languages. They were trying to erase the Indigenous. I couldn't learn my language, which is Ojibwe, Anishinaabe, or Algonquin, as it's known on the Eastern Seaboard, so I substituted poetry. Even today, if I want to explain a concept or idea, I use poetry instead of prose. It makes much more sense and is far clearer.

My mother died in a house fire when I was thirteen months old, and I was placed in a foster home. I didn't get back to my family until I was sixteen. During that first period, I only spoke English. I've been engaged in my own culture for the last sixty years, but I learned how Western civilization lived, acted, and thought and how different it was from the Indigenous way of life.

I traveled all over Canada and the United States on the folk circuit. That's where I met a wonderful musician, singer, and comedian Jud Strunk. He was a cast member of Rowan and Martin's *Laugh-In*. He would write a song, "Daisy a Day," that reached number thirteen on the country charts in 1973.

Jud's band, the Coplin Kitchen, opened for Glen Campbell, who invited me to go on tour with them. I'd recite a poem, and the curtain would open. There'd be Jud and his band. It was fun for the audience. They'd be expecting him to open the show, and this young Native guy would walk to the microphone and tell a poem. The audience would quiet down. When the curtain opened and Jud was there, there'd be big applause. We had fun trying different things.

It was during the Vietnam War, and there were lots of songs about peace. People who went to folk festivals or coffeehouses were very liberal in their ideas. Poetry coming out of the states spoke loudly about issues affecting American reality. Up here in Canada, it wasn't as harsh. I don't think any Canadian poet could write a poem like Allen Ginsberg's "Howl." Our politics are different.

For a while, Joni Mitchell and I lived in the same rooming house. As young kids, we were always looking for the cheapest rooms. We were all as poor as church mice. She moved into a room across the hall. She was in particularly bad shape, because she was about to have a child. We all helped one another.

The United States fought an Indian war and eventually conquered the Indigenous peoples, but we never had a war. We could share the resources of the land through the Dish with One Spoon Treaty [an agreement that traces back to 1142, agreed to by the Anishinaabe and Haudenosaunee, in Montreal, in 1701], but the French and the English reneged on all their promises and stole the land. Canada is the result of two land developers swindling Indigenous peoples out of their land. The English wanted to control the French, but the French said, "No way, we have a deal. We want our language recognized."

They have a province, Québec, where they're allowed to speak French, but the Indigenous people were never invited into confederations. We're still marginalized and left out of the political picture. It impacts my work every day.

Winston Wuttunee and I started working together in the seventies. We remain very, very close friends and speak regularly. We wrote poems and songs together. He's a very spiritual person. The same goes for Shingoose [Curtis Jonnie]. He had a stroke a few years ago and lives in a nursing home, but I keep in touch with him. He can't play the guitar anymore, but he's still writing songs. I met the Goose, as I call him, at folk festivals. We'd get together sometimes with Winston and travel as a group. It was a beautiful era.

Shingoose and I put out an EP in 1975. It was the size of a single, but it had four songs. "Living on Indian Time" and "Peace Pipe Song" were by Shingoose, and "Sweet Alberta" and "Silver River" were by me. We couldn't get a record deal, so we took what little money we had, created our own company [Native Country], and released it. Bruce Cockburn played backup guitar. We tried to get airplay by sending it to radio stations, but we didn't get any. We sold the copies we had, and then it disappeared. Years later musicologist Kevin Howes came across it in a used record store. He got in touch with me and said, "We'd like to put your songs on a compilation." *Native North America,* volume 1, *Aboriginal Folk, Rock, and Country 1966–1985,* came out on Seattle-based Light in the Attic in 2014.

My reports on CityTV broadcast in British Columbia, the Yukon, the Northwest Territories, and Newfoundland. I became known as the Seacoast Reporter, but the Canadian cable industry found it cheaper to purchase American programs than develop local talent.

In July 2020 "Power of the Land" reached the top ten on the Indigenous music charts. I recorded it with Chris McKhool and his band, Sultans of String, and Twin Flames. I had written the poem and recited it at Koerner Hall in Toronto, where Canada's Global Orchestra performs. They invited me to a land acknowledgment, which is important in Canada these days. At least the Canadian government has given us that much recognition, to say, "Indigenous people still have a claim on the land."

I met Chris McKhool at that event. He said, "I love that poem. Would you be interested in having us put music to it?"

I said, "I'd be happy for you to do it."

He brought Twin Flames—Jaaji [Mohawk and Inuk] and Chelsey [Métis and Algonquin] June—to the session. They're such lovely young people, real salt of the earth. The Creator wanted it to happen. The idea fell together in a cool way.

There are only forty million people in Canada; the market is small. Taylor Swift sells forty million records an hour; it's difficult to compete with that. We're mice in comparison, although, as you know, elephants are sometimes nervous about mice.

Leela Gilday (1974–) (Dene)

The official website of Northwest Territory–born Leela Gilday describes how she "weaves her experiences as a northerner, a member of the Dene Nation, and a traveler into a beautiful world that transports the listener."[13]

My brother, Jay, and I were born in Yellowknife, the capital of the Northwest Territory. We don't have a large enough population [forty-three thousand] to support a full-time music career. That's why I travel so much.

I'm used to having space around me and feeling like I belong to the land. Everyone who comes here is immediately taken by its vastness. That's not to say that it's pristine or uncharted. My people have walked these lands for thousands of years. Everywhere you see, my people have been. A couple of months ago, I was talking to the Yellowstone chief. He told me that in the 1920s, there were twenty-nine villages along the northern shore of Great Slave Lake [the deepest lake in North America]. The pandemic of the 1920s wiped out a lot of people.

The Dene are different from tribes in the South. We don't have the sun dance. The Dene worldview is of being an extension of the land. We're not separate from it. Our ceremonies revolve around that relationship. We acknowledge the land and water. We lay out tobacco. We feed the fire.

There are small ceremonies that are part of our lives. We don't go into tents and fast; that's not our tradition.

We were colonized last of all the places in Canada, but we experienced regressed colonization and conversion by the Catholic Church. Many of our people became Catholic, but everything Native American was frowned upon by the church. We lost our larger ceremonies. But every Dene community still has traditional drummers, and there's a movement to mentor more. We have dances on Easter, Christmas, weddings, and funerals. Every event is marked by a gathering.

Lots of Dene musicians sing George Jones and Hank Williams–style country music. There's folk music and old-timey scene, rock, and pop as well. The young generation is into rap and hip-hop. We run the gamut.

I started singing when I was a baby. I was eight when I did my first solo performance. My dad's a trombone player and composer. He's from Ontario and played in their symphony. He also played with swing jazz bands. When he moved to just outside of Yellowknife, he worked as a music teacher. He had a folk group, the Gum Boots, that played tradi-

tional Canadian, Scottish, and Irish music, and more modern stuff. My mom loved music too. I grew up surrounded by it.

I started with art songs, but when I auditioned for the University of Alberta in the tenth grade, I switched to classical singing. I have respect for classical music, but I realized that it wasn't the direction my heart was drawn.

I started writing songs as a teenager, but I wasn't serious about it. When I finished my music degree in 1997, I started focusing on songwriting as a way of expressing my own stories and my own reality. My first album was an experiment. I recorded it in Toronto, with John Switzer producing.

He held my hand through the process. He was really kind. We made the record over nine months. I was still working a full-time job. I'd come to the studio every Tuesday.

Since moving temporarily to Vancouver in 2003, I've been writing about missing and murdered Indigenous women. It became very personal to me. One of my dear friends lost her sister. Three weeks ago a relative of mine was murdered in Yellowknife. On a larger scale, these problems are the fallout of colonization, the legacy of displacement, and government policies designed to eradicate Indigenous people.

Another theme that flows through my music is mental health. I sing about people stigmatized by mental health issues and try to take the shame out of their struggle. We have a high rate of suicide in the North. Everyone's lost a friend or a family member.

"One Drum," from my second album, *Sedzé* [2008], was a unifying song. I get a lot of requests for it. I wrote it for, what we called at the time, a national aboriginal arts gathering. It was powerful. There were amazing artists from across the country talking about the planet, art, protests, and opportunities. We put our heads together and created a community. We put on a show, and I was asked to write a song for the finale. I was intimidated—there were some heavy hitters among us—but I sat in my hotel room and wrote it in a couple of hours. I wanted something that everybody could sing in harmony and express unity and togetherness.

Sedzé earned me my first JUNO award as the Best Indigenous Album of 2008. It made it possible for me to make a living playing music and moving forward. I got an agent, toured all over Canada, and reached out to other countries.

Eleven years later I got my second JUNO award for *North Star Crossing* [2019]. It was my best work. It was a long time coming. I was touring but going through personal struggles and not writing much. You've got to put new material out every two years, but my heart wasn't in it. There were five years between *Heart of the People* and *North Star Crossing*. I took time to think about what I wanted to say to the world. They were the most important messages I could deliver.

As an independent artist, I'm not putting records out to make the big bucks. The album was about healing and empowerment. It was a distillation of the things I wanted to focus on, like the water protectors at the

Dakota Access Pipeline protest. The refrain of "Rolling Thunder" is "We could choose money, or we could choose life."

Tanya Tagaq and I went to high school together. She's a dear friend, and I wanted to feature her on "Rolling Thunder." She's such a fierce performer, I felt she could get behind the message of the song. She did it with honor.

It's our responsibility as Indigenous peoples to stand up for our land and water and protect them for future generations. It's crazy to think there would have to be a fight, but we live in the middle of a capitalistic paradigm. The earth is crying; the pandemic is an expression of that. It's a warning bell to remind us to shift back into balance.

There were a couple of love songs on the album. One was to my husband ["Let It Roll"] and the other was to my land and territory ["Falling Stars"]. I made a video of it. It's based on a traditional Dene Teton song.

"K'eintah Natse Ju" [We are healing together] was very personal. It wasn't autobiographical, but it was about healing within our Indigenous family. I've struggled with depression all my life, but it became clear to me that it needed to be discussed. When you talk about something, it eliminates the mystery and takes the power away from it. If I talk about my depression, it makes it less stressful to step forward. I want people to know they're not alone. I was moved to write "North Star Calling" for anyone who needed to hear it.

I worked with a new producer, Toronto-born multi-instrumentalist Hill Koukoutis, who really pushed me. She involved me in every aspect, from choosing tracks to helping to set the mood of the record. I'm a strong singer, but that can be something singers hide behind. In the past, I relied on my voice to wow people, but I didn't allow myself to be as vulnerable as I wanted until Hill brought it out of me.

I had a summer of touring scheduled to promote *North Star Calling*, but everything was canceled. At first I was panicking about whether I'd be able to make a living, but I've come to where I'm at peace. It'll unfold the way it's going to unfold.

Jay Gilday (1977–) (Dene)

The Alberta Music Industry Association praises Leela Gilday's younger brother, Jay Gilday, for "[threading] together the colours of his own ancestral traditions: Dene spirituals, Irish ballads, Canadian folk and rock."[14]

I have a day job as a letter carrier. It's a good job for a musician. I get to take as many breaks as I want as long as I get the job done. John Prine was a mail carrier. Last year I played at the Edmonton Folk Festival. John was supposed to play, but he had a heart attack.

If you play six-string acoustic guitar in Canada, you're going to be playing a couple of Gordon Lightfoot songs. Stan Rogers too. I saw him right before he died in June 1983. His songs were some of the first I latched onto.

I acquired the folk tradition from my dad, but I got the fire of my louder stuff from Jimi Hendrix. I heard him when I was a teenager, and that was it for me. I played blues and rock on top of folk music for a long time.

There are lots of good songwriters in Canada. Ben Spencer and Ben Sures are phenomenal. They're always getting on me about my lyrics. My songs typically come music first.

I studied anthropology at the University of Alberta but never took a degree. After five years, I realized I wasn't going to be working in my field, so I took off. I did other things, but it taught me about research and collaboration. They're good tools to have.

I toured British Columbia folk clubs in 2019. They wanted something more than my solo act, so I put together a band. It's fantastic to play with a band, easy to take your ideas and build them as big as you want, but I write differently for my band than I do for myself. They're separate catalogs.

I have a fire inside me, but it doesn't present itself as Native. It's not up to me to teach you everything about my culture. You can do the work. I'm just trying to live my life. I've gotten gigs because I qualified, but I play music that's comfortable for the broader population.

In my teens, I visited my sister, Leela, in Edmonton, where she moved for a couple of years. I was supposed to go back to Yellowknife but ended up hitting the highway with friends and busking across Canada before making it back to Edmonton and setting up camp. I've been here since. I ended up meeting my wife here.

20. Jay Gilday

Yellowknife, where Leela and I were born, is in a beautiful part of the world. Our parents' house is on one of the largest bodies of water in North America. There's a huge amount of isolated territory, but Yellowknife has all the amenities of a tiny city. Within the Northwest Territories, it's considered a big city. Edmonton [more than eight hundred miles south] is the closest major center. That's where the university is. It's a natural evolution for any kid wanting to expand his or her horizon to go there.

Mom's family is Dene. She grew up about three hundred kilometers north of Yellowtail. She's our biggest fan. She does environmental reviews for the government, mostly under contract, and is close with the Dene people. She's a community liaison for the people in the North. Dad's family is from just outside of London, Ontario. He's been a music teacher for fifty years, but he's also a big band jazz trombonist. He plays Tommy Dorsey style.

It was interesting to grow up in two worlds, but I sometimes felt like I wasn't part of either of them. When I was in the city, I felt like a Dene. Out in the bush, I felt like a white kid in the Dene world. One foot in, one foot out.

When I came back to Edmonton, I wasn't looking to make music a career. I looked for jobs, but I didn't try making money with music until it started driving me nuts that I didn't have any records to my name. I made an album, but I was neck-deep with children and couldn't promote it. It wasn't until 2016, when I put out *Faster than Light*, that I started to have time to travel with my family or by myself. I was able to promote the CD. I stuck with it and started to get royalties. I felt good about it, so I kept going. *The Choice and the Chase* [2019] included songs that I'd been working on and some old songs that I needed to put down.

I'm going to be recording another record, but I'm taking time with the lyrics and trying to bring more cohesiveness to the songs. A lot of my songs are stand-alone, but I'd love to make a concept album.

I've been able to work through the pandemic. My wife's a registered nurse, so she's been working too. She does hospice home care. This pandemic has made the divisions between Canada and the United States clearer than ever. Hopefully, we can learn from each other.

Sandra Sutter (Cree Metís)

In a review of her album *Cluster Stars*, WRUV describes how Sandra Sutter's "original music speaks to her heritage/roots as a Metis/Cree woman and is so emotionally moving."[15]

It's going to take all of us to create a world we can survive in. You've got to make music that's accessible to everyone. The family that raised me wasn't musical. But my birth mother played piano, and my birth father played saxophone. I play both. That's where the music comes from.

I live in Calgary, Alberta, Canada. We're a million people geographically spread out. I was adopted, but I'm one of the luckiest people in the world. I've got friends whose stories haven't worked out as well as mine. My families are interconnected now. They're friends, and they hang out. I remember going to a wedding in rural Alberta, in the middle of nowhere. My birth uncle and his wife had been together for thirty years. But their granddaughter thought it was time for them to get married, so they did. I'd known them for ten years. The bride was an hour late. Everybody was sitting in the hot sun, waiting for her to show up, and talking. It wasn't a big deal. Somebody brought a case of beer out and cracked it open. We enjoyed a cold beer and talked about nothing, like it was normal. I knew I was with family, people I belonged to. It was an everyday experience for them and profound to me.

There are two significant things in my memory about music. My dad arranged for a piano to be brought to the house. That was an amazing thing for my brothers and me. My brothers didn't stick with music, but I fell in love with that piano.

I'm not sure why I was so attracted to Patsy Cline, other than the beautiful music she created and her tragic story. She and her mother sewed

21. Sandra Sutter

her costumes until their fingers bled. The Creator blessed her. Her voice connected to spirit, but it's easy to idolize a ghost. A fifteen-year-old First Nations girl, Tina Fontaine, was found in the river in Winnipeg in August 2014, and many women and girls are missing. Nobody talks about them except their families. We need to honor and recognize them. Why put so much attention on somebody in the public eye and so little on marginalized people?

I used to sing while standing on a hill [really a mound of dirt] next to our house while a house was being built. I'd make a neighborhood kid listen to me like he was my audience and that was my stage. That's appropriate for a girl from the prairie; he listened.

I wrote my first song when I was twelve. It wasn't too good, so I got away from writing for a while. I played in the high school band and took piano lessons. As a pianist, I backed people auditioning for the royal conservatory or a festival.

I saw in the paper that a jazz band, Shadowplay, was looking for a lyricist and singer. I called and went over to meet them. I took some tracks home and worked on them, trying to feel what the writers intended emotionally in the music.

They were advanced jazz players. When I went to my first rehearsal, I felt so intimidated that I shrunk into a corner. They gave me a mic and started playing one of the songs. I started singing. Thirty seconds into this first song, the drummer, this big guy named Jim Bailey, said, "Stop!"

I thought, "Oh no, I must be terrible," but he said, "Welcome." And that was it. We wound up playing together for four years. I wrote all the lyrics for them. They'd do crazy things like name a song something they thought I could never write lyrics to, and I'd have to come up with it. It was fun.

Years before my album *Cluster Stars*, I put out a three-song EP, *Peaceful Nation*. It was a good learning experience. I was blessed to be surrounded by people who encouraged me. We wrote the title song for the National Aboriginal Day opening ceremonies in Calgary.

I got my hands into so many things that I needed someone to help me stay focused on my creative output. The organization I was working with hired a professional coach for me, Marlene Cameron. We'd meet once a week and talk about my priorities and what was going on in my life. I would say, "I'd love to put out an album when I have enough money, enough time, and when I feel the product was ready."

She challenged me, saying, "What's stopping you?" and making me commit to a date to do it. That's how that EP came about. It was nerve-racking, but it was fun.

The Alberta Foundation for the Arts funded *Cluster Stars*. My grant writer, Stephanie Hutchison, said, "If you could have anyone you want to work on this album with you, who would you pick?"

I'm an Indigenous person in Canada, so I immediately said, "Vince Fontaine, of course."

"Find out if he'll work with you, and we'll add him to the grant."

Vince agreed to do it. He's an interesting person to work with. He said that his job was making sure I was ready when we went into the studio with [coproducer] Chris Burke-Gaffney [Orphan, the Pumps, and Harlequin]. The songs were already written. We workshopped a few, but he'd say that the best thing they could do was create an environment where I was comfortable enough for them to get the best performance out of me.

Vince would pick me up at the hotel in the morning. We'd have breakfast and drive around until he thought I was in the zone. Then we'd go to the studio and be there for hours. We recorded twelve songs in one weekend—the lead vocals and all the backup vocals.

We started each session with a ceremony with tobacco and a smudge. We made sure we were always grounded spiritually before we engaged in the work. We had elders praying that our album would create an understanding of things that impact Indigenous people and share our beautiful culture with non-Indigenous people and Indigenous people who didn't know our culture. We want our message to be heard by everyone.

Cluster Stars was an emotional journey. The elders taught me to let people learn in a way that they didn't know they were learning. "Mountain Song" was a reminder of our strength and our connection to our ancestors and to the land.

I used bagpipes on "Peaceful Nation" because they're part of my heritage too. The song teaches about things important to us like water, how to start the day, and the nature of people. That story I told about looking in mirror reflections until seeing what I thought was a warrior, that was the chorus. It says, "Do you know when you look at me, you see not only my history."

As to the last song, "Goodbye," we may think we've come a long way, but every day, for Indigenous people, the carpet is ripped out from under us. I could go on and on about the social issues, but how did we go from being strong and grounded to a place where children are still taken away?

At an event, Chief Vincent Yellow Old Woman [Siksika] and I were sitting beside each other at lunch. He leaned over and said, "You're a singer-songwriter, aren't you? Could you write a song for me?"

When an elder asks you to do something, you do it, so I said, "I can do that."

"Make sure it has these six words in it: 'kill the Indian in the child.'"

I got shivers, because I had just written those six words in the binder I was carrying. You know the Creator's got a plan when things like that happen. I worked on that song with Jim Peace. It's about Chief Vincent's journey to the non-Indigenous western society. Jim's a cowboy, but he's objective. We hashed out some ideas and came up with the skeleton of the song. Jim started making me mad, because he kept saying, "Sandra, you can't say this; you can't say that."

I didn't kick him out of my house. But he left, and I finished the song. I never gave him another chance to contribute to the lyrics, but I couldn't find the music for it. Both of us tried, but nothing was feeling right. Along comes this conference, and I'm supposed to perform this song, "Indian in the Child," for Chief Vincent. I'm freaking out, because it's not a song. It's a poem, a spoken-word piece. I turned to my band and said, "Can you play something Leonard Cohen–ish?"

There were about 150 people in the room—lots of people I knew and the chief. Most of the audience knew the subject deeply, so I kept my head down and occasionally looked sideways at Chief Vincent. When I finished,

I looked up and everybody was on their feet, not clapping, but crying. That was such a powerful moment. It taught me so much. You've got to listen to the Creator. Your instincts are almost always right if you're grounded.

Patriarchy contributes to Indigenous women going missing and being murdered. The story of Pocahontas devalues the role of Indigenous women. I might write a song called "Patriarchy and Pocahontas," but I'm not sure where the rhymes would be.

I've heard that the music business is cutthroat and competitive, but I don't find that in the Indigenous world. Country music is a brotherhood, like guys on motorcycles who have a secret wave as they drive down the highway, but for Indigenous people, music is a connection to all creation and to one another.

My birth certificate didn't mention that I was Native. When I was seven or eight, I sat on a bathroom counter, angled the mirror so I could see behind me, and looked at reflection after reflection. In the back reflection, I saw an Indigenous warrior. Were the ancestors reaching out to me or my imagination? I didn't know, but I questioned my parents regularly, "Are you sure I'm not Native."

I knew where I belonged, but I had nothing to back it up. When I was twenty-two, I got to look at a registry of baptisms at St. Paul's Cathedral in Saskatoon. It's an amazing building, and I felt intimidated. There was a mix-up with the name of the woman who adopted me. I talked to the administrators and told them that my mom's name was incorrect. Her name was Marie Lorraine Sutter. They said, "No, no, we took it right out of the baptismal registry. We wrote it exactly as your mom registered it."

They pulled out this big dusty book of baptisms, flopped it open, and turned to the year that I was baptized. There indeed was my name—Sandra Lynn Sutter. My mom's name was spelled incorrectly, but my dad's name was right. When my mom and dad showed me my birth certificate, they showed me the birth certificate that had my birth name on it—Rita June MacLeod. It showed that my ancestry was Scottish and German. The baby baptized immediately before Sandra Lynn Sutter was Rita June MacLeod. That was me. My birth mother had me baptized in that church—the baptism before. Is that crazy or what? That's how I found my birth mother's name, Loretta Catherine MacLeod. I hired a private detective to hunt her down. He worked for a couple of years but couldn't find her.

In the midnineties, when we were getting better at internet searches, a friend searched through the nonidentifying background history of my birth mother's family provided by Social Services. It showed a fair number of siblings, eight or nine of them, and revealed what they did for a living, so he could track my birth family. He found a woman. There was another woman in her family with the same number of kids, and all the men in her family were in the occupations that the nonidentifying history had said. My uncle Clayton was a firefighter. He was easy to confirm.

One of the women in that family was Rita June MacLeod, which was my name at birth. We thought, in all our wisdom, that the Catholic Church must have put the wrong name on my birth certificate. I figured they mixed up the information, but as it turned out, my birth mother named me after her sister Rita June MacLeod. My friend tracked her down. She lives in Calgary. We wrote her a letter. She wrote back and said, "I'm your aunt. Your mother is Loretta Catherine MacLeod. I'll connect you, but since you're in Calgary, why don't you come and meet your grandmother, your other auntie, Rose MacLeod [Constantine was her married name], and me?"

That was the non-Indigenous side of my family. Through them, I reconnected with my birth mother. She told me the name of an uncle, Will, on my birth father's side who lived in Saskatchewan, so I phoned him. We talked for a minute. I told him who I was. "My father's Darryl Ziegler."

Cool as a cucumber, he said, "Let me call you back."

My birth father never knew my birth mother was pregnant. He died tragically in a car accident before I was born.

After we hung up, Uncle Will called his brother Gyll and said, "This woman says she's Darryl's daughter; I don't know what to do."

Uncle Gyll said, "Call her back. Get her to come to Saskatoon, and we'll meet her."

I drove to Saskatoon and met Uncle Will, who told me stories about the family. At one point, I was sitting at his kitchen table. He had gone away to do something. I saw this picture on the wall. When he came back, he caught me staring at it and said, "Your father painted that when he was in prison."

After Uncle Will died, Uncle Gyll gave that painting to me. My mom, who adopted me, is an artist. She reframed it for me. She made it look beautiful and kept my father's handwriting so I could see it. It's a picture of the Last Supper.

It was a shock to hear that my father had been in prison. He did a decent amount of time, but he was so well-respected by the police that when he died, they had an honor guard at his funeral. In my mind, he was James Dean—this cool guy. Everybody who tells me about him says the same thing.

I look exactly like my birth father. I showed a picture of him as a young man to my dad who adopted me, next to a picture of me in the eighth grade, and he said, "Why are you showing me pictures of yourself?"

Some of the family was suspicious. They thought I wanted something, but like Uncle Gyll said, "We don't have anything. She can't want our money. All she wants is to know her family and her roots."

There were thirteen kids in my birth father's family. I got close to Uncle Gyll. I'd visit or talk to him on the phone about what I'd learned about the residential schools and the work done by the Truth and Reconciliation Commission in Canada. You talk about truth before you engage along the path to reconciliation. Uncle Gyll did some research of his own. He called his brother and sister. They were raised in Saskatoon, not on a reserve or Metís settlement. He asked them, "When you went away to school, did you go to residential school?"

Nobody in the family knew. That happens all over. People don't talk about painful things, but we've got to help them to experience them through music and work through what they need to work through.

That's the Cree Metís side of my family. Some family members embraced their history. Others didn't because of the racism that existed years ago and still does. They chose to identify with the German side of their roots and didn't advertise that they were Indigenous.

It's important to get young people involved. I met a young beatbox player, Deion Blackman, from Cold Lake First Nation, Alberta. He's going to come to the studio and record with us. We're going to do a traditional Christmas song. Before we met, his dad told me he was a beatboxer, and I thought to myself, "What's that?"

I wound up sitting next to him in a hotel restaurant and asked, "If I sing a cappella, could you beatbox to it?"

We started jamming, and it was so much fun. I said, "You're on my next album."

I'm working on a book of lyrics and music. There'll be photographs and cutaway pages that kids can color. We need to be accessible to our youth and have that balance that the elders talk about, but we also need to be role models so people don't think we're so untouchable they can't do it themselves. Our young people are just so beautiful, and so many are doing amazing things. I can't wait to see what the world looks like five years or ten years from now.

Kelly Margaret Derrickson (Syilx Okanagan)

In an article for *Revelstoke Review*, David Wylie describes Kelly Derrickson's songs as "often an honest perspective on the challenges facing Indigenous communities."[16]

My music is for every person, Native or not. I want it to be a learning experience. I hope that when the next generation is old enough to understand, they'll learn about our people through my music. Our history is peaceful. All we want to do is protect this planet, the land, and the spirit. Our ancestors are directing me in everything I do. I'm not doing it to be famous or rich but to send a message and elevate our people.

I've played bluegrass, country music, musical theater, and rock and roll. I was even in a metal band. Growing up, I listened to the Beatles and Elvis Presley. My mom, brother, and I used to play oldies and dance in the living room before supper. I love country music—Johnny Cash and Dolly Parton. It's raw and spoken from the heart. When I was going to the Berklee College of Music in Boston, I absorbed Ella Fitzgerald and Sarah Vaughn. I didn't have a clue about jazz before, but it opened a whole new universe for me.

I coined the term "country tribal rock." My music has all three aspects. Record companies wanted me to go R&B, pop, or country, but I couldn't do it. Music comes out of my soul. I embrace all of it. This is who I am. I don't care to be like anybody else.

I've been going, going, and going since my first album, *Warriors of Love* [2014]. It had songs, like "A Man like That," that resonated with me as soon as I heard them. I had been abused in a relationship and understood that there were many levels of domestic violence. It was important for me to sing that song.

I wrote the majority of *I Am* [2017]. Each album has to be not just a sequel but something more. If you're not better each time, you should go back to the drawing board. Time, learning, and experience go into it.

There was controversy over "All I See Is Red [Ten Little Indians]," written with my drummer Benny Cancino. I put all my love—my entire being—into what I do. I want songs to be meaningful and shake people. I don't want audiences thinking, "That was a pretty song."

They're not always perfect or pretty, but they're about what's going on. Life could be bittersweet and heartbreaking, but sometimes it's beautiful. I put it all into my songs.

The strongest feminine force I know is my mom. She stands up for what she believes and never backs down. We're all yin and yang, masculine and feminine. When I'm in my business mode, I'm more masculine. When I'm writing, I'm both. The feminine is where we take care of the earth, take care of ourselves, and have more of a nurturing, emotional side. The world is changing. We're no longer teaching young boys to be strong and brave and telling them they must fight. It's okay to cry and feel your feelings.

"We Are Love," written with Derek Miller from the Six Nations of the Grand River First Nation, in Ontario, came out as a single in August 2019. It's the story of the return of White Buffalo Calf, whose spirit embodies the feminine nature. As we walk through to the other side of this virus, that's when we'll see White Buffalo Calf. Her message is "Embrace the femininity," but it's not just the femininity in yourself. It's about valuing the females in your life, your children, your mother, and lifting them up.

I met Derek through Laura Milliken, co-founder of Big Soul Productions. When my dad received an Inspire Award for mentoring kids, Laura was the creative director of the awards ceremony. She's good friends with Derek. She said, "You should do a song together."

Laura and Derek came to Palm Desert, in California's Coachella Valley, where I spend my time, and we wrote "We Are Love." Derek's a great writer and performer, but I'm more into the message of lyrics than he is. If I write something that's not meaningful, I'm not going to sing it. But he said, "These words are just too much," and we came to a standstill. I said, "Trust me, you're going to love it," and finished recording it. When we listened to it, he said, "This is amazing!"

He couldn't believe in a million years that the lyrics would go with the music, but the message came through.

"Suicide Song" was about my dad, Grand Chief Ronald Derrickson. When he was nine, he kept being told, "You're just a dumb little Indian kid. You'll never get anywhere."

He told me he thought about committing suicide for a while. Then he told himself, "You've got to rise above."

That's where the song came from. Suicide is prevalent among our people. I was working on a project for missing Indigenous people, but the statistics were covered up. During the time of residential schools, so many Native children were killed and buried without it being reported. It's still going on. Native women, men, and children go missing, and no one looks for them. It's a hopeless situation, but we keep trying to shed light on it and change what's going on between our people and the government. It's getting better in some parts, worse in others.

My father is my fountain of knowledge, an amazing man. He was elected chief six times. He fights for our people, whether anybody's on his side or not. People praise him and tell him that he's doing a good job, but there are moments when he's completely alone. That's an important path you've got to walk. He did it because it was the right thing to do.

Everything I do goes past him first. We lock our minds together and brainstorm. His experiences are so much more than mine; he's been on the planet longer. I draw from his experiences—the boarding schools and what he went through, the pain and suffering.

I see my father as the strongest person on this planet. He's so strong-willed, and he's got a strong mind. He wanted to be a lawyer and was smart enough to do it, but he was beaten down. The principal punched him in the head and told him, "Indians don't go to universities; you're nothing."

That was his last day of school. He got his hands on every book he could read and educated himself.

My family used to visit my grandma and grandpa. My grandpa played guitar, banjo, and fiddle. My uncle Kelly did too. I remember Uncle Noll, the oldest brother, playing washtub bass. We had serious hoedowns every weekend. I grew up with bluegrass and country music. It got my blood moving. The way people crave food, I needed music; it's always been that way. I've always wanted to sing and write. As soon as I could write, I put words down on paper and sang them. I begged for singing lessons, but my mom would say, "You're too young."

Finally, when I was five or six, I started opera training with a local teacher. I had no idea what opera was. She asked, "Do you like opera music?" and I said, "No."

"Well, that's what you're learning."

I laugh now, but I took it all in.

I was planning to be an attorney. I got a scholarship to UBC [University of British Columbia], but I also applied secretly to Berklee. When they offered me a scholarship, I had to go. I couldn't deny my true path. I studied music business and performing arts. It was such a different world to me. I was in the college gospel choir, the only Native. Everyone else was African American.

I went home the first three times crying. I didn't know if I was going to be able to do it, but my teacher pulled me aside and said, "Don't quit."

Then she said, "I want to tell you something. You're a good singer. Everyone else is an apple or orange, but you're a cherry. Keep being a cherry. You're on the right path. It's okay to be different."

That was enough fuel to keep doing what I was doing. I've never wanted to be like anyone else. I just want to do what's in my soul, what I'm here to do.

I grew up on a farm in Westbank First Nation Indian Reserve, part of the city of Kelowna, British Columbia, across the Okanagan Lake Bridge. There were 10,000 people there when I grew up. Now there are more than 380,000. It's one of the fastest-growing cities in Canada. There's a lot of tourism. It's beautiful, with a lake and mountains. I still have a home there.

We were poor, but we never went without. We had everything in our backyard. I spent my days playing in cherry trees. We grew up with peaches, apples, horses, chickens, roosters, cows, bunnies, cats, and dogs. We lived good.

When I started going to public school, I was beaten up, bullied, and treated badly because I was Native. My dad was a radical and making waves in the news. There was a spotlight on our family. People either embraced us, or they were poisoned by jealousy. They hurt me because they didn't understand who I was. Someone tried to kidnap me. It was one thing after another. There was a lot of hatred.

When we moved to Victoria, I attended St. Michael University School. Nine of us were chosen to partake of classes at the Conservatory of Music. Students came to that school from all over the world. It wasn't as bad as the uneducated town where I felt prejudice. I still feel it among my own people. Sometimes your own people are the hardest on you. You've got to decide, like my dad did, that no matter what happens, you're going to get up and keep walking.

I moved to Switzerland to attend Neuchâtel Junior College. My grandfather asked me, "Why are you going? You have everything you could want right here. Whatever you want, Grandma will cook it for you."

It's important to see the world, experience how other people live, and find out that you're not the only person in the world, but my grandfather was right. I had to go away to find out who I was, but no matter where I went, when I came back, I'd look around and say, "This is a beautiful place."

When I started playing Native music and speaking about my people, there was Buffy Sainte-Marie, whom I still love, but there wasn't much more. Now there are so many talented Indigenous artists. Our generation has stepped up. I love what people are doing and the direction they're going. They're trying to make a change. That's what we've got to do. We've got to be our own people but also share it with the world. I'm Native, but my mom's white. It's important to have a message every person can relate to.

The world has shut down, but Mother Nature is winning for the first time in history. The turtles have made it to the ocean; the earth is healing. People are staying home; the pollution is less. Everything's glowing again. The air is cleaner. It's amazing what could happen in a couple of months. The time for being racist is fading. People are realizing that we can't live like this any longer. It's been done to Native people, but Natives aren't the only ones who have experienced hardship. No matter who you are, regardless of whether you're white, Black, yellow, or Irish, we've all had pain. That's our poison—jealousy and hatred.

We've got to look within ourselves and change. I don't want to see animals or people suffering. It affects me as an artist and a human being. I have internal heartbreak that I constantly deal with. That's why I write what I write.

Native people have been so misunderstood, but we come from a place of pure love and peace. We want what's best for the planet. It's what our ancestors direct us to do. We choose to walk a life of beauty or a life of sorrow. We can lie down and wait to die, hold grudges, feel bad for ourselves, or blame the rest of the world. We've got to make a good life for ourselves and our families and make a change.

Being positive is a choice. Treating people with kindness, love, and respect is a choice. It comes from everything we do, every day, every thought. It's not about my people or your people but about saving the planet.

I was proud to be the NAMA's Female Artist of the Year two years in a row [2016 and 2017]. Nobody else has done that, but if I never got an award, I'd still be doing what I'm doing. If you believe in something and you're directed by Spirit to do it, you've got to do what's in your soul.

Matt James (Naveau) (1987–) (Anishinaabe)

Matt James, the fun-loving bassist and vocalist of the award-winning Canucky Bluegrass Boys, turns to his Indigenous roots on his solo recordings.

You bare your life when you sing a song, knowing that people are going to judge you, but if I reach one person and change their life, all the criticism and negativity goes away.

I grew up on the Mattagami First Nation Reserve, near Timmins in Northern Ontario. My grandmother, Elizabeth Naveau, introduced me to country music. Shania Twain used to sing at our local church. I remember her singing in the bathroom while she was getting ready. I was invited to sing at her homecoming concert in Windsor, Canada, in 1999, selected out of thousands of applicants to be part of the choir for "God Bless the Child." I was just a kid. All these amazingly talented musicians surrounded me.

My aunts and uncles played on the Grand Ole Opry in the 1960s. My uncles [Norman, John, and Reno Naveau] played guitars and fiddles. Uncle Norman was a fiddle champion. They played at step dance festivals and fiddle competitions and were very well-known.

Hank Williams, Hank Snow, Patsy Cline, Loretta Lynn, and Roseanne Cash were my staples growing up. My grandma was a huge Johnny Cash and Kitty Wells fan. We listened to a lot of bluegrass too: Flatt and Scruggs, Ricky Skaggs, Alison Krauss, and Jim and Jesse. My next-door neighbor played banjo. You could hear it ringing across the whole reserve.

I'm a nine-time Canadian Bluegrass Awards winner with the Canucky Bluegrass Boys [formerly Grassbackwardz]. I've been Bass Player of the Year, Entertainer of the Year, and Songwriter of the Year. We've been the Most Promising Group and Vocal Group of the Year. My best friend, Lee D. Roy, was Guitar Player of the Year. R. J. Nelson plays banjo. Don Reed's been nominated several times as Fiddle Player of the Year. He won the Canadian Open Old Time Fiddle Championship, in Shelbourne, Ontario, in 1980, '81, and '82, and he recorded with Buck Owens, Dwight Yoakam, and Michelle Shocked. He plays with my country band as well.

When I was eighteen or nineteen, some friends said, "Let's go to a bluegrass festival."

I asked, "What's bluegrass?"

They played me a Del McCoury CD [*The Cold Hard Facts*]. "There's a Snake in the House" was the song. "Why would I want to go to a festival of that?"

"If you don't like the music, come for the party."

"Count me in."

When we got to the festival, banjo player Russell Moore and IIIrd Tyme Out were singing "Swing Low, Sweet Chariot." When they came in with the harmonies and the bass singer came in with his low part, you could feel the ground shake. It was quite an incredible experience. I got bitten by the bluegrass bug; I absolutely fell in love with the music.

The best part of festivals isn't watching bands perform—that's the cake—but the icing is when you go campsite to campsite and jam. No matter which way you walk, you find people singing harmony. There are beginners along with people who've won competitions. The humbleness of allowing anyone to play, regardless of their level, inspired me to pick up the doghouse bass. I learned to play during the winter.

When I went back a year later, people remembered me [I don't blend in], but they were surprised to see me playing bass. I won't say that it's in my blood, but I was meant to play music. It came quickly. People ask me how I learned so fast. I don't know how to explain it, but when I play bass, I not only hear it but see where my hands are supposed to go. My fretboard lights up for me. I just have to connect the dots.

By my third year, I had won Bass Player of the Year twice. In the third year, I received a nomination as Entertainer of the Year. I was the first person in Canadian Music Awards history to score a double whammy, winning Bass Player and Entertainer of the Year the same year. I pulled that off twice. How does a bass player do that? He's supposed to be the nobody in the background. I have an infectious personality on stage; I don't even know what I'm going to say. Everyone says, "Your show is so funny," but it came out of necessity. I was the only one in the band who wasn't too shy to talk on the mic. Back in the day, when we were just getting started, I'd have a little liquid encouragement, a beer or two, before getting on stage. I never let anyone know. I'd be spinning my bass, holding it over my head, running from one side of the stage to the other, and making it back in time to sing my part in three-part harmony. I drove those guys crazy. I ended up getting the nickname Tigger.

One of my friends gave me [bluegrass vocalist] Rhonda Vincent's DVD, *Ragin' Live: Rhonda Vincent and the Rage: Movies* [2005]. I must have burned a hole through it, watching it so many times. I thought she was the biggest thing in the world, as big as Shania Twain. The Gettysburg Bluegrass Festival was the closest she was playing. We were living in Ontario, thirty-six hours from Gettysburg, but we jumped in the motor home and made the trip.

The day she was performing, we saw her great big tour bus. "Oh, my God! I need a picture."

I had friends and bandmates with me. We were all big lovers of Rhonda Vincent's music. As we were walking up to the bus, we saw her sitting at a fold-up table in the little boutique set up by her pop-up camper, picking her mandolin. I walked up to her and said, "We just drove thirty-six hours to see you," and she went, "Do you pick?"

"Sure, I play bass. He plays guitar, he plays fiddle, and we all sing."

"Well, get your instruments. Let's jam."

We ended up picking and singing with her. The next thing we knew, two hundred to three hundred people were wondering, "How'd these guys get Rhonda to do this?"

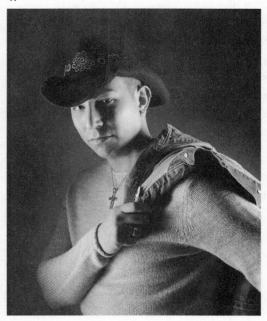

23. Matt James

After we played for a while, she asked, "Why don't you come to my [Sally Mountain] festival in Queen City, Missouri?"

She didn't have to ask twice. We brought a whole entourage, including everyone's moms. It was my mom's first time crossing the border into the States. We spent a week at the festival. Rhonda brought us on stage four or five times.

At the festival's open mic, on Thursday, we did a fifteen-minute set that turned into a forty-five-minute set. They wouldn't let us get off the stage. We did encore after encore. For our final song, Rhonda got on stage and played with us. I just about collapsed. She stood right behind me; I couldn't believe it was happening. When our set was done, she said, "Do you want to come back and play some more?"

The crowd gave us a standing ovation. The next day, we played an hour-long set. Rhonda joined us for the entire set. It was validation that we were doing what we were supposed to be doing. We had something special; the journey had begun.

Growing up on the reserve was humbling; there wasn't much to do. Once I started hitting eleven, twelve, and thirteen, the novelty of going outside to play wore off. I had to become creative at passing time and being productive.

I started singing in church; my grandma brought me there a lot. I was in a praise and worship choir at the age of fifteen. I learned to play the drums. I wasn't good, but they'd let me play a song or two. Then they'd say, "That's enough."

If they had let me keep going, I would have gotten good. I've always wanted to entertain, whether it was by telling jokes, hosting an event, or playing music. I got rid of my stage fright the first time my grandma made me sing in front of people. These days, I sing for close to ten thousand people. At Shania Twain's festival, I sang for forty thousand. People ask me, "Aren't you scared?"

I tell them, "Not at all. It's the one place where I feel the most at home."

I went through a lot on the reserve. My dad was an alcoholic. I had no choice but to grow up faster than the average kid. I have two younger sisters, and I was responsible for taking care of them. I didn't mind, because I loved them, but with our dad drinking and partying, it left it to me to be the parent.

When they say it takes a community to raise a child, it absolutely does. My community raised us. I saw a lot on the reserve that people don't like to talk about, but there's nothing wrong with talking about where you come from or the problems that are there. I take my experiences with me whether I'm writing songs or doing entrepreneurial, motivational, or self-esteem speaking for youth, which I do quite often. The first thing I do is introduce myself to these young people. I talk about my upbringing and the things I've gone through, the hardships, alcoholism, drug addiction, and how they affected me. I learned to deal with it, fight it, and overcome it. They realize I'm not so different from them.

My grandmother played guitar. She'd pick on her front porch just about every night. One night, she was playing Shania Twain's "What Made You Say That?" when I happened to walk onto the porch. When she got to the chorus, I sang. She stopped playing and asked, "Can you do that again?"

"Sure, Grandma, I can sing the whole song if you want."

She started over, and I sang.

We were isolated, about forty-five minutes from town, but Grandma went and bought a karaoke machine. You had to pop a VCR tape into a recorder that hooked up to it. My grandma bought all kinds of videos for it. I learned every song on those tapes.

I used to go to the corner store, put quarters in the jukebox, and play Rosanne Cash's recording of "Tennessee Flat Top Box," by her father, Johnny Cash. It was my favorite song. I'd play it until my quarters ran out. If I asked my grandmother for money, she'd say, "You know what to do."

I'd get my guitar and start playing, and she'd put money in the tip jar. The people at the corner store got sick of me coming in to listen to this one song. They'd see me coming, unplug the jukebox, and tell me it wasn't working,

My grandmother knew I was going to be an entertainer. Before she passed, she told me I'd be a big star one day and sing for lots of people. I asked if I was going to sing for a gazillion, and she said, "Yes."

We moved off the reserve to Timmins when I was fifteen. I was happy. There wasn't anything to do on the reserve. In Timmins I kept myself busy putting on concerts and fashion shows.

Songwriting was a release; I didn't want to talk to a therapist or a counselor. When you have abandonment issues, you have trouble trusting anybody. I was always cautious of whom I talked to and how I spoke to them. I didn't let many people into my life until I learned to release that and start using it as a positive. I use my experiences to help other people. I've gotten a lot of letters. One said, "I was about to commit suicide, and your song came on the radio and stopped me."

It choked me up that something I wrote could have that much impact on another person's life. It makes it all worth it.

After I lost my dad in 2017, I wrote "More Than a Memory." To this day, I have a hard time singing it. It reminds me that he's not with us anymore. It's only been three years since he's been gone. I'll sing it, look at the audience, and see people wiping tears from their faces.

My dad and I had a big falling out two years before he passed. We called each other awful names and said hurtful things. We broke each other's hearts. We're both so stubborn that we had a hard time forgiving one another. He passed away before we reconciled our differences. When I found out that my dad had passed, I was numb. I remember touching my face and not feeling anything. I blacked out.

If I didn't have music, I wouldn't be here today, but I learned to not hold a grudge. Time isn't forever. At any moment, it could be taken away. Garbage is disposable; people aren't. When I said, "I'm sorry," to my dad, he was lying in a casket. I didn't get to hear it back. That's what hurt the most. I'll never get to hear it from him.

I got caught up in drugs and alcohol. It was my way of coping. I was so numb and in pain. It made me better for the moment, but it didn't help my well-being. When you're traumatized, you don't care. Anything must be better than the way you feel.

I finally came to terms with everything. I no longer need a substance to make me happy or control my life. I absolutely feel free now. I have so much to offer the world. Being able to walk away from it and still have my health, dignity, and life in check has given me a lot to write about.

Before computers and cell phones, we had to go to our elders to find wisdom. My father might have been trying to teach me something; I'll never know. What I do know is that, deep down, he never stopped loving me. Even with all the hurt, I could walk away a better man.

My songs are gifts. I still can't believe that I wrote "Miner's Prayer," the title track of my album. My dad came to me in a dream. He was a miner who almost got killed underground, but his life was spared. In the dream, he got on his knees, prayed, and had a conversation with God. I heard every word. When I woke, I rushed to my garage and wrote down as much as I could remember. I picked up a guitar and started playing it as if I already knew it. I recorded it on my cell phone. When I listened back, I bawled my eyes out. It was so beautiful. I felt like I was listening to someone else's song. I was just the messenger.

I heard myself on the radio for the first time, on May 28, 2019. My next-door neighbor called and said, "Matt, you're on the radio."

I jumped out of bed, ran to my jeep, turned the key in the ignition, and put the radio on. I stumbled a little—I was shaking so badly. I had to turn the dial to 99.9 FM. Finally, I hit it and heard "Miner's Prayer." It was coming across the airwaves, and the whole world was listening. I had tears rolling down my face. I blasted it, with the windows down. I wanted the world to hear it. It was a mind-blowing experience, but it kept getting better.

I received my first nomination for Country Music Album of the Year at the 2019 Indigenous Music Awards [formerly Aboriginal Peoples' Choice Music Awards]. Don Amero [*Evolution*] ended up winning, deservedly so. He's paid his dues.

When I won the Best Country Americana Album NAMA, I didn't think that was even possible. Marty Stuart [*The Pilgrim—Deluxe Edition*] was in the same category. He's a living legend. The whole room went quiet. "The nominees are … Marty Stuart, Matt James," and they named some other people. The world stopped turning. You could hear a pin drop. Then they said the winner was me. I was so blown away that I ran out of the room and called my mom. I never went on stage to give my acceptance speech.

I'm going to have more opportunities. The future is bright. I'm not going to stop until I'm standing center stage at the Grand Ole Opry. That's my grandmother's prediction; it's just a matter of when. I've got the fire to do it. I'm just holding tight, waiting for it to happen. I know it will.

Gospel Music

The appropriateness of Indigenous Americans singing gospel music is debatable. "The very singing of these songs and belief in a Lord and Savior," said William Prince (Peguis), a Manitoba-based gospel singer and the son of a minister, "is the success of a plan to extinguish Indian identity."[17]

"It meant ridding them of their culture and their language," added Josh Charette (Turtle Mountain Chippewa), "and westernizing them by educating them and filling their lands with a Christian missionary presence. … They were told that they were wrong and devil worshipers for the way that they believed, and that … to be truly saved, they must abandon their traditional ways first."[18]

Others take a different view. "We believe in Jesus," said 2017 Best Gospel and Inspirational NAMA recipient Callie Bennett, "but my father taught us to balance being Christian and keeping our Navajo values. There are positive Diné values that line up with biblical teachings."

Callie Bennett (1988–) (South Korean and Diné)

Greg Miller, producer and founder of Immersion Productions, declares that Callie Bennett's "powerful voice and passionate soul resonate not only within her Native American culture but across the mainstream musical landscape. . . . She is a force to be reckoned with."[19]

There was a reason God placed the Red Nation in the Americas. He's the one causing us to continue despite all the opposition from the dark forces.

Whether it's the tribes in America or the First Nations in Canada and Australia, Natives have something we call *k'é* [kinship] in the Navajo Nation, the teaching of relating to one another. A lot of our young people, and even some elders, refer to k'é as their clan, but the teaching goes deeper than shaking hands and knowing who you're related to. It goes beyond that, to teachings of love and compassion, what my father calls "covenant kindness."

The teaching of k'é comes with responsibility. If you own a horse, you take care of it. It's the same with people. There's harmony when we're relating to each other. We have teachings and values that help to heal people, whether they're Native or not. I saw that growing up. It was part of learning the difference between the two worlds, but there can be unity amid diversity. That's what my father teaches; it's on the inside cover of *Awake, Arise, Shine* [2017].

We have the tribe known as the Diné, or Navajo, and we have family clans, which are like bloodlines. I introduce myself as Red Running into Water clan. That's my mother's clan, my very first clan. My secondary clan is the Áshįįhí [Salt People] clan—my father's clan. My maternal grand-father's clan is the Towering House Clan [Kinyaa'áanii], and my paternal grandfather's clan is the Deer People of the Red Running to the Water clan [Bįįh Diné Táchii'nii]. I always say my last name first. We identify ourselves not by our name but by where we come from, the family that raised us.

Much of the inspiration for *Awake, Arise, Shine* came from my family. My father, Ellson Bennett, is a nondenominational Christian minister. My faith-based beliefs inspired the CD, as did, of course, our Diné culture, my growing up, my surroundings, and all the ethnicities and nationali-ties in my family. I love world music. I love percussion and drums. All of that tied together.

Bill Miller [Mohican] was a huge inspiration, along with Robert Mirabal [Taos Pueblo]. On the pop side, I loved Michael Jackson because of how inspirational some of his songs were and how they reached the world. The same with Bob Marley and so many others whose music touched lives. Through the power of music and lyrics, people can inspire people.

I was born in Seoul, South Korea, two days after Christmas 1988, and adopted as a baby.

Growing up on and off the Navajo Reservation, I had to learn very quickly to bridge both worlds.

I love my family so much, especially my grandfather, uncles, and father. They taught me about Diné history and culture. I remember my grandfather sitting me down and telling me that he wanted to share something that was in his heart. He told me that when I was adopted, I was cut off from my heritage, culture, and language. He said, "You had no people or country," but he looked me straight in the eye and continued, "When we took you in, we gave you our culture and our language. You are Navajo."

That spoke great volumes. It can be a beautiful thing, being adopted. I'm very thankful for my heritage and my family.

I didn't grow up in a musical home, but my mother said that after I came off the airplane as a month-old baby, she took me to a function where there

was music playing. I hummed along and stayed on key. Because of that, she knew I was going to be musical. Singing came naturally, but my mom knew that I needed to be more rounded. So I took piano lessons at five, singing lessons at seven, and guitar lessons at eight. I learned to read notes, but I came to a point where I had to move on. My guitar teacher took me as far as he could before telling me, "You're one of my best students, but you can learn from here on your own."

I sang with a children's choir and had two vocal coaches. When I was a child, I learned to stand straight with correct posture, how to pronounce words, and about diaphragm support. I took vocal lessons again in my teens. The teacher taught me technical things, especially about supporting the diaphragm and opening the throat, but she said I was sounding "too mechanical" and told me to quit vocal lessons.

I had to stop worrying about technical things and start focusing more on feelings and the passion behind the music. When I sing, I put my heart into it. That passion comes out. People say practice makes perfect, but I don't know if we ever reach perfection. As artists, we're always learning and growing.

My father is my life coach, my pastor, my everything. He taught me the artistic side of things. We performed together at the 2019 NAMAs. He was taught by one grandfather about his Navajo traditional side, but he was also taught about Christianity by his father, a very well-known evangelist of our Navajo Nation. He went down a searching-for-himself path but learned from both sides and taught that to his daughters.

I have two sisters who were adopted in Arizona. One plays drums and sings. I'm working with her on vocal training. My other sister is more focused on her family. We knew we were adopted, but we were told to never think less of ourselves and to know who we were, not only as Indigenous people, but also spiritually. Lots of young people go through identity issues, wondering who they are. Being adopted, you go through that a little bit more. If it weren't for my family and our faith, it would have been much harder.

The Navajo Nation is in northern Arizona. Phoenix is the closest city. When you go off the rez, it's so not your surroundings. Navajo Nation is a hot desert, and there's barely any economic development. It's thirty or forty years behind in infrastructure.

I started elementary school in the Phoenix area, but we moved back to the reservation.

We also started traveling as a family. We were homeschooled for our high school years.

My first album, *Glorify* [2011], was a definite journey. I had songs based around our Christian faith. The project was taken from Texas to Mexico, all the way up to Oklahoma, where it landed with the producers. They took it to another level, but shortly after everything was recorded and mastered, their studio burned down. They contacted me and said, "We're sorry, but we can't produce your next album."

It took another five or six years before we hooked up with Greg Miller at Immersion Productions. He's also a video producer and a talented person. He previously worked with Earth, Wind, and Fire and opened the door to having their keyboardist and music director, Larry Dunn, on "Hope." Greg and I went back and forth about titling the CD after that song. It's one of the most unique songs I've ever written because of the bossa nova–sounding chords.

Larry was a huge deal, but my heart was set on the title *Awake, Arise, Shine*. I wanted to encourage people—not just our people—to wake up and take their place in society, to not pull back anymore, and go for their dreams.

"All Nations, Tribes, and Tongues" came together quickly. My father was encouraging churches to embrace the idea that all of us, no matter what nation or tribe, should be working together. I wanted a song that would not only be a message for us as Native Americans but also for Indigenous people around the globe and everyone else. It's going to take every nation, every tribe, and every tongue coming together to heal.

The closing track, "Amazing Grace," is one of our most beloved songs, not just by the Navajo Nation, but by people everywhere. It has such a resonating message. Singing it in our Navajo, or Diné, language meant so much to me. There was no way I could leave it off my first album in six years.

My video "Reach Who You Are" had my heart behind it, but it also had a powerful message. I wrote it with young people in mind, encouraging them to reach for who they are, especially with the pressures of today's world. My dad worked the camera; I totally trust his artistic side. The dancer was my sister China. It was all this coming together, the heart and passion, the time and effort, the art, and the powerful message. I've gotten emails from people saying how much that video touched them.

Right before this quarantine and isolation, I was finishing one of my shorter projects. It has only seven tracks, but I sang the most beloved hymns from the Navajo Nation. We were planning a CD-release party but had to postpone everything.

My next full-length album will consist of at least twelve tracks and be geared toward the younger generation. I want to include new sounds, with my producer getting more creative. On *Awake, Arise, Shine* we added acoustic instruments, like the didgeridoo. Everything was as natural as possible, but with this next one, I want to include not just natural sounds but also dive into pop culture.

Young people, including myself, are taking their place in society. We want to have a brighter voice. There's a lot that we can learn and build on.

Robby Cummings (1978–) (Tsalagi, Lumbee, and Scots Irish)

The son of a hard-living country singer who turned to Christianity, Robby Cummings is "an anointed singer/songwriter and musician whose call is to lead worship."[20]

Native Americans have always had a relationship with the one we call the Creator. The way I present it to Native people is by telling them that the Creator we talk about, and the God in the Bible, are the same. Most Natives know that, but they don't all know that he had a son who came to this world. The Bible called him "Chief of the Tribe of Judah."

Since the fall of humankind, when Adam and Eve sinned, there have been problems in the world. God sent his only son, Jesus Christ, to pay the price for that sin. His mama called him "Yeshua," which means "Salvation," but what we see all over the world, with all the evil and hate, is that sin is still a problem. God is calling for people to live peacefully, according to what his word tells us to do. Jesus said, "Love your enemies and pray for those who persecute you."

I'm Cherokee on my mama's side and Lumbee on my dad's. I'm also Scots-Irish. What I've learned by talking to elders is that there are two sides to it. Some Christian pastors don't agree with anything Native or traditional. Then you have the other side, those who believe that things Natives do traditionally are beautiful and not evil. That's where I am. In my musical ministry, I try to accommodate both sides. I don't get controversial when it comes to the two belief systems. God created all things. It was all meant for good.

Before I was born, my dad was a country singer. He played in honky-tonks and bars and ran around doing crazy stuff. He married my mom at

25. Robby Cummings

a young age. She was already going to church. She prayed every day that God would change his heart. Her prayers brought him to salvation and changed his life. He told me that he had been sitting in the bedroom and Mama was playing a tape of a sermon by some evangelist. Instead of getting angry and telling her to turn it off, he listened. What the pastor was saying sunk in. Suddenly, my dad felt sorry for doing the things he was doing. He felt like he needed help and cried out, "Lord, if you save me, I'll serve you."

He told me that he felt something inside of him going out the window like a spirit. It scared him. Looking back, we think it might have been an evil spirit leaving him. From that moment, his life was totally changed. God filled him, and he started writing Christian songs. He quit cheating on my mom and hanging out in bars.

Dad taught me to play drum kit when I was five. I played drums in his gospel band until I was a teenager and started playing guitar. He used to take country songs and turn them into gospel tunes. I just cut one of his songs, "Narrow Road." It refers to what the Bible calls, in Matthew 7:14, "a wide road and a narrow road."

Wide is the way to destruction, and narrow is the way to life. It's a good analogy. It's easy to do what you want, but it's a narrow road to do what's right, to be gracious and kind, put your life down for others. I've heard from Native elders that they call that the "red road."

It's the walk of peace and selflessness, the same message the Bible teaches us.

Starting so young, playing music was like eating dinner. I loved it, but as a teenager, I'd sometimes get weary and want to do something else.

Dad would offer me ten dollars or buy me something I wanted, just to get me to play another gig.

I could play any instrument. Somebody brought me a violin. Within six months, I was tearing it up. Guitar, keyboards, trumpet—the same thing. I started playing the Native flute, whistles, anything. I was like my dad. I just took it to another level.

Getting married was a hard thing to do, but my wife, Lindsay, got pregnant. We met at her father's church. Growing up in the Bible Belt, the right thing to do was get married.

Fortunately, we were madly in love. I would have married her anyway, just not at seventeen.

We had a hard road—so many trials and tribulations. That's why I started writing songs. I didn't know it when we were married, but Lindsay had been sexually assaulted at thirteen. She didn't tell anyone what happened to her. After we were married for five or six years, it started coming out. Because of the pain, distrust, and anxiety, she wound up having an affair. It broke my heart, but she was sorry and repentant. Instead of leaving her, we decided to try another way—choose God and walk this narrow way I sing about. It changed our lives. God restored our marriage. We've been married for twenty-five years and have four children. Our oldest is living with us. She's twenty-four, our only girl. Then we've got Ethan, Moloka'i, and Isiah.

Lindsay's working on a book, "Chosen but Silent: Journey to My Void." It starts with her mom being pregnant. Her husband is leaving her, and she's scared to death. At an abortion clinic, she sees the doctor, and it's about to go down. She's lying on a bed when she has a vision of cows being slaughtered. She feels like that's what she's fixing to do. She gets up, puts her clothes on, and runs out the back door before anyone can stop her. Nine months later my wife was born.

She's escaped death so many times; she shouldn't be here. She never had a voice and never talked about her problems. God opened all that up, and she healed. She's a nurse now.

My wife's stepfather, Arthur Lee, was a pastor. We went to Guyana together. It was our second trip to a Third World country. Our first had been to Honduras. He was establishing churches in the jungle. In Guyana we stayed in the small town of Guayana Esequiba [a disputed territory claimed by Venezuela], where the Jonestown Massacre happened on November 18, 1978. Since then, people in the town, including Native Guyanese [Arawaks, Wapisianas, and Caribs], have felt bitter and hurt. Our mission was to preach the gospel of love and truth and open a church. They didn't have one.

The Jonestown compound was closed, but we drove by. There was a big fence around it. People in town told us stories. Americans weren't the only ones killed. Natives would go there for work. Those people are never mentioned. One lady told me that one of her relatives wound up getting locked in. She ended up dying.

I brought my guitar on our trips and sang. People were excited to have live music. They didn't get that a whole lot, especially out in the jungle.

The first time I went to a meeting, there were Native Americans in full regalia representing their tribes, Jewish people from Israel and New York wearing yarmulkes, and Scots-Irish people wearing kilts. They were coming together to repent for the sins of their ancestors. I was just blown away; it was very humbling. It made me want to know more about my heritage.

I didn't grow up Native. I knew my great-grandmother was Cherokee, but we didn't talk about it. I was told I was white. Finding out I was Native American made me want to know more about who they were, where they came from, what they did, and what happened to them. That led me to the sad story of the Trail of Tears. The Cherokee were excommunicated from their land, gathered up, and shipped to Oklahoma. Four thousand died from cold, hunger, or disease. I didn't know that. We didn't learn about it in the history books. It was horrible; a lot of healing was needed.

Kevin Costner's miniseries 500 Nations, in 1995, was enlightening. I learned that the Cherokee were just one tribe. There were over five hundred other Indigenous nations treated the same way. Many were annihilated. When you're a kid, you just know what the movies show you.

What bothered me the most was learning that a lot of it had been done in the name of Christianity. The church took Native American children from their homes and placed them in residential schools, where they abused and mistreated them and tried to take the Indian out of them. They wouldn't let them speak their language. They cut their hair and wouldn't let them practice their beliefs. There were lots of things needing to be undone. That's what took me down the path of Native American worship music. It wasn't long before my songs caught on, and I started getting calls to do gatherings all over the country.

I wasn't just a white boy anymore. Now I had a history, a culture. I have a grandmama whose husband was murdered. She married into a Scots-Irish family so she wouldn't be killed or shipped to Oklahoma. It made me want to do anything I could to help. I'm a musician. I write songs, touch hearts, and bring healing. Nothing heals a soul better than a song. It's a powerful thing.

I've been collaborating with a Taino Indian from Puerto Rico, Alex Castillo. He's an incredible songwriter. We've written some great songs together. One of them, "If My People," won the Best Gospel Inspirational Recording NAMA in 2019. Its lyrics came out of Corinthians 14.

In Native communities, shame and anger are hanging over a lot of us. The first time I visited a western tribal community, I went to the Rosebud Indian Reservation in South Dakota. I'm not as dark as them, so they saw me as an outsider. I could feel their hatred—they had been mistreated so badly. But that hatred isn't going to help them. Somehow that must go away.

Natives must forgive the white man. If we carry hatred, it's going to destroy us.

The Bible teaches us that, in Christ, there's no male or female, no Greek or Jew. We're all the same; we've all got red blood. That's how we need to treat one another. Under God we're all one. I saw an analogy that said, "They took a white egg and a brown egg and cracked them open, and both eggs looked exactly alike."

Since moving to Cleveland, Tennessee, in 2017, I've met many incredible musicians and producers. They're everywhere. I used to live fifteen minutes from Walterboro, South Carolina, but I didn't have the opportunities I have in East Tennessee. There are lots of big churches, but I was invited to a small ministry of only fifty people. They fed the homeless ten thousand meals last year. That's where the need was. They wanted me to play music and lead them in worship, so I started going regularly. There are lots of people with messed up lives, but none of them want that life. They're trapped. They need someone to help them; I'm doing as much as I can.

10

Rockin' the Rez

As we have seen, Indigenous musicians have played an essential role in North America's music. "Our peoples were part of the origin story of blues, jazz, and rock," Joy Harjo told me in 2011.

When it comes to rock, "American Indians pose a challenge to what we typically see as rock history," contended John Troutman, music curator of the National Museum of American History, Washington DC, "which has been very black and white."[1]

"It's not necessarily that there is a Native American quality in rock and roll," said David Fricke of *Rolling Stone*. "What you're looking at is a hidden portion of the American population that is making quantitative and qualitative strides."[2]

Fred Lincoln "Link" Wray Jr. (1929–2005) (Shawnee and Mexican)

The executive producer of Catherine Bainbridge's documentary *Rumble: The Indians Who Rocked the World* (2017), Stevie Salas (Apache) played guitar for Rod Stewart, George Clinton, Bootsy Collins, Eddie Money, and many others. A turning point in his musical growth was hearing Link Wray for the first time. "My brain exploded," he remembered, "because Native American people didn't have any role models. Nobody wanted to be Native American. It was something we would keep to ourselves, something we didn't talk about. Native Americans were doing these things back then, but no one saw them."[3]

Wray, who was born in Dunn, North Carolina, struck gold with his Fuzz-Tone-heavy instrumental "Rumble" in April 1958. "There was no mistaking the creepy, overdriven, two-chord riff," said Matt Ashare of *Rolling Stone*, "and slow thudding backbeat that filled the room."[4]

"When you come to someone like Link Wray," explained Fricke, "he not only invented the power chord but wrote the song that popularized it. . . . A Native American had a thoroughly original idea, and that became the essence of a much wider thing."[5]

"[Wray] made an indelible mark on the whole evolution of where rock 'n' roll was going to go," said Robbie Robertson, "and then I found out [he] was an Indian!"[6]

Wray included Indigenous-themed tunes like "Shawnee," "Apache," and "Comanche" in his setlist, but he and his brothers—rhythm guitarist Vernon and drummer Doug—downplayed their ethnicity. They may have inherited their passion for music from their Shawnee mother, but she instructed them to keep their Indigenous roots to themselves. "Lillian Wray refused to teach her three boys the Shawnee language," said Dana Raidt, author of *Link Wray: The First Man in Black*, "for fear of what would happen if they were caught speaking it. She turned out lights and put blankets over windows when the Ku Klux Klan burned crosses nearby."[7]

"Music industry executives expected Wray and other Native artists to play ball," Raidt continued, "play dumb, and play white. Those artists didn't hide their Indian-ness because they wanted to. They did it because they had to—or it was done for them."[8]

Continuing to build on his guitar-slinger reputation, Wray would be inducted into the Rockabilly Hall of Fame, the North Carolina Music Hall of Fame, and the Native American Music Hall of Fame. The father of the reverberating power chord ranked forty-five on *Rolling Stone*'s list of top one hundred guitarists.

Jimmy Carl Black (James Inkanish Jr.) (1938–2008)
(Cheyenne and Scottish)

El Paso–born Jimmy Carl Black played drums and sang with Frank Zappa's original Mothers of Invention, calling himself "the Indian of the group" and elaborating, "Although I'm not full blood, I'm close enough for rock and roll."[9]

Born James Inkanish Jr., Black changed his surname after his mother married her second husband. A trumpet player in junior high and high school, he switched to the drums after seeing Elvis Presley in 1955. "There was no chance in rock'n'roll for a trumpeter," he said.[10]

Serving in the U.S. Air Force, in Kansas, Black began playing in Wichita nightclubs in 1958. Four years later, he recorded his first single, "Stretch Pants," backed with "A Matter of Time." Two weeks after moving to California in 1964, he met bassist Roy Estrada. The Mothers of Invention grew out of their band, the Soul Giants. The events leading to Zappa began three or four months after they formed. When their singer received his draft notice, Ray Collins replaced him. The guitarist didn't like Collins [and] quit. Zappa took his place after promising, "If you guys learn my music I'll make you rich and famous."[11]

"He took care of half of that promise," Black said years later, "because I'm damn sure I didn't get rich."[12]

The renamed Mothers of Invention would be one of the era's most adventurous groups. Black's singing of "Lonesome Cowboy Burt" was a highlight of 200 Motels (1971), but by its premiere, Zappa had phoned to tell him that he was making changes. Black went on to form Geronimo Black (named after his son) with Bunk Gardner, who had played woodwinds and tenor saxophone in the Mothers of Invention.

Supporting his family as a musician, however, remained an elusive dream. Returning to his childhood home along the Mexican border, in Anthony, Texas, Black took a job in a doughnut factory. "I certainly didn't stop playing music just because I wasn't in LA," he said. "I was pretty fed-up with the politics of the music business and still am. They don't even like—or know—what good music is even if it bit them in the ass. All they care about is how you look and how much money you can make for them. Listen to the radio or watch MTV for a perfect example of what I'm talking about here. Besides that, I was raising five kids and I thought that my small home town . . . was a better environment for them to grow up in—and I was right. Sometimes family must come before career."[13]

Resurfacing in the early eighties, Black joined Gardner and ex–Mothers of Invention keyboardist Don Preston in the Grandmothers of Invention. He would serve several stints with the Zappa tribute band over the next twenty years. The group played its farewell concert in 2018, a decade after his passing.

James Marshall "Jimi" Hendrix (1942–70)

Inducted into the Rock and Roll Hall of Fame in 1992 and the Native American Music Hall of Fame in its inaugural year (1998), Jimi Hendrix had Indigenous blood on both sides of his family. His Tsalagi paternal grandmother, Zenora "Nora" Rose Moore, a former vaudeville dancer, "would tell me little Indian stories," the left-handed guitarist remembered, "that had been told to her when she was my age. I couldn't wait to hear a new story. She had Cherokee blood. So did Gramma Jeter. I was proud of that, it was in me too."[14]

Jaime Royal "Robbie" Robertson (1943–)
(Mohawk, Cayuga, and Jewish Canadian)

Robbie Robertson was inducted (with The Band) into the Juno Hall of Fame in 1989 and the Rock and Roll Hall of Fame in 1993. Two years later the Toronto-born guitarist and songwriter scored Lifetime Achievement recognition from the National Academy of Songwriters.

Few fans knew of Robertson's Indigenous roots before 1994, when he assembled the all-Indigenous Red Rose Ensemble for a six-hour TBS documentary, *The Native Americans*. His Mohawk and Cayuga mother had encouraged him to be proud of his Indigenous heritage, but she warned him to keep it to himself.

Robertson's soundtrack—which featured an all-star cast including Montreal-based Kashtin and Walela, the trio formed by Tsalagi Baptist minister Richard Coolidge's daughters Rita and Priscilla and Priscilla's daughter Laura Satterfield—was "quite evocative," said *All Music Guide's* Stephen Thomas Erlewine, "recalling an American version of Peter Gabriel's Mediterranean exploration *Passion*."[15]

During the 2002 Winter Olympics opening ceremonies, in Salt Lake City, Utah, Robertson led the Red Rose Ensemble, along with Ute, Shoshone, Goshute, Paiute, and Diné drum groups and dancers, in an internationally televised celebration of Indigenous culture. Seen by sixteen million viewers, the enlarged ensemble performed "Stomp Dance (Unity)." Written by Robertson, coproducer Jim Wilson, and the Six Nations Women Singers, its refrain repeats, "This is Indian country. This is Indian country."

"When I think about it," Robertson told me, "my heart still takes wings."

Robertson was one of ten musicians profiled in *Rumble: The Indians Who Rocked the World.* "All over the world," he said, "there is an attention, a cultural curiosity towards American Indians: they are all fascinated by Mysticism, spirituality and Indian culture."[16]

XIT

Led by Motown songwriter and producer Tom Bee, Indigenous America's first rock band, XIT (X-I-T), was formed in 1971. The initials of its name stood for "Crossing of Indian Tribes."

"The press called us musical ambassadors of the American Indian Movement," Bee told me in 2013, "and we did a lot of benefits in conjunction with AIM. The message in our music was their platform, so it was a perfect combination."

Bee was as much an entrepreneur as he was a musician. Selling releases on his Lance Records label from the trunk of his car since the midsixties, he scored his first success after hooking up with Motown Records. The Jackson Five recorded his song "(We've Got) Blue Skies" in 1970, and Smokey Robinson included "Just My Soul Responding" (with Bee beating a powwow drum and chanting) on his 1973 solo debut, *Smokey.* A year later R&B vocalist Michael Edward Campbell recorded "Roxanne" and "Roll It Over." "Joyful Jukebox Music" became the title track of the Jackson Five's final album, in 1976.

Despite Motown owner Berry Gordy's hesitancy, XIT's first album, *Plight of the Redman* (1972), was released on the label's Rare Earth subsidiary to an enthusiastic reception. Songs like "The Coming of the Whiteman" and "War Cry" delivered a solid punch. XIT opened for Three Dog Night, the Beach Boys, Grand Funk Railroad, and Joe Cocker. "*Billboard* kept [the album] off the charts," Bee claimed, "and radio stations wouldn't play it. They were afraid of a Native uprising."

The album came out right before the February 27–May 8, 1973, occupation of the Pine Ridge Reservation.

XIT kept things sizzling with its sophomore album, *Silent Warrior* (1973), which included incendiary tracks like "Reservation of Education," "We Live," "Young Warrior," and "Anthem of the American Indian."

"President Nixon sent a letter to all the radio stations," Bee remembered, "encouraging them not to play it."

Gordy commanded Motown's sales office "to hold back on the record," Bee said, "but it was too late. The album went on to be a big underground hit on college campuses in the U.S. and all over Europe."

Beginning a third album in 1977, XIT disbanded before it was completed. Augmented by four tracks by a reunited lineup, five songs were recorded before the split was released as *Relocation* in 1990.

XIT filmed their May 2000 performance at the Mystic Lake Casino's Celebrity Palace in Prior Lake, Minnesota, for a DVD narrated by Floyd Westerman, *Without Reservation*. "The performance is resolute," said Germany's *Rock Times*, "the emotions are genuine, and the band's enthusiasm for playing is symptomatic."[17]

Former XIT members Lee Herrera, Jomac Suazo, A. Michael Martinez, and R. C. Gariss continued to play together (without Bee) as the Ox Boyz. Their 2012 debut, *The Red Album*, was nominated for an Album of the Year NAMA. They continue to perform as the Original XIT. "We've been playing since high school," said Herrera. "It just progressed into this sound of Native American rock."[18]

Bee parlayed royalties for writing "Red Hot," a 1979 disco hit by Chaka Kahn's sister Tara Boom, into the first Indigenous-owned record label, SOAR (Sound of America Records). Frustrated that Indigenous music was "limited to trading posts," he lifted recording standards and produced Native artists the way he would Motown stars. The result was more than three hundred high-quality releases by drum groups (e.g., the Black Lodge Singers, the Gray Horse Singers, the Cozad Family, the Cathedral Lake Singers), round dance singers (e.g., Jay Begaye), flute players (e.g., Douglas Spotted Eagle, Bryan Akipa), gospel choirs (e.g., Red Nativity), singer-songwriters (e.g., Derek Miller), and alt-rockers (e.g., Randy Bee).

Blue Mountain Tribe

Robin Hairston (1956–) (Chiricahua Apache)

Watching XIT on public TV, "Rockin'" Robin Hairston was brought to tears. "They were rocking the house with drums, flute, chanting, and rock and roll instruments," remembered the blues harmonica player and singer-songwriter. "I looked at my son and said, 'Caleb, we're going to start an all-Native blues-rock band.' That was the beginning of Blue Mountain Tribe."

It cost $10,000 to go to Tom Weir's Studio City Sound, in Hollywood, but it's where all the greats record—Rod Stewart, Kelly Clarkson, Soulja Boy, Toots and the Maytals, Keith Richards, Eric Clapton, Burt Bacharach, the Beach Boys. We needed to pay top dollar if we wanted top merchandise. We released *All My Relations* on our own Buffalo Creek Records. It sold well, and we started getting fans. Blue Mountain Tribe is now known around the world.

We live in Tehachapi. It's in Central California, high up in the mountains, away from the cities, and secluded from civilization. We love it. It's an Indian community—the Tejon, Paiute, and Kawaiisu are from here. You could walk through the mountains and find artifacts. I found an arrowhead on my property. I'm originally from Tujunga, twenty minutes from Los Angeles, but because of all the crime, we wanted to get away and up into the mountains as far as we could go.

Every day, every moment, I eat, breathe, and sleep Apache. We belong to the Chiricahua Apache [Tsokanende] Indian Nation. I was brought up in the city, but my mom taught me about our culture and history. When I was young, I pursued the Apache way of life. I was known as "Apache Boy," the only Indian in the whole town.

The Apache went through horrendous suffering as prisoners of war. We were attacked on both sides of the border and had to fight. We were one of the last Indian nations to surrender. We have ceremonies and gatherings, and we go to powwows. But we mostly pray to the Creator around the family circle. We ask for healing of the world.

Corporations are killing Mother Earth with coal mining and strip mining—stripping her skin. The two biggest metal mining companies in the world, Rio Tino and BHP Billiton, are trying to build a huge copper

mine on Apache sacred land underneath Oak Flat, an hour east of Phoenix. It's going to be four miles deep and ten miles wide and decimate the land, the water, and Chiricahua sacred sites. We pray that Ussen, or Creator, has the strength to stop the horrific things the government is doing. Mother Earth is in pain, and she's crying.

I was brought up in the sixties and loved Jimi Hendrix, Janis Joplin, and Cream. Steppenwolf's "The Pusherman" blew me away. It used profanity, but it was damning what the pusherman was doing—selling heroin and horrible drugs. I've known many people who have died of overdoses. The pusherman got my mom hooked. I was fifteen when she passed away. She was into rainbows, yellow jackets, mini whites, and other bad drugs.

As a teenager, I got involved with a gang, the Tajunga Angels. I was president, but I wasn't intelligent. I got straight Fs and barely got out of high school. I couldn't go to college or a trade school. I didn't have anywhere to go [I had been living in foster homes]. I didn't want to roam the streets, so I enlisted in the Marine Corps. When I went to boot camp, they said, "We're making you military police. With your background, you'll make a great cop. It'll straighten you out."

Later, when I was a marine reservist, I'd pick up prisoners and bring them back to Washington DC. One time, I had to pick up a very violent prisoner. I had to handcuff him to bring him back. We had to catch a bus, but we had to go through an alley to get to the bus stop. This alley was infested with drug addicts, gang bangers, prostitutes, and bums. We could see people bouncing off the walls. They were like zombies. They grabbed at our ankles, pleading, "Give me money. Give me money."

The prisoner even told me, "Sergeant, we're going to get killed, especially with me in handcuffs and you wearing a badge."

"If we don't make it, we don't catch our bus. Let's go."

Halfway through the alley, I heard someone playing harmonica. It wasn't a big deal. I was nineteen years old; I'd heard Bob Dylan and Canned Heat. As we got closer, the harmonica got louder. Then we came upon the person playing the harmonica. He was a Black man sitting in feces and waste. He was missing an eye. He was torn up on drugs, but he was playing the most beautiful harmonica that you could imagine. I've never heard a better harmonica player—Paul Butterfield, Charlie Musselwhite, or James Cotton. It brought tears to my eyes; I tried hard to fight them. Here I was—this big, tough military policeman—and the last thing I wanted to do was shed tears before a prisoner. I said to myself, "If this guy could play that good, just think what I could do if I tried to learn this instrument."

We watched the harmonica player play a song, then made it through the rest of the alley. On the corner next to the bus stop, you won't believe this, but there was a frigging music store. It had a sign saying, "Open for business," and a harmonica dangling in the window. We had twenty minutes before the bus. We walked into the store, and I bought my first harmonica—a Marine Band in the key of C. I started playing it and, of course, sounded horrible. The prisoner wanted to escape from me.

Wherever I could, I played. That man in the alley kept going through my head, motivating me to practice and practice, driving people crazy. One day my wife and I went to a party. I had my harmonica in my pocket. I pulled it out and said, "Do you want to hear a song?"

Everybody went, "Yeah, let's hear it," so I started playing. When I was done, someone walked over to me and said, "You suck!"

That was the beginning of my career. My inspiration had come from a drug addict in an alley, and when I played for people for the first time,

I was told I sucked. I believe in taking a negative and turning it into a positive. Look at me now—I'm a force to be reckoned with.

When Caleb was eight, he was diagnosed with autism. Psychiatrists told me that he'd never amount to anything and would need to be medicated for the rest of his life. It broke my heart. My life was ended as far as dreams for my son.

I had an old acoustic guitar in a backroom. It had only one string. As soon as we got home, Caleb walked straight to the guitar, picked it up, and played "Iron Man" by Black Sabbath—the whole song—on one string. I was blown away. When he was done, I said, "Caleb, where'd you learn to play guitar?"

He goes, "Dad, I didn't. We just heard the song on the radio."

I said, "Play this," and hummed Jimi Hendrix's "Fire." Caleb played it. I broke down in tears; it was so emotional. I took Caleb back to the doctor, who told me, "Mr. Hairston, your son might be a savant."

"What's a savant?"

"Somebody who appears to be retarded"—that's the word they used back then—"but get them on a piano or violin, and they'll play Mozart, Bach, and Liszt."

He told me, "Get this kid into music."

When I got home, I told my wife what the doctor said. Then I took Caleb to a music store and bought a chart with guitar tablatures. I also bought him a guitar and said, "If you learn this chart in one month, I'll give you $100."

Four days later he said, "Dad, pick a key."

I went through the entire chart. He had mastered it all. It usually takes months or years to do that. People come from all over when they hear that we're playing; they want to hear him.

Caleb started composing melodies and rhythms and bringing them to me. I'd put lyrics to what he wrote. The songs reflected Native issues and were a lot like what XIT did in the seventies. I told Tom Bee what we were doing—I didn't want to step on his toes—but he loved us. We've become close.

All Our Relations [2014] won the NAMA for Best Blues Recording, and "Children on the Rez" [2019] won as Best Video of a Live Performance. Those awards mean everything to me. We have them in our front room, with the medallions and trophies. They're a tremendous accomplishment; the competition is tough.

Blue Mountain Tribe just put out videos of "Going Crazy" and "Pray for Our Planet." We wrote them about the pandemic. Indians are social people who love getting together and barbecuing. We love having pow-wows and going to sweats. We love being around other people. That's our spiritual way, our tradition.

We don't play music for the money; there is no money. We do it for the love of our Indigenous people. We play uplifting songs to enlighten them and let them see the love and compassion we have, not only for our tribe but for all tribes.

Caleb's still autistic—you could tell if you talk to him or see his actions—but he became the youngest civilian employee in the history of Edwards Air Force Base. We got him a job as a menial worker. He progressed quickly because of his knack for numbers. Music is like mathematics. He's excelled at working for the Department of Defense. Nothing the psychiatrist told me turned out to jive at all.

Redbone
Patrick "Pat Vegas" Vasquez (1946–) (Tohono O'odham)
Candido "Lolly Vegas" Vasquez (1939–2010) (Tohono O'odham)

More commercially successful than XIT, Southern California–based Redbone eschewed the Eurotech sweeping through 1970s disco clubs, in favor of a dance-inspiring mix of rock, jazz, R&B, Cajun, and Indigenous music. Inducted into the Native American Music Hall of Fame in 2008, the buckskin-and-feathers-clad group broke into the top fifty with their third single, "Maggie," in 1970. "The Witch Queen of New Orleans," about a nineteenth-century practitioner of voodoo, reached number twenty-one a year later. "Come and Get Your Love" did even better. A top-five hit in 1974, it remained in the top forty for six months. Covered by a German band, the Real McCoys, in 1995, it topped *Billboard*'s dance charts. Redbone's original recording experienced a resurgence when it was included in the Marvel Studios film *Guardians of the Galaxy* (2014). The soundtrack CD sold over a million copies. "Come and Get Your Love" has been the theme song of Netflix's animated series *F Is for Family* and of the reality series *Big Shrimpin'*.

Born in the San Joaquin Valley city of Coalinga, California, Pat and Lolly Vegas grew up with migrant workers from their father's hometown in Mexico. "Now, the word 'Mexican' is already problematic," said Pat. "It's like saying 'Texan' or 'Philadelphian.' Everyone we call Mexican was Native American. The Spanish came and took over Mexico. Then the Germans came after them, and finally the French. And they all married Indians."[19]

Sung to by their mother since infancy, the brothers were inspired by their grandfather, a Robert Johnson–style blues guitarist. Displaying musical talent in their teens, they accompanied pianist Oscar Peterson at the Monterey Jazz Festival in 1962. The brothers went on to record with Odetta, John Lee Hooker, Tina Turner, Sonny and Cher, James Brown, Little Richard, and the Everly Brothers. They backed Dobie Gray on "The 'In' Crowd" in 1965 and P. J. Proby on "Nicki Hoeky" two years later.

Accompanying Elvis Presley in *Kissin' Cousins* (1964), Pat and Lolly ("The Mexican Elvis") also appeared on-screen with Tommy Kirk, Deborah Walley, and Bobby "Boris" Pickett in *It's a Bikini World* (1967). Pat went on to cowrite the instrumental theme of *The Munsters* TV show.

After recording as the Avantis, the Routers, the Markets, and the Sharks, the Vegas brothers toured with swamp pop teenage idol Jimmy Clanton. They joined Leon Russell, Glen Campbell, and pre-Bread David Gates in the short-lived surf music group, the Deuce Coups. Along with Russell and Delaney Bramlett, they comprised the Shindogs, the house band of ABC's weekly music series *Shindig!* (1964–66). Russell would coproduce, with Thomas Leslie "Snuff" Garrett, *Pat and Lolly Vegas: Live at the Haunted House* (1966).

Originally known as the Crazy Creole Cakewalk Band, Pat and Lolly's group became Redbone, the Creole term for a mixed-race person with some Indian blood, in 1969. Jimi Hendrix had been encouraging the brothers to embrace their Indigenous heritage for three years. "Jimi made me aware of my roots," Pat recalled. "He would say, '[Being] American Indian is beautiful, man. Be proud of that.'"[20]

Managed by Bumps Blackwell, who previously guided Little Richard and Sam Cooke, Redbone signed with Epic Records. Debuting with a funky, New Orleans–influenced two-disc album in early 1970, they incorporated Indigenous themes into its follow-up, *Potlatch*, a few months later. Along with their first hit, "Maggie," the album included a protest song, "Alcatraz," dedicated to AIM. "Chant: 13th Hour" was released as a single on the first Earth Day (April 22, 1970). Native influences continued on *Message from a Drum* (1971) and *Already Here* (1972).

The message was clear on "We Were All Wounded by Wounded Knee," the politically charged standout track of *Already Here*. The song not only recalled the 1890 massacre but also nodded to the ongoing reservation occupation at the time. Epic refused to release it as a single. The Vegas brothers financed five hundred copies. Selling out quickly during Redbone's overseas tour, Epic's European branch agreed to release it. Topping the charts in several countries, including Denmark and the Netherlands, it remained banned in the United States.

Redbone's fifth album, *Wovoka* (1973), included "Come and Get Your Love," but its title track irritated label executives. Written by Pat and Lolly, the song recalled the Paiute prophet and shaman, also known as Jack Wilson, whose vision during the New Year's Day 1889 eclipse inspired the Ghost Dance religion. Adherents believed that dancing and singing past exhaustion, wearing sacred shirts that protected them from bullets, and "strict observance of a moral code that emphasized harmony, hard work, and sobriety" would end westward expansion, establish peace and prosperity for Indigenous peoples, and resurrect ancestors.[21] The U.S. government's unease about the religion led to the death of Sitting Bull, on December 15, 1890, and the Wounded Knee Massacre, exactly two weeks later, when Colonel James W. Forsythe and the Seventh Calvary murdered more than three hundred Miniconjou and Hunkpapa Lakota, including flu-ridden Chief Big Foot. Two days later Charles Eastman (Ohiyesa) (Santee Dakota, English, and French)—Pine Ridge Reservation physician and future author of *Memories of an Indian Boyhood* (1902), *Old Indian Days* (1907), *The Soul of the Indian* (1911), *Indian Heroes and Great Chieftains* (1918), and seven other books—went to the snow-covered site to search for survivors and provide medical assistance. "Such trouble as we had," he said, "may justly be charged to dishonest politicians who, through unfit appointees, first robbed the Indians, then bullied them, and finally in a panic called for troops to suppress them."[22]

When Redbone's next album, *Turquoise Dreams through Beaded Eyes* (1974), failed to sell (possibly due to poor promotion), Epic dropped them from its roster. It didn't help that the era's leading impresario, Bill Graham, banned them for canceling an appearance at the last moment, after Lolly had injured his hand. Graham would apologize years later.

Signing with RCA, Redbone released *Cycles* in 1977. It would be their last hurrah. They continued to tour, but subsequent releases have been limited to reissues and live recordings.

Lolly Vegas succumbed to lung cancer on March 4, 2020, more than two decades after a stroke forced him to retire. A series of fine guitarists, including Raven Hernandez and Tracy Lee Nelson, took his place. "Lolly did amazing things on the guitar," Hernandez remembered when we spoke in 2012. "He played his guitar through a Leslie revolving speaker and got a unique sound."

Mixing "Native blues songs, powerful guitar riffs, and funky tunes,"[23] Nelson continues to record provocative songs about Indigenous issues, "because it's where I come from and it's about what we have been through and what we're going through."[24]

Tracy Lee Nelson (1964–) (Luiseño, Diegueño, and Kumeyaay)

Punk rocker–turned–bluesman Tracy Lee Nelson "talks of poverty, discrimination, genocide, writing power songs with a down-home feel."[25]

My brother Karl loved the Beatles. That's what got me into music. Now that I know more about chords and scales and writing songs, I see they were geniuses.

I started playing guitar at eleven or twelve. My neighbor Ray was also a big Beatles fan. He looked like Paul McCartney. One day, he said, "Let's get some instruments."

Being so young, I hadn't worked yet; I couldn't buy a guitar. But Ray was older than me, and he had a job. He bought himself a guitar, and then he bought a Les Paul copy and said, "Tracy, I'm giving this to you."

I didn't know anything about guitars, but the idea sounded fun. I gradually learned to play, just by picking at it. There were six strings; I figured I could do something with them. My first chord was a barre chord. My first song was "One Way or Another" by Blondie. It was the start of the new-wave era.

I hung out with a friend's band, Legal Weapon, in the punk rock days.

When I moved out of my parent's house, my roommate [D. H. Peligro] played drums for the Dead Kennedys. He'd go to gigs with Jello Biafra.

I started a band, the Side Effects, and played at local parties and gigs. One of our first shows, in 1982, was opening for Bad Religion at Valley West in LA.

A good friend who played bass, Donald Lee Durham, and I started Johnny and the Dingbats around 1985. Our single "In Transylvania" got some airplay on a local radio station, KROQ. Then we became the Mad Vampires.

Donald suggested that I write about what happened to the Indians and what's still going on. I never thought about racism growing up. I was a happy-go-lucky kid, loving life and wanting to play music and skateboard.

One day I went to a video store. A homeless guy was sitting outside the store. As I was walking by, he asked me for spare change. I looked at him; said, "I don't have a nickel or a dime, sorry"; and started walking into the store. He yelled at me, "You damn foreigner, go back to your own country!"

I thought to myself, "No respect," and kept walking, but it stayed with me. I started composing songs like "Native American Holocaust" and thinking that I should start a band to play Native blues. I certainly had a lot of blues to sing about.

Robert Johnson was a big influence on me, the old-style acoustic blues. He could make his guitar sound like three guitars were playing at the same time. I couldn't figure out how he did it, until I saw a video; it was fingerpicking.

I started learning more open-D tuning and slide guitar. That's when I decided to record *500 Years of the Blues*. I recorded it in my bathroom. I wanted to capture the natural echo like they did in the old days. I didn't have money to go to a real studio, but I did have an eight-track recorder.

I started playing in bars and clubs, which was cool and fun. Back then we

27. Tracy Lee Nelson

used to post flyers around town to get exposure. I did a few gigs opening for Redbone at local powwows. When Lolly Vegas had a stroke, their manager asked if I'd be interested in filling in. Then Lolly's brother, Pat, called and said, "Hey, Tracy, can you come over?"

I drove to Pat's house, and we talked about the songs. He gave me tapes. We met again at Sunset Studios, in Hollywood, where Redbone rehearsed. They had a lot of shows booked.

I was sad about Lolly. He was an idol to all Native Americans. He and his brother accomplished so much. I needed to learn Lolly's guitar picking and riffs to songs like "Witch Queen of New Orleans." He was popping his strings with his fingers. He played a ninth chord, not a barre chord, as you would think. It was cool; we sounded just like the record.

Redbone did a few shows in Hollywood, but we were focused on Super Bowl XXX at Sun Devil Football Stadium, Tempe, Arizona, on January 28, 1996. The Dallas Cowboys beat the Pittsburgh Steelers, twenty-seven to seventeen. We played during the pregame show with the Four Tops and Hootie and the Blowfish. Everything was strictly controlled. They picked us up at the airport and took us to the hotel. We couldn't go anywhere. After rehearsing, we were on our way back to our rooms, standing by the elevator. When the door opened, there were the Four Tops. They looked at us and said, "Redbone!"

Pat knew a few of them; he knows everybody. We all started talking. It was an honor to meet them.

Musicians in my Native Blues Band come from nearby reservations. I'm from the La Jolla Indian Reservation in northeast San Diego. My original drummer, Vince Duro, is from the San Manuel Reservation in San Bernardino County. He played with the legendary Ike Turner for two years, until Ike's passing in December 2007. Our bass player, Harold Hill, is from the Barona Reservation. We occasionally have a second lead guitarist from the Chukchansi Reservation, Ben Domingo. Ben and I hit it off right away and played benefits and casinos together. He lives in Fresno and has his own band, but once in a while, he plays shows with me.

Blues Loving Man [2017] was nominated for an Indigenous Music Award as the year's Best Blues Recording, and I was nominated as the Best New Artist. A few months later I got the Best Blues Recording NAMA. I had never applied for awards before, but I wanted to get more exposure. I was already working on my ninth CD, but I was honored that they recognized my years of hard work.

I composed "Khadijah" about a missing woman from the Round Valley Reservation. Her family is still searching for her. The song was nominated for Best Country Single at Dollywood. I want to bring more awareness to the issue.

I was honored to serve two consecutive terms [2002–7] as chairman of my tribe. My term was extended because of wildfires. I oversaw economic development and federal programs on the reservation. My focus was on negotiating with the governor of California, Arnold Schwarzenegger, for our casino.

My dad, Lester Lee Nelson, was chairman before me, as was my grandfather. My mom is from the Mesa Grande Reservation, up the hills from here. Our tribe is called Luiseno, and my mom's tribe is Kumeyaay. My mom is also Mataweer family.

I was a professional skateboarder from 1975 to 1978. Skateboarding and playing guitar were my outlets. When I was nine, my stepdad, Ralph Ebert, gave me a sip of beer. Since then, I haven't touched beer. The closest I come is root beer. I was always rebellious. People say, "You're Native American—you have to drink," but I wanted to smash that stereotype. It gave me the strength to never touch alcohol or drugs.

Native kids need an outlet, just to keep them from alcohol and substance abuse. My son, Blake Redwolf Nelson, and I talked about this and decided to open a skateboard company for kids on the reservation. I drew designs, and we had them put on skateboards. Being on a reservation, it took off in a different way. The Native kids thought it was cool to ride a skateboard that said, "Full-blood."

I started advertising online. An organization in New York saw the ad and called. They wanted to buy my skateboards and put them in the Smithsonian Institute's Museum of the American Indian in Washington DC. They put together a traveling exhibit with my skateboards and found other Natives who did it too.

I've been mostly performing solo lately, but I've been working with the band on a new CD titled "Relocation." We've recorded fifteen tracks that need to be mixed down.

"Hello San Diego" was released as a single in July 2021. For another song, "Cruise the Rez" I wanted screaming guitars like Stevie Ray Vaughn. It's a different perspective, as a Native American, of the blues. People forget that we went through genocide.

I've been hosting *Blues Mondays* on Facebook. I play three original songs each week, doing whatever I can to keep the blues alive.

Patrick Joseph "P. J." Vegas (1990–)
(Yaqui and Indigenous Mexican)

The son of Redbone co-founder Pat Vegas, P. J. Vegas "continues to break down discriminatory doors, an ability that has been passed down to him genetically."[26]

The recipient of a Best Independent Single NAMA ("Tears") in 2015, Vegas shared an MTV VMA (video music award) for Best Video with a Message ("Stand Up / Standing Rock"), two years later, as a member of Mag 7 (Magnificent 7), an intertribal supergroup that includes singers Taboo (Jaime Luis Gomez) (Shoshone and Mexican) of Black Eyed Peas, Kaala Hodges (Diné), and MC Drezus (Jeremiah Manitopyes) (Plains Cree); flutist Tony Duncan (Mandan, Hidatsa, and Arikara); and beatboxer, rapper, and dancer Christian "Supaman" Parrish (Crow). "[Vegas] is an unwavering advocate for his community . . . proudly merging his passions for music and social justice."[27]

Heritage is important to me. It's how we pray, how we have ceremonies, how we gather. There're always songs, chants, and telling stories through song. The beat of the drum is always in the background, representing life.

I'm an urban Native, an Indigenous singer-songwriter from Los Angeles. The opportunity to travel with my father to Indigenous communities was my connection. We'd go to powwows and other gatherings in Arizona every year, but I've had to rediscover most of the stuff I was accustomed to as a kid. As I got older and my father's schedule changed, I wasn't around my culture as much as I liked; I had to seek it out.

It was very cool to grow up with a living legend, a man who showed me things to strive for and allowed me to pursue my dreams. I got to hear a lot of music when I was growing up. I went to Redbone rehearsals, back and forth to shows, and learned to deal with people.

Until I was ten years old, Redbone was guitarist–keyboard player Tony Bellamy [1946–2009] [Yaqui], my father, and Uncle Lolly. They went through a couple of drummers. I went to powwows, concerts, and casinos with them. It was amazing to see my dad and uncle playing together. My uncle was an amazing player. I was a witness to the way he handled that guitar. He was able to do unique chord progressions. He could go from one end of a guitar's neck to the other incredibly fast. He was a real pro.

I took a different route, but I studied my father's and uncle's techniques, what made them great as musicians, and why their sound was so important. They taught me so much. It was a new way for Indigenous artists to be heard and seen.

Culture and tribal affiliation integrate into my music. Language and chants go on in the background. There are tribal drums, chanting, and things we use in our everyday ceremonies. I try for a happy medium between mainstream music and my Indigenous roots, something that fuses culture and mainstream. That's what my uncle and dad did. That's the biggest influence they had on me.

I tried playing different musical instruments but gravitated toward the keys. You could create lots of sounds on a keyboard. A piano is a piano, but when you're thinking production-wise and using a MIDI keyboard, there's a lot more that you could do. You could play drums, guitar, or flute on a keyboard and create any sound you want. If you know chord progressions, you can make it sound good.

Cody Blackbird is my bro. He was seeking to see if my father would play with him on a gig or collaborate on a song. That's how we met. I played him some of my music, and we got to talking. I had a song, "Better Dayz," that I had been working on for a while. I thought it should have some flute on it. I approached him with the idea. He said, "I'd love to do it."

We went to the studio, and he laid down the flute track. It was one of those things that you knew had to be. It turned out well.

"Better Dayz" was released as a single in late 2016. It's in a storytelling-type mode. A lot is going on in the world right now, a lot that's been going on for years. There are a lot of trials and tribulations that we, as Native people, go through, but it's not solely Natives. As a kid, I wished for better days. People are put in difficult situations every day. They keep pushing forward and praying for the sun to set, the moon to rise, and the sun to rise the next morning.

Priceless, the Free Album [2013] was my intro to the music game, the first time I was hands-on with the production. Before that, I was making records with my friends, until the music got good enough for me to feel confident that other people would want to hear it. Once I built that confidence, I knew I had to put out a project.

I've released singles—"Lose My Mind," "Not Today," and "Come My Way"—over the last two years, trying to get out as much music as I could. Things were pulling me in different directions, but I knew I needed music to thrust me forward.

I have my hand in everything I do. I coproduce everything I put out, adding sprinkles here and there of my own sauce, my beat. I listen to the basic track before writing the words and figure out if it should be happy or sad. That's when I put pen to pad.

Anyone who tells me they don't want to be in the mainstream, I just think they're lying. Why wouldn't you want your creation, something you put yourself into, to be heard on the highest level? But you can be successful without being mainstream. Social media has gotten the word out. Because of CNN, MSNBC, and other news outlets, people saw what was happening at Standing Rock. There are no such things as gatekeepers anymore. That's what was holding Natives back for so long—the people in charge. They feared that if the mainstream opened to Natives, they would have to deal with their bloody past. Colonization is still happening, but it's now called gentrification.

Native artists can stand on their own two feet. My father and uncle proved that it could be done. That was the beauty of Redbone. They showed the possibilities to Native kids all over the world who might have thought that, because of their race, culture, identity, and ethnicity, they didn't have an opportunity. Redbone was the pillar of that inspiration. Everything I do is community based, but it's geared toward the mainstream. I know it's possible.

I've been doing off-the-top freestyling, going to the studio with a subject or topic and writing as I go along. That's a key part to making my songs feel more real; they're coming directly from me. When I sit down to write, I think too much about what people want to hear, instead of what comes naturally.

I've been lucky to have people around me who are front liners—water protectors and people who are constantly laying their freedom, lives, and bodies on the line to put a stop to things that have been happening for so many years. I've been using my music to bring awareness to certain issues—activism through music. That's why I create songs like "Better Dayz," "Tears," and "Pecos." They're about issues that go on every day but get overlooked by mainstream media. If I bring awareness to these issues and, at the same time, make people feel good with my music, that's what I'm all about.

I'm going to be dropping a new track, "Smoke." The title stands for "Still My Own Known Enemy." It talks about the yin and yang of constantly being pulled in this direction and that direction, trying to find the confidence to put your stuff out to the world, allow it to do what it does, and not be your own worst enemy about it.

Vince Fontaine (1962–2022) (Anishinaabe)

Founder, leader, and guitarist of two of Indigenous Canada's top groups, Eagle and Hawk and Indian City, Vince Fontaine was described by Arlen Dumas, grand chief of the Manitoba Assembly of Chiefs (AMC), as "a musical beacon and a cultural ambassador for First Nations throughout North America and throughout the world."[28]

On January 10, 2022, Vince Fontaine recorded with his Indian City bandmate Jeremy Koz. The following day, the sixty-year-old guitarist, producer, and bandleader yielded to a fatal heart attack. A ceremony was held in Winnipeg, Manitoba, Canada, five days later. "It's a testament to the impact that he made in people's lives," said his niece Nahanni Fontaine, "and that commitment to community."[29]

Musicians in Canada love ice hockey. A bunch of us have been playing together for over twenty-five years, with eleven players on each team. It's the middle of August, but there are a handful of indoor rinks open. We're playing our last game until the fall today. It's going to be ninety degrees outside. Eagle and Hawk vocalist Jay Bodner and I have skated in a celebrity hockey game for fifteen years during JUNO Awards weekend. We've got some great players, including one who won the Stanley Cup. Of course, they're a hundred times better than us.

Growing up in North Kildonan, Manitoba, about eight miles from Winnipeg, there weren't many other Native kids, but I was like any kid in North America. I was a baseball pitcher, the only Native on the team. I really liked it. Of course, I watched Major League Baseball. When I lived in Montreal, I went to see the Expos play.

I knew I was an Indian. I didn't go to ceremonies every day or wear turquoise and beads. But my skin was dark, and we went to powwows. I got called names like "Dirty Indian."

I was proud of who I was, but—I hate to say this—there were times when I was more inclined to say I was French because of the prejudice.

I dropped out of school and worked in construction, later going back and earning a psychology degree from the University of Winnipeg. I also played guitar. In the early to midnineties, I was playing with bands in western Canada, looking for that elusive record deal. We were like any other band, long-haired rock and rollers covering Aerosmith.

During the summer of 1990, a crisis erupted over a proposed golf course on Mohawk sacred land in Oka, Quebec. It became a big thing across Canada and then the world, one of many historic incidents of protest and confrontation. It gave me the first sense of being a voice for Indigenous people.

Around 1992 or '93, I met Troy Westwood, a placekicker for the Winnipeg Blue Bombers of the Canadian Football League and a major celebrity. He was a good football player. He started the Banjo Bowl [now an annual game

29. Vince Fontaine

between the Blue Bombers and the Saskatchewan Roughriders], and he got a tryout for the San Francisco 49ers. They didn't take him because he's a lefty.

Troy was hilarious. He called one rival football team "banjo-picking inbreds."

He was young, with long hair. He was also a great singer-songwriter. We jammed at one of the big clubs in town, and people really liked it. We had chemistry.

My cousin, Larry Phillip "Phil" Fontaine, was chief of the Assembly of Manitoba Chiefs, the chief of all chiefs. He invited Troy and me to a sweat lodge and said, "Start this partnership with a ceremony."

That gave us confidence and direction. I felt entrusted to be a vehicle and bring music to the community. It became my responsibility.

Troy was busy during the summer, with practices and the game once a week, but that didn't stop us from having a vision. We didn't have a name yet, but our first song was a Led Zeppelin kind of a thing called "Eagle and Hawk."

We shopped our demo cassette around and played at local clubs. We released our first album, *The Vision*, in 1997. Troy wasn't a guitarist or piano player, but he could sing on pitch. He understood melody, and he made every lyric count. We'd talk about dreams or about seeing something, and he'd go away and write lyrics. Most songs on our first album were written off a guitar riff. Troy put words to the melody. We'd take it to the studio, bring the band in, and play. Let the producer manage it.

I was already in music, and people knew my name. But it helped to be connected with Troy. Critics wrote about a Blue Bombers player appearing at the Marvel Club, one of the clubs where football fans went after games. They got a kick when he got up and sang and, sure enough, he was good.

Eagle and Hawk started getting a high profile, but it would have been difficult for Troy to give up a football career to be in a band struggling to make a living. Country music was jumping up the charts. Rap, hip-hop, and rock and roll were taking a back seat to Seattle grunge and Nirvana. We didn't know what we were going to do, but we kept playing music and writing songs.

I started going to Europe with Keith Secola and the Wild Band of Indians in 1996, and my summers were taken up with that. We played festivals and the Olympics in Atlanta. I was getting a reputation for doing original songs in a new genre of Indigenous music and traveling the world. Newspapers were taking note.

When it became evident that Troy wasn't going to return to Eagle and Hawk, Jody Gaskin [Anishinaabe], from Sault Ste. Marie, Michigan, took his place. He could do it all—dance, play flute and guitar, and he had a heck of a voice. It was a fantastic opportunity for him, but he had his own thing going on. Sometimes we'd go to Europe, and I'd be his guitar player. Then we'd do a tour two months later, and he'd be the singer for Eagle and Hawk. It was the best of both worlds, but I wanted to do a new album and needed a full-time singer. That's when I started eyeballing Jay Bodner. We had been in the same music scene for years. He had a long history in the clubs, playing music and writing songs. He had energy; he was hip. I approached him in November or December of '97 and said, "I've got a tour in Europe—want to come? We're going to Paris, Zurich, Munich, and Berlin."

Jay was intending to go once, but it turned into years. Troy and I had our specific roles. He was the lyricist, and I was the guitar player. But I could send Jay a riff, and he'd expand on it. We'd jam and toss ideas around. We had chemistry from the start.

My community [Sagkeeng First Nation] wanted to book Buffy Sainte-Marie and asked if I could do it. I said, "Okay, I'll check into it," and entered the world of contracts. Then I was asked to book Susan Aglukark and Kashtin. I started putting on events a few times a year. Keith Secola told me, "I'll give you points any time you book me."

I started understanding how managers and booking agents negotiated. I realized how much people were making and gauged how much I should get paid. I wore multiple hats, but I was fair, keeping in mind that I had integrity to uphold.

Eagle and Hawk did a show at the George Pompidou Center in Paris. The keynote speaker was Dennis Banks. He was doing a Sacred Run across Europe and talking to the media and communities about the plight of American Indians and how they needed support. At the show, he walked onstage carrying his big powwow drum with seven, eight, or nine people following him. They looked European, not Native. There was even an Asian person. Dennis placed the drum down and put chairs around it. Those folks sat around the drum. Dennis hit it once, and they went into a song. They sounded like any champion drum group. When they stopped, he said, "When you've been entrusted as the vehicle in your circle and you bring people in, they can partake of the circle to its full extent."

He had taught them songs and invited them into his circle. That became a rallying point for Eagle and Hawk. I've brought dozens of people into my entrusted responsibility of Native American heritage and circle. Since Troy handed the keys to me and went back to football, I've brought in singers, bass players, drummers, dancers, and keyboard players to partake of this experience.

Songs for Turtle Island [2011], my solo CD, won a NAMA for Best Instrumental Album. As an artist, I was stretching my legs. Eagle and Hawk was idle, and Indian City had yet to hit the gate. *Songs for Turtle Island* was mostly instrumental, with some chanting and vocals. It had tracks like "Water Song," "White Buffalo," "Buffalo Song," and "Raven Fanfare."

I was watching PBS and saw the Fania All-Stars, this fantastic Latin group from New York that had coined Salsa. They featured three or four singers. I thought it'd be cool to do that. Later that summer, I flew to Colorado with a good friend to see the incredible Carlos Santana. He had the blueprint. He's not the lead singer, but he has two or three vocalists. That showed me the path, along with the Fania All-Stars, for Indian City.

We got a lot of hype, but I really enjoyed our music. I was part of every songwriting effort. It was different from Eagle and Hawk. I wasn't confined to guitar-driven things. I could step out and do something different. I had great vocalists at my disposal. Pamela Davis was incredible. Don Amero [Cree Metís and Eastern European] was a star by himself. He's gone on to win JUNOs. It was a great opportunity to bring them together, one of my favorite experiences.

Eagle and Hawk put out a seven-track album, *Liberty*, at the end of 2019, our first in ten years, but we had to hold off on promoting it. Our keyboard player [Gerry Atwell] died suddenly of a heart attack, and it set us back. Then Christmas came. January and February were slow. We thought we'd pick it up in March, and what happened? COVID!

The title song was an immediate response to the Trump administration's approach to immigration and open borders. American Indians were generous people who welcomed people and helped them out. You're going to close the borders?

We released "She's Come of Age" as a single. It's centuries overdue. One of the things we're trying to do is come of age.

The opening track, "Great Divide," is about climate and political division, whether it's in Canada, the U.S., or the world. After we released the CD, the unfortunate incident with George Floyd happened. As Indigenous people, we align with Black Lives Matter. We have issues to address in our community, government, and society, and we'll continue to address them—poverty, residential schools, history, and broken treaties. But there's hope. Look at what happened in Oklahoma in July 2020. The state court sided with the Muscogee Tribe and gave some of their land back. We want to see more justice like that.

Don Amero (1980–) (Cree Metís and Eastern European)

A founding member of Vince Fontaine's Indian City and a NAMA-winning solo artist, Don Amero's "golden voice bear-hugs each song with warmth and tenderness."[30]

Drinking at a bar and having a party isn't my brand. I'm about family and integrity. I have songs about love between couples, but I mostly sing songs that have something to say and cause people to think more intently about their life. That's the caveat for me. Musically, I've been on a slow escalator ride. I signed with Mike Denny's MDM Recordings in Toronto in 2018. They're a country music label. I just released a seven-song EP, *The Next Chapter*, my eighth album. There's never a dull day in my world.

I'm a singer-songwriter in my heart. Those vibes are still part of me, but I felt like I had hit the ceiling in my growth in the folk and roots community.

I was already dipping my toes in the country music community. Songs like "Right Where I Wanna Be" and "Turn These Grey Skies Blue" fit right in.

I grew up in Winnipeg and had a great early life. My parents were blue-collar, hardworking folks. I stuck with being a kid, playing in the yard from morning to night. I wasn't a great student. I wasn't terrible, but I didn't get straight As. Things went awry when I was eleven or twelve. My mom witnessed a murder at the restaurant where she worked. It was one of her friends. She got involved and tried to help him. He died in her arms. That set my mother on a tough course for a while. She and my dad hadn't been happy for years, but that was a catalyst in terms of her realizing the life that she had wasn't the one she wanted, particularly when it came to being married to my dad. She left abruptly and ended up with somebody else very quickly. He was abusive and a drug addict. As her son, watching my mom going through that was heavy for me. It was destroying my life, but it was tempered by love. I believe in something greater than myself. I was able to push through, knowing that I had a purpose, a reason I'm here. I have something to offer. That got me through those dark days.

Mom came from Cree and Metís roots in Manitoba, but I had almost no connection to that growing up. She was raised to be ashamed of her history. Many people have a similar story. Being Indigenous was frowned upon. People strayed from identifying as Indigenous. Mom fell into that camp.

When I was growing up, my parents would say, "You're Heinz 57," because my dad is from Nova Scotia and of eastern European descent. He wanted us to connect with our Nova Scotia roots, but I was a prairie boy in the middle of the country without a connection to the East Coast, other than my dad's stories.

As I grew up, I saw hurt and pain in the Indigenous community and thought about how I could be a game changer. That led to me wanting to be an ambassador of Indigenous thoughts and ideas, making sure people knew the issues. If you look at my catalog, you'll find songs about social injustices and mental health conversations, but I try to deliver some cake too, some sweetness, some sugar. Having heart-to-heart talks, you need to have a relationship with folks. If the first thing out of your mouth is going after them with injustices and depressing issues, it builds a wall between you and the people who don't agree with you. My idea is to build a relationship first. Then we can have those deeper conversations. Without that relationship, you don't have much of a foundation to stand on. That's what's lacking the most in Canada—community and connection. Without them it's hard to have those deeper conversations. I would venture to guess that it's the same in the States.

The music I'm delivering these days is a handshake, my way of saying, "Hello, nice to meet you. Here's what I do," and then going deeper on the journey.

Indian City put forward the Indigenous issues of the day. Vince [Fontaine] was hoping it would continue the conversation he had going on with Eagle and Hawk. He needed a breath of fresh air from his own music. Indian City served that purpose. I loved my time with them. We could hang our hats knowing that we did something worthwhile. The community appreciated it, and it still does. It was great for my personal growth and my connection to the Indigenous community, but I struggled with having my musical career, balancing my home life, and trying to be connected with Indian City. I couldn't juggle all three; something had to give. I had to step away from Indian City.

Before jumping into music, I did floor installations. I needed to make a living, but my tremendously understanding wife and partner got what I was trying to do. In the early days, she worked to make sure we had enough to pay our bills.

As my career grew, we had children. Oscar is eight; Stella, five; and our youngest, Elliott, is one. When Stella was born, my wife stepped away from her job as an administrator at our church and became a stay-at-home mom. Taking care of kids is the hardest job in the world, but music has provided for us. That's not to say there's no room to grow, but we invested in our early years to get where we are now.

I auditioned for *Canadian Idol*. It wasn't as big a platform as Lil Mike and Funny Bone had on *America's Got Talent*. I was on TV for three seconds. That's all I got, but I did well. I made it to the Golden Ticket in Winnipeg.

They flew us to Toronto. I made it to the final cut. I was in the final seventy-five people, out of ten thousand people who auditioned. What I learned was that those shows were looking for characters. I wanted to showcase my music and didn't care much about being a character. That was my downfall. I didn't understand the entertainment industry at that point. I was frustrated and sad when they sent me home, but I grew from that. I understood the music business quite a bit more.

Change Your Life [2007] was my first album. I was sitting around a table with my manager at the time. She asked me, "So, what do you want to do?"

I told her, "I want to put music out that, when people hear it, they want to change their life for the better."

She immediately said, "That's the title of the album."

When the album came out, it did indeed change my life, as well as others'. People have written to me saying my music spoke to them and became part of their medicine. That was when I first put the pedal to the metal. I haven't looked back since. That's not to say I haven't had my white flag moments when I wanted to give up.

The Long Way Home [2010], my third album, received a NAMA as Best Folk Recording. *Heart on My Sleeve* [2013] was nominated for an Aboriginal Album of the Year JUNO Award [my first of three] and a Canadian Folk Music Award. It won an Aboriginal People's Choice Music Award for Best Folk/Acoustic Album. *Evolution* received an Indigenous Music Award for Best Country Album of 2019. "Church" was the Best Music Video.

Awards have never been the reason I do this, but they validate the work I've done. Music isn't like any other industry where you get a promotion or raise if you do your job well. If you stand out, you get an award. The people you're nominated with are what makes it such a great honor, but when you get to walk away with the hardware, it's a testament to the work you've put in.

Other than "On Down the Road," a teaser of a tune, I didn't write anything on *The Next Chapter*. I sang songs by Nashville writers who are good at the craft. Knowing that we were aiming toward commercial country music, it was a different vibe than I could create.

Amero Little Christmas came out in 2019. Christmas is a big part of my life. It's more than Santa Claus and presents. It's the one time of year when family comes together. The spirit of the season is the connection with family, joy, and love. That's what I hope to spread.

For the first ten years, I'd think of going back to the day job. Then something great would happen, another door would open, and I'd be encouraged to keep going. For the last three or four years, I've settled into the idea that this is what I'm going to do. It's not just about music and stories but about how I'm going to inspire the next generation; I've settled into being a role model, doing workshops [Music Is Medicine] and speaking engagements.

I'm hoping my journey leads to festivals, without having to play the everybody's-sleeping-through-your-set time. Success will be the story there, but my trajectory is heading to where I'll be more of an artist developer, somebody who gives opportunities to the next generation. There's a growing movement to support Indigenous people in Canada. Industries and corporations are beginning to acknowledge our history. They know they're part of changing the future, so they're finding new Indigenous initiatives. We still have a long way to go, but everybody is doing a lot better and thriving. The social fabric is changing.

Idle No More and Standing Rock caused a shift in people talking about their rights. We're either going to band together, or nobody's going to pay attention. The world stopped to look, but the outcome was bleak. Big oil won. That's our shame. I don't know what to do about that. At the same time, solidarity is the reason we're in our much better current state. When the virus hit, we stopped talking about those issues. I hope we get back to the conversation again.

Indigenous musicians continue to impact contemporary rock. Joey Belladonna (1960–) (Haudenosaunee) sings with New York–based Anthrax, and Chuck Billy (1962–) (Pomo) fronts Testament, from Berkeley, California. Navajo Reservation–based Testify plays what it calls "Rez Metal."

Performing with drummer, bassist, and producer Pohonasin since 2005, Nechochwen (Shawnee) applies a modern twist to the tribal history and legends of West Virginia. "We all learned about Sitting Bull, Seattle, Chief Joseph and Geronimo in school," he said, "and that's wonderful, but even here in West Virginia, I learned about Tecumseh, Brant, Black Hawk and Half King on my own, not from school or movies. I want to shine a light on the amazing things we never seem to hear about. This is just part of our focus."[31]

The Cody Blackbird Band

Cody Sun Bear Blackbird (1991–) (Tsalagi, Dakota, and Romani)

In late 2021 the Cody Blackbird Band became the first Indigenous rock group featured in *Rolling Stone* when they collaborated on a single, "Backup," with Alaskan alt-rockers Portugal, the Man.

Our music is globally conscious. It has a positive message, whether it's about overcoming the challenges of our community, regaining our culture and language, or revitalization. We've got a platform we never had in the past.

We've been compared to Blues Traveler, not only based on our music, but also on how we coexist as a band and how we want our music to be perceived. [Blues Traveler front man] John Popper had the dream of taking a rarely featured instrument [harmonica] and making it the prime component of his music. That's what I've done with the flute. I was NAMA's Debut Artist in 2010 and Flutist of the Year a year later, the youngest to win the award.

I learned to play the flute by ear. It's taken a lot of practice and a lot of work to fit into different genres, but it comes from instinct.

I met Frank Waln at the NAMAs years back. We have a mutual uncle-through-ceremony who kept telling me, "You ought to hit him up."

At the time, I was based in Chicago and doing a lot of American Indian Center events and powwows. Frank was studying audio production and music design at Columbia College of Music. I went over, and we used one of the school's recording rooms to work on my 2017 album of traditional flute music, *Wicohan*. Frank did the engineering. One day, he said, "I've got an idea for a song, 'Hear My Cry,' and could use your help."

He burst out the lyrics and played the song on a piano. I came up with a riff, and we built around it. It was a true collaboration, Frank bringing his fire and me bringing mine. It won the NAMA for Song of the Year and was the most played song on Native radio in 2012. I learned a lot by working with Frank, but it was mutually beneficial. We were able to bring our knowledge together—him on the recording side and me on the melodic. We did shows with Keith Secola and Mvskoke and Seneca hoop dancers Lumhe and Samsoche Sampson.

I don't know much about my Cherokee side; I grew up with Dakota ceremonies. I was born in Bemidji, Minnesota, but we moved to Idaho when I was a year and a half and to Anchorage, Alaska, when I was eight or nine. I spent my school years there. During the summer, we'd go to South Dakota, a five-and-a-half-hour flight away, to visit family and have our ceremonies and sun dances. Then we'd go back home, and I'd start school again.

My dad, Thomas Blackbird, was an American Indian cowboy poet. A few years after we moved to Idaho, he started writing more songs. He performed at the Cowboy Poetry Gathering in Elko, Wyoming, and shared the

31. Cody Blackbird

stage with Michael Martin Murphy and Guy Clark numerous times. He did powwows and cultural festivals. His music and poetry were exceptional.

I grew up on the road, going to shows with my father, but I was too young to remember much. I've asked elders what it was like before social media—when they had to make phone calls, put ads in newspapers, and do physical marketing. They didn't have the online presence to say, "I'm going to be in Des Moines or Kansas City," and have everybody show up.

I was diagnosed with ADHD as a child, but it turned out to be a false diagnosis. They gave me Ritalin for fourteen years, but no matter how much they counteracted it with meds, I was still rambunctious. The only things that calmed me were ceremony music and flute music; that was it. I'd sit there listening and zone out. I was meditating, but I didn't know that as a kid. It helped me sleep, helped me get by.

When I was nine, we went to the Indian Market in Anchorage. It takes place in the summer. Thousands of tourists pass through on the weekends. It's a big to-do with artists, vendors, food, and music. The day we went, an intertribal First Nations band, Medicine Dream, played. They're an alternative rock group that incorporates Native flute. I heard them and wanted to play the flute.

We ordered a flute-making kit. I still have that flute, but it was breathy and homemade. I found a High Spirits flute at a music shop and begged my dad to get it for me. He said, "No, you'll play it a few times and never touch it again."

I said, "No, I swear," so he got it for me. I wouldn't put it down. They had to take it from me so I'd do my homework. My bedroom was beneath my parent's bedroom. My dad clogged the vent with a towel when I was learning to play so he wouldn't have to hear me. He never said anything. I had a drum set too. He was pleasantly pleased when I picked up the flute and put the drums away.

Within a year, I was able to emulate whatever I heard. Medicine Dream did a flute song that was fast and poppy. I was eleven years old when I heard it. I went to one of their concerts and brought a G flute. They played that song in F-sharp, but I sat in the audience playing it note for note.

I've got fifteen flutes that don't leave the house. I tour with others that come and go. I work with Brent Haines's Woodsounds Flutes. He sends me flutes and says, "If you find someone who wants this flute, I'll make you another."

I'll sell those, or do some trade, and get the flutes out to other homes. They don't have to live with me all the time.

I have a flute that belonged to Joseph FireCrow. It stays at the house, but I play it quite a bit. I have another made by Hawk Littlejohn, one of the last twenty flutes that he did. His widow, Geri Littlejohn, finished it after finding the blank. I have a couple of much older flutes. They're very sentimental. You'll hear them on my recordings but not during live shows.

When I was eighteen, I did an album that's no longer available, *Coming Home*. I recorded it in Alaska, thus the title. I did traditional songs. The title track had a guitar, vocals, and flute. *Raven Speaks* [2009] came out after that. That got me a NAMA nomination as Debut Artist. The next year, I released *The Journey* and won the NAMA for Flutist of the Year.

People were asking me to add more of my singing, along with my flute, so I wanted the album to be a mash-up. There were songs with singing and flute, songs with just flute, traditional singing, and round dance music. My brother and I went into a studio in Minneapolis and knocked it out in a night. I sent it to a mixing editor, and he did the magic on it.

I was booked to perform at a fundraiser for the Clean Water Alliance in South Dakota. The organizers said, "We'd like you to have a band. Do you think you could do it?"

I told them, "I'm traveling from North Arizona; there's no way I could bring a whole band."

"What if we hook you up with some players?"

I already knew John Frazier, a Grammy-winning percussionist from South Dakota. My brother, Caleb, has been with me the whole time. He's been on percussion, flute, and drums, as well as backing vocals. He's got a free-flowing style. We had Kurt Olson, whose resume includes drumming for Brulé, Keith Secola, and Indigenous. He's a Nashville cat. He was in town with Brulé. He came over and drummed for us. Brian Lebrun was on guitar, and Mike Riordan played bass. We got together once or twice before the show and came up with jams. There were no vocals. It was just flute, rock, and reggae. I liked it; it was what I wanted to do.

Brian and Mike continued playing with Caleb and me. John joined us when he could. When I moved to Arizona, I brought on a couple of acoustic guitarists from Morgantown, West Virginia—Xavier Torres and Lewis Schenk. They moved on after a couple of years. We had Will Benjamin for a while. Now we've got Justin Hyland [drums] and Neci Night [bass, guitar, and vocals]. Neci is also a songwriter; she's working on her own album. We've been partnering up and writing songs. Justin is a phenomenal drummer. He brings a lot of great ideas about arrangements.

I recorded the flute for P. J. Vegas's "Better Dayz" in 2014. He has an amazing voice and great charisma. It's in his blood. I got to share the stage with him during Indigenous Day in Los Angeles. His dad, Pat Vegas of Redbone, hit me up, "Cody, would you work with my son? He's got a song, and flute would go really good with it."

The Cody Blackbird Band's third CD, *Euphoria* [2017], placed number seventeen on iTunes' new age chart and number eighteen on *Billboard*'s new age chart. We were happy. The album came out exactly how we wanted it. It was something different, something that took you on a trip with instrumental jams. We worked on it with Terrance Jade [Lakota] from Wounded Knee. When I moved to Arizona, we brought him down. Terrance is an amazing producer. He came up with great concepts. He'd crank out a track, call me in, and say, "What do you think about this?"

The album I'm working on, *Immortal*, should be done by August 2021. The rest of my repertoire has been a mash-up of alternative rock, blues, reggae, and R&B, but this is in-your-face rock. There's no holding back. The music's taken a shift and has a lot more elements. We've got Sage Cornelius playing fiddle, and we added keyboards and horns. Our lyrics are still derived from tradition, but they're about who we are, the things we're fighting, and the things we're going through on the front lines of water rights and mental health.

Sihasin

Jeneda Benally (1980–) (Diné, German, and Polish American)
Clayson Benally (1986–) (Diné, German, and Polish American)

IndigenousWays describes Jeneda and Clayson Benally's Sihasin as "an explosive [sibling] duo of just bass, drums, and vocals with a traditional Navajo backbone bridging folk, rock, world, pop and a little punk."[32]

JENEDA BENALLY (JB). Clayson and I are celebrating thirty years of playing music together. We played with our brother, Klee, as Blackfire, from 1990 to 2012, but since then, we've been Sihasin [See-ha-sin]. In the Diné language, it means "hope." It's one of our values, as Diné people, to think positively.

CLAYSON BENALLY (CB). We went through a huge transition from Blackfire and hardcore punk rock to Sihasin. There was a piece missing—Klee—but there was so much creative energy. It was spiritual growth. Music for Indigenous people, not just Sihasin, reflects what's happening in the world. It's an illustration of who we are as storytellers, carrying on our culture's rich traditions and legacies. It's something that hopefully will never be erased from us. Our music is about sharing that message—who we are and what we're doing and reflecting on the world today.

JB. We're Indigenous, but we're also punk rockers, alt-rockers, or whatever label people want to give us. We don't have to be called Indigenous artists.

I'm a Diné woman, but I'm a human being too. We don't make a conscious effort to include traditional Diné vocals [though they're occasionally sung by Jeneda and Clayson's father, Jones Benally, a traditional hetáli, or healer] and rhythms into our contemporary music. It's who we are. We're traditional people who utilize modern tools to remind the world that our culture is cool. It has value. It's not a stereotype.

CB. We've been part of the Ramones family going back to the early nineties, when Jeneda and a friend went to see the Ramones. They were so knocked out that they drove to Austin to see them again. She thought they were a family band, because of their stage name, and sent them a letter. After the show, she connected with their bass player, C. J. Ramone [Christopher Joseph Ward], and it became a brother-sister relationship. He gave us a lot of guidance when we started Blackfire. For our first recording experience, CJ flew out and produced us.

On my sixteenth birthday, in 1994, we released our first EP. It helped define our sound and led to Blackfire winning a **NAMA** as the year's Best Debut Group.

We've always had people coming to spend time with my family and rejuvenate, get their heads straightened out before going back to Hollywood or the music scene. After CJ, Joey Ramone [Jeffrey Ross Hyman] came into our life. He had been diagnosed with lymphoma. Doctors gave him a short period to live. After the Ramones' last tour, in 1996, he came out, and my dad helped him significantly. He ended up sticking around for quite a bit longer, passing in 2001 at the age of fifty. He was our spiritual producer when we recorded *One Nation Under*, the **NAMA**'s Best Pop/Rock Recording of 2001. We had that kind of mentorship and support from the Ramones.

JB. Joey wanted to produce us, but it didn't work out. Blackfire already had a producer, Don Flemings, whom we still love very much, who produced Sonic Youth, Screaming Trees, and his own Velvet Monkeys. Joey's last recordings were the two songs he sang on *One Nation Under*. After we did "What Do You See," he said, "Okay, I understand why you're using Don Flemings."

CB. We last worked with Don on *Woody Guthrie Singles* [2003]. We wanted to keep Woody's spirit alive. He wrote about dust bowls and unions, but he also wrote about American Indian issues. After we performed "Mean Things Happenin' in this World" at Woody Fest, Pete Seeger came up to us and jokingly said, "Great job. It sounded nothing like the original."

We didn't have any guide other than Woody's words, but we wanted to do complete justice to the song. Cyril Neville covered our version.

"Indian Corn Song" talked about wastefulness and how Indigenous people are living in a balanced way.

JB. After Joey passed, Blackfire was asked to do a couple of Ramones tunes—"I Believe in Miracles" and "Planet Earth 88"—for a compilation CD. After it came out, I was reading the liner notes and saw that Ed Stasium mixed it in Durango, Colorado. We had heard about him from Joey. He not only produced the Ramones but also Living Colour, the Smithereens, the Talking Heads, Mick Jagger, Soul Asylum, and Joan Jett and the Blackhearts. Durango was just up the road from us, and we had a performance coming up at the college, so we put a call out to him and said, "Joey wanted us to meet a long time ago and work together. We'd be really excited, in this wild world of complications, if we could work it out."

CB. It was a natural relationship. There must be a lot of trust between an artist and a producer. It's nice to have him as part of our team.[33]

JB. We're not commercial mainstream music but a confluence of musical styles, history, and messages. Ed gets that, like a family member. You can't ask for anything better.

JB. He produced Blackfire's *(Silence) Is a Weapon* [2007]. My brothers and I thought it important for people to hear the full traditional songs we were combining with electric music, so we made it a double album. One disc was contemporary, and the other traditional. We owe it to our ancestors to pass on our traditional knowledge. We still exist. And we're going to use modern tools and crank it up to eleven, because as Indigenous people, we've got something to say, and we need you to hear it. That was the concept of the album's art, too, a postapocalyptic Western civilization in which people continue to thrive.

CB. The cover showed Lebanon after it was bombed. It was a vintage photo. We put images of Indigenous horseback riders next to the bombed-out rubbish. What's sustainable when humans destroy everything? We're a virus on this planet, exploiting the resources without giving back. People look at our Indigenous culture as if it's something in the past, but what's preserved is the cultural knowledge and the teachings from our elders. That's the future.

JB. [Peter LaFarge biographer] Sandra Hale Schulman asked us to record "I'm an Alien, I'm an Indian." She's made it so much her life's work to connect the younger generation with his songs. It was an incredible honor. We recorded two of Peter's songs but only put one on the album.[34]

CB. I remember creating the melody for "I'm an Alien, I'm an Indian" and thinking, "This sound's nothing like the original."

That school of thinking comes from having a mother, Berta Benally, who came out of the Greenwich Village folk generation. She encouraged taking a song and making it your own, stressing the importance of being an individual without trying to sound like anyone else. We weren't going to sound like the original, so we did what gave us the emotional satisfaction needed to convey the story. That's why the guitar riff is there, to give it the upbeat energy that Peter LaFarge initially had. We dropped the tempo to give more power to the emotion.

[Stasium] was skeptical when he produced Sihasin's first album, *Never Surrender*, but he found it liberating. It created more space and gave it a unique sound. The songs we recorded were direct. It felt natural to allow them to speak in their own voices and not get buried.

JB. In an article in the *Huffington Post*, Evan Greer called Sihasin one of the top "freedom fighting bands to get you through the Trump years."[35]

That was the motivation we needed to get back into the studio. We started working on *Fight like a Woman* in February 2017 but, for the first time, took our time. As Blackfire, we were used to the punk rock concept of two weeks maximum for an album, but Ed said, "Allow the songs to breathe."

Having time to experiment and let the songs sing was one of the most amazing processes I never knew existed. We've recorded without Ed, but I always feel insecure. With *Fight like a Woman* he wanted us to be credited as coproducers. He said we did enough of the work. That was huge. We got to collaborate with a legendary producer.

Fight like a Woman's theme was empowerment.[36] They're songs of honoring, not only our matriarchal culture, but also our Indigenous knowledge—learning to grow our own plants, being self-sufficient and as resilient as our ancestors were. We wanted to honor our ancestors but find ways to inspire future generations; that was the driving force.

The album was the most personal I've ever written. It's easy for me to write love songs for change and justice, love songs about equality, and love

32. Sihasin

songs about the environment, but this was the first time I wrote love songs for my heart. I wasn't being a champion or a cheerleader for change but writing about what was happening in my life. I shared it, hoping listeners connected in a different way.

"See You" was written to help me deal with the grief of losing my three-year-old godson. He was killed in a parking lot crosswalk, by a distracted driver, while he was holding his mother's hand. It took time for me to write it, but I couldn't sing it. As much as I wanted to, as much I wanted my godson in the spirit world to hear my voice, I couldn't do it. Clayson sang it, but that song is so personal to me. The loss of any family member is difficult, but the loss of a child, without warning, is incredibly painful. I wrote the song with an amazing singer-songwriter, Brianna Lea Pruitt [Tsalagi, Choctaw, and Chickasaw]. She took her own life at the age of thirty-two in 2015. We never finished the song, but I had a dream after she died. In the dream, she asked me, "So, did you record the song yet?"

We had been working on five songs, but I knew the song she was asking about. I told her, "You died. How can I finish it?"

It hurt so much when she died—she hadn't reached out to me—but in my dream, she insisted, "You've got to record the song."

Inspiration for "Don't You Ever Give Up" came when I stayed up all night on Facebook Messenger with a kid who was contemplating suicide. Clayson and I do volunteer work to help young people recognize the power of creativity and use that creativity to come out of the darker spots and deal with so-called negative emotions. I ended up writing two songs that night. The kid is still alive. The next day, after lots of sleep, I couldn't stop thinking about our messages and how people need to shine. If you don't like something, change it. You have that power.

"Drive" was inspired by a relative who was being abused. She was living in an unsafe home. I kept trying to get her to leave, but she was fearful that her partner would come after her. The song is about physical abuse, mental abuse, emotional abuse, financial abuse, sexual abuse, and domestic violence. When I was writing it, I realized that part of me was in that song. I was in a long-term emotionally abusive relationship.

"Vengeance" is incredibly personal. I found out that my partner of over a decade was cheating on me. It was incredibly painful. "Vengeance" is about coping with a relationship that's not healthy and taking your power back.

"Big Shot in the Dark" came from friends who used to be in Timbuk 3.[37] We were asked to record it for a 2016 compilation, *Begging His Graces: The Songs and Sins of Pat McDonald*, Timbuk 3's lead singer and songwriter.

CB. People think you can't do it without a guitar. When you think about what Jeneda and I are working with, the drums are the backbone, very much a part of the foundation, and Jeneda's bass is the pure tone. I worked with a friend to develop a splitter box for Jeneda's bass. It splits into a bass amplifier and a guitar amplifier. Most people don't realize that there isn't a guitar when they hear us; so much sound is produced from that setup.

JB. Our sound is as big live as it is on our albums. We like to stay true to the performance. Some people do a lot of production on their albums, but we want to be able to perform what we record.

CB. We're old-school. We prefer everything to be in the moment, not prerecorded. The energy must be authentic.

JB. Our mom comes from a generation when there were no rules. It might be the Indigenous teachings in me, but I recognize and respond to that concept. I don't see rules when it comes to making music or needing to have a guitarist or keyboard player. You work with what you have, be as resourceful as you can, and do the best you can.

CB. We're very blessed to have grown up with positive role models, people who could give us guidance and knowledge.

JB. During my preschool years, we lived on the reservation. We hauled water and didn't have electricity. It was a beautiful, peaceful life. I got to be with sheep and with my grandmother. When it came time to go to school, my parents didn't want me to go to boarding school. My father's a survivor of the boarding school era. They moved off the reservation, beyond the government boundaries, so I could have an education. Growing up meant school during the week and going to the reservation every weekend, a two-and-a-half-hour drive. We spent a lot of time in our truck singing traditional songs; we didn't have a radio. We had to be resourceful and creative. That was my childhood, my adulthood as well.

CB. I'm the baby of the family, but I wanted to start a band. I sketched out what its name would be. First, it was going to be the Bad Brains or the Dead Heads. My mom vetoed the Dead Heads. I ended up sketching out Blackfire. My initial sketch was a reference to where we came from—Black Mesa. It's in the heart of the Navajo Reservation, where a lot of coal mining goes on. When you burn coal, it's one of the darkest substances. I saw black fire enveloping the whole world. I tried to get friends to join the band, but they were all too busy. Eleven-year-olds just want to play and do their own thing. Klee had a practice pad and drumsticks but never really connected with them. I ended up taking them. I started drumming on everything. Pretty soon Klee picked up a guitar from a pawnshop. Jeneda picked up a Fender Jazzmaster bass.

JB. I never wanted to play another instrument besides bass. I toyed with the idea of a ukulele because it had four strings. The first time I heard a bass, I went "Whoa!"

That sound was all the emotions I was feeling but didn't know how to put into words. Before I found my voice, the bass was my voice. It communicated my feelings for me.

When I started playing, I faced a lot of sexism. I was told by one of my first teachers that if I wanted to learn to play the bass, I would have to cut my hair. He said that, anatomically speaking, women were just not made to play bass. That was fuel for me. It made me want to prove folks like that wrong. These days, I don't experience sexism as much. The grunge era was kinder to women musicians. Women could play an instrument without being objectified, but pop music marketing is still all about objectifying women. We're not objects. I'm not going to wear leotards on the cover of our album just to sell CDs.

CB. Mom produced concerts when we were growing up. She had Taj Mahal come to the Grand Canyon to play. She brought Albert King, Jackson Browne, and Jesse Colin Young out. She put on John Trudell's first concert, a benefit to bring attention and aid to the relocation that was happening to our people at Black Mesa.

JB. We grew up falling asleep in packing cases backstage. We had the privilege of hearing live music and being at arm's length from so many legendary musicians, but when you're a kid, you don't realize how fortunate you are.

CB. I'd watch drummers at my mother's shows, but they'd tell me not to copy their stuff. I had to learn the hard way. I saw how much they loved playing, the way the music moved them. That was a big part of my learning.

JB. I'm grateful for the care and the nurturing my parents took in giving us a musical life, whether it was singing ceremonial songs or being backstage playing someone's guitar. It was normal to sing all night at a ceremony and be at a rock concert the next night.

CB. Everything that I'm utilizing as an adult, a lot of those teachings come from my father. He grew up on the reservation in the 1930s, without seeing white people. Everything was pristine.

JB. My father went to a boarding school when he was twenty. When the school found out that he could do hoop dancing, they started sending him all around the world. He toured with a Wild West show before going to Hollywood and acting in films by John Wayne, Gene Autry, and Roy Rogers.

CB. He wasn't the oldest, but the second born. My grandfather wasn't a nice person. He was very cruel and cared more about his cows. I'm blessed that my dad didn't go in that direction. He followed his mother, an amazing woman who was always joking, always transforming whatever hardships, negative energy, or things that might be perceived as difficult into something positive.

It's hard to be an Indigenous person, with cultural foundations and teachings, and also in the contemporary modern world. It can be very confusing, especially as a youth, not knowing where you fit in or belong. There are two worlds—the contemporary and the traditional. My father did an amazing job at helping us to navigate that foundation. We know who we are when we travel out to the world. We're not afraid to question and learn. To this day, my father is still teaching and sharing traditional knowledge and wisdom, being a healer, and helping people in their journey.

JB. I have my brother to fall back on, and he has me. But growing up was realizing that there were, and still are, vast injustices in the world of Indigenous people. There's economic disparity, educational disparity, and disparity in resources. I wondered if everybody had these problems. Was it normal for a five-year-old to see her grandmother pleading with men in suits to get off our homeland and allow us to live a traditional life?

CB. We were living in the southern part of the Grand Canyon. It was a large, diverse community—Hopis, Navajos, and millions of tourists—but at the end of the day, it was just an isolated community. We'd go back and forth to the Black Mesa Reservation and help our grandmother and elders with ceremonies. We went to powwows, performed with traditional Navajo dancers, did the hoop dance, and lived this natural synthesis of culture.

JB. Electricity wasn't something I missed. With every drop of water and every drop of oil in our lanterns, I learned not to be wasteful. That's the opposite of how society lives today.

CB. You have the urban Indian and the reservation Native. There's always been this weird distinction. I come from the heart of the Navajo Nation; that's where my umbilical cord was placed. It was uprooted by bulldozer, Peabody Coal, the forced relocation, and the division that exists with the federal government. Having part of my roots uplifted allowed me to function and thrive in both worlds. I can articulate what my grandmother's wishes and needs were and why we stand up and fight for our sacred places, our families, and our right to exist. We travel around the world and share that message.

JB. When we, as Indigenous people, open the door to our culture, we allow people to be tourists and provide a window for them to see us. When we're visible, it breaks down stereotypes. It allows people to appreciate our resilience and the richness of our culture. That leads to bridges of understanding. When we can understand each other, we're less fearful. That's when the real work begins on equality, justice, and building healthy communities based on respect.

CB. Our love of punk rock came out of learning that the United States government was implementing a policy of relocation against our family. We were resisters. We learned to scream at the top of our lungs. That way, people could hear the message of our music. That message is still relevant, and it holds. We're still fighting to protect our lifestyle, traditional way, and sacred sites.

JB. Blackfire came together right before midnight on New Year's Eve 1989. We had been toying around with music, but that was our first gig. We only had three songs; we didn't know anyone else's songs. We played music as a mouthpiece against the injustice we saw growing up, the relocation, the assimilation, the genocide of our people, and the loss of our ancestral homeland.

CB. Being the people at the source of that coal, we're the canary in the mine, trying to say, "This is impacting us. It's affecting our people, the water, and the air. What are we going to do about it? We need your help."

JB. We lost our lawsuit against the National Forest Service in 2012, after a five-year battle to prevent the Arizona Snowbowl from using wastewater for artificial snow.[38]

CB. They've been making artificial snow on our holy mountain. Elders, spiritual leaders, and medical practitioners, not just the Navajo but all the tribes, hold the mountain significant. It's our mountain of the west. Our elders warned that if they did the development, there would be drought. We prayed to the mountain deities to bring rain.

JB. Suing the federal government was one of the most frightening things I've ever done, but it was also one of the most empowering things I've ever done.

CB. Man-made snow was bound to have an impact. We've seen drought, wildfires, and very severe conditions. The mountain's not going to take it anymore. As an Indigenous person, I'm not going to say, "I told you so," but this is what happens when you mess with Mother Nature and put toilet water on a sacred mountain.

JB. *Never Surrender* was therapy for me to heal and grow. We sang about border issues, the call for peace, and the idea of never surrendering. Every time Clayson or I tried speaking about reclaimed wastewater or the holy San Francisco Peaks, we were sued. The ski resort took us to court for over a quarter of a million dollars; they lost. We got the ACLU, Bar Association, and Ralph Nader involved, but [the ski resort] sued us for the cost of the lawsuit. They continued harassing us for six years; it was brutal. They bullied us, but there's a song waiting in the wings. The statute of limitations is up.

CB. Once you're a punk, you're always a punk. It's about honesty, being truthful and authentic.

JB. We're Sihasin, but we'll always be Blackfire. Clayson and I have so much fun playing Blackfire songs. We did a punk version of "Winter Wonderland." Cleopatra Records asked us to pick a song for a compilation [*Punk Rock Christmas*] that also included tracks by Iggy Pop, Smash Mouth, the Vibrators, and Eddie and the Hot Rods. I'm a huge fan of the label. I was surprised when the song was picked for a Hyundai commercial, paired with Tony Bennett. That, to us, was a game changer, beyond the scope of reality.

CB. We wanted a Christmas song that wasn't Christian-biased. Religion has been used as a tool and weapon to force assimilation and destroy our traditional, cultural lifeways. Everybody celebrates Christmas, regardless of religion or faith. The holidays are a time to give and be around the family. "Winter Wonderland" connected with us, but the line "We'll frolic and play the Eskimo way" was a problem. I've got in-laws up north. I talked with them to find a more appropriate word. We did a lot of research and came up with "the Inuit way," as an alternative. There are so many tribes in Alaska, Canada, and the maritime coast that used to be called "Eskimos." It's the same with Navajos. That's a name that was given to us, not the name that represents us. We are Diné.

JB. One of the films that used Sihasin's music, *The Dancer Diaries*, was controversial to me. When it was first pitched to us, I thought its story was demeaning to women. Set in a strip club, it was about the dancers. Andy Norris, who wrote and directed the film, asked for our music to be included. I was hesitant until he sent me the book he wrote. I read it, and it changed my entire perception. The stories were empowering; they fit my comfort zone.

CB. When everything's shut down, people realize, as parents, that we're educators. Even though our kids may not be in school, this is our opportunity to share our family's traditions and rich legacies with the next generation.

JB. The first episode on our YouTube channel debuted on June 1, 2020. It's a punk rock way to keep Indigenous culture alive. We're looking to inspire our youth to appreciate and truly invest in our Indigenous ways.

CB. Everyone's Indigenous in this world. Our teachings are our connection to the land and show us how to be respectful, grow food, nourish our children, and live in balance. Those traditions are crucial, part of the solution to the problems that we're facing today.

Sihasin comes full circle with songs that represent our authentic selves as Diné. We sing the message people need to hear. Music is how we heal, how we mend, and how we find inspiration to improve our lives as humans and for the different species we coexist with.

JB. We're three generations in this house, so it's important to stay protected. Clayson's wife is a health-care worker, so we keep a social distance from him. I intended to spend the summer building a hogan on our two-and-a-half-acre ranch on the reservation, but the lockdown is strict. Weekends are fifty-seven-hour lockdowns, and weekdays have curfews. It's not safe at all.

CB. We've been in isolation, but we've been working on new material. I've been recording into my iPhone when I've been in the forest. I pay attention to my dreams and write them down. I'm blessed that my sister doesn't live too far from me. We're trying to continue to make music, but we're social distancing. We had a lot of gigs fall through, but if there's a way to safeguard and protect our father, we've got to do it. He's ninety or so; we don't know how old he is. It's a challenge to find time to sit down and start writing.

JB. We have a cow for milk, a duck that lays eggs, a sheep for mutton, and we've got our garden planted. But 30 to 50 percent of our people don't have running water or electricity. We need to wash our hands and be as sanitary as we can be. We need electricity to, at least, have a refrigerator so we can store produce and medication to keep our people healthy. We need access to the internet so our kids can continue their education. It's a continuation of the genocide. The Indian Wars never ended. The government hasn't lived up to its treaties or agreements.

CB. We pray to heal this world. Singing together, we have the responsibility to have one ear connected to the past and our voices moving forward into the future.

JB. If there's a gift from the pandemic, it's that Klee has come back into our lives. That's been beautiful. He came out with his own acoustic album, *The Unsustainable Sessions*, in 2016. We played an online concert together recently; that was cool.

11

Rocksteady

Surrounded by the much-larger 27,000-square-mile Navajo Reservation, the eleven villages of the Hopi Reservation are squeezed into a 2,532 square mile, northern Arizona desert highland the size of Rhode Island. Despite its diminutive size, the Hopi Reservation became a hotbed for Jamaican reggae after teacher-turned-entrepreneur Gerry Gordon of Cultural Connection launched Reggae Inna Hopiland in 1984. More than fifty of the Caribbean's greatest musicians appeared at the Hopi Veterans Center. "The artists really seemed to relate to the Hopi," remembered Gordon. "The Hopi women would cook them food, and we'd throw them in the back of a pickup truck—the 'Hopi limo,' we called it—and show them around the reservation. The Hopi would always present a gift to the artist on stage, like pottery or a kachina doll. Time slowed down. It was an *interaction*, as opposed to them playing at a bar."[1]

Arthur "Casper Loma Da Wa" Lomayesva (1967–) (Hopi and Diné)

A regular attendee of the Reggae Inna Hopiland series, Casper Loma Da Wa absorbed what he heard and formed the Mighty 602 Band and, later, Higher Conspiracy.

> I saw the best artists at Reggae Inna Hopiland shows before opening for them, the cream of the crop. Freddy McGregor was the first. They call him "Hopi Freddy" now. He went back to Jamaica and told everybody, "If you go to Arizona, this is where you need to go."
>
> I learned from the best and took it up a notch. It wasn't long before we were headlining. The Mighty 602 Band was one of the hottest groups in

the Southwest. It was a great twenty-year run. Thirty-three musicians came and went. They were true musicians; they didn't have anything but the drive to play music. They didn't even have driver's licenses. I had to pick everyone up and take them to rehearsals. There were times when the drummer didn't have sticks. It wore me out. I wasn't used to taking care of grown men. The music was powerful, but we had real issues.

We were a hardworking band; but like anything else, if you're not watering the plant or feeding the spirit, it goes away. That's what happened. After the 2008 economic collapse, there was no work. I was broke like everyone, but I kept getting my guys into the studio to record. It wasn't working fast enough for me, so I ventured out on my own.

Taida Pinda had been playing with a local band, the Black Bottom Lighters, in Phoenix. I call him "MGT." He's an awesome guitar player, singer, and songwriter. It was a godsend that our paths crossed—the best thing to happen for both of us. He was also in transition, so we hooked up and started Highest Conspiracy. It wasn't immediate, but we realized it was what we wanted to do.

I've got twenty years on the second-oldest musician in Highest Conspiracy. That's why it's so vibrant. I don't have to do all the legwork. All I do is show up, play bass, and sing.

Until COVID, my drummer, Matthew Bracamonte, was going to college. He gets nothing but support and love from me. Steve Freund is our newest addition. He plays guitar and keyboard, as well as bass. It frees me to do what I do. When I'm playing bass, it hinders my singing. I can only do so much.

I played bass for the first time when Highest Conspiracy came together in early 2017. I was tired of counting on someone else to do it. I figured if I could get through geometry and trigonometry classes, I could surely learn to play bass. That's how I approached it. Nothing is impossible.

I wrote ten songs, and we went into the studio. We recorded *Reality and Dreams*, but a lot was going on in my life at the time. I went back to school and got a degree in engineering management at ASU [Arizona State University]. I'm a surveyor by trade; I've done it most of my life. It paid for the 602 project for more than twenty years. We released seven albums. I used money saved for retirement to pay for them.

I shouldn't have been going to college with sixteen- and seventeen-year-olds, but I managed to get through it and get my degree. It was one of the hardest things I've ever done. A couple of times, I took my knapsack and thought about putting it in the trash. I didn't want to go to school anymore. I didn't have to do it. I already had a job. I didn't need a degree. I was working as a civil engineer and going to school full-time. Time management was tough, but my spirit wouldn't let me quit. Building roads and highways were right up my alley and assignments were easy.

During my sophomore year of college, my wife sustained a serious injury and left her job as a hospice nurse. I changed my schedule. I was going to school during the day. When it happened, I changed to night classes and went back to work during the day. Going to school was the hardest thing I've done, but I didn't miss a mortgage payment, and we always paid our bills.

Hopiland isn't a reservation but the home of the original people of North America. Hopis have been here for four thousand years, long before America was America. They never relocated. Their only border disputes have been with the Navajos. Hopi used to be much bigger, but as the years went on, the Navajos kept taking more land. The U.S. government set

up the Navajo Reservation, with the Treaty of 1868, for one reason—to have access to the coal mines. I'm not saying that because I'm biased—I'm half Navajo—but it's the truth. That's why Hopi is in the middle of Navajo land.

There were millions of dollars of natural resources on that land. The operator of the coal mine, Peabody Energy, Inc., was based in England. The U.S. government gave them permission to go into disputed Hopi and Navajo land and take coal out, but the company took it a step further. Not only did they take coal out, but they used water from a ten-thousand-year-old aquifer. It was the most pristine water on Earth, charcoal filtered through the coal. The aquifer was one of the biggest in North America. That's why it was disputed land.

The Hopis got royalties from the coal mine, but the Navajos got a much bigger chunk. There's no rhyme or reason for that. It isn't fair at all. It created a lot of problems in the 1970s and '80s. It's been an uphill climb for the Hopis. The tribal chairperson, LeRoy N. Shingoitewa, knew the coal mine was going to shut down and didn't do anything. The prior chairperson, Ben Navumsa, tried kick-starting green energy programs. He knew the coal reserves weren't going to last forever. He looked at all kinds of possible solutions. He even looked at casino revenue, though the Hopis were against it.

There was no longer revenue coming from the coal mine. The Hopi were lucky to get enough coal to heat themselves in the winter. There were no jobs. People left the rez, taking their families, so there are no kids. The population of the schools dwindled, and the government had been giving them money per student. It was dismal. There was no water—the aquifer had drained. The Hopi didn't start alternative programs like the Navajo, who had solar power, wind farming, and casinos.

Timothy Nuvangyaoma, the Hopi tribal chairperson since 2017, is younger, but I don't know how he's going to stimulate the economy. There's nothing there unless the government starts granting the green stuff. The Navajos already have the lead; it's bleak.

My grandfather used to tell me that Hopiland can be two things. It's so far from civilization, it can be a sanctuary like it was in the old days. Hopis were praying for the world and farming. That's why so much prosperity happened. People still come here for solitude, culture, or to get back to their roots, but it could also be a prison. It's so isolated. All that's there is alcohol and drugs like meth, cocaine, and heroin. Bootleggers are right across the street. It's like any reserve. If you're in the middle of nowhere, what do you do?

People are split between two worlds—the cultural heritage of the Hopi and Navajo and the modern world with the internet and cell phones. Those who return to the reserve don't last long. They succumb to what happens if they drink too much or do drugs too much; their addiction kills them. My late twenties and early thirties were my experimental time. I lived in Las Vegas and hung out in the City of Sin. All we did was smoke, gamble, and drink.

My Hopi name is Loma Da Wa. *Loma* means "beautiful," and *da-wa* means "sun." When I was small, I had a bulb-shaped head. My grandfather said, "You look like that ghost, eh, what's his name ... Casper?"

It stuck to me. As I got older and became an artist, I started using that name—Casper from Hopiland. It followed me.

Living in Tucson, I was exposed to everything on the radio, but when my friends and cousins were listening to AC/DC, Metallica, and other hard rock bands, I was listening to Michael Jackson, the Parliament-Funkadelics, and Rose Royce. When people harmonized, that's what grabbed me. Hip-hop and reggae have always been what I do.

I'm careful with the songs I put out. They should be uplifting for humanity, not about putting people down. They should be about your culture, your lineage, and your generation. My records have been played all around the world. I've heard from soldiers who've come back from Iraq. They tell me, "Casper, you're not going to believe this, but I ran into someone playing *The Sounds of Reality* on a makeshift CD player—in the middle of a freaking war zone."

I'm not a rapper, but I can tell a story. It doesn't have to be "Knick-knack paddywhack."

I touch on subjects that people relate to, whether it's alcoholism, drug addiction, love, hate, or technology.

It's an honor to be compared to reggae master Pablo Moses. Our lyrical styles are similar. We sing about the reality going on around us. For me it's Hopiland and Peabody's coal mine. Pablo Moses is no joke. He's the direct descendent of an African warrior, and he runs a tight ship. If you cross him the wrong way, you might get cut. It was the same with the Mighty 602 Band. I was "The Dude."

I was an artist, as well as a manager, booking agent, and babysitter. I drove the van and set up hotel accommodations. I did it all.

I wrote my first song at work, in 1997, standing in the middle of a freeway, holding a surveyor rod, doing it the old-school way, before GPS. I sang about reggae artists coming to Hopiland and about what was current— police brutality, living two lives, on and off the reservation.

I had two groups—Rude Awakening on the West Coast and the Mighty

602 Band in the Southwest—and I was doing things on my own. I was fortunate to work with some heavyweights. John Trudell sang "Brother Leonard [Set Him Free]" on *Honor the People* [2009]. Our first meeting was nothing spectacular. He said, "Hello," and kept going. That continued for five years. During that time, he was at his peak with his music. We did shows together all the time. He was the headliner. We were on the bill, but we didn't hang out. I found out later why. He didn't trust anybody. He had gone through that whole bout with the FBI and was weary of people. He had people around him who weren't his friends but spies. I didn't know anything about it, but I asked Quiltman, John's right-hand man, "What's up with this? John won't give me the time of day."

He said, "Don't take it personally. He does that to everybody. You'll see—when he trusts you, he won't brush you off. You'll join the circle."

I respected that. After that, every time I saw John, I'd give him something he could use for meditation. I'd shake his hand and say, "Have a good show."

That went on for three years. I'd run into him and give him some good herb. One time, instead of just taking it from my hand, he grabbed me in a handshake and pulled me toward him. That was exactly what Quiltman had told me. John and I were friends from that time on. He became like an uncle to me because of the lessons he taught me in his last days. I told him, "I have a song that I want you to be a part of," and I gave him a time frame of when I wanted to do it. He told me he had only one day off in the next five months, so I scheduled the session for that day. The night before, he flew into Los Angeles from Italy. He had one day off before flying to Barcelona. He took a plane to Arizona the next morning and laid down the track with me. He flew back that afternoon. He had a two-hour layover before the flight, so I took him to lunch. He wanted to eat Mexican food. Our conversation changed my life. He told me, "Bro, you're on a radar, but you don't realize it. If you're singing anything about the uplifting of your people, you're on a radar. Take it from me—you need to be careful about where you go, what you say, whom you congregate with. They will bring you down, do anything they can to discredit your work."

John taught me to be true to what I was doing but careful of whom I was doing it with. He said, "You're dangerous, Casper."

He was true to his game.

The Mighty 602 Band's last release, *Elemental*, was in 2013, but I've brought that energy, along with an older mindset, to Highest Conspiracy. Our music is going to do good things; I'm happy about it. We finished recording the *Nowadays* EP in February 2020. We sent it to LA to get CDs printed, but the virus delayed everything. It finally came out at the beginning of May.

We've been rehearsing for our next album. It's not spoken word but my own style incorporating harmony and song. In Jamaica they call it "Singjay."

I'm also trying to get the 602 Band into the studio, but it's harder with them. I can't work around their schedules; I work full-time as a surveyor. I have a full-length album planned, but there aren't enough hours in a day.

My wife keeps me busy. We've been together for twenty years. We're trying to grow our own food. We've got an apple tree, a guava tree, peach trees, and tomatoes—a Garden of Eden.

I wish I could do music more, but I'm happy with what I do. I've been lucky, but I've worked hard to get to where I'm at. I'm going to keep making records until I die.

Innastate

Adrian Wall (1970–) (Pueblo of Jemez)

Rylan Kabotie (1994–) (Pueblo of Santa Clara, Hopi, and Jicarilla Apache)

Innastate's "sound is modern yet honors their Indigenous heritage, musical roots, and love of music."[2]

ADRIAN WALL (AW). I love reggae music. For the last ten years, I've been really into it. It's fun to play, and it's got a good message. Rylan and I started Innastate in Santa Fe, New Mexico, in 2014, but our story goes further back. I was on the roster of Albuquerque-based Native Roots. I played bass for them when they first started. I was also with a band, Red Earth, that won a couple of NAMAs—Debut Group of the Year in 2000 and Best World Music Recording in 2003. We played funk, reggae, metal, and hip-hop and mashed it all together; it was a lot of fun.

RYLAN KABOTIE (RK). I started playing guitar when I was thirteen, but I didn't like it and dropped it fast. Then I heard Metallica's "Anesthesia (Pulling Teeth)," with Cliff Burton playing bass. I was so amazed—I wanted to play

34. Innastate

like that. I had a band, From the Ashes, with my father, Ed Kabote; brother; and brother-in-law. My dad is still involved in music. He plays with a reggae rock band, the Yoties, in Flagstaff. He was a big influence on me. He taught my brothers, sisters, and me to sing church hymns when we were young.

AW. Rylan's dad is my father's best friend; we grew up playing together.

RK. Adrian became part of my life.

AW. I live in North Central New Mexico, a mile from the Jemez Pueblo line. When I was growing up, there weren't many Indigenous musicians. It was a different life. The values were different than what they are in Western culture. They were all about community, elders, kids, our traditions, and our language. That was the focus of Pueblo life.

RK. I don't live in a pueblo—our drummer does—but Santa Clara Pueblo is where I'm from. I'm of Hopi descent; Apache as well. I used to live in Española, which is a Native community close to Santa Clara Pueblo. I was raised in the Christian church. When my dad became a Christian, we became conservative Baptists. The Native lifestyle was stigmatized by the church. They looked down on Native religion and spirituality. I still go home every year for Santa Clara Pueblo Day in September. Once we were Christianized, the pueblos were given patron saint names.

AW. I stopped playing music for three years when I went to school. By my fourth year, I was itching to play. Rylan's the first person I called. I had a few songs I wanted to put together. Rylan said, "Yeah, let's play."

RK. I had quit music for a few years as well, but we started getting together once a week. We hit up a few different people to play drums, but everybody flaked out on us. Eventually, Adrian sent me an email with a Craigslist posting. It was early in the morning. I woke up and looked at it. It was a drummer looking for like-minded musicians. Adrian's message said, "I think this is our guy."

It turned out that he was from the same place that I'm from, Santa Clara Pueblo. It's funny—I had never met him. We wound up getting together at Adrian's. It stuck from there.

AW. We've got a wide age span. Karlo Johnson, our guitarist, is the oldest. I'm next at fifty, and Rylan's the youngest at twenty-six. It's the way we function as a community. We honor our elders and children. It's how we learn, how we create. We have multigenerational homes.

RK. Innastate was a big encouragement for me to listen to reggae music. Adrian has more of that influence. It hones our songs into something special.

AW. The syncopations of reggae music and Pueblo music are similar, but our brand of reggae isn't roots reggae or one-drop kind of stuff. We're all over the place. Rylan and I have heavy metal backgrounds. Growing up on the reservation, if you had a guitar, you played metal, sometimes country music too. When you grow up riffing odd-time, chunky stuff, you get good at playing guitar. That's something that sets our band apart—we-re good musicians.

RK. We've got a lot of energy when it comes to performances. We're a fun band to come and see.

AW. Red Earth started the Electric 49 at the Launchpad, in Albuquerque, in April 1998. We built it around the Gathering of Nations Powwow. It was well received. There wasn't much of a Native music scene at the time, but it was a jumping-off point. We brought in Keith Secola, Casper Lomayesva, and Native Roots. Hip-hop was on the rise. We presented as many genres as we could. There was a great waila band, Cisco, from Arizona with a metal thing going on.

Red Earth played in Phoenix, Albuquerque, and occasionally Flagstaff. I still have my bass, but I switched to guitar out of songwriting necessity.

Innastate is the first band I've sung in, so I've had a huge learning curve. Rylan is a great singer, and he's taught me a lot.

RK. We have a lot of input when it comes to the music. Our tunes, after someone brings them to the table, go through quite a bit of changing before we perform them for the public.

AW. We can't discount our drummer. Lawrence is a great timekeeper. That's what makes the songs work. Songwriting is split between Rylan and me. Rylan's got a ton of tunes, I've got a ton of tunes, and there are tunes we've worked out together.

RK. Lyrically, we come from different places. I have a song, "The Way," relating to being raised Christian and trying to find a balance between my religious and spiritual background and my Native American side.

AW. I've never tried to be overly political in my songs. I gear them more toward a mass audience, but there are issues that I bring up. When I was younger, incorporating Native themes was deliberate. I was searching for my identity through my art. I don't need to do that anymore. I'm confident in who I am as a Native person.

A lot of what we put into our songs is coded. I used to sing powwow music, and I'd like to include some of that. But it doesn't have to be in there for it to be Native music. It's about having voices as artists and being visible as contemporary Native people. We're a small portion of the population, and a lot of people don't know that we exist. They'd be surprised to hear our music and wonder, "That's a Native band?" But listen to Redbone's "Come and Get Your Love." Is that a Native song? We're a continuously evolving culture. I don't want somebody to say that it's not Native music because it doesn't have a rattle or a flute. We write what we feel; it's our right to make music the way we want.

RK. I tell people, "We're a band that just happens to be Native. We make the music we make."

AW. The title of our CD *Verde* [2018] means "Green." We had bloomed into a solid band. We did some new songs, but mostly it was songs we'd been playing since we started. Some were old. I wrote one when I was twenty. Afterward, the band said, "We're done with these songs—let's move on."

RK. For the album cover, the centerpiece was a yucca plant. It paid homage to where we come from and signified our growth. When we first came together,

I remember working on a couple of the songs. There were others we worked on as a band. It was great to have that collection of songs in one place.

AW. It took six months to record. We had been talking about getting into the studio for a while. We were playing with a keyboard player, Doug Bellen. He helped to produce some of it, more than we give him credit for. We had been using a producer from Santa Fe who was quite expensive.

RK. We add Romeo Alonzo [alto sax], Carly Marshall [tenor sax], Justin Pucila [guitar], MC T-Bone [trombone], and Mikey Jaramillo [percussion] for live performances. Each of us has our own life, but last year we played forty to fifty shows. We're going to focus on playing larger shows and writing music. We're highly creative individuals.

AW. We love what we do...

RK. and each other.

12

Tongue Twisters

Like reggae, hip-hop has been enthusiastically embraced by young Indigenous Americans. Talking "about the ghetto life, poverty, crime, drugs, alcohol, [and] teen pregnancy," rapper and dancer Supaman (Christian Parrish Takes the Gun) (Apsáalooke) says, "all that crazy stuff that happens in the ghetto is similar to the reservation life. We can relate to that."[1]

Melvin "Grandmaster Melle Mel" Glover and his brother Nathaniel Glover, better known as Kid Creole or Danny Dan, were the first Indigenous Americans to embrace hip-hop. The Bronx-born Tsalagi brothers' Rock and Roll Hall of Fame–inducted group, Grandmaster Flash and the Furious Five, however, was led by Barbadian American rapper Joseph "Grandmaster Flash" Saddler and focused on urban New York life.

The first hip-hopper to rap about Native issues was Litefoot (Gary Paul Davis) (1969–) (Eastern Cherokee). Success as a movie actor in Disney's *Indian in the Cupboard* (1995), *Mortal Kombat Annihilation* (1997), *Kull the Conqueror* (1997), *Song of Hiawatha* (1997), *Adaptation* (2002), and *29 Psalm* (2002) enabled the six-time NAMA-winning rapper and actor to finance high-quality recordings. "The music I was making was ahead of its time," he told me, "and the messages were definitely ahead of their time."

Since cofounding Red Vinyl Records in 2011, Litefoot has not only released eleven solo albums but also provided an outlet for rap artists, including Liv, Carmen, and Sten Joddi. "Young Native people didn't have a musical way to hear about important points of view," he said. "I thought I could be that voice."

In addition to Red Vinyl Records' roster, Indigenous rappers include Drezus (Jeremiah Andrade) (Plains Cree), MC Red Cloud (Henry Andrade)

(Wixáritari), Gearl Francis (Mi'kmaq), Lindsay "Eekwol" Knight (Muskaday), Tall Paul (Anishinaabe and Oneida), and Russell Means's son Natananii Means (Lakota).

The youngest recipient of the Best Producer NAMA, in 2010, Frank Waln (Sicangu Lakota) scored a Best Rap/Hip-Hop Recording Award a year later. "Something big is on the horizon," Waln told me. "I can feel it in my heart and my gut. I know I'm on the right path."

Gabriel Night Shield (1979–) (Lakota and Irish)

Gabriel Night Shield was in high school when he attended a performance by Litefoot. It was life changing. Night Shield would score the Best Rap/Hip-Hop NAMA for *Savage Display: The Total Package* (2006) less than a decade later.

> I've never liked being called a Native rapper. I'm a hip-hopper who just happens to be Native. When I started, Native hip-hoppers were pariahs. There were only a few of us doing it. The elders didn't know what to do about us. They'd say, "Stop acting Black."
>
> It's a whole different scene now. Because of the internet, I started finding out about War Party, Red Power Squad, and other Canadian groups. Litefoot had the biggest influence on me. He came to my high school and did a show. It was one of the coolest things I had ever seen. Hip-hop was something I saw on MTV—Dr. Dre and Snoop Dogg. To see someone who looked like me rapping was a fantasy come to life.
>
> My mom's roots are Irish. She grew up in Boston's Hyde Park. She's a schoolteacher. When she got out of college, St. Francis Indian School was the only school hiring. They gave her a house, and she moved to the Rosebud Reservation in South Dakota. I was born on the reservation, but I grew up in Brockton, Massachusetts, about forty-five minutes south of Boston.
>
> My stepdad was Native. He showed me a little, but there wasn't a strong connection between us. He was abusive and an alcoholic. After my mom had me, she became pregnant with my younger brother. She didn't want to do it by herself, so she decided to move back to her family in Massachusetts. That's where I grew up.

35. Gabriel Night Shield

My mom taught in Massachusetts until being laid off in 1991. St. Francis Indian School offered her a job again, so we moved back to the reservation. I went to St. Francis Indian School and took Lakota language classes. My mom wasn't necessarily part of the culture, and it wasn't heavy in our house, but I can't say that reservation life was foreign to me. The two summers before we officially moved back, I spent a couple of weeks with my dad's family. I still had a Boston accent, but I learned to lose it quickly. I was tired of being made fun of. My mom, who lives on the reservation, still has her Boston accent thirty years later.

The Rosebud Reservation is poverty-stricken. Alcoholism is everywhere. Barely anybody has a job. Kids run around at all times of day or night very unfocused. That was foreign to me. My mom was strict; I didn't grow up running wild.

I deejayed at high school dances, but when it came time to decide what I wanted to do with my life, I wasn't sure. I thought of going to school for video production but, at the last minute, switched to audio production and music business. I went to the Art Institute of Seattle for two years. A few other students and I didn't know anyone to record for class assignments, so we got together and recorded our own songs. I hadn't had any inclination to be an artist or to write music, but I fell in love with it immediately.

After I graduated, my mom got sick, and I went back to the reservation to take care of her. Once she was well enough, I moved to Sioux Falls, South Dakota, and tried to find a job. There's a great hip-hop scene in Sioux Falls. It's like a mini-Minneapolis, three and a half hours away, but I couldn't find any openings. I decided to create my own job and formed a record label, Night Shield Entertainment. We put our first project out the following year. I liked rapping, but I wasn't planning on being an artist. I wanted to support my artist friends. I thought they needed to be heard. I was going to be the Puff Daddy of the label.

My first three projects were compilations of other artists' work. My fourth project, *It's Official*, featured a Black Mexican rapper from Seattle, Cin'Atra [David Lee]. I had a verse here and there.

I put my first solo album, *Kataztrophik*, out in 2005. It caught fire and propelled things forward. That album was about me learning to be an artist. I wasn't comfortable making music by myself, so Cin'Atra and Overflow, from Ithaca, New York, helped me. I had gone to school with them. They taught me how to write verses and hooks and helped me grow as an artist.

Every day is a different song. I like it when songs are relatable to me. When I listen to them, I remember my mind frame, where I was in my life, and the mistakes I made. I use music as a journal; it's therapeutic. If something is stressing me out or on my mind, I write it down, put it together in the studio, and get it off my chest. Music frees my mind.

Savage Display: The Total Package [2006] won the Best Rap/Hip-Hop Recording NAMA. The following year, I won Single of the Year for "Broken Dreams," from *Loved and Hated*. Hoop dancer and singer Jackie Bird sang on its chorus. It was the first time that I mixed traditional Native music with hip-hop, as well as being socially conscious. I had been searching for the right opportunity. Jackie and I discussed a few things. I showed her a song I had been working on, which I didn't have a chorus to. She liked it and, on her own, started singing between my verses. It was incredible what she was doing. She came to the studio, and it was like lightning in a bottle. That song got a lot of radio play ... a lot of love. We sold tons of CDs; this was before the digital age. It was played all over the country.

Loved and Hated [2007] was when I truly became Night Shield, the person I was going to be as an artist. Since then, I've been completely confident. On the albums before, I was still feeling my way, rather than knowing what I was doing. I didn't want to follow the trend and do the same thing everybody was doing. I made the conscious decision to lean as far into the other lane as I could. That's why my next album was *Sex, Drunks, and Hip-Hop* [2008]. It was how I was living, partying all the time, living that "rapper life," and I wanted to talk about it in my music. I didn't want to hide what I was doing. But I was reckless, and it caught up to me. I got into legal trouble and got a couple of DWIs. I was facing going to prison, but I was lucky enough to be spared.

The Addiction [2015] was a continuation of *Sex, Drunks, and Hip-Hop*, but after the partying came *The Hangover* [2016]. *Savivor* [2018] was the next step. That album was a rebirth, as far as accepting that I wasn't living up to my potential.

"Killing Strangers" is one of my favorite songs on the album. It might be my most successful streaming song. Marilyn Manson had a song that I sampled. I listened to it nonstop for close to a year. I loved its theme. I wanted to remix it and do my own version. I thought of cool things to say. We added guitars and drums and sped it up. It turned out great.

DC Comics featured me in a graphic novel, *Scouts*, on their adult imprint, Vertigo. It was promoted as "*The Sopranos* on the reservation." It took place on the fictional Prairie Rose Reservation in South Dakota. When the book was coming out, the *Argus Leader* did a three-way interview with the writer, Jason Aaron, and me. I sent him a press kit with a CD. He liked it so much that he included it in his comic book. There's a scene where one of the characters, Dino, is in a car. He's got a Night Shield CD, a Tupac CD, and an MF Doom CD. It was a nerd's dream come true.

I'm aware that my fourteen-year-old daughter looks up to me. I wouldn't put *Sex, Drunks, and Hip-Hop* out now. I'm more conscious about what I represent, but I'm still having fun. I would still do "Killing Strangers" but maybe not as sexually graphic. It'd still be me, just a forty-one-year-old me.

Mike Bone/Lil Mike and Funny Bone

Jesus "Lil Mike" Silva II (1981–) (Pawnee and Choctaw)

Jesus "Funny Bone" Silva IV (1986–) (Pawnee and Choctaw)

Cast members of the all-Indigenous series *Reservation Dogs* (Hulu), brothers Lil Mike and Funny Bone are "Oklahoma City's only on-call, full-time, American Indian, little people, hip-hop artists."[2]

FUNNY BONE (FB). We have fans who don't like rap but enjoy our music. They say, "Man. I don't know what it is, but I like it." Being Native Americans, we use our platform for the betterment of our people. Touring reservations, hearing stories about how police are treating Natives, it just built up. We looked at each other and said, "Man, we've got to do something."

We came up with a beat and got to work.

LIL MIKE (LM). We wanted to spark a fire in people so they would join the fight—something that would start a revolution.

FB. People are becoming more aware of Native issues. There's still a lot to bring out, but we've made progress. There's going to be a cleansing, because you've got to weed out all the people that are trying to jump on the bandwagon. The Black Lives Matter movement made a difference. The media is picking up on it, but I need to see the proof in the pudding. I'm not going to just believe that it's pudding and stick it in my mouth.

LM. We grew up in an urban area, Oklahoma City, and our passion for Native culture didn't start until our late teens. Where we lived, you either hung out with the white folk, the Mexicans, or the Black folk. We didn't fit in with the white folk, and we didn't speak Spanish, so we hung out with the Bloods.

FB. We lived in a low-income neighborhood with a single mom—four kids. She put in a lot of work to get us where we're at today, but growing up, we had roaches. We made the best of it, but we slept on the floor. We thought we were Black. Our grandfather, just the other day, told us that we were mixed. We're not full-blooded Indians, but we have a lot in there.

LM. In high school we started learning about Native American history. They had a Native American Club, and I went to that. Somebody invited me to a powwow and snap! I could see a connection between the powwow drum and hip-hop. Hip-hop has always been the easiest way for me to speak.

FB. I like R&B and contemporary rock, anything that's clean. He loves heavy metal.

LM. We're both named Jesus Silva, as are our brothers, but we didn't go by our birth names. My brothers and I had nicknames. Through our growth process and characterisms, our names slowly evolved. We grew out of the childish nicknames and became Lil Mike and Funny Bone.

FB. Funny Bone is the acronym for Fully United New Nourished Young Brother of Noble Ethnicity. I picked it when I started rapping. I took to my character, being funny and out of the bone.

LM. I used to dance, so they called me Little Michael Jackson. Lil Mike stuck... forever.

FB. He did his high school talent show with the hat, the jacket, and the shiny glove—everything. He was always dancing.

LM. At one of our churches, they gave me the name Big Faith. No matter what situation I was going through, I treated it like I didn't care. That's big faith right there. We try to not get too preachy when we're performing unless a song calls for it. We always want to keep our faith at the forefront. It's a lifestyle.

FB. You don't have to be preachy to play music. There are a lot of Christian artists whose every song is gospel, but not everybody wants to hear preaching.

You can know God and still play. One of our slogans is "Love God and party." Jesus spoke in parables. That's how we do our music. We've got a song "Off the Wall." It sounds like we're rapping about dancing. But we wrote it when we were going to different churches, and it seemed like everybody was stuck in their robotic cycles. We were like, "Man, they're saying this church is awesome, but they're not acting like it. They're singing like they're bored. Their preaching is mediocre. There's no fire, no life."

In my head, I was thinking, "Why are these people in this church?" There are so many different churches where they could get what they're looking for. Change it up a little bit. It doesn't just take the preacher, but the whole congregation.

LM. We're not the tallest straws in the barrel.

FB. It makes us more marketable and more recognizable.

LM. You don't have to be big to be a big deal. It helps us on stage when we're dancing. If we were average height or bigger, we'd get tired faster.

FB. "Rain Dance" was born in my senior year [2005]. The school didn't have a talent show, which was something I did every year. The principal told me they were having a cultural day instead. If I was going to do something, it had to be ethnic and educational. Over the years, it evolved into what people saw on *America's Got Talent* in 2013. A year before, we came out with a remix version. I wrote the original to a mixtape. Mike wasn't on the original. When we started working together, we had our producer make another beat, similar and better. Mike wrote a verse, and we rerecorded it. That's why we called it "The Remix." We had to remix it to make it our own.

LM. We've been on TV, but *America's Got Talent* was more than just another show.

FB. We watched *America's Got Talent* a lot.

LM. We enjoy seeing people showing off their gifts.

FB. When we got to *America's Got Talent*, we saw all the things happening in the background. Some of it disappointed us, and some of it was cool. We tried treating it as if it were any other show, not a major TV outlet. We didn't want to get nervous. By that time, we'd been doing it for over ten years. I told Mike before we got on stage, "Treat this like we're in a church, about to do a Sunday morning service, and we want to get kicked out."

We figured the audience wasn't going to get up and start dancing, but we won unanimously. They aired it on the same night as something we shot for

PBS. Young people saw us on *America's Got Talent*, and older people saw us on PBS. We were at a church camp when it aired. Our phone started ringing off the hook. Three months later we moved to the next level of *America's Got Talent*, in Las Vegas. We went in knowing we didn't want to win. There would be a big contract involved if we did. We just wanted exposure.

LM. The contract would have been like jail time.

FB. We didn't want to be locked under contract for ten or fifteen years. Winning is not always winning. Every time someone says we should have won, I say, "We did. We got the exposure."

While we were filming, they started sending people straight through to New York without a performance. They were just calling out names. Mike and I were freaking out, thinking they were going to call us and we were going to be locked under the contract. We started praying, "Lord, please don't let them pick us."

They didn't call our name, thank God. We did everything we could to piss off the producer and get under his skin. We did a mediocre performance. It was still cool; it just wasn't our best.

We've gone through a lot since we started. If we played you some of our older stuff, you'd say, "That's amazing," but if we told you how much we spent on recording equipment, you'd be "No way."

We used a five-dollar microphone that we found at a dollar store.

LM. It plugged into a radio transmitter and broadcast out of a radio. We used that mic in the studio. We put a sock on it to block the *p* words. We used a twenty-five-dollar Hip Hop DJ Beat Maker. Funny Bone figured out how to manipulate the sound. Whenever anyone who's had that program hears us, they say, "I've never heard that sample before."

Funny Bone tells them, "You've got to do this. You've got to do that." But they say, "That's crazy."

FB. We set up in a bedroom. We took out the mattress, brought in a computer, and put pillows on the walls. It sounded good. Sometimes it's the budget, and sometimes it's your ears, if you base your music on who the world is saying is the best producer, like Dr. Dre, and line up the lyrics and the beats. We'd play a Dr. Dre track and hear what we had to do. Turn this up; turn that down. That's how we figured out how to do it on a very low budget. Two years after that, radio stations started playing our stuff.

We started going to studios and recording, until we found one that we liked. We did "Fist in the Air" with Rob Swan [Cree], a rapper from Vancouver. He goes by the name KASP [Keeping Alive Stories for the People].

LM. That was our first single. With the topic of missing and murdered Indigenous women so important, we felt it was time to release it.

FB. "Fist in the Air" addresses a touchy subject. We don't want to look like we're trying to exploit it or make money off it, but we're using our platform to raise awareness. We looked at other songs about the same issue. They were all in Native tongues and either sappy or sad. We wanted something different.

LM. The song had to be catchy enough to make people say, "This is what they're rapping about. This is what we need to stand up for."

FB. We love collaborating with other artists. We get to share our fame and gain some of their fame. It's a win-win. That's how we look at growing our brand, but we have standards. If they want to get on a track with us, it must be clean, positive, and with no cursing. They can't talk about anything raunchy—sex, drugs—nothing like that, no alcohol. Through that, we changed some artists' approaches to music and, sometimes, their lives. It's preaching life.

LM. We've done tracks with Jim Conway from Oklahoma City. Every time we collaborate, we make a hit.

FB. My brother and I write to the beat that we're attacking. And then I write my part, and he writes his part. We come together when we're done. I listen to what he's got and tell him, "You should probably change this right here."

Then he critiques me. We go at it again and see if we like it. "Yeah, that's the one."

We record it, let it sit for a day, and listen to it. "Is that the one we're going to keep, or are we going to change some things?"

The recording process is a lot of critiquing. You've got to be your worst critic.

LM. If he writes something better, it will inspire me to trash what I did. I've done that twice. There are songs we've released that I could have done so much better.

FB. We challenge each other when we're going over lyrics and listening to each other. That challenges us to make our verses better.

LM. We perform at all kinds of events, even nursing homes. The first time an elderly person told us she was a big fan, she booked us for a birthday party. She was turning eighty-seven years old. We thought we were going to a teenager's birthday party. Elderly people enjoy us. I don't know if it's our spirit or our energy.

FB. Maybe it's because we scream. They can hear us.

LM. It's about how you market yourself, how you put yourself out there. A lot of people spend time begging other people to promote their music, when they could just find out ways to promote it themselves. *America's Got Talent* found us because we took every chance that we could to get attention.

FB. We put our videos on YouTube and our music on various websites.

LM. We have a song, "We Ain't Backin' Up," that just came out as a single. We did it with hip-hop lyricist T'ai Pu from Winnipeg. We're working on a remix. We have another song that talks about how we're not going to let certain topics in our lives determine if we're going to give up or not. We're also working on a protest song about police brutality and the racism going on. We're almost done with the chorus. I'm not sure of the title yet, maybe "That's Enough."

FB. We're going to do a rock version of "Rain Dance." We had a band in the past, and one of the guitarists played the melody on guitar. We did it at a nightclub. The video is on YouTube. The sound is terrible, and it's a little graphic. But it's a lot of fun.

LM. It's the last time we hand our phone to a drunk.

Shon Denay (Shantel D. Haynes) (1983–)
(Oglala Lakota and African American)

Hip-hop is one hue in Las Vegas–based vocalist Shon Denay's palette. Her "distinct sound" incorporates "raw neo soul, jazz, cabaret and quiet storm—reminiscent of past jazz artists from the early- to mid-20th century but mixed with contemporary R&B."[3]

I'm Native American—Oglala Lakota—on my mother's side and Black on my dad's. I wanted to honor my mother and our heritage, so I took the route of Native artist. But I was raised in the city, not on a reservation like my mother. I consider myself an urban Native. When I meet someone, they'll ask if I'm mixed with Dominican or Mexican blood. I tell them, "No, I'm Native American."

They'll look at me and say, "What! You still exist?"

"Yeah, we're still here. We're just not what you've been conditioned to believe; we're normal people like everyone else."

My five-month-pregnant mom, Debra Marie Black Crow, was murdered by her husband, Rodney "Patrick" McNeal, in 1997. He was a parole officer in San Bernardino, California. In 2015 I found out that his defense had been picked up by the California Innocence Project. I called them, and we had a meeting. I told them they had picked the wrong person. He was guilty; why hadn't they reached out to the family? They told me that even if he was guilty, they were still going to push his story, because they had invested money in him. It reopened a wound. I realized a lot of people, including me, were naive. Things happen after a trial. Most people think the bad guy goes to prison, and that's the end of it. But when the bad guy is in prison, he has nothing but time on his hands. He can work on getting out, try different angles.

When my mother was murdered, I was still a teenager. It was a few weeks before my fourteenth birthday, a pivotal time when I needed my mother. It was difficult to go through the trial and have the attorney ask me if I wanted to go for the death penalty. I wanted him to get as much time as possible so he could think about what he did. He not only murdered my mother and unborn sister but completely changed the trajectory of her children's lives and all the people who knew my mom. It wasn't just her.

I was lost for the longest time. I felt alone. I'm just one person, trying to get justice for my mother, and the California Innocence Project is this giant organization with celebrity backing. I was almost giving up hope, but the Missing and Murdered Indigenous Women's campaign reignited my drive. Through them I had an opportunity to meet a lot of talented Native Americans. I felt blessed. I'm still fighting as hard as I can to make sure that my mother's murderer stays where he belongs. People have told me, "Let it go. Forgive and forget." But I can't. He changed everything in my life. I don't feel that justice is served if he gets out without acknowledging what he did.

Before singing, I wrote poetry, did theater, and danced. I won second place in a national poetry contest. Once I was out of high school, I signed up to win a *Glamour* magazine hair makeover in New York. I had to write about why I should win. I didn't think anything of it. Months later they called me and said, "We read your essay and loved it. It had everybody laughing. We'd like to give you the grand prize."

It was crazy, but I went to New York. They paid for my flight and hotel, gave me spending money, and did the hair makeover. It was awesome. It gave me trust in myself that if I put my mind to it and believed in the product I was sharing, goodwill would come to me.

I lived in Boston for a year; my dad was in the air force. We bounced around. Because of that, I was a loner. I stayed in my room, listening to R&B singers like Brian McKnight and

37. Shon Denay

Jade on the radio. It morphed from singing in the choir with my best friend, Sarah, and in my room at home, to Las Vegas.

I started with a high school group called Illusion. It helped me, because I was taking theater classes. I was working on getting emotions across to a large group of people, but I was at a loss about what I was going to do with it after school. That's when I fell upon the Twisted Dance troupe, which allowed me to stay on stage. I stayed with them for eight years. We were backup dancers for well-known artists. It gave me courage and conditioned me to not fear the stage or a big group of people. I'm still friends with the other dancers. They're in my music video "Comeback."

I fell into the hip-hop scene in 2003. There was an eighteen-and-up venue that had hip-hop every Tuesday. There were other venues, but I was underage. I'd sit outside, listen, and be around people.

Karaoke came to me around the same time. It's a major part of my life, even now. There's a place near here, Ninja Karaoke, where I go almost every week. I should have a job there; I've become the informal host. I love making people smile and getting them to sing. We do some of my tracks; it's a good opportunity to get fans.

Producer Bosie T [Thompson] found me through Sarah. He heard me sing "Tyrone," by Erykah Badu, and told me, "I love your voice; I need to work with you."

We wound up doing a track, "Gotta Move On," in 2009. It was eye-opening. I had never experienced the back end of recording before. I didn't realize all the mechanics and patience you needed, along with talent and discipline, but from the first moment, Bosie was on it. "You're flat—do it again. You need more emotion—do it again."

It was like boot camp. It took thirteen hours to record a three-minute, twenty-two-second song. It almost made me quit. In fact, I wound up taking a hiatus after the track came out. When I came back in 2014, the scene had changed. I had to change quickly. It was a bridge from my hip-hop days to this new hip-hop scene. I fell into it at the right time.

I had to get my mother's story out. The best way to reach as many people as possible in a short time was through music. I hit Bosie up and said, "I've got all these songs written. Would you help me record them?"

He became my producer. That was the beginning of my EP *On the Rocks* [2018]. I wasn't ready to translate my mother's murder directly into songs—it's a difficult topic to sing about—but my songs were about being without a mother and the hard lessons you learn when you don't have a maternal figure. Recording was a release, very therapeutic. I knew, deep down, that my songs could help someone know they weren't the only one going through something like this. We can get through it together; it's possible to go beyond what's happening.

My original idea was an album that I was going to call *Crumbled Paper Spots*. I had lots of songs, but as I continued to build on the EP, it created a story about a failed relationship. It started with me being in love: "Everything's amazing." Then it's "Oh my gosh, this isn't what it's cracked up to be." "Am I supposed to be with this person?" And "I can't stand this person; I fell for it again."

The last track, "Comeback," was my way of saying, "Yes, it happened. It wasn't what I expected, but I was strong enough to get out of it. It didn't break me. I was able to come back."

When it was completed, I looked at the finished product and said, "Now what?"

Bosie said, "Now the hard part begins. You've got to start marketing it. It'll go nowhere unless you believe in it and push it."

He was right; it was difficult. Once the EP dropped and we started to market it, I thought, "How far can we take it?" and submitted it to the Indigenous Music Awards [formerly the Aboriginal People's Choice Music Awards] in Canada. They nominated me as the year's Best Female Artist. Going to Winnipeg for the awards ceremony, I saw all this amazing talent. Coming back to the States, I went with my sister to the NAMAs in November 2019. I was nominated in five categories and won Best Female Artist. It was unbelievable. The banquet hall at the Seneca Niagara Resort and Casino, where they held the awards ceremony, was full of talented human beings. The energy was electrifying. I was awestruck. When they called my name, no one knew me. It was just my sister and me screaming. Afterward, it was humbling when people congratulated me. Nineteen years is a long time for an awards show. I'm humbled to be one of the alumni.

I want to do more collaborations, but I'm not sure if they're going to be for a CD or singles. I'm working on a track that has a boom-back feel. I have another that touches on addiction and depression, which is a step closer to singing about my mother.

Update: Convicted of second-degree murder, Rodney "Patrick" McNeal was sentenced to thirty years to life, in 1999. California governor Jerry Brown Jr. denied him clemency in 2014, but six years later, Brown's successor, Gavin Newsom, shortened McNeil's sentence by eight years. In September 2020 the prisoner came before the parole board. The hearing ended in a rare split decision, but parole was granted two months later. That left Denay less than 120 days to reverse the parole board's decision. It was enough. More than seven thousand people signed Denay's Change .org petition demanding accountability and justice. In February 2021 Governor Newsome rescinded McNeal's parole. Its reversal "shows that justice can be retained for domestic violence victims, collateral victims, missing and murdered Indigenous women," Denay said, "and proves that people in law enforcement will be held accountable. . . . My mother deserved her life. My sister deserved her life. Now that they can no longer fight for themselves, I am here to maintain what they deserve. . . . JUSTICE."[4]

Sten Joddi (Muscogee)

Sten Joddi "credits his ability to overcome obstacles by maintaining his priorities of family, healthy lifestyle, tattoos, music and reconnecting with the Creator and Earth."[5]

The two-time NAMA-winning hip-hop artist appears semiregularly on *Reservation Dogs* as Bear's absent father, Punkin Lusty.

They do stories about Indigenous people on 20/20 and TV shows like that, but the reporters go to the poorest reservations and show the worst situations. We know about our problems. We don't need to be reminded. What we need are avenues to create our own economies so we can build generational wealth like the rich people of this country.

Our voices can't be shut off. They can't pull the plug on us when we start talking about real issues or bring out the truth and rewrite the history they state as fact. It's none of that. It's Standing Rock, the Columbus Day issue, the Idle No More movement, and everything in between.

Hip-hop has had a big influence on Indian country's youth and even on some of the older generation, my generation. When I was a kid—I'm sure my father was the same way and his father and so on—I couldn't find an Indigenous hero. We were always the token Indian on TV or in the movies.

When I talk about youngsters today, I'm talking about kids nine and ten years old. They've got iPhones, smartphones, and tablets connecting them to other Natives. They could get on the internet and watch videos. That's why we've come out of the woodwork. We have an abundance of rappers, singers, drummers, flutists, and powwow groups.

We were divided by disconnection, separation, and language barriers. We couldn't defend ourselves in large enough numbers. Now we can. That's one of the prophecies of the seventh generation. Everyone is coming back together and becoming one circle again. Whichever way we're doing it, if we continue doing it, we're going to grow in all industries across the board. Our opinions matter. You're going to listen to us. There's no more asking. We're in the building, at the table, and in the conversation.

I have fun on my records, but I speak from an Indigenous perspective. Some people like it, and some don't. It's not up to me to worry about it. I speak about what I know.

Hip-hop came from New York gangs trying to stop the killings and bring conflict resolution. It was dancing. It was graffiti. It was fashion.

I grew up in Okmulgee, Oklahoma, forty minutes from Tulsa. We had all kinds of influences, as far as hip-hop. Litefoot was one of them. I saw him for the first time at Creek Fest in Okmulgee. It was a weird feeling, because I was seeing somebody who looked like me, talked like me, and had stories about things I understood. I saw him as very cool. He was wearing an Oklahoma jersey and rapping, something I wanted to do. Years later we met. We're good friends to this day.

In Oklahoma it was mostly southern rock, country music, and some pop. We had a record player in the front room, and my mom played records. I was introduced to R&B and hip-hop by my uncles and aunts. They were ten or fifteen years older than me, but they were jamming on old-school back in the day. I gravitated toward that a little, but when I was eleven, Tupac, NWA, Public Enemy, KRS-1, and all these great artists started coming up. I'd be at a friend's house watching BET or MTV and see all this amazing music. That influenced me to start writing songs.

When I turned thirteen or fourteen, a friend got a karaoke machine, and we started rapping over other people's songs and making tapes.

I looked up to the older guys in my neighborhood. Some had nice cars, nice shoes, and gold chains, but they did bad things for the money. I gravitated toward that. My dad left when I was young; it came with the territory. My life between twelve and sixteen was a blur of growing up. I did a lot of living in that block of time. I did a lot of mistake making after sixteen, but I made good choices too. I went to Job Corp and got my GED. I got a culinary arts certificate, so I could work.

I moved to Murfreesboro, Tennessee, about a half hour from Nashville, but continued making bad decisions. Alcohol came into my life whenever I was able to buy it. I tried selling drugs but got addicted to coke. I spent time in jail, reflecting on things while I was locked up.

38. Sten Joddi

After I got out, I stayed on the road to recovery for two years, trying to do the right thing, but I was homeless. I got it in my head that I couldn't be around anybody, so I got on a Greyhound bus and ended up in Tulsa at a buddy's house sleeping on his couch. Then I moved to another person's house. I rode that situation for two years, trying to figure out what I wanted.

I kept a few jobs and did a little of this and a little of that, but I was always hustling tattoos. That's how I paid my way. I was trying to stay away from the streets and avoid trouble. I learned to tattoo when I was thirteen. It was always part of my life. As I said, I lived a lot between thirteen and sixteen. I look back now at teachers and my mom—not that it was their fault—but they never looked at tattooing as an avenue to go down. I never thought of it as a profession or a logical way to make a living but lived my young life thinking it was wrong to do.

Tattoos were illegal in Oklahoma. That had a big part to do with why they wouldn't tell a kid to look to it as a career. It wasn't as socially acceptable as it is today, but telling me to do something with my art would have been better than telling me to quit drawing.

I was working every second. Fast-food restaurants and steakhouses hired me in any town I was in. I'd get to know the people that I was working around. We'd have a few drinks after work, and I'd tattoo them and make side money. I found myself in Iowa tattooing at parties and got a little name for myself. I ended up meeting the woman who became my wife and the mother of my children. I was able to leave the street and focus on the better things in life. We don't live a wealthy life, but with my grinding, we're okay. Our kids have food and clothes. All the bills are paid, and that's all I could ever ask for.

I have songs where I'm talking to a younger me, saying, "Don't let anybody discourage you from any dream they think you can't do. They're going to try to discredit it or bring it down, because they don't understand it. What people don't understand, they hate. You may have the closest people to you trying to discourage you, but that should give you self-motivation, the internal fire, to prove them all wrong."

When I started doing music, I was single. Some of my music was wild and raw. There were vulnerable songs sprinkled in, but my structural ideas and the way I created music were different than they are now. It's more effortless now. If I'm writing something, I'm no longer trying to stay on a subject. If it doesn't come out like I turned on a water faucet, I delete it, because I'm thinking too much about what I'm going to say. I want songs to just come out. Those songs are the best, the ones that are most shared, the ones most listened to.

The Singles included songs that I had built up in a folder. I put them on one album, and it worked. People liked it. It's humbling when you work on something, but you realize that it's the songs that you didn't work on so hard that people love the most. They're easy to make and easy for people to love. I'm not bashing anybody that takes their time with their music and tries to create the most perfect song, but sometimes you've got to just let it flow. That's where freestyle rapping came from, where battle rapping came from. It's all improvisation. It's unexpected and spontaneous. It's the truth, because you don't have time to think about lying. When songs come out of me like that, I record them quickly.

The first time my wife and I went to the NAMAs, *7th Generation Prophecy* was nominated for Best Hip-Hop Album of 2017. Standing Rock was just heating up. Social activist Erin Schrode shared her video of the protest in November 2016. When I saw it, it had already been seen six thousand times. I shared it, and it went up to a million views by the next morning.

My thoughts were there from the beginning. I was bombarded with thoughts. I started going on YouTube, grabbing a beat, and writing a hook. Then I'd grab another beat and write another hook. I had fifteen hooks in half a day. I didn't have anyone in the shop. I wrote all these hooks—bang, bang, bang, bang—and sent them to artists I had in my head that would be good for each song. I got nine replies. I had that album finished, from the beginning of the idea to mixed, in a month. I was sitting on the artwork when everything got started at Standing Rock. It was close to December. Police started shooting everybody with water cannons and tear gas. I released *7th Generation Prophecy* so I could put it up for a NAMA. It was crazy.

All the bros on *7th Generation Prophecy* stepped foot on Standing Rock. I didn't go. My wife opposed it. She didn't want me to get hurt or arrested. She begged me, "Don't do it. They'll understand. Help with your music and get your words out there."

We did a protest in my town, standing in solidarity. You'd be surprised at the backlash we got for supporting the protesters at Standing Rock, but people came and supported us. They'd heard about the whole ordeal, but at the end of the day, it turned out good. The album reflected that experience, that atmosphere, and that whole situation. It's continued to be timeless, because the music didn't just reflect that time. It reflected the last five hundred years. The point was to say, "Our voices will be heard. We're not going anywhere. We've been here, and now you're going to know we're still here. You will listen."

Number one of all my songs is "Red Revolution," featuring Thomas X [Ojibwe] from Red Lake, Minnesota. It's sold a lot of copies. We haven't made a video, but it's gotten so many plays and great reviews.

Chase Manhattan from the Twin Cities is on "Broken Promises." He's in the thick of things in Minneapolis. His album *Tribal Tribulation* [2010] won the NAMA for Best Hip-Hop/Rap Recording. We're hustlers in the same game—Muscogee Creek boys. We know that we have to come up with our own way, but we're the most creative people in the universe. We're resilient people who will figure out a way to survive.

I had Lil Mike and Funny Bone on "One Ride." When I was writing the hook to the song, they came to my mind. I said, "I'm going to get those two bros on here. And we're going to tell people that you've only got one ride—you'd better ride it to the fullest. Take advantage of every minute, and don't take it for granted."

Tall Paul's another Minneapolis artist I respect. He's got a Jim Thorpe song that's just insane. He came up and was willing to get on "Daydreams." He killed it on that song.

Saskatchewan-born and Toronto-based Joey Stylez [Joseph Dale Martin LaPointe] [Cree-Métis] featured on "Urban Nativez." He's a crazy, influential, Native rapper who's been doing his thing for a long time. He's set high goals and standards for Native artists.

Russell Means's son Nataanii Means sang on "Lots of Love." I put his father in the sound bite. I put [Oglala Lakota activist and attorney] Chase Iron Eyes's broadcast from Standing Rock on the end of the CD. I hit him up on his inbox and said, "Can I use a tape of your live-feed audio?" He said, "Do whatever you want with it. We want the message to be heard, and we want people listening."

I had Baby Shel from Red Lake on "Addicted to the Life," which looked into the life of being a Native. Whatever may be your reality, embrace it, instead of looking at it as the wrong thing. It used to not be cool to be Indian, but everybody wants to be an Indian now for some reason. The ones who are Native are having an identity crisis because of our environment. We don't know where to go. Should we be this; should we be that? I'm a basketball player, but I love to go to powwows and dance. You can be all those things and be addicted to that life and not the drugs and the bad things you're forced to be around, like alcohol. That's just the way life is, just being Native. It's right there in your face. It's no different from any other community that walks past a bar, a pawnshop, or a crack house. We know that struggle, that feeling you have when your back is against the wall. Now that we have these connections, that beacon of light in the darkness says, "Hey, man, you don't have to go there. Check out what we're doing. Find something you love to do, and when you love yourself, you can make yourself the best you can be."

Even the critics loved the CD. I was up for the NAMA against some really dope artists—Shining Soul [Tohono O'odham and Diné], Artson [Rarámuri or Tarahumara], Rellik [Metís], and Gabriel Yaiva and DJ Soe [Navajo, Hopi, Yaqui, and Cree]. I didn't think I was going to win. I didn't have an entourage, just my wife and me. When they called my name, we sounded like two kids in the middle of a hayfield. We got to walk on the red carpet and meet Felipe Rose of the Village People. I consider that dude my big brother now. We worked together. We won a NAMA for the Best Dance Song, the following year, with "Going Back to My Roots."

In Indian country we help each other. If you see somebody who's hungry, you feed them. You help in any way you can. I've started to see that with Indigenous artists.

The truth is not always pretty. If you're trying to understand another culture, the truth may not be what you want to hear or in the way you want to hear it. Nonetheless, it is still the truth. If I use a word here or there that people may not like, I leave it to their spirit to digest.

I talk to communities, to troubled youth, to my children the same way. There's no filter, because the world doesn't have a filter. The world isn't going to tell you, "We're going to make you sleep in this gutter tonight, but we're going to do it nicely."

The police aren't going to get you out of your car softly or use rubber handcuffs so your wrists don't hurt. No, they're going to mess you up. You're going to sleep in the gutter, and it's going to be cold. You're going to be hungover and jonesing for the next hit of crack or whatever you're on. The world doesn't care. It'll beat you down.

We can point fingers, place blame, and cry about our environmental situations, but at the end of the day, we can choose to change. It may take longer for some but not so long for others. There's always a chance to do better and be better. That's what I try to do every day, be better than I was yesterday.

We've got to get back to doing things the way our people intended us to do them. I'm talking sweat lodges, sun dances, taking medicine, praying, and finding the creative balance to live a happy life.

Elders can take you back to the way. They want to tell people to be more understanding and more accepting. Don't push youngsters away because they like rap or rock and roll. It's going to take all of us.

13

Connections

The modern European violin, or fiddle, arrived in North America in the seventeenth century. Scottish and English traders introduced fiddle playing to the Cherokee. Adopting the instrument, several tribes developed unique traditions. Metís fiddlers are known for "a rather unassuming style of stepdance, far removed from the flashing feet of Riverdance that so many [people] associated with traditional stepdancing. It's similar to French-Canadian stepdancing, or the older Scottish styles of stepdancing found on Cape Breton Island."[1]

New York's Metropolitan Museum of Art possesses a *tsii'edo'a'tl* ("wood that sings"), or Apache fiddle. Made from the agave plant, the instrument was "used in social settings, especially for ceremonial and love songs."[2]

"Some ethnomusicologists reckon that the Apache just copied the European violin," said British violinist Jon Rose, "[but] it doesn't look like a copy to me."[3]

"[The Apache] say it's been in ceremonial use," Rose continued, "since before the red-faced white men arrived on their land. Certainly the very appearance of an Apache violin is closer to ancient Mongolian string instruments than anything European."[4]

The symphonic world has provided opportunities for Indigenous musicians. R. Carlos Nakai, Calvin Standing Bear, Connor Chee, and the Blackfoot Confederacy are some who have appeared as featured soloists. The relationship, however, has not been easy.

"Orchestras can be very hierarchical places," said Matthew Loden, CEO of the Toronto Symphony Orchestra, "[but] we are trying to take a page from Indigenous learning, which is more collaborative."[5]

Composing for Zeitgeist, the Kronos Quartet, Joffrey Ballet, the National Symphony Orchestra, and Chanticleer, Wisconsin-born Brent Michael Davids (Stockbridge Munsee) is one of a growing number of classically trained composers who "proudly identify their heritage as American Indian."[6]

"They've studied the Western tradition," said flutist Timothy Nevaquaya (Comanche), "and they've studied their own American Indian traditions, which are dying out. You hear that merging with Western tonality and harmony, and that is intriguing; that is something totally new."

"Not only are American Indians expressing contemporary expressions," added pianist Jerod Impichchaachaaha Tate (Chickasaw and Irish), "but they're also going back and learning their traditions very well, along with dancing and language."

Louis Wayne Ballard or Honga-nó-zhe (Stands with Eagles) (1931–2007) (Cherokee, Quapaw, French, and Scottish)

Called the "Rosetta Stone of Native American classical composition,"[7] by Jerod Impichchaachaaha Tate, Louis Ballard was born near Miami, Oklahoma. Raised on the Quapaw Reservation, in northeastern Oklahoma, and spending most of his adult years in Santa Fe, New Mexico, "his lineage traces back to the medicine chief of the Quapaw Nation of Oklahoma on his mother's side and the principle chief of the Cherokee Nation of Oklahoma on his father's side."[8]

Ballard's chamber music, symphonies, vocal works, and ballets were performed in Carnegie Hall and Lincoln Center in New York, the John F. Kennedy Performing Arts Center in Washington DC, and concert halls in Argentina, Austria, England, China, the Czech Republic, France, Germany, Hungary, Italy, Russia, and Spain. "The expressiveness in art, and the language of the American Indian," Ballard explained, "has universality possessing the power to touch and speak to every one of us in America, and everyone in the world. It can make a magnificent contribution to the mainstream of . . . world literature, music, education, architecture, design. The list is endless. The possibilities are unlimited."[9]

"The Native community liked and respected Ballard a lot," recalled

Ballard's housekeeper, Lydia Talache, in 2015. "They enjoyed his music and felt that Ballard had a lot to offer. He was openly welcomed into the community."[10]

The Chamber Symphony Orchestra in St. Paul, Minnesota, under Dennis Russell Davies, commissioned Ballard's masterpiece, *Incident at Wounded Knee*, in 1974. Premiered at New York's Town Hall, its composer described it as "a series of musical episodes [that] depict the emotional procession toward the town, the state of the souls in torment, and the violent conflict. The work culminates in musical and dance forms affirming the essential spirituality of Native American people."[11]

A powwow dancer as a youngster, Ballard was sent to the Seneca Indian Training School in Wyandotte, Oklahoma, at the age of six. He would describe the Quaker-run boarding school as a "brainwashing center for young Indians."[12]

Ballard found refuge in music. "Piano became my surrogate mother and father," he remembered. "It was reliable; It was always there . . . Periodically, we were sent to live with Mother. . . . We were often ostracized because we were Indian. The teacher would ask us to draw tom-toms and tomahawks, while others drew trees and puppies. After school, the white students often chased us and threw rocks. . . . I continued to live in two worlds."[13]

Obtaining a master's degree from the University of Tulsa, Ballard served as music director of Santa Fe's Institute of American Indian Arts (1962–68) and music curriculum specialist for the BIA (1968–79), working with more than 350 schools nationwide. His *Music for the Classroom*, combining curriculum and recordings, was published in 1973. "Ballard largely remade music education in Native American schools," reads his entry in the Encyclopedia of World Biography, "introducing both traditional and modern Indian materials and encouraging the teaching of Indian instruments in an attempt to familiarize students with the musical systems of various tribes."[14]

"It is not enough," Ballard asserted, "to acknowledge that Native American Indian music is merely different from other music. What is needed in America is an awakening and reorienting of our total spiritual and cultural perspectives to embrace, understand, and learn from the Aboriginal American what motivates his musical and artistic impulses."[15]

Zitkála-Šá (Gertrude Simmons Bonnin)
(Yankton Dakota) (1876–1938)

Collaborating with Brigham Young University (BYU) music professor William F. Hanson (1887–1967) (Yankton Sioux), South Dakota–born Zitkála-Šá (Red Bird) wrote the libretto and songs for *The Sun Dance Opera* (1913), the first Indigenous opera. Hanson based its melodies on her violin playing. "We have tried to use the Opera," Hanson explained in the program for the 1935 revival at BYU, "as a medium to interpret the inner and human side of the Red Man."[16]

Raised by her mother on the Yankton Sioux Reservation, Zitkála-Šá did more than provide words and inspiration for Hanson's opera. Her English-language books, including *Old Indian Legends* (1901), the auto-biographical *American Indian Stories* (1921), and dozens of articles in magazines like *Atlantic Monthly* and *Harper's Monthly*, added to the mainstream's understanding of Native Americans. "I thank you for your book on Indian legends," Helen Keller wrote to her in 1919. "I have read them with exquisite pleasure. Like all folk tales, they mirror the child's life of the world. There is in them a note of wild, strange music. You have translated them into our language in a way that will keep them alive in the hearts of men. They are so young, so fresh, so full of the odors of the virgin forest untrod by the foot of white man! The thoughts of your people seem dipped in the colors of the rainbow, palpitant with the play of winds, eerie with the thrill of a spirit-world unseen but felt and feared."[17]

Zitkála-Šá was eight years old when missionaries came to the reservation to recruit students for White's Indiana Manual Labor Institute. Opened in 1850, the school had been one of several founded by Quaker Josiah White. A mill owner and engineer, White made his fortune as the inventor of a method to bring coal down the Lehigh River in Pennsylvania.

In 1882 "the Indian Aid Society with the cooperation of the Indian Bureau arranged to send Indian children from the Sac and Fox Agencies in Indian Territory to White's Institute."[18] Within two years, the school included students from a variety of tribes. Despite her mother's objections, Zitkála-Šá was one of the youngsters chosen. She remained at the school for three years.

Returning to the reservation in 1887, Zitkála-Šá found herself so assimilated that she no longer fit in with her own people. After three uncomfortable years, she returned to the school, studying piano and violin and earning a scholarship to a teacher training program at Earlham College. Health problems and financial difficulties would cause her to leave the Richmond, Virginia, college six weeks before graduation, but she continued to study violin at the New England Conservatory of Music in Boston.

Speaking against slavery, Zitkála-Šá placed second in the 1898 Indiana State Oratorical Society contest. Hired as a music teacher at Carlisle, a year later, she appeared as a featured soloist when the school's band performed in Washington DC for President William McKinley and his guests in 1900. Upon their return, Carlisle's longtime superintendent, Richard Henry Pratt, sent her to the Yankton Reservation to recruit students.

During her first trip home in more than a decade and a half, Zitkála-Šá was appalled by the impoverished conditions and the number of whites occupying land after the allocations mandated by the Dawes Act were distributed.

Escalating arguments with Pratt culminated in Zitkála-Šá's leaving Carlisle in 1901. Returning to the reservation to care for her ailing mother, she collated the stories published in her first book, *Old Indian Legends*. "The American Indian must have a voice," she said. "Let us teach our children to be proud of their Indian blood. Let us stand up straight and continue claiming our human rights."[19]

In addition to writing numerous articles condemning the boarding schools, Zitkála-Šá worked as a BIA clerk on the Standing Rock Indian Reservation and toured the United States for the General Foundation of Women's Clubs. Shortly after her 1902 marriage to Raymond Talefase Bonnin, another boarding school survivor, the BIA assigned her to the Unitah and Ouray Reservation in Utah. She and her husband would remain on the reservation for the next fourteen years, raising their son, Raymond Ohiya Bonnin, and working with the Ute.

Zitkála-Šá based *The Sun Dance Opera*'s libretto and songs on a sacred ceremony that was prohibited by the federal government at the time. "I have been trained in the concepts of the Christian religion," she said during a 1913 interview, "but I do not find them more beautiful, more noble, or more true than the religious ideals of the Indian. Indeed, if one allows for a change in names, the two sets of concepts are much the same. I should not like to see my people lose their ideals or have them supplanted by others less fitted to influence their lives for good."[20]

The Sun Dance Opera premiered at the Orpheus Hall in Vernal, Utah, in February 1913. Some members of the Ute tribe participated, but major roles were played by non-Indigenous actors in redface. The opera toured through Utah, running for fifteen performances.

Hanson included only his name on the title page of the score and its copyright registration. When the New York Light Opera Guild revived *The Sun Dance Opera* at the Broadway Theater in April 1938, only its composer was credited.

Zitkála-Šá devoted the rest of her life to activism. A member of the advisory board of the Society for the American Indian (SAI) since 1911, she moved to Washington DC with Bonnin and their son, Raymond Ohiya Bonnin (1903–39), after being elected secretary in 1916.

When the United States declared war on Germany, in 1917, and entered World War I, Bonnin enlisted in the army. He would be honorably discharged as a captain in 1920.

Founding the National Council of American Indians with Bonnin in 1926, Zitkála-Šá served as president until her January 1938 passing, three months before the Broadway premiere of *The Sun Dance Opera*. She and her husband are buried in Arlington National Cemetery.

In 2022 Minnesota-based AOT (An Opera Theatre) produced a thirty-minute opera film, *Mináǧi Kin Dowán* (My spirit sings), based on Zitkála-Šá's life. Featuring a libretto by Hannah Johnson (Anishinaabe and Ojibwe), the opera's music was composed by Lyz Jaakola (Fond du Lac Anishinaabe). "Some of the music is like you'd expect from the Indigenous palette," the composer told an interviewer, "but some is more classic, I even quote some Mozart in there. . . . We are decolonizing opera!"[21]

Maria Tallchief (Elizabeth Marie Tallchief)
(1925–2013) (Osage, Scottish, and Irish)

Remembered for her electrifying passion, technical ability, and stunning beauty, Maria Tallchief was America's first major prima ballerina. Born in Fairfax, Oklahoma, she began studying ballet at the age of three. Noticing the talents of Maria and her sister, Marjorie, her parents moved the family to Los Angeles in 1933. Initially training with Ernest Belcher, Tallchief transferred to Bronislava Nijinska's studio at the age of twelve. Five years later she headed to New York with dreams of a career as a dancer. Nijinska arranged an audition with Ballet Russe de Monte Carlo. Tallchief failed to get the role, but it would be a harbinger of things to come. After Nijinska agreed to stage a Chopin concerto for Ballet Russe, Tallchief was hired as an understudy. She advanced quickly. When the lead ballerina failed to get along with the rest of the cast and was fired, Tallchief took her place. She would remain with the prestigious ensemble for five years, working with groundbreaking choreographers and directors. During rehearsals for *Rodeo (The Courtship of Burnt Ranch)*, in 1942, Agnes DeMille convinced her to change her name to Maria, a derivative of her middle name.

After working with George Balanchine, twenty-two years her senior, in *The Song of Norway* (1944), Tallchief married the famed choreographer two years later. When Balanchine cofounded what would become the New York City Ballet, she became his lead ballerina and starred in *The Firebird* (1949). Despite their marriage being annulled in 1952, she continued to work with Balanchine, appearing as the Sugarplum Fairy in his staging of *The Nutcracker* (1954).

Having served as the Lyric Opera of Chicago's director of ballet in the 1970s, Tallchief founded the Chicago City Ballet with her sister in 1981. Inducted into the National Women's Hall of Fame in 1996, she received a National Medal of the Arts in 1999 and was posthumously voted into the National Native American Hall of Fame in 2018. Two years later the U.S. Mint issued a specially designed quarter, with Tallchief's image and Osage name, Wa-Txthe-thonba (Woman of Two Standards), as part of its series honoring American women for their contributions to culture. The reverse side shows Laura Gardin Fraser's 1932 sculpture of George Washington.

A year younger than Maria, Marjorie Tallchief is best remembered for choreographing the Harkness Ballet of New York's 1964 production of *Koshare*, based on a Hopi creation myth. Louis Ballard composed its score. After premiering in Barcelona, Spain, the thirty-minute piece toured the United States and Europe.

Jeremy Dutcher (1990–) (Wolastoqiyik)

A two-spirit member of the Tobique First Nation (one of six Wolastoq-iyik, or Maliseet, reserves in New Brunswick, Canada), Jeremy Dutcher finds inspiration in wax recordings of his ancestors. The conservatory-trained composer and vocalist's "decision to make music that centres on Wolastoqiyik, his people, to sing in the language, and to weave in electronic samples of his ancestors' sounds, is all part of his desire to revive the culture."[22]

There's real positivity among Indigenous people making music today. Because of technology and social media, we don't have to tell our story to anyone else. It's possible to find an audience without signing over your music, power, and sacred songs.

I'm a bridge person, a person between cultures. My mother comes from the Wolastoqiyik [Wool-las-two-wee-ig] people in Northwest New Brunswick, but my father's not Indigenous. He jokes, "You saved me," but we brought him into the fold and taught him the language.

As maternal people, we pass through our mothers. Mine was insistent that we knew who we were, where we came from, our history, and our language. You can't understand the differences between European ways of thinking and Indigenous ways until you go out into the world and interact with all kinds of people. We're different, but we're the same too.

Wolastoqiyik is what we call the river. It means "Peaceful Wave." We're the people of that river. When Europeans first arrived, they were greeted with such generosity, kindness, and friendship that the 1726 treaty governing the land is called the Peace and Friendship Treaty. Despite our problems, we've remained peaceful and open to dialogue, maintaining good relations in the face of inhumanity.

39. Jeremy Dutcher

The Wolastoqey [Wool-las-two-gway] language was always around me, whether my mother was talking to her mother or her sisters. She'd command us to "do that" or "go there" in language. My father's an English speaker, and I stuck with that. But I'm comfortable speaking Wolastoqey. More and more, I get to do it. Traveling with this album reconnected me with the language and my people. Everywhere I go, it feels like there're relatives.

My childhood experiences were different than most people's—it wasn't just because I was darker than everyone else—but those experiences helped me understand what resiliency looks like and how to survive. You choose to live with terror, or you move on more lightly.

I grew up singing traditional music around the drum, but I also had a deep appreciation for jazz. When I got into high school, I started reading music. I went on to study opera and composition at Dalhousie University in Nova Scotia. Opera turns a lot of people off—it turns me off if I'm being honest about it—but I like to say that I've taken the good parts and left the rest.

I'm thirty, but I always say that I spent twenty-seven years writing Wolastoqiyik Linuwakonawa [Wool-las-two-wi-ig Lint-two-wah-gun-ah-wa], the recipient of a Polaris Music Prize and a JUNO for Indigenous Music Album of 2018. It was the culmination of my work till then. It started in 2012 when an elder, Maggie Paul, told me about wax cylinders at the Canadian Museum of History in Gatineau, Quebec. She said, "You've got to bring them back for the people."

That set me on a journey that led to field recordings of my ancestors. Their voices connected with me. I had never heard anything like it. Canada prohibited our ceremonial songs and gatherings, attempting to erase our culture, until 1951. The songs wanted to be back with the people again, but it wasn't just my people who needed them. Indigenous people coast-to-coast needed these songs.

At one time, there were lots of people collecting our songs. I worked with the collection that musicologist William Mechling [a former University of Pennsylvania student of Franz Boas] put together between 1907 and 1913. I wrote twelve arrangements, but there were over a hundred songs collected.

I'm not going to be recording from wax cylinders my whole life, but those songs are so beautiful. I used a neoclassical frame of a piano with a string quartet and then had a percussionist round out the sound. You can hear those ancient voices if you listen.

There aren't many who can understand the words—less than a hundred fluent speakers—but everyone can get the meaning. The songs are about our life, language, and the beauty of our culture. There's so much to grieve about and work to change, yet if we dazzle at the beauty of what we have, we're much better served.

There were three trading songs in the collection. "Essuonike" [Let's trade] journeyed through those three melodies. "The Canoe Song" is sung when we're out on a canoe. We don't sing a song at any other time than when it's connected to the action.

Some of the songs tell stories; some are mythologies. Some are like legal texts, statements made to hold leadership accountable and remind chiefs to think about all of us. The songs are never about one thing.

Winning the Polaris Music Prize brought increased awareness outside my community and allowed me to tour and create new work. The awards ceremony was exciting. My mother and father were there. The elder who pointed me in the direction of the wax cylinders was there. I don't do it for the awards or statues, but it was a beautiful celebration.

The first time that I went to the JUNO Awards [March 2019], I was stoked. When I won my category at the pretelecast gala dinner, I went up to the stage. At the time, troubling things were going on. Justin Trudeau had just sent military police into our territory. There were Indigenous people without clean drinking water. I started to speak to that, but as I spoke, they raised the music. And I went away, not thinking anything more about it.

Later that night, when Arkelis won for Best Rock Album, they invited me to finish my speech during their time. They had my back. I'm grateful that they let me say what was important to me. It was a beautiful act.

The next night, my band and I performed "Sakomawit." I prefer intimate spaces where people can witness a musical event. To blow that up to a stadium of screaming people was surreal. The museum collection includes more than music. I enlarged a few photographs to poster size and hung them from the rafters. The ancestors were there; it felt special. My niece was in the front row.

The "Mehcinut" video came through a collaboration with a director from Toronto, Chandler Levack [Anishinaabe]. She was one of the dancers as well. We wanted to tell a story of death and rebirth. Indigenous people lost a lot in the process of colonization, but there's a deep, truthful understanding that we never lost anything. It's always been here, it's still here, and it will always be here. I wanted to celebrate that beauty, but it wasn't just my nation that I wanted to honor. In the middle of the video, there's what I called the Table of Excellence. I invited people from nations coast-to-coast to sit at that table and be a star in a constellation. None of us can do it alone. We had filmmakers, writers, musicians, and all kinds of inspiring people going beyond beads and feathers and existing in our diverse beauty. We've been unlearning a lot quickly—faster than we've ever done as a species on this planet—but buckle up.

We're going to seize the moment and rise.

Connor Chee (1987–) (Diné)

The grandson of a Diné healer, Connor Chee sets "Navajo texts" to "succinct wooden flute and piano passages that flesh out the mood."[23]

Whether I was going to the Eastman School of Music or the University of Cincinnati's College-Conservatory of Music or giving piano lessons, people would ask me, "Do you live in a tepee?"

I'd tell them, "It's not like the cowboys and Indians you've seen on TV or in the movies," but they'd be perplexed. They'd ask about my background, and I'd tell them, "Navajo . . . Native American."

They'd say, "That's funny, but we know they're all dead."

Navajo music is passed through oral tradition. My goal was to write our songs down so they wouldn't get lost. I started with recordings of my grandpa Keith Chee. I tried writing them down, but they didn't fit standard European notation. I ended up composing new pieces based on traditional Navajo chants. I combined my background in classical piano and my cultural traditions and came up with *The Navajo Piano* [2014]. It won a NAMA as the year's Best Instrumental Recording. *Emergence* came out in 2018. There were differences in the way I approached the piano and how I incorporated my grandfather's vocals. He's a healer, deeply rooted in tradition. He doesn't even speak English. Growing up, I attended ceremonies with him. My music is not only tied to Navajo culture but also to prayers. Prayer was integral to everything my grandfather did; it was something I grew up with.

I've met other Native piano players, thanks to social media, but growing up, I didn't know any. One of my professors told me, "You should find Navajo piano music to play at your recital."

The only pieces I could find were by people who weren't Native but had seen a ceremony once or twice and based a piece on that. It had nothing to do with actual Native culture. I was at a loss. I didn't have anyone I could look up to. I had teachers who said, "You're Native—you'll never stand up against Russia-trained pianists or disciplined Chinese and Koreans."

That was a challenge but also a motivator. I knew I could do it as well as anyone. My background didn't mean I had to be held back.

My parents were always supportive. My dad gave me a toy keyboard one Christmas. I took to it and started making up my own tunes. He and my mom saw that I was interested and got me piano lessons. There were few music teachers in Page, Arizona, so we ended up driving to Flagstaff, a couple of hours away, once a week, so I could take lessons. It was a commitment. You can't take a four-hour round trip casually.

We moved to Cincinnati when I was ten, and I went to the School for Creative and Performing Arts. It went from the fourth grade through the twelfth. I wasn't used to being in the same building as high schoolers, but I was serious and willing to put in the work.

When I was training for competitions, I'd go to school during the day. They mixed in academic classes, but I had a daily piano lesson. And after that, I'd go home and spend another three hours with my teacher at a piano. I'd get up the next day and do it all over again.

During the summer, my teacher ran a camp. Everyone involved in competitions came five days a week, like a regular school day, but we focused on the piano. It was a different way of growing up than any of my friends. There were times when they'd say, "Let's do this or that," and I had to tell them, "No, I'm still in school."

I didn't always want to practice, but my parents kept me on track. It was all worth it. I acquired valuable knowledge, but I struggled with it. I doubted myself, and that made me doubt the amount of time and commitment I was putting into it. I questioned whether it was the right path for me and whether I wanted to spend all that time practicing. It wasn't easy.

Performing in Carnegie Hall when I was twelve, as gold medal winner in the World Piano Competition's Young Artist Division, is one of the best memories I have. It was my first time in New York, my first time in a venue that size. It was the most exciting thing and the most terrifying. My friends in the piano department made the trip. So did a lot of family members, including my grandfather, who had never been on a plane before. It was motivation to keep going.

Navajo music is usually monophonic, but I've added harmony to my music. Repetition plays a big part in the chanting, repeating phrases or rearranging words and musical fragments in interesting ways. Most music has a climax or resolution, but that's not always the case with traditional Navajo music.

When I write, I have to wait for inspiration. There's always a worry that it's not going to come, but I turn to nature or my spirituality and reconnect with the process of making music.

There are always new challenges and opportunities; I can't predict what's going to happen. When I was in college, I didn't see myself as a composer or recording artist. The traditional path for a pianist is getting educated and teaching at a university, but I didn't want to be on that path.

Orchestras including the Cincinnati Pops and the Hamilton-Fairfield and Blue Ash / Montgomery Symphonies ask me to play with them. I was supposed to do a concert with an orchestra in Gallup, New Mexico, but it was canceled due to the pandemic. We were going to play a Mozart concerto.

Coda

When I was writing *Heartbeat, Warble, and the Electric Powwow*, I was repeatedly asked what made Indigenous music Indigenous. Was it simply because it was played by Native Americans, or was there a more meaningful connection? What links R. Carlos Nakai's flute melodies and Redbone's funky grooves? What ties Northern Cree's round dance songs and Buffy Sainte-Marie's ballads? How about Indigenous music that doesn't reflect Indianism?

I wracked my brain seeking an answer, until stumbling upon Richard Erdoes and Alfonso Ortiza's *American Indian Myths and Legends*.[1] Its concluding chapter stressed Indigenous belief in the interconnectedness between human beings, the natural world, and the spiritual realm. Doing interviews for this book and listening to songs, example after example of this came through.

Not only are Indigenous virtues worth preserving, but we would all be better off if we embraced and incorporated them into our lives, regardless of our ethnicity. The U.S. Constitution is based on the Haudenosaunee Great Law of Peace, which some say goes back to August 1142, but we continue to divide by race, religion, wealth, and politics, rather than working together for the preservation of the planet.

The obstacles facing Indigenous North America are numerous. In the opening paragraph of the Rockefeller Foundation-funded Meriam Report (official title: The Problem of Indian Administration), President Herbert Hoover and Vice President Charles Curtis, who was one-quarter Kaw, reported that "an overwhelming majority of the Indians are poor, even extremely poor, and they are not adjusted to the economic and social system of the dominant white civilization."[2]

That was in February 1928. Seven years shy of a century later, it isn't much better. The *Gallup Independent* called conditions on reservations "comparable to Third World."[3]

Over 25 percent of Indigenous peoples are below the poverty line, the highest rate among minority groups. On reservations, the rate is even higher (38–63 percent). The median income is $23,000. The employment-to-population ratio is 57 percent. The scarcity of jobs leads many to rely on social security, disability, and veteran's income. Only 15 percent hold bachelor's degrees, less than half the percentage of Caucasians.

Housing is a serious problem. Overcrowding affects 30 percent of reservation homes, sheltering multigenerational families. Less than half of the houses are connected to a public sewer, contributing to poor health. The infant death rate is 65 percent. Compared to Caucasians, Native Americans are more than twice as likely to experience heart disease before the age of sixty-five. There were 3.5 times more COVID-19 cases among Native Americans, and life expectancy is 5.5 years less than the total U.S. population. Natives are 82 percent more likely to die of suicide.

The trauma goes even further. Four out of five Indigenous women have experienced violence, more than double the rate for Caucasians. The United Nations claims, "An indigenous woman is more likely to be raped, with some estimates showing that more than one in three indigenous women are raped during their lifetime."[4]

The Indigenous murder rate of American Indian and Native Alaskan women—according to the National Crime Information Center, the United States' central database for tracking crime-related information—is more than ten times the national average. Homicide was the leading cause of death for Indigenous females between the ages of ten and twenty-four, and it was the fifth leading cause for those between twenty-five and thirty-four. This murder rate is triple what it is for white women.

Farther to the north, an inquiry found that, although comprising only 4 percent of Canada's female population, Indigenous women and girls made up 16 percent of the country's femicides.

The abduction of Indigenous women, men, and two-spirit people is problematic on both sides of the border. Seattle's Indian Health Board reported 128 Indigenous females missing in the United States and Canada in 2017. Their ages spanned from less than a year old to eighty-three years old, with a median age of twenty-nine.

Not all is gloom, however. Despite more than a half millennium of systematic genocide, Indigenous pride has not been extinguished. Rather than defeat, the music reflects resilience and determination. Native peoples are building toward the future, making sure the lessons from the past are not forgotten.

New artists and established veterans are continuing to release stimulating recordings. The internet provides an avenue for reaching fans, but Indigenous musicians haven't given up on the mainstream. In July 2021 the Cody Blackbird Band became the first Indigenous group featured in *Rolling Stone*. A month later *Reservation Dogs* premiered on Hulu. Chronicling the exploits of four teenagers in rural Oklahoma, the show was co-created by Sterlin Harjo and Taika Waititi and features an all-Indigenous cast. The inclusion of Indigenous musicians including Sten Joddi, Redbone, and Lil Mike and Funny Bone provides a much-needed platform.

Stereotypes are increasingly breaking down. In 2012 the ska-punk band No Doubt, from Anaheim, California, withdrew their highly derogatory video for "Looking Hot," the second single from *Push and Shove*, and issued an apology. Two years later hip-hopper Pharrell Williams was similarly remorseful after being criticized for wearing an eagle-feather headdress on the cover of *Elle UK* magazine.

On March 31, 2022, Pope Francis met First Nation, Inuit, and Metís delegates at the Vatican. The next day, the Argentina-born pontiff addressed the Roman Catholic Church's participation in Canada's residential schools, stating, "I feel shame—sorrow and shame—for the role that a number of Catholics, particularly those with educational responsibilities, have had in all these things that wounded you, in the abuses you suffered and in the lack of respect shown for your identity, your culture, and even your spiritual values."[5]

Anglican, Unitarian, and Presbyterian churches had previously apologized for abuses at their schools. "It is chilling to think," admitted the Holy Father, "of determined efforts to instill a sense of inferiority, to rob people of their cultural identity, to sever their roots, and to consider all the personal and social effects that this continues to entail: unresolved traumas that have become intergenerational traumas."[6]

The pope continued to apologize to Canada's First Nations in July 2022. The Vatican called the eighty-five-year-old pontiff's weeklong trip a "penitential pilgrimage."[7] Chief Randy Ermineskin of the Ermineskin Cree Nation said, "For survivors from coast to coast, this is an opportunity— the first and maybe the last—to perhaps find some closure for themselves and their families."[8]

Some believe change isn't coming fast enough. During a mass at the shrine Sanctuaire Sainte-Anne-de-Beaupré, outside Quebec City, on July 29, 2022, the pope was greeted by a banner pleading for him to rescind the *Doctrine of Discovery*. "The Pope and the Catholic Church are ground zero for the genocide that we've endured,"[9] said Eva Jewell (Anishinaabe), research director at Toronto Metropolitan University's Yellowhead Institute.

The pontiff took it to heart. Speaking for the Catholic Church, on March 30, 2023, a year after the Vatican meeting, and the day before entering the hospital to be treated for infectious bronchitis, he repudiated "those concepts that fail to recognize the inherent human rights of indigenous peoples, including what has become known as the legal and political 'doctrine of discovery.'"[10]

He further acknowledged and apologized for the suffering "due to the expropriation of their lands . . . as well as the policies of forced assimilation, promoted by the governmental authorities of the time, intended to eliminate their indigenous cultures."[11]

The papal repudiation of the *Doctrine of Discovery* is indeed a positive step. An official release from the Holy See Press Office, on the day of the repeal, explained that "the Church has acquired a greater awareness of [Indigenous peoples'] sufferings, past and present, due to the expropriation of their lands, which they consider a sacred gift from God and their ancestors, as well as the policies of forced assimilation, promoted by the governmental authorities of the time, intended to eliminate their indigenous cultures. . . . Their sufferings constitute a powerful summons to abandon the colonizing mentality and to walk with them side by side, in mutual respect and dialogue, recognizing the rights and cultural values of all individuals and peoples."[12]

"We could begin our journey of healing," said Grand Chief George Arcand Jr. (Confederacy of Treaty Six First Nations), "and change the way things have been for our people for many, many years."[13]

More is still needed. "I've always said we need a new papal bull," explained Assembly of First Nations national chief Rose Anne Archibald, "to talk about the value and worthiness of Indigenous people and cultures around the world."[14]

Enough said . . . It's time to listen.

INTERVIEWS

Amero, Don, October 2, 2020

Bee, Tom, February 6, 2011

Benally, Clayson, December 11, 2011, May 28, 2020

Benally, Jeneda, December 11, 2011, May 28, 2020

Bennett, Callie, May 26, 2020

Blackbird, Cody Sun Bear, May 16, 2020

Chee, Connor, May 21, 2020

Ciliberti, Lucas, May 26, 2020

Coane, Donna, May 22, 2020

Cummings, Robby, June 4, 2020

Davis, Gary Paul "Litefoot," November 19, 2011

Denay, Shon (Shantel D. Haynes), May 20, 2020

Derrickson, Kelly Margaret, May 23, 2020

Dutcher, Jeremy, July 1, 2020

Eagle Tail, Desja, May 13, 2020

Faithful, Jacob, July 28, 2020

Fontaine, Vince, August 4, 2020

Fox, Theresa "Bear," May 14, 2020

Fralick, Paco, June 25, 2020

General, Dan "DJ Shub," June 10, 2020

Gilday, Jay, July 14, 2020

Gilday, Leela, May 22, 2020

Hairston, Robin, June 11, 2020

Harjo, Joy, July 9, 2011

Hernandez, Raven, June 11, 2012

Holland, Jack "Crazy Flute," May 19, 2020

Hollis, Robert "Bobby Bullet" St. Germaine, May 15, 2020

James (Naveau), Matt, May 19, 2020

Joddi, Sten, June 11, 2020

Kabotie, Rylan, June 4, 2020

Kirkpatrick, Jane, July 12, 2022

Kokopelli, Bearheart (Bernhard Mikuskovics), via Skype, May 19, 2020

Lomayesva, Arthur "Casper Loma Da Wa," May 14, 2020

Lee, Barry, May 27, 2020

Mahal, Taj, March 6, 2013

Morin, Cary, June 5, 2020

Nakai, Raymond Carlos, June 2012

Nelson, Tracy Lee, May 23, 2020

Nevaquaya, Timothy, July 14, 2011

Night Shield, Gabriel, June 9, 2020

Orona, Roman, May 12, 2020

Oxendine, Jamie K., June 22, 2012

Rainwater, Marvin Karlton, September 15, 2012

Ramon, Thomas Ehren "Bear Witness," June 8, 2020

Redbird, Duke, August 6, 2020

Redhouse, Vince, May 21, 2020

Robertson, Jaime Royal "Robbie," May 13, 2013

Rushingwind-Ruiz, Steven, May 14, 2020

Sainte-Marie, Beverly "Buffy," via email, June 19, 2011

Schulman, Sandra Hale, February 6, 2012

Shenandoah, Joanne Lynn, May 12, 2020

Silas, Wayne, Jr., July 18, 2011

Silva, Jesus, II, "Lil Mike," June 25, 2020

Silva, Jesus, IV, "Funny Bone," June 25, 2020

Standing Bear, Calvin Ishoni, May 20, 2020

Sutter, Sandra, June 28, 2020

Tate, Jerod Impichchaachaaha, October 25, 2011

Vavages, Stevie Ray, May 27, 2020

Vegas, Patrick Joseph "P. J.," May 12, 2020

Wall, Adrian, June 4, 2020

Waln, Frank, November 18, 2011

Ware, John, December 14, 2013

Wood, Fawn, July 30, 2020

Wood, Steve, July 15, 2011

Photographs provided courtesy of artists.

All quotes from personal interviews unless otherwise indicated.

NOTES

PREFACE

1. Katharine Q. Seelye, "Ladonna Brave Bull Allard, Pipeline Foe," *New York Times*, April 21, 2021.
2. Craig Harris, *Heartbeat, Warble, and the Electric Powwow: American Indian Music* (Norman: University of Oklahoma Press, 2016).
3. Peter d'Errico, "John Marshall: Indian Lover?," *Journal of the West*, Summer 2000, https://www.umass.edu/legal/derrico/marshall_jow.html.
4. Devon A. Mihesuah, "Introduction," *American Indian Quarterly* 20, no. 1 (1996), http://www.jstor.org/stable/1184935.

1. FINGERPRINTS

1. Juliette Appold, "Appreciating Native American Music," NLS *Music Notes* (blog), Library of Congress, November 4, 2021, https://blogs.loc.gov/nls-music-notes/2021/11/appreciating -native-american-music/.
2. Lee Shaw, "Russell 'Big Chief' Moore: Stellar Native American Jazzman," *Syncopated Times*, March 1, 2016.
3. "Oscar Pettiford," All about Jazz, last updated April 27, 2022, https://www.allaboutjazz .com/musicians/oscar-pettiford.
4. Barry Kernfel, ed., *The New Grove Dictionary of Jazz* (New York: Macmillan, 1994), 44.
5. "Mildred Bailey's Native American Roots," *Bibliolore* (blog), February 27, 2017, https:// bibliolore.org/2017/02/27/mildred-baileys-native-american-roots/.
6. John McDonough, "Mildred Bailey's Belated Accolade," *DownBeat*, August 11, 2020.
7. McDonough, "Mildred Bailey's Belated Accolade."
8. Jessica Robinson, "Search for Jazz Singer's Roots Brings Together Two Julias," NPR, May 2, 2012.
9. Robinson, "Search for Jazz Singer's Roots."
10. Associated Press, "Jazz Great Illinois Jacquet Dead at 81," *Today*, July 23, 2004, https:// www.today.com/popculture/jazz-great-illinois-jacquet-dead-81-1C9492135.
11. Illinois Jacquet, "It's a Struggle," interview by Les Tomkins, *Jazz Professional*, January 1, 1973, quoted in John Rosie, "Illinois Jacquet (1922–2004)," National Jazz Archive, https://nationaljazzarchive.org.uk/explore/interviews/1633367-illinois-jacquet?.
12. Roy, "Witchi Tai To—Jim Pepper," *Just a Song* (blog), January 19, 2010, http://justasong2 .blogspot.com/2010/01/witchi-tai-to-jim-pepper.html.

13. Roy, "Witchi Tai To—Jim Pepper."
14. *DownBeat*, quoted in "Witchi-Tai-To: Jan Garbarek—Bobo Stenson Quartet," EMC Records, https://www.ecmrecords.com/shop/143038750651/witchi-tai-to-jan-garbarek-bobo-stenson-quartet.

2. ANTHROPOLOGISTS

1. Rachel Parsons, "Anthropology Association Apologizes to Native Americans for the Field's Legacy of Harm," *Scientific American*, March 28, 2022, https://www.scientificamerican.com/article/anthropology-association-apologizes-to-native-americans-for-the-fields-legacy-of-harm/.
2. Quoted in Parsons, "Anthropology Association Apologizes."
3. Joe Watkins, "Writing Unwritten History," *Abstracts*, November/December 2001.
4. Parsons, "Anthropology Association Apologizes."
5. Parsons, "Anthropology Association Apologizes."
6. Theodore Roosevelt, First Annual Message to the Senate and House of Representatives, December 3, 1901, https://www.apstudent.com/ushistory/docs1901/tr1.htm.
7. Kristina Gaddy, "Meet the Socialite Who Helped Preserve—and Destroy—Native American Culture," Ozy True Stories, June 11, 2018, https://www.ozy.com/true-and-stories/meet-the-socialite-who-helped-preserve-and-destroy-native-american-culture/86969/.
8. Partnership with Native Americans, "Standing Bear—1829–1908," accessed March 18, 2023, http://www.nativepartnership.org/site/PageServer?pagename=PWNA_Native_Biography_standingbear.
9. Partnership with Native Americans, "Standing Bear—1829–1908."
10. Maggie, "Alice Cunningham Fletcher," *History of American Women* (blog), May 26, 2015, https://www.womenhistoryblog.com/2015/05/alice-cunningham-fletcher.html.
11. Alice C. Fletcher, "Indian Songs, Personal Studies of Indian Life," *Century Illustrated Magazine*, 1894, 1.
12. Fletcher, "Indian Songs," 4.
13. Gaddy, "Meet the Socialite."
14. Francis Densmore, "She Heard an Indian Drum," in *Francis Densmore and American Indian Music: A Memorial Volume*, comp. and ed. Charles Hofmann (New York: Museum of the American Indian, 1968), 2; quoted in Dorian Brooks, "Francis Densmore," Fembio, https://www.fembio.org/english/biography.php/woman/biography/frances-theresa-densmore/.
15. Densmore, "She Heard an Indian Drum," 2.
16. Brooks, "Francis Densmore."
17. Brooks, "Francis Densmore."
18. Natalie Curtis, *The Indians' Book: Authentic Native American Legends, Lore, and Music* (New York: Harper and Bros., 1907).
19. Natalie Curtis Burlin, *Negro Folk Songs* (New York: G. Schirmer, 1918).
20. Curtis, *Indians' Book*.
21. Elbridge L. Adams, address at Hampton Institute, January 31, 1926, *Southern Workman*, March 1926.

3. ASSIMILATION

1. Ron Gurley, "Two Worlds," Amber Alert in Indian Country, May 31, 2017, https://www
.amber-ic.org/tribal-connections/two-worlds/.
2. Erin Tapahe, "Maintaining Traditional Native American Values in a Modern World,"
Universe Narratives, April 30, 2019, https://universe.byu.edu/narratives/maintaining
-traditional-native-american-values-in-a-modern-world/.
3. Murray Lee, "Leon Hale, Walking in Two Worlds," *Partnership with Native Americans*
(blog), March 3, 2015, http://blog.nativepartnership.org/leon-hale-walking-in-two-worlds/.
4. Ryan Winn, "George Washington and the Resiliency of Indian People," *Tribal College Journal*, July 2, 2018, https://tribalcollegejournal.org/george-washington-and-the
-resiliency-of-indian-people/.
5. Colin Calloway, "George Washington's 'Tortuous' Relationship with Native Americans,"
Zócalo Public Square, August 2, 2018, https://www.zocalopublicsquare.org/2018/08
/02/george-washingtons-tortuous-relationship-native-americans/ideas/essay/.
6. Alysa Landry, "Thomas Jefferson: Architect of Indian Removal Policy," Indian Country
Today, September 13, 2018, https://indiancountrytoday.com/archive/thomas-jefferson
-architect-of-indian-removal-policy.
7. Landry, "Thomas Jefferson."
8. Bryan Newland, *Federal Indian Boarding School Initiative Investigative Report* (Washington DC: Department of the Interior, Bureau of Indian Affairs, May 2022), 21, https://
www.bia.gov/sites/default/files/dup/inline-files/bsi_investigative_report_may_2022
_508.pdf.
9. Landry, "Thomas Jefferson."
10. Landry, "Thomas Jefferson."
11. Landry, "Thomas Jefferson."
12. Mato Canli Win, "Civilization Act," *Lakota Times*, June 17, 2021, https://www.lakotatimes
.com/articles/civilization-act/.
13. ReconciliAction YEG, "The Gradual Civilization Act," *University of Alberta Faculty of
Law* (blog), October 4, 2018, https://ualbertalaw.typepad.com/faculty/2018/10/the
-gradual-civilization-act.html.
14. *The Doctrine of Discovery and Its Enduring Impact on Indigenous Peoples* (Onondaga
Nation NY: Onondaga Nation Communication Office, 2012), https://www.onondaganation
.org/mediafiles/pdfs/un/Doctrine%20of%20Discovery.pdf.
15. Indigenous Values Initiative, "Dum Diversas," *Doctrine of Discovery* Project, July 23,
2018, https://doctrineofdiscovery.org/dum-diversas/.
16. Joan Huyser-Honig and Mark MacDonald, "Indigenous Christian Worship Resources:
Where to Start," Calvin Institute of Christian Worship, March 19, 2020, https://worship
.calvin.edu/resources/resource-library/indigenous-christian-worship-resources-where
-to-start/.
17. Frances Gardiner Davenport, ed., *European Treaties Bearing on the History of the
United States and Its Dependencies to 1648* (Washington DC: Carnegie Institution of
Washington, 1917), 61–63.
18. Tim Giago, "Why Did the Native Americans Convert to Foreign Religions?," Indianz,
March 19, 2020, https://www.indianz.com/News/2020/03/09/tim-giago-why-did-the
-native-americans-c.asp.

19. Pope Paul III, *Sublimis Deus: On the Enslavement and Evangelization of Indians*, May 29, 1537, Papal Encyclicals Online, last updated February 20, 2020, https://www.papalencyclicals.net/paul03/p3subli.htm.

20. Seminole County Government, "Seminole Indian Wars," Seminole County Museum Resources and Historical Information, accessed March 18, 2023, https://www.seminolecountyfl.gov/departments-services/leisure-services/parks-recreation/museum-of-seminole-county-history/about-the-museum-of-seminole-county-hi/museum-resources-historical-informatio/seminole-indian-wars.stml.

21. Johnson and Graham's Lessee v. M'Intosh, 21 U.S. 543 (1823). https://supreme.justia.com/cases/federal/us/21/543/. See also Robert J. Miller, "American Indians, the Doctrine of Discovery, and Manifest Destiny," *Wyoming Law Review*, January 2011, https://scholarship.law.uwyo.edu/cgi/viewcontent.cgi?article=1254&context=wlr.

22. "Manifest Destiny and Indian Removal," Smithsonian American Art Museum, February 2015, https://americanexperience.si.edu/wp-content/uploads/2015/02/Manifest-Destiny-and-Indian-Removal.pdf.

23. Alysa Landry, "James Monroe: Pushed Tribes off Land, but Boosted Indian Education," American Indian Today, last updated September 13, 2018, https://indiancountrytoday.com/archive/james-monroe-pushed-tribes-off-land-but-boosted-indian-education.

24. "President Andrew Jackson's Message to Congress on Indian Removal," National Archives, last updated December 6, 1830, https://www.archives.gov/milestone-documents/jacksons-message-to-congress-on-indian-removal.

25. Dylan Matthews, "Andrew Jackson Was a Slaver, Ethnic Cleanser, and Tyrant. He Deserves No Place on Our Money," Vox, April 20, 2016, https://www.vox.com/2016/4/20/11469514/andrew-jackson-indian-removal.

26. Thomas A. Britten, "Hoover and the Indians: The Case for Continuity in Federal Indian Policy, 1900–1935," *Historian* 61, no. 3 (October 2007).

27. Cherokee Nation v. Georgia, 30 U.S. 1 (1831), https://www.oregon.gov/ode/students-and-family/equity/NativeAmericanEducation/Documents/sb13%20curriculum/sc%20summary%207_Cherokee%20nation%20v%20georgia.pdf.

28. Worcester vs. Georgia, 31 U.S. 515 (1832), Oyez, https://www.oyez.org/cases/1789-1850/31us515.

29. "Federal Trust Doctrine First Described by Supreme Court," 1831, U.S. Department of Justice, last updated May 14, 2015, https://www.justice.gov/enrd/timeline-event/federal-trust-doctrine-first-described-supreme-court.

30. John Bethune, *A map of that part of Georgia occupied by the Cherokee Indians, taken from an actual survey made during the present year 1831, in pursuance of an act of the general assembly of the state: This interesting tract of country contains four millions three hundred & sixty six thousand five hundred & fifty four acres, many rich gold mines & many delightful situations & though in some parts mountainous, some of the richest land belonging to the state* (Milledgeville GA: John Bethune, 1831), Library of Congress, G3920 1831.B4, https://www.loc.gov/item/2004633028/.

31. Constitutional Rights Foundation, "Indian Removal: The Cherokees, Jackson, and the 'Trail of Tears,'" *Bill of Rights in Action* 21, no. 1 (Winter 2004), https://www.crf-usa.org/bill-of-rights-in-action/bria-21-1-c-indian-removal-the-cherokees-jackson-and-the-trail-of-tears.html.

32. "Trail of Tears," History.com, last updated July 28, 2022, https://www.history.com /topics/native-american-history/trail-of-tears.

33. "Trail of Tears," History.com.

34. R. H. Pratt, "The Indian Policy: The Advantages of Mingling Indians with Whites," *Proceedings of the National Conference of Charities and Correction at the Nineteenth Annual Session Held in Denver, Col., June 23–29, 1892*, ed. Isabel C. Barrows (Boston: Press of Geo. H. Ellis, 1892), https://carlisleindian.dickinson.edu/sites/default/files/docs -resources/CIS-Resources_1892-PrattSpeech.pdf. See also "'Kill the Indian in Him, and Save the Man': R. H. Pratt on the Education of Native Americans," Carlisle Indian School Digital Resource Center, accessed March 18, 2023, https://carlisleindian.dickinson .edu/teach/kill-indian-him-and-save-man-r-h-pratt-education-native-americans.

35. Barbara Landis, "Carlisle Indian Industrial School History," 1996, http://home.epix .net/~landis/histry.html.

36. "National Day for Truth and Reconciliation in Canada in 2022," Bentway, September 29, 2022, https://www.thebentway.ca/2022/09/29/national-day-for-truth-and-reconciliation /?gclid=CjwKCAiA9NGfBhBvEiwAq5vSy2t0ekQtMMtCmyjch0f9ZYvNs9afd-cCRIEnc OQB1h4sBS-ks5Z-TBoCpIYQAvD_BwE.

37. Graham Lee Brewer, "U.S. Counts Indian Boarding School Deaths for First Time but Leaves Key Questions Unanswered," NBC News, May 11, 2022, https://www.nbcnews.com /news/us-news/indian-boarding-school-deaths-interior-department-report-rcna28284.

38. United States v. Kagama, 118 U.S. 375 (1886).

39. Brewer, "U.S. Counts Indian Boarding School Deaths."

40. Philleo Nash, "Philleo Nash Oral History Interview, June 5, 1967," interview by Jerry N. Hess, Harry S. Truman Library, June 5, 1967, https://www.trumanlibrary.gov/library /oral-histories/nash13#693.

41. Max Nesterak, "Uprooted: The 1950s Plan to Erase Indian Country," APM Reports, November 1, 2019, https://www.apmreports.org/episode/2019/11/01/uprooted-the -1950s-plan-to-erase-indian-country.

42. Nesterak, "Uprooted."

43. Nesterak, "Uprooted."

44. Carolyn Casey, "Crossing Cultures: A Growing Number of Christian Churches Work to Support, Not Destroy Indian Spirituality," *Tribal College* 6, no. 2 (1994), https:// tribalcollegejournal.org/crossing-cultures-growing-number-christian-churches-work -support-destroy-indian-spirituality/.

45. Richard Twiss, "Another Path of Jesus," *Christianity Today*, October 8, 2012, https:// www.christianitytoday.com/pastors/2012/summer/anotherpath.html. See also Richard Twiss, *One Church Many Tribes: Serving Jesus the Way God Made You* (Minneapolis MN: Chosen Books, 2000).

46. Casey, "Crossing Cultures."

47. United Methodist Church, "Regarding Native American Culture and Traditions as Sacred," in *Book of Resolutions* (Washington DC: United Methodist Publishing House, 2016), Resolution 3334, https://www.umcjustice.org/who-we-are/social-principles-and -resolutions/regarding-native-american-culture-and-traditions-as-sacred-3334.

48. Michael Waasegiizhig Price, "Sacred Ceremonies in Unsacred Places," *Tribal College* 30, no, 2 (2018), https://tribalcollegejournal.org/sacred-ceremonies-in-unsacred-places/.

49. David Amram, "No More Walls—A Conversation with David Amram," interview by John McLaughlin, *Folk Life*, February 1977.

50. Brian Wright-McLeod, *The Encyclopedia of Native Music* (Tucson: University of Arizona Press, 2005), 285.

51. Curtis, *Indians' Book*.

52. Canyon Records, "Peyote Healing Chants," liner notes to *Healing Chants of the Native American Church*, sung by Ralph Turtle, 1972, Drumhop, accessed January 11, 2023, https://drumhop.com/music.php?page=237.

53. Isaac Radner, "Indigenous Religions and Christianity: Acculturation and Assimilation—A Summary," *Indigenous Religious Traditions* (blog), accessed January 11, 2023, https://sites.coloradocollege.edu/indigenoustraditions/6-%e2%80%a2-independent-projects/indigenous-religions-and-christianity-acculturation-and-assimilation-a-summary/.

54. ReconciliAction YEG, "Ruth Bader Ginsburg: Legacy, Reconciliation, and the Doctrine of Discovery," *University of Alberta Faculty of Law* (blog), September 25, 2020, https://ualbertalaw.typepad.com/faculty/.

55. Lisa Wangsness, "Massachusetts Clergy Join Pipeline Protest in North Dakota," *Boston Globe*, November 4, 2016.

4. STEREOTYPICAL

1. "Hawikuh and the Zuni-Cibola Complex, New Mexico," National Park Service, accessed January 11, 2023, https://www.nps.gov/nr/travel/american_latino_heritage/hawikuh_zuni-cibola.html.

2. Lyn Garrity, "John M. Barry on Roger Williams and the Indians," *Smithsonian Magazine*, January 1, 2012, https://www.smithsonianmag.com/history/john-m-barry-on-roger-williams-and-the-indians-9322792/.

3. Lloyd Custer Mayhew Hare, *Martha's Vineyard: A Short History and Guide* (Edgartown MA: Dukes County Historical Society, 1956), 98.

4. W. L. Hubbard, *The American History and Encyclopedia of Music* (New York: Irving Squire, 1908).

5. Gabriel Swift, "Indian Melodies by Thomas Commuck, a Narragansett Indian," *Princeton Collections of the American West* (blog), December 9, 2013, https://blogs.princeton.edu/westernamericana/2013/12/09/indian-melodies-by-thomas-commuck-a-narragansett-indian-1845/.

6. "Symphony No. 9 ('New World')," Redwood Symphony, accessed January 11, 2023, https://redwoodsymphony.org/piece/symphony-no-9-new-world/.

7. Kansas Historical Society, "Thurlow Lieurance," last updated January 2013, https://www.kshs.org/kansapedia/thurlow-lieurance/12131.

8. Paul Mayberry, "Hiawatha and the Indian Intermezzo," *Chatfield Music Lending Library* (blog), March 26, 2008, https://chatfieldband.lib.mn.us/uncategorized/hiawatha-and-the-indian-intermezzo/.

9. Sudip Bose, "A Composer in an Antique Land: The Legacy of Arthur Farwell," *American Scholar*, November 1, 2019, https://theamericanscholar.org/a-composer-in-an-antique-land/.

10. Rocky Productions, "Sheb Wooley," Rock and Country Encyclopedia and Discography, September 28, 2020, https://www.rocky-52.net/chanteursw/wooley_sheb.htm.

11. Spencer Leigh, "Marvin Rainwater: Rock 'n' Roller Who Led the U.S. Invasion of 1950s Britain," *Independent*, September 27, 2013, https://www.independent.co.uk/news /obituaries/marvin-rainwater-rock-n-roller-who-led-the-us-invasion-of-1950s-britain -8845096.html.

12. Bear Family Records, "Marvin Rainwater," accessed January 12, 2023, https://www .bear-family.com/rainwater-marvin/.

5. DEFIANCE

1. Liam Clancy and Pat Clancy, "Patrick Humphries Interview (Liam and Pat Clancy)," *Telegraph* 18 (Winter 1984), 62–68, http://www.bobdylanroots.com/inter02.html.

2. "The Doctrine of Discovery: 'By the Authority of Almighty God,'" Friends Committee of National Legislation, September 25, 2016, https://www.fcnl.org/updates/2016-09 /doctrine-discovery.

3. Patrick Humphries, "Liam and Pat Clancy Interview," *Telegraph*, London, UK, October 18, 1984.

4. *Indian Studies Journal*, 1984, quoted in José Barreiro, "An Appreciation of Floyd Westerman," Indian Country Today, last updated September 12, 2018, https://ictnews.org /archive/an-appreciation-of-floyd-westerman.

5. Charla Bear, "American Indian Boarding Schools Haunt Many," NPR, May 12, 2008, https://www.npr.org/2008/05/12/16516865/american-indian-boarding-schools-haunt -many.

6. Dianne Meili, "Floyd Red Crow Westerman Fought against Injustice throughout His Life," Windspeaker, November 3, 2017, https://windspeaker.com/news/footprints/floyd -red-crow-westerman-fought-against-injustice-throughout-his-life.

7. Floyd Red Crow Westerman, "Indigenous Native American Prophecy from Floyd Red Crow Westerman," *Awaken*, October 25, 2020, https://awaken.com/2020/10/indigenous -native-american-prophecy-from-floyd-red-crow-westerman/.

8. "Westerman Launches Native Studio," Indianz, September 8, 2000, https://www.indianz .com/News/archive..asp?ID=ae/982000-1&day=9/8/00.

9. Max Mertens, "The Story of Trailblazing Indigenous Folk Singer Willie Dunn," Bandcamp, March 25, 2021, https://daily.bandcamp.com/features/willie-dunn-creation -never-sleeps-creation-never-dies-feature.

10. Jacob Pagano, "The Pirate Radio Broadcaster Who Occupied Alcatraz and Terrified the FBI," Narratively Hidden History, January 16, 2019, https://narratively.com/native -radio-alcatraz-fbi/.

11. Emily Chertoff, "Occupy Wounded Knee: A 71-Day Siege and a Forgotten Civil Rights Movement," *Atlantic*, October 23, 2012.

12. Erik Ortiz, "Leonard Peltier, Imprisoned Native American Activist, Has New Message for Biden in Clemency Push," NBC News, March 24, 2022, https://www.nbcnews.com /news/us-news/leonard-peltier-imprisoned-native-american-activist-new-message -biden-rcna19731.

13. Ortiz, "Leonard Peltier."

14. Ortiz, "Leonard Peltier."

15. Pagano, "Pirate Radio Broadcaster."

16. Sarah Sunshine Manning, "Manning: The Picture in Our Hallway: My Story Growing Up with the (Manning) Trudell Family," Indian Country Today, last updated September 13, 2018, https://ictnews.org/archive/manning-the-picture-in-our-hallway-my-story -growing-up-with-the-manning-trudell-family.

17. Josh Righthand, "The Pop Charts' Native Roots," *Smithsonian Magazine*, October 2010.

18. Erik Ortiz, "A Sioux Poet Whose Fiery Protests Now Come in Jewel Boxes," *New York Times*, February 19, 1995, https://www.nytimes.com/1995/02/19/books/pop-music-a -sioux-poet-whose-fiery-protests-now-come-packaged-in-jewel-boxes.html.

19. Neal Ullestad, "American Indian Rap and Reggae: Dancing to the Beat of a Different Drummer," *Popular Music and Society* 23, no. 2 (1999): 62–90.

20. Ty Burr, "Johnny Damas and Me," *Entertainment*, March 4, 1994, https://ew.com/article /1994/03/04/johnny-damas-and-me/.

21. Native American Music Awards, "National Association of Native American Music," accessed January 17, 2023, https://www.nativeamericanmusicawards.com/national -association-of-native-american-music.

22. Robbie Wolliver, "Italian-Irish for American Indian Music," *New York Times*, April 20, 2000.

23. A Tribe Called Geek, "Joel Rafael with John Trudell's Bad Dog to Perform Summer Festival Dates in Support of John Trudell Archives Re-Release of John Trudell's 'AKA *Grafitti Man*,'" ATCG, May 12, 2017, https://atribecalledgeek.com/joel-rafael-with-john-trudells -bad-dog-to-perform-summer-festival-dates-in-support-of-john-trudell-archives-re -release-of-john-trudells-aka-grafitti-man/.

24. Gary Graff, "Jason Mraz Joins Joel Rafael on 'Strong': Exclusive Premiere," *Billboard*, April 17, 2019.

6. BEATING OF THE HEART

1. Paul Gowder, "Pow Wow Drum and Singing/Importance and Explanation/Native American," Powwows, July 19, 2011, https://www.powwows.com/pow-wow-singing2/ #:~:text=Without%20the%20drum%20and%20the,Drum%20can%20connect%20with %20spirit.

2. Sam Scott, "50 Years of Powwow," *Stanford Magazine*, May 2021, https://stanfordmag .org/contents/50-years-of-powwow.

3. Luther Standing Bear, *My People, the Sioux* (Boston: Houghton Mifflin, 1928).

4. Paul Fees, "Wild West Shows: Buffalo Bill's Wild West," Buffalo Bill Center of the West, accessed January 18, 2023, https://centerofthewest.org/learn/western-essays/wild -west-shows/.

5. Fees, "Wild West Shows."

6. GW Main, "'Indian Princess' Do-Hum-Me (1824–1843)," Green-Wood, November 26, 2010, https://www.green-wood.com/2010/indian-princess-do-hum-me-saved/.

7. Jamie K. Oxendine, "History of the Powwow | Origin and Background | Native American," Powwows, last updated February 27, 2020, https://www.powwows.com/history -of-the-powwow/.

8. Oxendine, "History of the Powwow."

9. "Powwow (n)," Online Etymology Dictionary, last updated September 30, 2020, https:// www.etymonline.com/word/powwow.

10. Nanticoke Indian Association, "What Is a Powwow?," Nanticoke Indian Tribe, accessed January 18, 2023, https://www.nanticokeindians.org/page/what-powwow.

11. Liz Przybylski, "Indigenous Survivance and Urban Musical Practice," *Revue de recherche en civilisation américaine* 5 (2015), https://journals.openedition.org/rrca/706.

12. Joe Medicine Crow, introduction to *Native Spirit: The Sun Dance Way*, by Thomas Yellowtail, recorded and ed. Michael Oren Fitzgerald (Bloomington IN: World Wisdom, 2007), http://www.worldwisdom.com/public/viewpdf/default.aspx?article-title=Intro_by_Joe_Medicine_Crow_to_Native_Spirit_The_Sun_Dance_Way.pdf.

13. Johnny Arlee, *Over a Century of Moving to the Drum: Salish Indian Celebrations on the Flathead Indian Reservation*, ed. Robert Bigart (Helena: Montana Historical Society Press, 1998), quoted from the "About" page of the Arlee Celebration official website, accessed March 19, 2023, http://www.arleepowwow.com/more/about.

14. Autumn Whitfield-Madrano, "History of a Warrior's Dance—Gourd Dancing," American Indian Today, last updated September 13, 2018, https://ictnews.org/archive/history-of-a-warriors-dancegourd-dancing.

15. Whitfield-Madrano, "History of a Warrior's Dance."

16. Charles Hudson, *The Southeastern Indians* (Knoxville: University of Tennessee Press, 1976), quoted in Rufus Ward, "Ask Rufus: Green Corn and Dancing under a Full Moon," *Dispatch*, August 16, 2014, https://cdispatch.com/opinions/2014-08-16/ask-rufus-green-corn-and-dancing-under-a-full-moon/.

17. Admin, "The Green Corn Ceremony," Native American Netroots, May 5, 2011, http://nativeamericannetroots.net/diary/951#:~:text=The%20green%20corn%20ceremony%20was%20also%20associated%20with%20the%20quest,lasted%20until%20the%20second%20sunrise.

18. James Taylor Carson, *Indians of the Southeast: Searching for the Bright Path: The Mississippi Choctaws from Prehistory to Removal* (Lincoln: University of Nebraska Press, 2003), 166.

19. Associated Press, "Powwows across US Adapt to Pandemic for a Second Year," *U.S. News*, April 23, 2021, https://www.usnews.com/news/us/articles/2021-04-23/powwows-across-us-adapt-to-pandemic-for-a-second-year?context=amp.

20. Reginald Laupin and Gladys Laupin, *Indian Dances of North America: Their Importance to Indian Life* (Norman: University of Oklahoma Press, 1977), 78.

21. Deb Reger, "Oskiyak Kisik (Young Spirit)—Mewasinsational (Round Dance Songs)," WRUV Reviews, November 2, 2018, https://wruv.wordpress.com/2018/11/02/oskiyak-kisik-young-spirit-mewasinsational-round-dance-songs/.

22. "About Fawn Wood," Buffalo Jump Records, accessed January 19, 2023, https://buffalojumprecords.com/fawn-wood/.

23. Katie Bain, "With His New Single 'The Social' and Forthcoming Album, DJ Shub Is Using Music as a Weapon," *Billboard*, July 30, 2020, https://www.billboard.com/music/music-news/dj-shub-the-social-interview-9423197/.

7. SOUND OF THE WIND

1. Sofia Rizzi, "Hear the World's Oldest Instrument, the 50,000-Year-Old Neanderthal Flute," Classic FM, October 1, 2021, https://www.classicfm.com/discover-music/instruments

/flute/worlds-oldest-instrument-neanderthal-flute/#:~:text=Archaeologists%20have
%20found%20a%20pre,musical%20instrument%20in%20the%20world.

2. Dani Rhys, "Kokopelli—What Does This Symbol Mean?" Symbol Sage, https://symbolsage
.com/kokopelli-symbol-meaning-and-significance/.

3. Rhys, "Kokopelli."

4. Kevin Brewer, "The Cultural Significance of the Pueblo Indian Flute" (master's thesis,
Ouachita Baptist University, 2004), https://scholarlycommons.obu.edu/cgi/viewcontent
.cgi?article=1027&context=honors_theses.

5. Brewer, "Cultural Significance of the Pueblo Indian Flute."

6. Cabeza de Vaca, "The Atlantic Crossing," trans. Fanny Bandelier (1905), Houston Institute for Culture, http://www.houstonculture.org/devaca/1a.html.

7. *The Journey of Coronado, 1540–1542: From the City of Mexico to the Grand Canon of
Colorado and the Buffalo Plains of Texas, Kansas, and Nebraska, as Told by Himself
and His Followers* (New York: A. S. Barnes and Company, 1904).

8. Brian Freeman, "The Kiowa: Plains; Comanche, Cheyenne, Kiowa, Caddo, Wichita,
Pawnee," Collections of the Archive of American Folk Song, L39, recorded and edited
by Willard Rhodes, Drumhop, accessed January 22, 2023, https://drumhop.com/music
.php?page=135.

9. "The Indian Arts and Crafts Act of 1990," U.S. Department of the Interior, accessed
January 23, 2023, https://www.doi.gov/iacb/act.

10. Cecily Hilleary, "Native American Flutist Shares Authentic Sounds and Stories," VOA
News, February 18, 2019, adapted by Jonathan Evans for Learning English, https://
learningenglish.voanews.com/a/native-american-flutist-shares-authentic-sounds-and
-stories/4787484.html.

11. Quoted from the expanded "Biography" page on Calvin Standing Bear's official website,
accessed March 19, 2023, https://www.calvinstandingbear.org/#!/page_BIO /.

12. "Band Bio," Crazy Flute website, accessed January 25, 2023, https://www.crazyflutemusic
.com/band.

13. Steve Wildsmith, "Steve Rushingwind, Other Native American Performers Head to
Townsend," *Blount County (TN) Daily Times*, August 24, 2016, https://www.thedailytimes
.com/entertainment/steve-rushingwind-other-native-american-performers-head-to
-townsend/article_1aee1a92-094a-5b9c-ad33-ea5a0f490e79.html.

14. Kimberly Haas, "Vince Redhouse Jazzes Up the Native American Flute," Voice of America,
March 14, 2004, MP3 audio, 5:33, https://www.voanews.com/a/2001920.html.

8. ANCESTRAL VOICES

1. Dana Lepofsky, Álvaro Fernández-Llamazares, and Oqwilowgwa Kim Recalma-Clutesi,
"Indigenous Song Keepers Reveal Traditional Ecological Knowledge in Music," Conversation, January 2, 2020, https://theconversation.com/indigenous-song-keepers-reveal
-traditional-ecological-knowledge-in-music-123573.

2. Quoted from the homepage of Roman Orona's official website, accessed January 29,
2023, https://www.romanorona.com/.

3. "Spirit Wing," Philadelphia Folksong Society, accessed March 19, 2023, https://pfs.org
/folkies/spirit-wing/.

1. Alice Cunningham Fletcher, *A Study of Omaha Indian Music*, aided by Francis La Flesche and with a report by John Comfort Fillmore, (Cambridge MA: Peabody Museum of American Archaeology and Ethnology, 1893), 10.

2. Willard Rhodes, *Indian Songs of Today* (Washington DC: Recording Laboratory, Library of Congress, 1987), 6, https://loc.gov/folklife/LP/AFSL36_AIToday.pdf.

3. Tom Barnes, "Native Americans Are Writing the Most Powerful Country Music Today," Mic, December 10, 2014, https://www.mic.com/articles/106178/native-american-country -music-is-the-truest-kind-of-country-we-have.

4. Simon Romero, "Navajo Country Music Shatters 'Cowboys and Indians' Stereotypes," *New York Times*, November 30, 2019, https://www.nytimes.com/2019/11/30/us/navajo -country-music.html.

5. Kristina Jacobson, "Why Navajos Love Their Country Music," *Sapiens*, July 23, 2019, https://www.sapiens.org/culture/navajo-music/.

6. Romero, "Navajo Country Music."

7. Sesi King, "Bear Fox Nominated as NAMMY Debut Artist," *Indian Time*, September 22, 2011, https://www.indiantime.net/story/2011/09/22/news/bear-fox-nominated -as-nammy-debut-artist/05022012144787675326.html.

8. Quoted from the homepage of Desja Eagle Tail's official website, accessed January 29, 2023, https://www.desjaeagletail.com/.

9. Ryan Miller, "Singer Lucas Ciliberti Wins Prestigious Music Award," *Enid News and Eagle*, November 7, 2017, https://www.enidnews.com/news/entertainment/singer-lucas-ciliberti -wins-prestigious-music-award/article_510c72a6-8336-566d-a118-98795ec715e6.html.

10. "Bobby Bullet, Ojibwe Singer-Songwriter, to Perform at Warehouse," *Minocqua (WI) Lakeland Times*, October 12, 2021, https://www.lakelandtimes.com/Content/Default /Community/Article/Bobby-Bullet-Ojibwe-Singer-Songwriter-to-perform-at-Warehouse /-3/85/48582.

11. Quoted from the biography on Paco Fralick's official website, accessed January 29, 2023, https://pacofralick.com/bio.

12. William Rees, "Canada's First Nations," *History Today* 68, no. 9 (September 9, 2018), https://www.historytoday.com/history-matters/canada%e2%80%99s-first-nations.

13. Quoted from the "About" page on Leela Gilday's official website, accessed January 29, 2023, https://www.leelagilday.com/about.

14. "Jay Gilday," Alberta Music Industry Association, accessed January 29, 2023, https:// www.albertamusic.org/directory-profile/jay-gilday-2/.

15. Deb Reger, "Cluster Stars—Sandra Sutter," *WRUV Reviews* (blog), December 5, 2018, https://wruv.wordpress.com/2018/12/05/cluster-stars-sandra-sutter/.

16. David Wylie, "Kelly Derrickson's Music with a Message," *Revelstoke Review*, November 18, 2018, https://www.revelstokereview.com/life/kelly-derricksons-music-with-a -message/.

17. "Musician William Prince Melds Indigenous and Christian Roots; Boston Marathon Is Back," *Here and Now*, hosted by Scott Tong, NPR, October 11, 2021, MP3 audio, 41:36, interview with William Prince begins at 10:30, https://www.npr.org/2021/10/11 /1045023877/musician-william-prince-melds-indigenous-and-christian-roots-boston -marathon-is-.

18. Ethnic Field Ministry, "Nations: The Native American Ministry of Cru," Cru, accessed January 29, 2023, https://www.cru.org/us/en/train-and-grow/leadership-training /starting-a-ministry/launching/nations.html.

19. Quoted from the homepage of Callie Bennett's official website, accessed January 29, 2023, https://www.calliebennett.com/.

20. Quoted from the homepage of Robby Cummings's official website, accessed January 29, 2023, https://robbycummings.com/home.

10. ROCKIN' THE REZ

1. Louis Beale, "The Kickass Native American Rock Bands Music History Forgot," Daily Beast, last updated July 15, 2017, https://www.thedailybeast.com/the-kickass-native -american-rock-bands-music-history-forgot.

2. Beale, "Kickass Native American Rock Bands."

3. Stevie Salas, "An Interview with Rumble's Executive Producer Stevie Salas," by Cynthia Biret, *Riot Material*, May 1, 2018.

4. Matt Ashare, "Live Report: Link Wray," *Rolling Stone*, May 29, 1998, https://www .rollingstone.com/music/music-news/live-report-link-wray-108677/.

5. Beale, "Kickass Native American Rock Bands."

6. Catherine Bainbridge and Alfonso Maiorana, dirs., *Rumble: The Indians Who Rocked the World* (Montreal QC: Rezolution Pictures, 2017).

7. Dana Raidt, "Link Wray Grew Up Hiding from the KKK in Rural North Carolina. Over the Course of His Career, He Refused to Be Erased," *Indy Week*, February 6, 2019, https://indyweek.com/music/link-wray-kkk-rural-north-carolina/.

8. Raidt, "Link Wray Grew Up."

9. Jimmy Carl Black, "Geronimo Black, 1972—1st Half," MP3 audio from Jimmy Carl Black's official website, 5:07, https://www.jimmycarlblack.com/en/content/geronimo -black-1972-1st-half.

10. Alan Clayson, "Jimmy Carl Black: Drummer and Sometimes Lead Vocalist Who Worked with Frank Zappa and Captain Beefheart," *Guardian*, November 4, 2008, https://www .theguardian.com/music/2008/nov/04/popandrock.

11. "Jimmy Carl Black," United Mutations, accessed January 29, 2023, https://www.united -mutations.com/b/jimmy_carl_black.htm.

12. Clayson, "Jimmy Carl Black."

13. Jimmy Carl Black, "Jimmy Carl Black Interview," by Steve Moore, Stephen Moore Books, March 29, 2000, https://www.stevemoorebooks.com/frank-zappa-tribute/jimmy-carl -black/.

14. Eve Lazarus, "Nora Hendrix: Jimi Hendrix Plays the Pacific Coliseum—September 7, 1968," *Every Place Has a Story* (blog), September 1, 2018, https://evelazarus.com/tag /nora-hendrix/.

15. Stephen Thomas Erlewine, review of *Music for the Native Americans*, by Robbie Robertson and the Red Road Ensemble, AllMusic, accessed January 29, 2023, https://www .allmusic.com/album/music-for-the-native-americans-mw0000118845.

16. "Robbie Robertson: Palacongressi, Agrigento., Italy," Sugarmegs, February 2, 1995, http://tela.sugarmegs.org/_asxtela/asxcards/RobbieRobertson1995-02 -11palacongressiAgrigentoItaly.html.

17. Olli "Wahn" Wirtz, "Xit / Without Reservation," Archiv, August 20, 2005, https://www
    -rocktimes-info.translate.goog/Archiv/gesamt/xyz/xit/without_reservation.html?
    _x_tr_sl=de&_x_tr_tl=en&_x_tr_hl=en&_x_tr_pto=sc.

18. Shondiin Silversmith, "Re-enter XIT," *Navajo Times*, October 10, 2013, https://www
    .navajotimes.com/entertainment/2013/1013/101013xit.php.

19. Sonia Paoloni and Christian Staebler, *Redbone: The True Story of a Native American
    Rock Band* (San Diego CA: IDW Publishing, 2020).

20. Michael Limnios Blues Network, "Pat Vegas: Redbone Movement," *Blues.Gr* (blog),
    January 30, 2104, http://blues.gr/profiles/blogs/interview-with-pat-vegas-of-redbone
    -a-native-american-mexican.

21. Kathleen Kuiper, *Native American Culture* (Chicago: Britannica Educational Publishing,
    2011).

22. Charles Eastman, *Living in Two Worlds: The American Indian Experience*, ed. Michael
    Oren Fitzgerald (Bloomington IN: World Wisdom, 2010), 117.

23. Rey Roldan, "PJ Vegas Fights for Racial Justice with His Single 'Pesos,'" *American
    Songwriter*, 2020, https://americansongwriter.com/pesos-pj-vegas-song-interview/.

24. Stan Bindell, "Tracy Lee Nelson, Former Chairman of Lajolla Tribe and Blues Legend,
    Releases New Album," *Navajo-Hopi Observer*, February 6, 2018, https://www.nhonews
    .com/news/2018/feb/06/tracy-lee-nelson-former-chairman-lajolla-tribe-and/.

25. Gordon Lee Johnson, "Tracy Lee Nelson: Skate Rat with a Rez Kid Heart," KCET, Febru-
    ary 26, 2013, https://www.kcet.org/shows/artbound/tracy-lee-nelson-skate-rat-with
    -a-rez-kid-heart.

26. Roldan, "PJ Vegas Fights for Racial Justice."

27. "PJ Vegas—Music with a Message," Indigenous Rights Radio, accessed February 11,
    2023, https://rights.culturalsurvival.org/pj-vegas-music-message.

28. Sam Thompson, "Manitoba Music Icon Vince Fontaine Dies at 60," *Global News*, Janu-
    ary 12, 2022, https://globalnews.ca/news/8505880/manitoba-music-vince-fontaine
    -dead/.

29. "'It's a Great Loss': Musician Vince Fontaine Remembered at Winnipeg Event," CBC
    News, January 16, 2022, https://www.cbc.ca/news/canada/manitoba/vince-fontaine
    -eagle-and-hawk-memory-of-life-1.6317046.

30. Kim Hughes, "Album Review: Don Amero, Nothing Is Meaningless," Parton and Pearl,
    October 12, 2021, https://www.partonandpearl.com/blog/album-review-don-amero
    -nothing-is-meaningless.

31. Nechochwen, "The Serpent Tradition: An Interview with Nechochwen," by Matt Solis,
    Decibel, October 15, 2015, https://www.decibelmagazine.com/2015/10/15/the-serpent
    -tradition-an-interview-with-nechochwen/.

32. "Wisdom Circle with Sihasin," IndigenousWays, November 17, 2021, https://www
    .indigenousways.org/events/wisdom-circle-with-sihasin.

33. Stasium won a Best Producer NAMA for Sihasin's *Fight like a Woman* in 2019.

34. "Drums" is so far unreleased.

35. Evan Greer, "12 Freedom Fighting Bands to Get You through the Trump Years," *Huff-
    ington Post*, December 28, 2016, https://www.huffpost.com/entry/12-freedom-fighting
    -bands-to-get-you-through-the-trump_b_5862a39ae4b014e7c72ede3a.

36. The title song of *Fight like a Woman* paid tribute to Rosa Parks, Anne Frank, Angela Davis, Winnie Mandela, Harriet Tubman, and other powerful women.

37. "Big Shot in the Dark" was the title track of Timbuk 3's 1991 album.

38. The Arizona Snowbowl is a ski resort on the western flank of the sacred San Francisco Peaks. Klee, who produced a documentary, *The Snowball Effect*, about the conflict, was arrested during an early protest.

11. ROCKSTEADY

1. Niki D'Andrea, "Rasta Redmon: Hopi Reggae Artist Casper Lomayesva Brings Redemption Songs to the Desert," *New Phoenix Times*, October 1, 2009, https://www.phoenixnewtimes.com/news/rasta-redmon-hopi-reggae-artist-casper-lomayesva-brings-redemption-songs-to-the-desert-6431432.

2. Eiteljorg Museum of American Indians and Western Art, "Virtual Artist Talk Series with Innastate," event press release, accessed March 25, 2023, https://eiteljorg.org/eiteljorg-events/virtual-artist-talk-series-with-innastate/.

12. TONGUE TWISTERS

1. Tom Barnes, "8 Songs by Native American Rappers That Deserve to Be Heard," Mic, April 30, 2015, https://www.mic.com/articles/116942/8-songs-by-native-american-rappers-that-deserve-to-be-heard.

2. Ken Raymond, "Faith Takes Brothers from Gangsta to Gospel: Lil Mike and Funny Bone Await Their Big Break in Unique Niche as an Indian, Christian, Hip-Hop Act," *Oklahoman*, April 29, 2006, https://www.oklahoman.com/story/news/2006/04/29/faith-takes-brothers-gangsta-gospel-mike-funny-bone-await-their-break-unique-niche-indian-christian/61887552007/.

3. Shawn Menders, "Shon Denay: Best Female Artist," *Say Magazine*, December 3, 2019, https://www.pressreader.com/canada/say-magazine/20191230/282041919049282.

4. Rae Rose, "Justice for the Family of Debra Marie Blackcrow: California Governor Reverses the Decision to Commute Sentence," Last Real Indians, February 1, 2021, https://lastrealindians.com/news/2021/2/1/reversal-of-parole-verdict-for-rodney-patrick-mcneal.

5. "Rapper/Actor/Tattoo Artists Sten Joddi to Speak about Indigenous Representation," KWBG, November 23, 2021, https://www.kwbg.com/2021/11/23/rapper-actor-tattoo-artists-sten-joddi-to-speak-about-indigenous-representation/.

13. CONNECTIONS

1. "Metis Music," Canadian Studies Center, University of Washington, accessed February 18, 2023, https://jsis.washington.edu/canada/music-collection/metis-music/.

2. Athabascan Family, *Tsii' Edo' Ai* (fiddle), ca. 1900, agave flower stalk, wood, paint, horsehair, 17 15/16 x 2 1/4–3 9/16 cm (body), 2 1/4 cm (peg), 21 1/16 x 3 1/8 cm (bow), Metropolitan Museum of Art, New York, https://www.metmuseum.org/art/collection/search/502761. See also "Apache Fiddle," National Museum of American History, accessed February 18, 2023, https://americanhistory.si.edu/collections/search/object/nmah_606930.

3. Jon Rose, "The Apache Violin: Indigenous Violin Music in South and North America," Jon Rose Web Archive, 2005, https://jonroseweb.com/archive/c_articles_apache_violin .html.

4. Rose, "Apache Violin."

5. Rita Pyrillis, "Native Sounds," *Symphony*, Spring 2021, https://americanorchestras.org/wp -content/uploads/2021/05/Native-Sounds.pdf?fbclid=Iwar0rcef7uoSf7tyq9ftrkl4ky7irk _zrdnqhaNpdboht7uJbTkr9nrfexhI.

6. Gail Wein, "Native American Composers," NewMusicBox, April 8, 2009, https:// newmusicusa.org/nmbx/native-american-composers/.

7. Pyrillis, "Native Sounds."

8. Courtney Crappell, "Native American Influence in the Piano Music of Louis W. Ballard" (master's thesis, University of New Mexico, 2008), 12, https://www.academia.edu /1821580/Native_American_influence_in_the_piano_music_of_Louis_W._Ballard.

9. Karl Erik Ettinger, "Louis Ballard: Composer and Music Educator" (PhD diss., University of Florida, 2014).

10. Adam Eric Berkowitz, "Finding a Place for *Cacega Ayuwipi* within the Structure of American Indian Music and Dance Traditions" (master's thesis, Florida Atlantic University, 2015), 177, https://fau.digital.flvc.org/islandora/object/fau%3A31263/datastream/OBJ /view/Finding_a_place_for_Cacega_Ayuwipi_within_the_structure_of_American _Indian_music_and_dance_traditions.pdf.

11. KaleidoMusArt, "Louis Wayne Ballard," Kaleidoscope MusArt, January 25, 2021, https:// kaleidoscopemusart.com/louis-wayne-ballard/.

12. Louis W. Ballard, "Louis Ballard, Quapaw/Cherokee Composer," in *This Song Remembers: Self-Portraits of Native Americans in the Arts* (Boston: Houghton Mifflin, 1980), 128.

13. KaleidoMusArt, "Louis Wayne Ballard."

14. Encyclopedia of World Biography, s.v. "Ballard, Louis Wayne," accessed February 18, 2023, https://www.encyclopedia.com/history/encyclopedias-almanacs-transcripts -and-maps/ballard-louis-wayne.

15. Wayne Louis Ballard, "Louis Ballard, Quapaw/Cherokee Composer," in *This Song Remembers: Self-Portraits of Native Americans in the Arts*, ed. Jane B. Katz (Boston: Houghton Mifflin, 1980), 132–38.

16. William F. Hanson, program for the 1935 production of *The Sun Dance Opera*, William F. Hanson Papers, BYU Library, L. Tom Perry Special Collections Repository, Provo UT.

17. Helen Keller to Zitkála-Šá, August 25, 1919, American Indian Stories, CUNY, https:// cuny.manifoldapp.org/projects/american-indian-stories.

18. Ronald L. Woodward, "White's Indiana Manual Labor Institute," *Wabash Weekly Courier*, March 30, 1888, https://images.indianahistory.org/digital/api/collection/p16797coll68 /id/7162/download.

19. "Zitkála-Šá / Gertrude Simmons Bonnin: Composer, Author, and Indigenous Rights Activist / 1876–1938," Unladylike Productions, 2020, accessed February 18, 2023, https:// unladylike2020.com/profile/zitkala-sa/.

20. Zitkála-Šá, interview by N. L. Nelson, *Deseret News* (Salt Lake UT), May 15, 1913.

21. Ann Klefstad, "Why Indigenous Creatives Chose Opera to Celebrate a Dakota Activist and Artist," The Current, November 23, 2022, https://www.thecurrent.org/feature/2022 /11/23/why-indigenous-creatives-chose-opera-to-celebrate-a-dakota-activist-and-artist ?fbclid=IwAR176JTa4c2sxvhZgp_GSbgLiBSLq0di12zNO0kdtsjIKI5NOGjI0OkEUU0.

22. Kate Adach, "'I Hope to Be That Beautiful Complication for People': Jeremy Dutcher on His Signature Style," CBC, June 1, 2021, https://www.cbc.ca/radio/unreserved/indigenous -fashion-the-politics-of-ribbon-skirts-runways-and-resilience-1.6034149/i-hope-to -be-that-beautiful-complication-for-people-jeremy-dutcher-on-his-signature-style -1.6047222.

23. Grego Applegate Edwards, "Connor Chee, Scenes from Dinetah," Gapplegate Classical-Modern Music Review (blog), November 23, 2020, https://classicalmodernmusic.blogspot .com/2020/11/connor-chee-scenes-from-dinetah.html.

CODA

1. Richard Erdoes and Alfonso Ortiza, eds., American Indian Myths and Legends (New York: Pantheon Books, 1984).

2. Nesterak, "Uprooted."

3. Gallup Independent, May 5, 2004, quoted in "Living Conditions," Partnership with Native Americans, 2022, http://www.nativepartnership.org/site/PageServer?pagename =naa_livingconditions.

4. "Human Rights," Department of Economic and Social Affairs Indigenous Peoples, https://www.un.org/development/desa/indigenouspeoples/mandated-areas1/human -rights.html.

5. Hannah Brockhaus, "Pope Francis Expresses 'Sorrow and Shame' for Catholic Role in Abuse against Indigenous Peoples," Catholic News Agency, April 1, 2022, https://www .catholicnewsagency.com/news/250857/pope-francis-expresses-sorrow-and-shame-for -catholic-role-in-abuse-against-indigenous-peoples. See also Deepa Shivaram, "The Pope Apologizes for Abuse of Indigenous Children in Canada's Residential Schools," NPR, April 1, 2022, https://www.npr.org/2022/04/01/1090213962/pope-francis-apology -indigenous-people-canada.

6. Shivaram, "Pope Apologizes."

7. Associated Press, "Pope Arrives in Canada on 'Penitential Voyage,'" Politico, last updated July 24, 2022, https://www.politico.com/news/2022/07/24/pope-francis-canada -apologies-00047610.

8. Associated Press, "Pope's Indigenous Tour Signals a Rethink of Mission Legacy," Crux Catholic Media, July 24, 2022, https://cruxnow.com/ap/2022/07/popes-indigenous -tour-signals-a-rethink-of-mission-legacy.

9. Stephanie Taylor, "Papal Apology Sparks Calls to Renounce 500-Year-Old Doctrine of Discovery," Canadian Press, July 30, 2022.

10. Bill Chappell, "The Vatican Repudiates 'Doctrine of Discovery,' Which Was Used to Justify Colonialism," NPR, March 30, 2023, https://www.npr.org/2023/03/30/1167056438 /vatican-doctrine-of-discovery-colonialism-indigenous.

11. Native News Online staff, "Vatican Rejects Doctrine of Discovery," Native News Online, March 30, 2023, https://nativenewsonline.net/currents/vatican-rejects-doctrine-of

-discovery?utm_source=Native+News+Online&utm_campaign=7ffd0d59d9
-EMAIL_CAMPAIGN_2021_11_24_COPY_01&utm_medium=email&utm
_term=0_dfd2540337-7ffd0d59d9-1412482955.

12. "Joint Statement of the Dicasteries for Culture and Education and for Promoting Integral Human Development on the 'Doctrine of Discovery,' 30.03.2023," Summary of Bulletin, Holy See Press Office, Vatican City, March 30, 2023, https://press.vatican.va/content/salastampa/en/bollettino/pubblico/2023/03/30/230330b.html.

13. Associated Press, "Pope Arrives in Canada."

14. Taylor, "Papal Apology Sparks Calls."

Wayne, John, 32, 239
Weather Report, 103
Webb, Chick, 3
Webb, Jimmy, 145
Wells, Kitty, 1, 182
Westerman, Floyd "Kanghi Duta" ("Red Wolf") 36–41, 124, 203
Westwood, Troy, 219–22
White, Aaron, 109
White, Josh, 33
Wicohan, 228
Williams, Hank, 1, 135, 143, 144, 164, 182
Williams, Mason, 135
Williams, Roger, 28
Wind Traveling Band, 76
Winner, Septimus, 30
Winter, Paul, 6
Wonder, Stevie, 68, 81
Wood, Earl, 61. *See also* Northern Cree
Wood, Fawn, 58–62, 63
Wood, Randy, 58, 61, 62, 76
Wood, Steve. *See* Northern Cree

Wooley, Frederick "Sheb," 30–31
Wray, Fred Lincoln "Link," Jr., 198–99

X Files, 37
XIT, 63, 202–8

Yacoub, Gabriel, 76
Yañez, Larry, 76
Yazzie, Kevin, 62
Yoakam, Dwight, 182
Young, Neil, 122, 135
Young Ancients, 137
Youngblood, Mary, 122
Young Spirit, 48, 50

Zamora, Albert, 116
Zappa, Frank, 199, 200
Zeno, Lee Allen, 138
Zitkála-Šá (Gertrude Simmons Bonnin), 280–82
Zlokowski, Korczak, 79
Zydeco, Buckwheat, 138